Vicente Ximenes, LBJ's Great Society, and
Mexican American Civil Rights Rhetoric

Vicente Ximenes,

LBJ's Great Society, and Mexican American Civil Rights Rhetoric

Michelle Hall Kells

Foreword by Juan C. Guerra

Southern Illinois University Press
Carbondale

Southern Illinois University Press
www.siupress.com

21 20 19 18   4 3 2 1

This publication has been supported by a generous Publication Subsidy Grant provided by the College of Arts and Sciences at the University of New Mexico.

Cover illustration: Vicente Ximenes and President Lyndon B. Johnson at the White House following the Viva Johnson campaign, 1965 (tinted). Personal Papers of Vicente T. Ximenes.

Library of Congress Cataloging-in-Publication Data
Names: Kells, Michelle Hall, author.
Title: Vicente Ximenes, LBJ's Great Society, and Mexican American civil rights rhetoric / Michelle Hall Kells, foreword by Juan C. Guerra.
Description: Carbondale : Southern Illinois University Press, 2018. | Includes bibliographical references and index.
Identifiers: LCCN 2017022016 | ISBN 9780809336395 (pbk.) | ISBN 9780809336401 (e-book)
Subjects: LCSH: Ximenes, Vicente, 1919–2014—Oratory. | Mexican Americans—Politics and government—20th century. | Ximenes, Vicente, 1919–2014—Influence. | Chicano movement—History—20th century. | Political activists—United States—Biography. | Mexican Americans—Biography.
Classification: LCC E184.M5 K453 2018 | DDC 320.0868/72073—dc23
LC record available at https://lccn.loc.gov/2017022016

To María Castillo Ximenes, the
love from which this story grows.

*La casa no se reclinar sobre la
tierra, sino sobre una mujer.*

Contents

Gallery of illustrations beginning on page 89

Foreword

Juan C. Guerra

*M*ichelle Hall Kells and I have known each other for almost twenty years. In that time we have influenced each other's work in dramatic ways because we share a sense of how rhetoric and pedagogy can be utilized in college classrooms and communities to change lives for the better. This new book by Michelle follows her powerful 2006 book about Héctor P. García's efforts to establish the American GI Forum (AGIF) as a key player in the post–World War II political arena.[1] Just as that first book grew to encompass García's commitment to the role of everyday rhetoric in the civil rights struggles of Mexican Americans in South Texas, this book establishes a broad historical context that helps explain Vicente Ximenes's efforts to bring about institutional change through his expansion of the AGIF's influence across the nation and its affiliation with other civil rights organizations. Both the 2006 book and this one reflect recent efforts by scholars in various fields to recover the lesser known, but equally important, voices throughout history that have shaped American civic reform. As someone who became implicated in a Chicano movement that demanded an allegiance to oppositional counternarratives and belittled the resistance work of individuals like García and Ximenes because we were unwilling to accept their argument that we should undertake institutional change by integrating ourselves into the various institutions that governed our lives—especially the more political ones shaped by state power—I must admit that I had little respect at the time for those we perceived as *vendidos*.

Among other things, I realize that my generation and I were the beneficiaries of the affirmative action policies Ximenes helped to write. Although it pains me to say it, especially after everything I've learned from Michelle's vivid illustration of the incredible impact that García and Ximenes's rhetorical work has had on the civil rights movement, neither of them originally fit into the panoply of revolutionary heroes I worshipped as a young man (the times were heavily gendered back then) in the late 1960s and into the 1970s and 1980s, among them Rodolfo "Corky" Gonzáles, César Chávez, and Reies López Tijerina. It's important to note, however, that before I became politicized by the antiwar, Chicano, Black Nationalist, and Puerto Rican Independence movements while I was at the University of Illinois at Chicago, I was an apolitical child who knew nothing about the world beyond the limits of the housing project I grew up in or the highly segregated schools I attended in Harlingen, Texas, about 240 miles south of Floresville, a small town near San Antonio where Ximenes came of age around the time I was born. I'm sure it will not come as a surprise that in the years since (getting older has that effect on many of us), I have developed greater respect for García and Ximenes's pragmatic understanding of the critical role we must play as *citizens in the making* in a country that belongs as much to us as it does to anyone else. But I'm getting ahead of myself.

Because I was the first child in my family born in the United States (my two older sisters were born in Mexico), I came into a world very similar to the one that Ximenes and his siblings experienced after Anglos moved into Floresville, his father lost his business as an independent general store owner, and they all suddenly became, in Ximenes's words, "aliens and dirty Mexicans in our own land." Four years after I was born in a labor camp set up to accommodate the growing influx of Mexicans in the post–World War II era, the very people that Ximenes worked so hard to represent in the civic and political spheres, my family and I (my stepfather was a World War II veteran) moved into a brand new housing project on the west side of Harlingen, where almost everyone I knew (African American families in the complex were strictly segregated from us) was of Mexican origin. Schooling for me was not much different from what it was for Ximenes: I too attended a highly segregated public elementary school where, by law, we were not permitted to speak Spanish in class. Until I moved to Chicago after my junior year at Harlingen High School in 1967, I too knew the consequences of having been at an educational institution where "a preponderant majority of teachers," as Ximenes put it, "did not value my culture, customs, national origin, music, or food." Even though I was a good student, not a single teacher or counselor in my South Texas high school ever suggested that I should consider college. It's no surprise, then, that of the six older children in my family (the younger three who came of age in the 1980s attended college), I was the only one who completed high school.

As soon as I arrived in Chicago, my life took on a different trajectory that in some ways paralleled Ximenes's after he left his hometown. I can only imagine how much more similar our lives might have been from that point on if I could have credited my father, as both García and Ximenes did theirs, for my success in the political and civic spheres. Instead, I remained an introverted student in a culture of silence who, despite his ability to pass (because of my light skin), knew his place in the world only too well and made every effort to become invisible in the eyes of certain others to avoid being discriminated against. After working a full-time job during the night shift in a local factory while attending my senior year of high school in Chicago, I unexpectedly came across Mr. Piper, a biology teacher who urged me to apply for a scholarship offered to Mexican American youth by a group of Mexican Americans from Ximenes's generation who shared many of his values and beliefs. Once I was admitted to the University of Illinois at Chicago (UIC), the only university I applied to, I suddenly found myself having to make difficult decisions about where I stood in regard to civil rights and the Vietnam War. Before long I began participating in marches and demonstrations against the war, a practice that morphed into a consideration of the place of Chicanos in the larger society and our struggle for social justice.

After I completed my undergraduate degree, I stumbled into a job as a lecturer in basic writing at UIC and found myself in one of the many educational opportunity programs established across the country in the late 1960s to provide disenfranchised students with an opportunity to go to college. I also started teaching some of the most woefully underprepared students that Chicago high schools were producing at the time. In the midst of this new pedagogical endeavor, I became immersed in conversations with faculty, staff, and students at UIC who were profoundly committed to Chicano, black, and Puerto Rican liberation. By the time the Vietnam War had ended, I was deeply embroiled in social justice issues and committed to doing everything I could to ensure that more underrepresented minority students like myself would have an opportunity to go to college and gain access to the range of options that mainstream Anglo students took for granted. In time, my campus activism expanded to include community activism in the Chicano/ Mexicano and Puerto Rican communities of Chicago, and I found myself in much the same place (but for different reasons) that Ximenes did when he elected to enter public service through the Civilian Conservation Corps and the military. Because times were different, I took an alternative path, one that led me to question the very idea of engaging in institutional change from inside the system. *Opposition*, rather than *resistance*, was the operative word in my vocabulary of motive.

Over the course of the last twelve of the sixteen years I worked full-time at UIC as a basic writing teacher and engaged in campus and community activism, I pursued graduate study on a part-time basis and completed an MA and PhD in language, literacy, and rhetoric. Despite my commitment to oppositional politics and my direct involvement with Rodolfo "Corky" Gonzáles and other Chicano, Puerto Rican, and African American activists committed to social justice, in time, I began to realize just how important it was for us to engage in political change by also working inside the systems of power that informed our personal, professional, and political lives. My lived

experience helped me understand that one could not remain forever outside
the walls of the institutions that controlled our lives if our goal was to change
rather than destroy them. After many years of speaking out against those
many of us cast as *vendidos*, I came to understand that external opposition
to institutional power and authority was necessary but insufficient. We had
no choice, as Ximenes consistently argued, but to engage in institutional
change from the inside if we were ever going to increase the educational and
economic opportunities available to disenfranchised youth in our communities of belonging. This brings me to where I am now, or more accurately,
to where I've been for the last twenty-five years.

After I left UIC in 1990 and took a tenure-track position at the University
of Washington in Seattle, I immersed myself more fully in scholarly work that
explored the difficult lives of undocumented Mexican immigrants and the
challenges they faced in light of the varied literacy practices they had developed in out-of-school contexts. My goals at the time were, first, to intervene
in unjust representations of the participants in my field research as ignorant
or naïve individuals whose lack of literacy kept them from advancing in the
larger society and, second, to draw attention to the range of discriminatory
practices that kept them in their place. At about the same time that Michelle
and I met fifteen years ago, the focus of my work shifted back to theoretical
and pedagogical work I had been doing in the college classroom with disenfranchised students who did not yet possess the rhetorical and discursive
skills necessary to succeed in the academy. Around that time I coined a term
I thought scholars in the field would find useful to describe the repertoire of
rhetorical and discursive sensibilities I had noticed disenfranchised students
using in my writing classes. *Transcultural repositioning*, which I defined as
a rhetorical ability many disenfranchised students enact as they move back
and forth across "different languages and dialects, different social classes,
different cultural and artistic forms, different ways of seeing and thinking
about the increasingly fluid and hybridized world emerging all around us,"
became for me a way to highlight what students who had no choice but to
cross borders and boundaries all their lives brought to the classroom and in
so doing enriched everyone's ability to develop the kind of critical language
and cultural awareness that Ximenes promulgated, as Michelle recounts in
her book.[2]

In the course of reading Michelle's book and learning more about the
rich repertoire of rhetorical and discursive practices that Ximenes called
on over the course of his involvement in varied forms of civic and political
engagement, I have come to appreciate just how much what Michelle has

learned from her archival research and her interviews with Ximenes informs our (hers and mine) shared conceptions of teaching and learning in the academy. As Michelle readily demonstrates, what set Ximenes apart in many ways was how effectively he could reposition himself transculturally as he moved in, between, across, and beyond the challenging social spheres that he occupied in his efforts to address the needs of Mexican Americans and other peoples of color who faced similar forms of discrimination and disempowerment at the hands of the state and its privileged allies. In Michelle's own words, Ximenes learned early in his life that "to spark and sustain a social movement is a hermeneutic problem distinctly different from institutionalizing and implementing social reform. Making a system shift and taking an ecological approach to social change demand agitators as well as agents of healing." As a representative of the latter, Ximenes used his hard-earned repertoire of rhetorical and discursive skills to "occupy diverse social spheres" and "exercise the agency of belonging." And he did it in the context of the varied leadership tasks he undertook before and after expanding the AGIF from Texas into New Mexico and beyond: as a program coordinator in Quito, Ecuador, during the Kennedy administration; as chairman of the Viva Johnson election campaign of 1964 (I personally shook LBJ's hand at the age of fourteen when he visited our hometown during the campaign); as deputy director of the U.S. Agency for International Development in Panama during the Johnson administration; and as the U.S. commissioner of the Equal Employment Opportunity Commission and chairman of the president's Cabinet Committee on Mexican American Affairs.

In the context of our current political scene, I have no doubt that you will discover just how radically current Ximenes's vision of an engaged citizen's role is, especially when it comes to navigating the treacherous waters that a discursive democracy produces as a consequence of the multiplicity of perspectives everyone must negotiate. The lessons that emerge from Michelle's critical examination of Ximenes's personal, civic, and professional lives readily provide educators with a sense of what the "full quiver of semiotic modes" that Cynthia Selfe has often referred to looks like. More than ever, our students need a full quiver of linguistic and cultural practices they can call on to address the "wickedly complex communicative tasks" we all face in an increasingly "challenging and difficult world."[3] In invoking the work of Chantal Mouffe, Michelle also reminds us of the critical difference between an adversary and an enemy to illustrate how Ximenes repeatedly worked to overcome an us/them opposition in the political arena by thinking of those whose views were different from his as adversaries rather than enemies.[4] In so doing, Ximenes found ways to participate in and continue the critical conversations that must be sustained in any community to ensure that just and meaningful change occurs. Through his life's work, Ximenes taught us that *compromise* need not be a dirty word—a valuable lesson in light of the intransigence that informs our current political discourse—particularly if we practice it in a principled and respectful manner that acknowledges the important role of difference in all of our lives.

Acknowledgments

Under history, memory and forgetting.
Under memory and forgetting, life.
But writing a life is another story.
Incompletion.

     —Paul Ricoeur, *Memory,*
      History, Forgetting

This book has been a long time coming. Reflecting on the journey of more than ten years, I echo Michelle Ballif's lament: "The answers are beyond me, impossibly possible, but the question itself poses to historiography a uniquely ethical task: how to historicize the impossible?"[1] The initial research was formally launched in the summer of 2006 with a University of New Mexico faculty research grant and was further enhanced with the Lyndon B. Johnson Research Fellow grant in the summer of 2008. I returned to the archives at the Lyndon B. Johnson Presidential Library and other libraries many times through the research phases of this project. The rhetorical influence of Vicente Ximenes in post–World War II civil rights reform became evident early in my research on Mexican American civic activism, beginning in 1997 when I was working on *Héctor P. García: Everyday Rhetoric and Mexican American Civil Rights.*[2]

Over the course of his rhetorical career, Vicente Ximenes contributed to one of the most comprehensive archives of twentieth-century civil rights rhetoric, helping to build an extensive body of discourses related to post–World War II Mexican American issues. Vicente Ximenes and I met for the first time in November 2002 in Corpus Christi at the premiere release of Jeff Felts's PBS film *Justice for My People: The Héctor P. García Story.*[3] I instantly appreciated Vicente's wry sense of humor and deep understanding of the ironies of his own position in the historical moments that catapulted him into the national limelight in 1967.

Vicente and I began talking over lunch at the La Vida Llena Retirement Community situated on a street named Lagrima de Oro in Albuquerque, New Mexico, in 2004 and continued our conversations for some ten years. He was the first person I called when I joined the University of New Mexico faculty in 2004. It is fitting that the site of our discussions was La Vida Llena, a Spanish term that translates as "the full life" or "the rich life." Lagrima de Oro, a concept that roughly translates as "tears of gold," represents another fitting trope for the spatial poetics of our collective remembering. Vicente once aptly described the process of gathering history into a book as "a gem of memories."[4] The metaphorical juxtaposition of these tropes sums it up beautifully, this journey of documenting a full life amidst the struggle of living. As a living legacy, a national treasure, Vicente lived abundantly.

If there is one take-away message that our extended conversation has illustrated to me over this past decade, it is this: democracy as commodity, or as Ralph Cintron asserts, "democracy as fetish" (the political economy of capitalism that historically inflects democracy and masks the opacity of economic relationships between the haves and have-nots), is indeed alive and well in this post-Obama moment.[5] Truly, the reassertion of white privilege and unabashed reification of racial stratification as *topoi* are in fierce circulation, evidenced fervently with the 2016 presidential election. But this is not the only story. The life and work of Vicente Ximenes represents, among other things, the efficacy and value of democracy as a cultural rhetorical ecology and gift-giving economy. It is through the transformative and generative work of the citizen that we as the *polis* protect what southwestern poet Terry Tempest Williams calls "the open space of democracy."[6] These are the generous stories, the inductive moments I will never forget that have shaped the evolution of this book. Certainly these occasions will endure in my awareness well past the process of writing this book.

The research journey also led me early on to the offices of Henry Cisneros on Soledad Street in San Antonio, Texas. As the former mayor of San Antonio and secretary of Housing and Urban Development in the Clinton administration, Cisneros was a leading voice for Latinos through the twentieth century. Cisneros has also served as the narrator for several significant documentaries on Mexican American issues such as Héctor Galán's series *¡Chicano! History of the Mexican American Civil Rights Movement* as well as the PBS documentary *El Senador: The Life and Times of Senator Dennis Chávez* produced by the Center for Regional Studies at the University of New Mexico.[7] In July 2006 Cisneros kindly cleared his schedule for an hour to discuss how Ximenes paved the way to Washington, D.C., for Latino leaders like himself in government, business, and education. Cisneros openly recognized the generational bridge that Ximenes represents for contemporary Mexican Americans. Quite simply, he argued, the story of Mexican American civil rights reform is incomplete without acknowledging World War II activists like Ximenes. Cisneros asserted, "Vicente Ximenes is a giant in Mexican American history."

At the close of our discussion, Henry Cisneros posed one question to me, a question that calls for an answer again and again. Cisneros asked, "What can we tell emerging democracies who look to America and ask, 'How did we do it?' [how did we incorporate and enfranchise a nation of immigrants to form our enduring democracy]?" Part of the answer rests with recovering the rhetorical lives of leaders like Vicente Ximenes, reformers who opened the door to political incorporation through dissent, dialogue, and deliberation.

To the family of Vicente Ximenes, especially his children, Ana, Olivia, and Ricardo, thank you for your enduring confidence and faith in this project. A special note of appreciation to Vicente's siblings Joe Ximenes and Madge Ximenes Valdez for your thoughtful conversations and support. My gratitude to my own huge and diverse tribe that is my extended family, a noisy and vibrant embodiment of what Vasconcelos perhaps meant when he coined the term *la raza cósmica*.[8] I attribute my love of history and language to a very long line of loquacious women, especially my grandmothers, Elma Lynn Hall and Angela Louise Jones. The racial, cultural, and national diversity that constitutes millennial U.S. immigrant identity is reflective of my own family *mestizaje*: Mexican, Irish, French, Polish, Africana, Vietnamese, Venezuelan—these are my people. I extend a special thanks to *mis tíos* los Gallegos, whose generosity and love have supported me for a lifetime, and *mis hermanos* los Medinas, whose faith and perseverance endure with grace and good humor in all things. My sisters, Beth and Stephanie, never cease to inspire me. *Mis vecinos y compadres* in Tierra Amarilla, New Mexico, especially los Polacos, who encourage me to keep up the fight, keep me company, and give me wise counsel. To my good friend and guide through all things political, a special thanks to Robert McNeill for offering his sage insight of the past fifty years navigating civil rights law. My children continue to move me forward. To my husband, Ross, who shares this journey (who always helps me find my way—with and without a map), thank you. Most of all, I remain indebted to the gifts of joy and hope for the future from my granddaughters, Bailey Elizabeth and Anna Michelle.

Sections of this book have been presented at the Texas State Historical Association (2006); Rhetoric Society of America (2008, 2010, 2012, 2014, 2016); American GI Forum Sixtieth Anniversary Conference (2008); University of Texas–El Paso Frontera Retórica Symposium (2011); and Texas A&M—Commerce Writing Democracy (2011) and Albuquerque Cultural Conference (2011). A University of New Mexico faculty research grant (2006) and the Lyndon B. Johnson Presidential Research Fellowship (2008) funded archival work for the book. Research sabbaticals in 2009–10 and 2014 at the University of New Mexico allowed me to complete the archival and field research in Texas. Segments of this book have been previously published as articles.[9]

To my colleagues at the University of New Mexico who have shared this journey, especially Anita Obermeier, Mark Peceny, Phil Ganderton, Jesse Alemán, and Steve Benz, your support has been invaluable. I wish to acknowledge my colleagues at the Southwest Hispanic Research Institute and offer my sincere appreciation to Barbara Reyes, Irene Vásquez, Christine Sierra, Manuel García y Griego, Richard Santos, Gabriel Meléndez, Eliseo "Cheo" Torres, and Felipe González. My soulful gratitude to Erin Penner Gallegos and Karl Kageff for your insightful editing assistance along the way. A thank-you to Southern Illinois University Press, especially Linda Buhman, Amy Alsip, and Robert Brown Jr. for their astute editorial guidance.

Lyndon B. Johnson Presidential Library Reading Room specialists Bob Tissing, Will Clements, Allen Fisher, and Brian McNerny have been helpful beyond measure. To Grace Charles and Anne Hodges at special collections and at the Texas A&M University–Corpus Christi, *muchismas gracias por todo*. To the folks in Silver City, New Mexico, especially Felipe de Ortego y Gasca, Terry Humble, and Ken Dyer, you helped to make this research journey a joy. Thank you to Andrea Jaquez and Gilda Baeza-Ortego at the J. Cloyd Miller Library at Western New Mexico University for your kind assistance.

For their enduring generosity and encouragement, I need to recognize my esteemed colleagues in history, especially Anthony Quiroz, Julie Leininger Pycior, Carlos Blanton, Carl Allsup, Neil Foley, Cynthia Orozco, David Montejano, Juan Gómez-Quiñones, and Ignacio García. To my colleagues in rhetoric and composition studies, particularly Juan Guerra, Jaime Mejía, Ralph Cintron, Victor Villanueva, Jacqueline Jones Royster, Shannon Carter, Cristina Kirklighter, and Keith Gilyard—thank you for the work that you do.

Finally, after reading the first complete draft of this book in 2011, Vicente offered a long list of acknowledgments extending across the course of his public life. His list of names reads like a litany of thanksgiving: Santiago Campos, Avelino Gutierrez, Manuel Chávez, Ben Chavez, Bob Esparza, Victor Gonzales, Alfonso Proo, Vicente Jasso, Zeke Duran, Toby Duran, Frank Martinez, Ruben Anaya, Humberto Aguirre, Felix Salinas, Monsignor José Garcia, Victor Proo, Helen Proo, Josephine Proo, Hobart LaGrone, Tibo Chávez, Fabian Chávez, Ray Powell, Ray Powell Jr., Albert Amador,

Andrew Yslas, Duven Lujan, Emma Lujan, Rose Cordova, Raul Cordova, Clarence Gailard, Ana Gailard, Leo Hernandez, Minnie Hernandez, Lorrenzo Chavez, Shirley Driggs, Ernest Sanchez, Pete Anaya, Mary Anaya, Rudy Baca, Joe Flores, Max Cisneros, Bob Saavadra, Frank Jaramillo, Tony Nunez, Albert Romero, Juan Burciaga, Edwin Mechem, Zeke Hernandez, Drew Cloud, Ralph Edgel, Blanca Hernandez, Dave Cargo, Frederic Groves, Reies López Tijerina, Art Tafoya, Polly Baca, Molly Galvan, José Ontiveros, Ben Hernandez, Edmund Engel, Meril Esquivel, Carlos Truan, and Henry Cisneros.

Vaya con dios.

Vicente Ximenes, LBJ's Great Society, and
Mexican American Civil Rights Rhetoric

Introduction: The Cultural Rhetorical Ecology of the Mexican American Civil Rights Movement

*I*n August 1968 Vicente Ximenes delivered the keynote address for the Twentieth Annual Convention of the American GI Forum in Corpus Christi, Texas, in his capacity as the chair of the White House Inter-Agency Committee on Mexican American Affairs. It was a heady occasion for the esteemed orator and the enthusiastic audience. For a fleeting moment, Ximenes and his *compadres* recognized the gravitas of their collective success and the power of political presence. In Ximenes's eloquent act of epideictic rhetoric commemorating this landmark event, his remarks situate the post–World War II Mexican American generation in the narrative of Western and U.S. history:

> Han habido epocas en el pasado en cuales hombres llegaron a realizer desarrollos progresivos a base de un sueño. La historia ha inscribido a esas gran epocas como El Renacimiento, La Revolucion Industrial, y la Edad de Razon. Hoy, somos nosotros participantes en otra gran epoca que, en fin, dara luz el conocimiento de la dignidad de todas razas y del valor de cada hombre. Quizas, sera designado simplemente La Epoca del Hombre.[1]
>
> We, the members of the American GI Forum of the U.S., have helped to write this chapter of history-in-the-making. We believed, when few others did, that someday we would see a focus on Opportunity for the Mexican American. We were the movers before our nation understood that changes had to be made. We believed what we wrote and said the Forum stood for. We sacrificed and worked and argued and defended our program before all people.
>
> We vowed that ". . . Freedom should be everybody's business" and we knew that, to be free, a man first has to be confident and proud of what he is. If a man cannot get a job or gain admittance to a school because his name happens to be Gonzalez or Chavez, he is not free. If a man must seek cover under some other term rather than use the words "Mexican American," he is not free. If he is made to feel that his language and attitudes are inferior, he is not free.[2]

Coming full circle, returning to the birthplace of the American GI Forum and his home state of Texas, Vicente Ximenes sat at the table with his longtime friend and colleague Héctor P. García and the members of the

American GI Forum. He not only found himself celebrating among friends and fellow grassroots organizers but also rubbing elbows with the framers and functionaries of Lyndon B. Johnson's Great Society. Thirty days later President Johnson approved the first national Hispanic Heritage Week, a rhetorical act of civic recognition that Ximenes as chair of the Inter-Agency Committee on Mexican American Affairs ushered into effect on September 17, 1968. Civic inclusion seemed possible at last. The victory dance was short lived, however, not only for Ximenes and the postwar Mexican American generation but for the nation as a whole.

History of the post–World War II civil rights era represents a complex overlay of events spanning the two decades between 1948 and 1968. Historians frequently mark the death of Martin Luther King Jr. as the end of the movement. Scholars such as J. Mills Thornton argue that "the Civil Rights Movement died like a fire deprived of oxygen, when it burned beyond Americanist ideals."[3] Historian William E. Leuchtenburg concludes in *The White House Looks South*, "The Voting Rights Act of 1965 promoted by Johnson ushered in an era not of Democratic but Republican hegemony."[4] The results of civil rights activism and legislation in the 1960s "was not at all what they had anticipated."[5] Activists and liberal Democrats alike could not forestall the forty years of backlash, reversal, and countermoves that followed.

Despite the widely held belief that civil rights activism fizzled out by the end of the 1960s, a few scholars claim that the movement never died completely but has continued to smolder like smudge pots in vast corners of the nation. In *Making Aztlán: Ideology and Culture of the Chicana and Chicano Movement, 1966–1977*, Juan Gómez-Quiñones and Irene Vásquez assert, "Multiethnicity and multiculturalism are ongoing processes of social definition within U.S. boundaries, whose parameters Mexican Americans have advanced. The United States is continually being socially and institutionally defined and Mexican American communities are part of that definition."[6]

As counternarrative to the rhetorical construction of postwar civil rights history, scholars like Gómez-Quiñones and Vásquez acknowledge that the battle for inclusion has been waged by an array of everyday voices. Civil rights narratives that rest on binaries exclude the stories and histories of those between and outside the poles, those who nevertheless struggled, and continue to struggle, for inclusion and equality on behalf of their peoples. Mexican American civil rights narratives rest between the poles of black and white, continuously complicating the canon of U.S. civil rights history.

Rhetorical scholarship over the past decade has begun recovering these lesser-known voices through history who have shaped American civic reform. In her article "The Long Civil Rights Movement and the Political Uses of the Past," Jacquelyn Dowd Hall calls for "a more robust, more progressive, and *truer* story."[7] Renee Romano and Leigh Raiford's *The Civil Rights Movement in American Memory* takes up the call.[8] Stirring the current of recovery rhetorics, Jacqueline Jones Royster's *Traces of a Stream: Literacy and Social Change among African American Women* chronicles the rhetorical biographies of little-known public figures through the nineteenth century who served as harbingers for African American voices and activists of the twentieth century. Cornel West's *American Evasion of Philosophy: A Genealogy of Pragmatism* signals the growing "renascence" of academic scholars, public intellectuals, and social activists "moving into the frightening wilderness of pragmatism and historicism" to engage and resist institutional structures of domination and subordination.[9] Finally, Minrose Gwin's *Remembering Medgar Evers: Writing the Long Civil Rights Movement* eloquently defines this historical moment as "an aesthetics of memory."[10]

We are hungry for new stories. In this turbulent post-Obama moment, we need scholarship across the disciplines to help expand recovery rhetorics that make visible the conspicuously absent, those figures who remind us of the possibilities of leading public lives and enacting the possibilities of democracy. Who are the shadow figures of the past who can shed light on our present? In *The Public Work of Rhetoric: Citizen-Scholars and Civic Engagement*, John Ackerman and David Coogan ask, how do we as educators cultivate citizen scholars for the twenty-first century?[11] The anxieties of public life in government, industry, health, and the spectrum of cultural arts press the limits of rhetorical imagination. Ackerman and Coogan contend, "Though we enter these scenes as citizen-scholars, and in fact we often use our academic training sometimes as a moral compass and discursive divining rod, in most of our narratives we discover a preexisting conspiracy against the common good in public life that cannot be determined through the intellectual prism of the hermeneutic interpretation."[12] In brief, we need the rhetoric of story, not only as history but as imaginative fiction. As West contends, "in this world-weary period of pervasive cynicisms, nihilisms, terrorisms, and possible extermination, there is a longing for norms and values that can make a difference, a yearning for principled resistance and struggle that can change our desperate plight."[13]

The erosion of civil rights reforms throughout latter decades of the twentieth century and into the early twenty-first century in all facets of American life, combined with the failure of the New Left within the academy to offer pragmatic strategies or maps of resistance, stirs the shadow of history. Since the landmark presidency of Barack Obama, the backlash of the political right—the beneficiaries of hereditary privilege—reverberates in all facets of public life: government, education, media, environment, and international diplomacy. To echo West's own words, "I am disappointed with the professional incorporation of former New Left activists who now often thrive on a self-serving careerism while espousing rhetorics of oppositional politics of little seriousness and integrity."[14] Nevertheless, these lacunae of the New Left give us occasion to contemplate the stories of leaders making a difference through acts of everyday citizenship. As a scholar and educator, I am heartened by those leaders, those everyday figures that West would call prophetic pragmatists, who resist despair and endure.

Emerging voices within academic and civic culture are beginning to reconcile the fact that the struggles of twentieth-century civil rights movements emerged from the far corners of the nation—the Deep South as well as deep in the Southwest. These new evolving narratives are slowly complicating and transforming the national historical narrative. As Raúl Yzaguirre observes, "precious little has been written about the civil rights struggles of Mexican Americans, Puerto Ricans, and other Latinos. And it is largely unknown even to otherwise well-informed decision-makers, much less the average politically sophisticated citizen."[15] The challenge of obscurity is not limited to any one group or subject position. The burden of obfuscation is political and rhetorical. In a recent tribute celebrating the fiftieth anniversary of the 1964 Civil Rights Act, President Barack Obama remarked on April 10, 2014, at the Lyndon B. Johnson Presidential Library:

> Those of us who have had the singular privilege to hold the office of the Presidency know well that progress in this country can be hard and it can be slow, frustrating, and sometimes you're stymied. The office humbles you. You're reminded daily that in this great democracy, you are but a relay swimmer in the currents of history, bound by decisions made by those who came before, reliant on the efforts of those who will follow to fully vindicate your vision.[16]

Resisting despair, Obama reminds us that our nation needs to recover the talisman of history to help us read not only the past but to divine our place in the present.

Civil Rights Reform and Rhetorical Resilience

There are a few national leaders telling their stories, those who took the long view and offered a hand to draft the larger map of U.S. civil rights reform. There are a few figures whose lives and legacies complicate the accepted grand narrative of the postwar civil rights era, whose voices provide contour and dimension to the linear, flat surface of history making. They reassure us that the currents of history do not level the "impossible possibility."[17] As Michelle Ballif reminds in "Writing the Event: The Impossible Possibility for Historiography," the historicity of an event like the civil rights era is "beyond categorical systems of knowledge and certainly beyond programmatical systems of agency."[18] History is the rupture of the linear narrative, the counternormative, the traumatic event. For Mexican American civil rights activists, the traumatic event of exclusion never ended.

To spark and sustain a social movement is a hermeneutic problem distinctly different from institutionalizing and implementing social reform. Making a system shift and taking a holistic ecological approach to social change demands agitators as well as agents of healing. As a historical commonplace, it is generally acknowledged that revolutionary leaders rarely finish the revolutions they begin. They break through the surface of the habitual. It is the uncommon figure who endures the turbulence of revolution and remains in circulation to promote the necessary process of healing and reconciliation.

Vicente Ximenes is one of those rare historical figures, an activist who fought for inclusion on many fronts. He made the unusual leap from community organizer to national insider, navigating the postwar political landscape all the way to Lyndon B. Johnson's administration. As a grassroots leader who extended his scope from the mesquite-covered plains of South Texas to the White House, Ximenes represents a study in rhetorical resilience. He is a figure who both ruptured the normative social structure and helped repair the violence of history. This book foregrounds the ruptures and the lacunae that Ximenes filled. It describes the ruptures in the commonsense world of the post–World War II United States through an examination of Ximenes's rhetorical and political moments. My aim is to tell old stories in new ways and to introduce complex voices that help to enlarge the evolving historical recovery project of twentieth-century U.S. civil rights rhetoric. Ximenes's life and work answer the question, how can rhetorical action help us condition our environments for health, wholeness, and justice?

While the story of Vicente Ximenes invokes the mnemonics of "the historiographical operation" as a kind of discourse-based hermeneutic practice explored by Michel de Certeau's *The Writing of History* and Paul Ricoeur's *Memory, History, Forgetting*, I am reading the text for its present purposes—its epistemic as well as pedagogic value. The Ximenes story helps to answer several critical questions about the (re)distribution of power for a nation pitted against itself over the politics of hereditary privilege. As a consumer nation coming to the end of its current ecological shelf life, we need models of citizenship and leadership that engage the rich ecotones of difference.[19]

The cultural rhetorical ecology represented by the life and work of Vicente Ximenes offers a vision for what it means to be a citizen, to occupy diverse social spheres, and to exercise the agency of belonging.

The scenes of the Ximenes story are described here as inductive moments of rhetorical action. The events of Ximenes's rhetorical career are more akin to methodological moments woven into one another than to discrete phases of development or periodization.[20] Envisioned as inductive moments expanding into overlapping spheres of influence, Ximenes's immersion into public life represents a dynamic ecology of cultural rhetorical fields of experience. He engaged history by practicing resilient presence and persistent action in his expanding ecological spheres of relationships over an extended span of time. As de Certeau asserts, "making history is a practice."[21] Ximenes made history through action not pontification. He made history by doing history. Telling his story necessitates a similar practical approach.

While I share the historian's imperative to authenticate the record through evidence, as a rhetorician I also remain keenly aware of the metadiscourse of history, the selectivity and partiality that shape all texts.[22] In the epistemic universe of rhetoric, the rhetor, the text, and the audience are inextricably co-constitutive. As such, I foreground each chapter with Ximenes's own public discourse to situate him as agent in the dynamic ecology of his own story. His letters, speeches, reports, testimonies, and lectures encapsulate the cultural rhetorical ecologies of his own experience. As a rhetorical history, the scholarly task invites us to historicize, contextualize, narrativize, theorize, analyze, intertextualize, and synthesize these texts in order to glean significance from the extant material and to catalyze meaning for present purposes.

As an author and scholar, my first obligation is to cast my subject as an active participant, or agent, in the narrativization of his own experience against the rhetorical construction of history. I have structured this book to give Ximenes center stage. Here is my bias: to cast Ximenes as the lead actor in his own story. This is where my principal duty rests. While other key actors, like Lyndon B. Johnson, share this historical platform, this is Ximenes's rhetorical liturgy.[23] Although there are many features of this project that align my work with political biography, engaging the hermeneutics of the text is the primary task. As a historical rhetorical scholar, I assume a stance of critical distance with the extant material under examination. Nevertheless, I also acknowledge my unique connection to the subject of this study. Like Jacqueline Jones Royster confesses, "I realized fairly early in the project that I had no desire to be totally dispassionate, nor to assume a 'pseudo-objective stance.'"[24] The connections and ethical implications are the very exigences for this work.

Why Vicente Ximenes?

Ximenes belonged to a vibrant and engaged generation of Mexican American leaders who extended the work of their predecessors beyond the barrios of their communities toward national reform.[25] They were born during the first two decades of the twentieth century and emerged from their experiences of World War II into one of the most politically engaged generations in U.S. history. Beneficiaries of Franklin D. Roosevelt's New Deal liberalism, they reimagined their place in U.S. democracy and claimed the rights and privileges of belonging. They acquired educations, served their communities, assumed positions of authority, and confronted the disparities of institutionalized discrimination. Physician Héctor P. García, labor organizers Ernesto Galarza and César Chávez, community organizer Bert Corona, youth organizer Rodolfo "Corky" Gonzáles, legislators Edward Roybal and Joe Bernal, attorney Gus García, court justice Albert Peña Jr., organizer and economist Vicente Ximenes, and many others constitute a pantheon of groundbreaking post–World War II activists who individually and collectively reconfigured the local and national lives of Mexican Americans.[26]

The recovery of new narratives in American civil rights reform reminds us that social displacement and political dispossession sparked resistance and catalyzed activism throughout U.S. history among many different groups: African Americans, Mexican Americans, Native Americans, labor organizers, feminists, and gay and lesbian organizers. Some efforts were more visible than others, some more efficacious than others. The constellation of rhetorical influences moving the nation into the twentieth-century civil rights era was convergent as well as divergent; resisting marginalization emerges, however, as the unifying theme among twentieth-century civil rights organizers.

Ximenes offers one such story:

> My ancestors helped build the Villa de Flores and prior to the Texas Revolution conducted the government and business affairs of the town. After the revolution a great influx of Americanos, Polish, and German immigrants flooded the town and eventually took over the government and business of Floresville, Texas. My father who was an independent general store owner soon lost his business and became an employee of the Americano store owners. We became aliens and dirty Mexicans in our own land.[27]

The struggle for visibility, the exercise of rhetorical agency, the necessity for coalition building, and the evolution of civic community reflect some of the critical mobilization practices at the heart of every social movement like the Cold War Mexican American civil rights movement.

Why Rhetoric?

This rhetorical history of Ximenes offers a unique case study of civil rights activism informed by a fifty-year perspective—the product of enduring pragmatism, democratic practice, and perseverance. As a rhetorical project, Ximenes offers an uncommon constellation of lifelong associations and efficacious moves that enhanced his agency of belonging across diverse social spheres. It is not just that Ximenes gained access to so many spheres but that so many others gained access with him. As a world-class leader, Ximenes forged a public service career spanning the globe for over five decades. Ximenes retired as an Air Force major after World War II and was awarded the Distinguished Flying Cross and the Air Medal for combat duty. During the 1960s he took a leadership role in the Alliance for Progress programs in Latin America, accepting an appointment under President John F. Kennedy as an economist and program coordinator in Quito, Ecuador (1961–64), and an appointment as deputy director for the U.S. Agency for International Development in Panama (1966–67) during the Johnson administration. He then served as the U.S. commissioner of the Equal Employment Opportunity Commission (EEOC) (1967–71) and chairman of the White House Cabinet Committee on Mexican American Affairs (1967–69). He retired to New Mexico, where he remained active in human rights issues and helped to establish the New Mexico Youth Conservation Corps, coming full circle by returning to the places and projects where his professional life began. Ximenes realized early on as a young clerk serving in the Civilian Conservation Corps that environmental justice (across natural, constructed, and social spaces) is both a human rights and civil rights issue.

Ximenes is one of the few postwar activists who joined the ranks of Johnson's cadre of leaders, the stewards of Great Society policies. Moving into national policy making, Ximenes joined Johnson's Great Society at the front lines in Sargent Shriver's War on Poverty program in 1965, serving urban neighborhoods torn apart by poverty and the violence of explosive race riots. Three years later Ximenes emerged not only as one of the highest ranking appointees in Johnson's administration but as one of most influential government representatives of Mexican American issues in post–World War II U.S. history.[28]

Ximenes's public service record and lifetime achievements have been lauded locally and nationally. He served as chairman of the New Mexico Youth Conservation Corps Commission, appointed by New Mexico Governor Bruce King in 1991 and reappointed to the commission by Governor Bill Richardson in 2003. President Jimmy Carter appointed Ximenes commissioner of White House Fellows (1977–81). Additionally, Ximenes was the recipient of the Common Cause Public Service Achievement Award, Washington, D.C., in 1982 and the State of New Mexico Distinguished Service Award in 1981. The Vicente Ximenes Scholarship in Public Rhetoric and Community Literacy, first established at the University of New Mexico in 2005, has been awarded to over a half-dozen recipients who are now tenure-line professors in rhetorical studies and Chicana/o studies programs across the nation.[29] The Ximenes Scholarship continues to honor his rhetorical legacy and enduring humanitarian commitment by providing educational support to members of historically underserved groups.[30] In recognition of his half-century association with the University of New Mexico, Ximenes was also awarded an Honorary Doctorate in Humane Letters in 2008.

This is the first book to privilege the perspective of a Mexican American leader exercising rhetorical authority inside the White House. The emergence of new scholarship in Mexican American civil rights history over the past ten years is slowly seeping into the national consciousness. Nonetheless, studies of Mexican American civil rights rhetoric, and of the impact of Mexican American civil rights activists on current rhetoric surrounding Mexican Americans' place within the larger landscape of American democracy, are few. The recent release of Anthony Quiroz's *Leaders of the Mexican American Generation* (2015) places Ximenes in the pantheon of Mexican American civil rights activists of the post–World War II era.

Why Now?

This book's release marks the fiftieth anniversary of the historic 1967 White House Cabinet Committee Hearings on Mexican American Affairs in El Paso. This event signaled a watershed moment for the Cold War Mexican American civil rights movement. The unprecedented El Paso Hearings represented a major shift in national visibility and Latino/a leadership, an event guided by Ximenes as the first Mexican American cabinet committee member serving in dual administrative appointments as commissioner of the EEOC and chair of the Inter-Agency Committee on Mexican American Affairs.

This 2017 post-Obama moment also marks an era when we as a nation are roiling from the surge of "white-lash" and the most overtly racist national rhetoric since the Reconstruction.[31] Whereas the "won cause" narrative of progress and a binary representation of civil rights struggles prevail within historical scholarship and public culture, the civil rights story is not over.[32] Enhancing the tapestry of civil rights rhetoric scholarship, this book picks up the narrative thread to examine the key role of Mexican American leaders like Ximenes in the institutionalization of civil rights reform during Lyndon B. Johnson's Great Society era.

Ximenes's rhetorical career in twentieth-century Mexican American civil rights history indicates that in order for social movements to effect enduring institutional change, they must become part of governing organizations. They must shape and exercise policy and practice from the inside out. It is not enough to mobilize a movement for social change. Activists must mentor advocates to implement and administer institutional transformation. The efficacy of a movement is ultimately assessed by the effective and strategic placement of representatives from the counterpublic within the dominant social structure. As an appointee to the Johnson presidential administration, Ximenes made that pivotal shift from hometown civil rights agitator to high-level government policy maker.

What then moves a figure from regional lore to national history making? For civil rights activists like Ximenes, the *chispa* of distinction was ignited by an exigence, a discursive dissonance, an act of resistance. Ximenes describes the moment he took his place on the political stage of his generation:

> I attended a Mexicano school through the fourth grade and then trans-
> ferred to the integrated school for the rest of my elementary and secondary
> school grades. There was an elementary school for black students and no
> secondary or high school for them. Mexican Americans were grudgingly
> admitted. "You are prohibited from speaking Spanish in class or on the
> school grounds" was my first instruction at the integrated school. Little
> by little, the Mexican Americans at the integrated school were driven
> out by persistent discrimination by some biased teachers. The last dis-
> criminatory act at the integrated school occurred at the PTA banquet
> for high school graduates. Five of us Mexican Americans survived the
> war against us and the nice PTA ladies placed us all at one table in the
> back of the banquet room. All five of us came to the table and looked at
> each other and without a word walked out just as the minister began the
> invocation. I and two other graduates took our caps and gowns and left
> them on the principal's doorstep. It was my first act of symbolic resistance
> to discrimination.[33]

Over seventy-five years later, an *Albuquerque Journal* article titled the "Front Line Warrior" labeled Ximenes the "father of affirmative action."[34] This book traces the journey from those first symbolic acts of resistance to a legacy of civil rights activism and reform.

An Unfinished Story

The story of Ximenes appears briefly in the footnotes of history. Hugh Davis Graham's portrait of Ximenes in *The Civil Rights Era: Origins and Development of National Policy 1960–1972* is factual yet incomplete. Advancing a grand narrative of civil rights history, Graham argues that "the civil rights movement, first led by blacks, then joined by women formed the expanding edge of the New American administrative state."[35] Graham's examination of postwar civil rights policy making chronicles a rhetorical and political climate in which Mexican American activists are invisible if not altogether absent. The only mention of Mexican Americans in Graham's history of the U.S. civil rights era is Vicente Ximenes's name, noted in his examination of EEOC appointments.[36] However, Graham fails to describe in detail Ximenes's rhetorical efficacy as a leader. Focused through the lens of Johnson and his cadre of political actors from within the White House, Graham's portrait characterizes Ximenes as little more than a pawn on a chessboard of political gamesmanship. History hinges on perspective and privilege. Graham offers this account of the Ximenes appointment:

> In the fall of 1966, Johnson moved to shore up his troubled Hispanic flank, where his senior appointments had been far less visible than his female or black appointments. Johnson was responding to stirrings of discontent among the restive Hispanic leaders. They were voicing their resentment of being generally ignored, and at being putatively represented on the EEOC by a Negro woman with a Spanish surname derived from her former spouse. . . .
>
> As a Democrat, Ximenes replaced Aileen Hernandez on the EEOC, thereby swapping a Hispanic male for a black female. Joe Califano confirmed for Johnson Ximenes's assigned role on the EEOC with unmistakable clarity: he "will actively take charge of the Mexican American problem and keep it away from the White House."[37]

The details that Graham omits ultimately constitute a misleading representation of Ximenes's role in the civil rights era. Serving as deputy director of the U.S. Agency for International Development in Panama at the time of the 1967 EEOC appointment, Ximenes was not privy to the gamesmanship that eventually forced Hernandez's resignation from the EEOC. Even more importantly, what Graham fails to include in this account of civil rights history is that Ximenes had consistently maintained strong collaborative relationships with the National Association for the Advancement of Colored

People and black activists during his community organizing throughout the 1950s and early 1960s in New Mexico.

Graham's incomplete portrait of Ximenes unwittingly replicates and exploits the contentious political dynamic that historically characterized Texas race relations—not the complex political world from which Ximenes evolved as a leader.[38] Without the context of a cohesive narrative that fleshes out Ximenes, providing the available means of persuasion of the rhetorical situation as well as his political stake in the story, these brief references constitute, at best, a multitude of fragments in the shifting kaleidoscope of history and, at worst, a misrepresentation of the history itself.

In another problematic representation of Ximenes and of Mexican Americans, Joseph Califano acknowledges Ximenes's role in the Johnson's administration, albeit in a brief footnote to a rowdy depiction of Johnson's introduction of Mexican American activists to the White House in 1966, in *The Triumph and Tragedy of Lyndon Johnson: The White House Years*. Califano, whose office once referred to Ximenes as "LBJ's wetback," however, blurs the lens on Mexican American leaders.[39]

In a portrait more fitting of a slapstick scene featuring the Three Stooges (or Three Amigos) bouncing on the bed in the Lincoln Bedroom than of the president of the United States ushering his honored guests through the White House, Califano perpetuates common stereotypes of Mexican-origin peoples. Califano's description of the May 1966 formal visit of key Mexican American leaders, including Bert Corona and Héctor P. García, details a boisterous evening in which the president refrains from drinking as his country-bumpkin guests imbibe and bumble through the hallowed corridors of the White House. Califano writes, "The Mexican Americans moved from room to room in wide-eyed amazement, raising their glasses as they shouted, 'Viva LBJ!'"[40] Although Ximenes was not actually present for this reportedly inglorious White House visit, he nonetheless appears in Califano's account of the first time a gaggle of Mexican Americans leaders were ever formally entertained at the White House.

The perpetuation of myths and stereotypes and the promulgation of portraits of Ximenes and his contemporaries as shadow figures in U.S. history reifies the black-white binary of civil rights history making. Califano projects onto Ximenes and his colleagues a host of negative stereotypes. A 1967 internal White House memo from Califano's office announcing Ximenes's administrative appointment to the EEOC and Inter-Agency Committee on Mexican American Affairs invokes these same stereotypes in the hand-scribbled moniker "LBJ's wetback" used to designate the newcomer to the White House.[41] Extending the racist jest, White House aides, in turn, would label Ximenes "Califano's wetback" in the stream of interdepartmental memos confidentially circulated to establish his office.[42] As the only person of color on LBJ's cabinet committee, Ximenes was the convenient whipping boy for the internalization of explosive racial tensions that defined the era.

Pluralism and Discursive Democracy

In *The Democratic Paradox*, Chantal Mouffe argues that the defining feature of modern democracy is not a single totalizing discourse but the cacophony of pluralisms. Amid this noise of diversity, modern democracy demands "a profound transformation in the symbolic ordering of social relations."[43] Rhetoric, democracy, and citizenship forge nearly coterminous relationships. The representation of citizens within the *polis* relies on the circulation of pluralistic rhetoric. The valences of difference constitute the hermeneutics of the public sphere. The history of twentieth-century civil rights reform is, among other things, a story about making profound transformations in the legal, social, symbolic, and economic ordering of civic relations. Affirming pluralism in U.S. social institutions, although "axiological" to liberal democratic society, remains a highly contentious public rhetorical process more than forty years since the postwar civil rights era. Twenty-first-century pluralisms—political, cultural, racial, linguistic, ideological, sexual, transnational, religious—continue to problematize how we govern ourselves and impose new demands on democracy.

As the framers of the U.S. Constitution realized early on, self-governance is an ongoing, collective, and generative endeavor. In *Doubt and the Demands of Democratic Citizenship*, David Hiley argues, "The legitimacy of democratic decision making depends on the political process being equally open to all citizens, or at least to legitimate representatives of all citizens."[44] Accordingly, studies of social mobilization that do not examine the institutionalization of civil rights reform represent incomplete portraits of the evolution of U.S. democracy. The ineradicable nature of political discord and the complexity of power relations integral to modern democracy necessitate the inclusion of historical narratives that both complicate and affirm our notions of pluralism.

The constellation of public discourses that contributed to the major civil rights reforms of the twentieth century was pluralistic and dynamic. These multiple dimensions of discursive diversity are critical to invigorating pluralistic democracy. As John Dewey observes in "The Ethics of Democracy," democracies are organic systems that function as parts of the greater whole. The participation of diverse individuals and communities in the exercise of citizenship both transforms and sustains the nation. The greater the variations, the greater are the possibilities for cultural survival. In the spirit of American pragmatism, Dewey reaffirms the integral role of the individual within the aggregate. It is the individual who "realizes within himself the spirit and will of the whole organism."[45] Rather than advancing abstract, normative models, rhetorical studies of civil rights activists like Ximenes provide descriptive portraits of leaders grappling with and shaping pluralist democracy.

The dangers of monolithic versions of civil rights history are no less serious today than they were forty years ago. In his 2007 address commemorating the fortieth anniversary of the historic 1967 White House Committee Hearings on Mexican American Affairs in El Paso, Henry Cisneros, former secretary of Housing and Urban Development, paid tribute to Ximenes's role in U.S. civil rights reform. Cisneros also noted the present state of civil rights, equality, and liberty for Latinos in America. Cisneros asserts:

> If we Latinos are going to make our full contribution to American society we cannot do it without health insurance, without adequate jobs, without completed educations, and without sufficient skills. The task that lies before us is a major one that our civic activists and our political leaders must commit to with the same courage, the same vision, the same uncompromising spirit, the same relentlessness, and the same sense of belief in America and an unwillingness to be ground down as Dr. Ximenes and his contemporaries showed. That is the task of our national leaders today.
>
> In the 1960s and 70s organizations such as the American GI Forum and LULAC [League of United Latin American Citizens] defined a new level of Latino engagement with the larger society. They engaged on a broad front: education, senior issues, children's concerns, disability programs, economic progress, corporate board representation, discrimination—in short, the gamut of life for Latinos in America. Much of the energy for establishing these organizations came out of that period and Dr. Ximenes not only encouraged but facilitated the conditions in which these organizations could prosper. At this point Latinos had capable leaders backed by foundations, churches, and labor organizations and sustained by their own sweat equity and recognition of the need to advocate on behalf of our community. So what started in the earlier era with individuals like Dr. García and like Dr. Ximenes ended up later being an army of activists who could change things dramatically—and have. Today we have some 45 national Latino organizations under the roof of the National Hispanic Leadership Agenda. They meet together to focus on what is important to the 44-plus million Latinos across the United States who are of diverse

origins: Mexican, Cuban, Puerto Rican, Dominican, Central American, and South American.[46]

The need for an expanded scholarship on Mexican American civil rights activism continues to evolve as rapidly as our demographic patterns are changing. As Cisneros further argues in *Latinos and the Nation's Future*, "the Latino population is now so large, its trajectory of growth so rapid, its contrast in relative age to that of the general population so stark, that it will not be possible for the United States to advance without substantial, and so far unimagined, gains in the economic, educational, and productive attributes of the nation's Latino population."[47]

Twentieth-century Mexican American civil rights history offers a valuable and productive heuristic from which to consider strategies that enhance Latino political inclusion, leadership, and community mobilization. The decisive role of the Latino vote in the presidential elections of John F. Kennedy and Lyndon B. Johnson in the 1960s foreshadowed, in many respects, the history-changing role of the Latino vote for the presidential elections of Barack Obama in 2008 and 2012. The efficacy of Latino political participation and the growing *mestizaje* of the American electorate in U.S. history is more than a footnote. It is a central chapter to the story of the American democratic project in the new millennium.

Passing the Torch: The Civil Rights Generation

In his journey from civil rights activist to White House cabinet appointee, Ximenes encountered many of the destabilizing forces of identity politics: racism, shifting constituencies, and the vacillating currents of insider/outsider dynamics. He maintained a leadership role through the turbulence of national change, surviving the cultural, social, and political upheavals of the era by cultivating an unassailable professional reputation and engaging in an unrelenting program of coalition building. Ximenes recalls the challenges of bridging the ideological gap between the World War II generation of reformers of the 1950s and the emergent Chicano generation of the 1960s. No stranger to controversy, Ximenes recounts:

> As EEOC commissioner, I conducted a series of Los Angeles movie industry hearings about negative stereotypes. Some ten or twelve members of MAPA (Mexican American Political Action) charged into the Federal Building hearing room with placards that said "Ximenes sells out," "Ximenes is a Tio Taco." As security guards began to usher them out to

regain order during the hearings, I requested that the protestors not be removed from the hearing room. About ten minutes after my question and answer dialogue with the movie executives, the placards came down and the protest group became a cheering section.[48]

Ximenes was among the local grassroots leaders that evolved with LBJ's visionary and short-lived administration; he served as chairman of the Viva Johnson campaign in 1964 and as an assistant inspector general for the War on Poverty initiative in 1965. Fifty years after President Johnson's Great Society speech, skeptics and pundits revisit this restorative act of epideictic rhetoric held at the University of Michigan commencement in May 1964. LBJ's Great Society remains a bold vision that, in many respects, seems like a quixotic quest in today's climate of polarized partisan politics. It was a utopian vision distorted by the shadows of the Vietnam War. The Great Society represented a constellation of social values that Ximenes and his contemporaries never abandoned.

The broad interconnectedness of LBJ's Great Society resonated deeply with Ximenes's own cultural rhetorical perspective and rich sociocultural affiliations that spanned the globe. As an educator and economist, Ximenes had an intuitive and cultivated sense of the *polis* and *oikos* (the public sphere and the private sphere). It was no mystery to him why the disciplinary fields of economics and ecology emerge out of and align with the classical Greek construct of *oikos* (the home). The cultivation and circulation of energy that are the provenance of both economics and ecology defined Ximenes's ethos. The Spanish notion of *querencia* (love of home, culture, and community) rested at the very center of his personal and professional universe.

Ximenes continued to subscribe to the *topoi* of Johnson's Great Society throughout the postwar social welfare state both at its apex and at its nadir. Ximenes advanced a political worldview promoting economic growth, global peace, and deliberative democracy.[49] He was an unwavering advocate of an expansionist program of social democracy at home and abroad—spending the first half of the 1960s working in Latin America. Serving the advancement of LBJ's domestic and foreign agendas provided Ximenes with the upwardly mobile opportunities he sought professionally for himself and politically for his people. Ximenes keenly understood the organizing tropes of Johnson's Great Society, the literal and metaphorical spaces Johnson described throughout his landmark 1964 University of Michigan commencement address: the city, the countryside, and the classroom.

Ximenes was not only a witness to but also an actor in this rise and subsequent fall of postwar social democracy. He recalls:

In March 1968, President Johnson asked me and Dr. Héctor García to travel to Mexico City with Vice President Humphrey to witness the nuclear non-proliferation treaty signing with Mexican President Díaz Ordáz. On the return flight to Washington, D.C., Humphrey told us that President Johnson announced he would not run for the Presidency. My twenty-seven-year close association with Lyndon Johnson came to an end on that flight. Nixon won the 1968 election and our access to the oval office ended for Dr. García and myself.[50]

Dreams and disappointments were delivered equally.

As Albert O. Hirschman argues in *The Rhetoric of Reaction: Perversity, Futility, Jeopardy*, "the lengthy postwar honeymoon" of universal suffrage and the social welfare state deteriorated rapidly at the close of LBJ's administration, refurbishing a host of reactive rhetorics with the events of the late 1960s and early 1970s as well as launching a forty-year backlash against Great Society legislation and programs. The postwar optimism and near-universal endorsement of expanded social welfare legislation during the first two decades following World War II quickly unraveled with the assassinations of Martin Luther King Jr. and Bobby Kennedy, and the loss of Democratic control of the White House with the election of Richard Nixon. Political tensions over the next four decades frayed the nation as evidenced in the fragmentation of the African American and Mexican American civil rights movements, the erosion of the feminist movement and the failed Equal Rights Amendment, the protracted and demoralizing losses of the Vietnam War, the wars in the Middle East, the oil crisis, and economic stagflation.

The deaths in recent years of Ximenes (February 27, 2014) at the age of ninety-four and his contemporaries Sargent Shriver (director of the Office of Economic Opportunity), Willard Wirtz, (secretary of the Department of Labor), and Dorothy Height (prominent African American civil rights activist for over seventy years) together index the closing chapters of liberal democracy and the administrative order of the civil rights era. Wirtz and Height died within a week of each other in April 2010, each at the age of ninety-eight, stalwart guardians of the postwar social contract of equal opportunity and voting rights.[51] Shriver's death followed in January 2011.

All four leaders were behind-the-scenes actors in the struggle for economic and social equality. Ximenes, in contrast to Wirtz, Shriver, and Height, played on both sides of the administrative aisle, however, as both a mobilizer and an administrator. No other civil rights activist of the period made the shift from community organizer to White House appointee. A gifted mediator like Wirtz, Ximenes worked to resolve many thorny issues related to equal employment during his tenure in Johnson's administration and carried on through the Nixon administration. An efficacious organizer like Height, Ximenes remained a humble and self-effacing champion of civil rights who deserves a place of honor in American history. A capable statesman like Shriver, Ximenes continued to promote social democratic programs well after the political right took hold of the White House. These nearly forgotten figures in the national narrative of postwar civil rights reform represent social cartographers mapping out the protracted possibilities embedded in a collective will to justice.

Ximenes cultivated and carefully constructed the ethos of the quintessential point person, both cultural broker and go-to liaison. He was the reliable agent, the network operator capable of generating enduring results and sustaining tenuous coalitions. Throughout his rhetorical career, Ximenes contended with the central question eloquently posed by Martin Luther King Jr. in his analysis of white backlash in *Where Do We Go from Here: Chaos or Community?* (1967): "Why is equality so assiduously avoided?"[52] Like King and other contemporaries in the civil rights struggle, Ximenes grappled with the Americanist dilemma of liberty and equality. He responded to the interlocking systems of oppression through collective mobilization and political deliberation, pressing for national policy making and demanding government accountability. Both King and Ximenes imagined a nation served and governed by its citizens—regardless of race, sex, linguistic heritage, or national origin. The cultural rhetorical ecology of America for Ximenes, like King, included the complex margins—the ecotones of difference and the rich transition zones of diversity.

The vision crafted by Martin Luther King Jr. in 1968 for the Poor People's Campaign represented a brilliant depiction of an equitable multicultural, multiracial nation, a "beloved community" inclusive of all citizens, all people of color—a nation capable of one day electing a black man to the office of president. Tragically, the Poor People's Campaign that King envisioned, inclusive of black, Latino, and Native American citizens, was never realized.

Ximenes carried on advocating for vulnerable communities long after the loss of his contemporaries Martin Luther King Jr., Stokely Carmichael, Bayard Rustin, Medgar Evers, and Malcolm X. For Ximenes, the civil rights era did not end in 1968. Ximenes and other civil rights leaders continued to step up on behalf of the historically underserved groups of this nation and persevered in the march toward social justice. Ximenes expanded his campaign for civil rights to include organizing on behalf of human rights, including immigration rights, throughout the next forty years. Speaking out on behalf of Latinos, blacks, women, immigrants, workers, youth, the environment, and the poor, Ximenes remained an enduring voice breaking through the long national silence that followed the postwar civil rights era.

When the Lyndon B. Johnson Presidential Library hosted the 2014 Civil Rights Summit to celebrate the fiftieth anniversary of the 1964 Civil Rights Act, President Obama and three former presidents (Bill Clinton, Jimmy Carter, and George W. Bush) were in attendance. Not since the first Civil Rights Symposium hosted at the Lyndon B. Johnson Presidential Library in 1972 (chapter 6) have so many luminaries gathered to commemorate the great civil rights events of the twentieth century. It was Lyndon B. Johnson's last public event before his death. Ximenes, who was a featured speaker in 1972, died just six weeks before the 2014 Civil Rights Summit. Only Julian Bond, who attended the first civil rights symposium in 1972, was present at this most recent civil rights celebration.[53] No other representative of the historical Mexican American civil rights era was present.

The legacy of Vicente Ximenes is part of the conversation on what it takes to build an equitable society, to practice an inclusive democracy, and to exercise the role of citizen of a national community as well as a global community. His enduring presence resonates in an era when social progress and political backlash stand in seemingly unrelenting gridlock. We are a nation at risk of despair. When the presence of thousands of Central American children—starving political, economic, and environmental refugees pressing our southernmost borders—is met with the virulent resistance and political attacks of well-fed white U.S. citizens, we cannot deny that something dark and dehumanizing grips the soul of this nation. The explosive anti-immigration rhetoric over the Fourth of July weekend in 2014 in Arizona and throughout the 2016 presidential election represents a bold contrast to the invitational rhetoric extended to "huddled masses yearning to be free" who pressed our shores over a hundred years ago.[54]

Ximenes reminds us that the great political and social impasses that have deprived so many groups and individuals of basic human rights must be confronted not once and for all, but for all times. Reading the role of Ximenes in the history of Mexican American civil rights activism, moreover, disrupts and complicates the dominant narrative of U.S. civil rights reform. The cultural rhetorical ecologies constituted through Ximenes's life and work represent a descriptive map of Mexican American activism and a topography of civil rights history poignantly reflective of our current twenty-first-century Chicano political ecology.[55]

Recovering Mexican American Civil Rights Rhetorics

This book traces the rhetorical career of Ximenes through six key spheres of his public life: (1) the formative Texas years through World War II military service (1919–47); (2) Ximenes's educational transition and acculturation process in New Mexico (1947–51); (3) the apprenticeship years organizing the American GI Forum in Albuquerque, New Mexico (1951–61); (4) the international service period in Latin America with U.S. Agency for International Development appointments in Ecuador and Panama (1961–67); (5) the national-level appointment phase beginning with the Viva Johnson campaign through the Equal Employment Opportunity Commission years (1964–69); (6) the senior statesman period through the closing of the Great Society and Ximenes's featured speaker role in the first Lyndon B. Johnson Presidential Library Civil Rights Symposium (1969–72). These six spheres of Ximenes's cultural rhetorical experience constitute a rich array of civic discourses illustrating the broad spectrum of his public life.

The rhetorical career of Ximenes situates him securely within the twentieth-century American rhetorical tradition. The Ximenes story is a narrative of process: grappling with exclusionary social structures in twentieth-century America and negotiating the nexus between political outsider and insider. His political journey is illustrative of what Mouffe calls "agonistic pluralism." According to Mouffe, an adversary, in contrast to an enemy, is "somebody whose ideas we combat but whose right to defend those ideas we do not put into question."[56] Antagonism, from this point of view, represents a conflict between enemies whereas agonism represents a conflict between adversaries. Going beyond the limits of deliberative democracy where rational consensus remains elusive and the public sphere remains exclusive, Ximenes again and again found ways to overcome the us-them opposition in the political arena by constructing "them" not as enemies but as adversaries. Demonstrating liberal democratic tolerance in numerous political situations, Ximenes found ways to engage his adversaries and acknowledge the multiple modalities of rhetorical engagement within a democracy.

As a World War II veteran, educator, economist, political activist, government official, and social reformer, Ximenes successfully negotiated multiple roles and discourse communities to institute and promote affirmative action policies on behalf of historically disenfranchised groups. Over the course of his long-standing career, Ximenes migrated from community organizer to Washington insider. From activist to administrator, Ximenes joined the "new American administrative state" of Johnson's Great Society.[57] He successfully navigated geographical, political, class, and cultural borders, forming associations with the poor as well the prominent, including national-level figures such as Kennedy and Johnson. Ximenes was a member of the Mexican American counterpublic as well as the government bureaucratic culture, a leading voice of the counterdiscourse resisting racism and discrimination in public and private institutions as well as a national custodian of the new dominant discourse of affirmative action and civil rights legislative reform.

When cabinet appointments and policy practices failed to implement the promises of the civil rights and voting rights acts, African American and Mexican American activists alike registered their displeasure and disappointment with the White House. "The Great Society is only a phrase so long as no date is set for the achievement of its promises," Martin Luther King Jr. once charged.[58] Mexican American leaders likewise became vocal gadflies to Johnson's Great Society. Héctor P. García publicly lambasted President Johnson in 1965 for forgetting his Spanish-speaking constituencies and failing to hold a White House conference on Mexican American issues.[59] Building on the social reforms of Roosevelt's New Deal, Johnson turned to leaders like Ximenes to implement the vision of a more equitable and just social system.

The civil rights reforms achieved during the Great Society were ultimately fortified by the coordination of all three branches of the federal government—executive, legislative, and judicial. The Great Society reflects a moment of constellation of social democratic leadership, not repeated in over forty years. As Graham observes, "indeed the judicial rulings of the civil rights era show a striking continuity in empowering the executive agencies and their custodians, extending the reach and reinforcing the authority of a new edifice of social regulation that was being constructed without blueprint or even conscious awareness."[60]

Ximenes served as one of the critical custodians and architects of Johnson's Great Society on behalf of his community, representing the needs and interests of the Mexican American constituency. Ximenes directed the historic 1967 White House Cabinet Committee Hearings on Mexican American Affairs in El Paso, Texas, the first national forum of its kind focusing on Mexican American issues. Ximenes invited Chicano activists into dialogue with members of President Lyndon B. Johnson's cabinet and postwar Mexican American reformers. Additionally, Ximenes helped to launch bilingual education initiatives and initiated the Model Cities Program that advanced urban renewal in cities throughout the Southwest.

For Ximenes, the exigencies and the rhetorical situation of civil rights activism extended beyond the typical characterization of the civil rights era. What was initially constructed as the cover term to represent the fight for constitutionally based rights of civic inclusion, *civil rights* now more broadly represents an umbrella term denoting movements for social justice advanced by diverse groups and issues. The problem with unpacking the meaning of a term or construct is not limited to concepts as slippery or as constantly evolving as civil rights.

This book offers a portrait of the rhetorical career of Vicente Ximenes that does not pretend to be biographically objective but that seeks instead to reflect the inherent ambiguities and preserve the shady edges of a complex leader in a complex historical moment. Constructed through archival research, fieldwork, and oral history interviews, this description of postwar Mexican American civil rights sharpens critical focus on the discursive action of Vicente Ximenes as a pivotal rhetorical agent of U.S. civil rights reform—moving from mobilization to inclusion.[61]

I am indebted to the work of my colleagues in history, sociology, and political science for invaluable research that has helped to contextualize the efficacious relationship between Ximenes and Lyndon B. Johnson—a political alliance that was shaped by (as well as helped to shape) national history. The rhetorical legacies of Vicente Ximenes and Lyndon B. Johnson illustrate that the essence of discursive democracy is not only exercising the vote but also participating in sustained and productive public deliberation. Ximenes and Johnson rallied as sparring partners (often at opposite corners of the political boxing ring) for several decades around questions related to Mexican American access to the ballot, to social goods, and to the political platform as well. Together they enacted a number of discursive democratic practices, acting on the conviction that deliberative processes allow citizens to discover their political interests, to make sense of the issues that influence their lives, to cultivate public opinions, and to take positions on problems. As rhetorical actors, Ximenes and Johnson affected not only post–World War II civil rights reform but the topography of Mexican American civic life into the twenty-first century.

1. *"Chente": Interrogating Histories, Negotiating Rhetorics*

*I*n an October 2006 guest lecture delivered to students at the University of New Mexico, Ximenes invited college writers to tell their own stories. Offering his own narrative as a model or heuristic, Ximenes illustrated how to interrogate the art of memory and engage the rhetoric of testimony. In this brief narrative, Ximenes candidly describes his experience growing up during the Dust Bowl years in Depression-era South Texas. He reflects on openly confronting enduring patterns of racism in U.S. society:

> From the time I was a grade school student in the 1920's until today the subjects of discrimination, race, color, national origin, and human rights have been a part of my life. From the first grade in a Mexican American segregated school in the 1920's until I received a Master's degree at UNM, I had a preponderant majority of teachers that did not value my culture, language, custom, national origin, music, or food. Even my mother's tasty bean burrito tortillas were ridiculed in school. I never had a Mexican American or Hispanic teacher during my formal education.
>
> I grew up in Floresville, Texas, a town of about two thousand inhabitants and divided into barrios of Mexicanos, Polish, German, Americanos and Negroes. I use these politically incorrect labels because these were the terms used to identify each other in our town. We attended a Mexicano school through the fourth grade and then we were transferred to an integrated school for the rest of secondary and high school. The Negroes had an elementary school and could not transfer to the integrated school, but would have to travel thirty miles to San Antonio to a Negro high school. The Negroes could not attend the Mexicano school and the Mexicanos could not attend the Negro elementary school. Texas racists were smart that way.
>
> Floresville was a violent town and Mexican Americans killed each other in family feuds. The annual Cinco de Mayo celebration lasted a week and included dancing, singing, and emotional speeches about the victory of the Mexicans against the French. But when the Castros and the Coys entered the fiesta area excitement and apprehension permeated the crowd. We all knew a shoot-out with one death was about to take place. The Diez y Seis de Septiembre was just as enthusiastic and lively as the Cinco de Mayo but we could expect violence as well.[1]

At the age of eighty-seven, with his long silver hair tied back in a ponytail and wearing a turquoise bolo tie and tennis shoes, Ximenes told his story to a group of young New Mexican students. Keenly aware that the majority of the class were first-generation bilingual college students, Ximenes described the texture of cultures, communities, and histories of his own South Texas beginnings. Resisting division, discrimination, and the denigration of difference represents a common thread weaving throughout Ximenes's story. As Paul Ricoeur argues in *Memory, History, Forgetting*, "everything starts, not from the archives, but from testimony."[2] Critical consciousness for Ximenes was not the product of academic theorizing; rather, it evolved out of the stories, experiences, and social conditions into which he was born and raised.

Mapping the Cultural Rhetorical Ecologies of History

The challenge of tracing the public life of Vicente Ximenes demands enhancing the notion of the rhetorical situation to map the dynamic influences or exigencies shaping social action. How does a social actor expand a sphere of concern into a sphere of influence? Rhetoric is the discursive conduit invigorating our environmental spheres, or cultural ecologies. Cultural rhetorical ecologies, therefore, represent the energy systems that vitalize social, cultural, political, and linguistic action and that, ultimately, condition rhetorical situations.

Just as microclimates and geologies condition the ecologies of bioregions, human environmental factors such as political economies, linguistic patterns, and cultural formations, literally and metaphorically, condition the ecologies of our shifting social configurations. Rhetorical situations constitute (and are constituted by) social actors engaging with their cultural ecology, or environmental terroir.[3] In *Chicano Culture, Ecology, Politics: Subversive Kin*, Devon Peña offers the concept of Chicano ecology to represent cultural and environmental Indo-Hispanic ways of life.[4] Extending Peña's notion of Chicano ecology, I offer the construct of cultural rhetorical ecologies to account for the interdependent and dynamic influences of rhetors acting within their social environments and the social environments stirring rhetors to act.

This chapter chronicles the evolving rhetorical career of Ximenes, beginning with his formative years in Floresville, Texas, and extending through his three-decade association with Lyndon B. Johnson. Their association began in the mesquite-covered plains of Texas and culminated in the nation's capital. Their South Texas spheres of belonging overlapped and included a number of important mutual associations such as Héctor García. The political, educational, economic, and personal dimensions of these multilayered sociohistorical contexts generated the exigencies and cultural rhetorical ecologies that ultimately shaped Ximenes as a leader. The South Texas social situation both cultivated and compelled Ximenes to acquire the rhetorical resilience that would serve him over the course of his long and varied career.

Fondly known as "Chente" among family and friends, Ximenes had an engaging style, easy smile, and vibrant eyes that inspired trust and confidence. His robust sense of humor and deep appreciation of irony allowed him to weather the incessant setbacks and roadblocks along the way. The contradictions of politics left him untroubled. He reveled in paradox. Ximenes stood a compact figure, less than five and a half feet in height (a striking contrast to the looming figure of Lyndon B. Johnson, who was over ten years his senior and nearly a foot taller). Ximenes made up for disparities in age and height with confidence, charm, tenacity, optimism, determination, and generosity of spirit. He was a worthy counterpart to Johnson's signature strong-arm style. The qualities that made Johnson so effective as a politician—his domineering mien, calculated ambition, and unrestrained drive—made him less effective in the art of cultivating durable and equitable relationships. Ximenes, in contrast, was characteristically faithful, affable, and measured. Their relationship was a dance. Ximenes flirted with power; Johnson devoured it.

Throughout his life Ximenes lived in constant tension between two competing desires: the desire for distinction and recognition, and the desire to be useful. Steeped in the anguish of poverty, Ximenes was moved by a deep need to mitigate the suffering of others. Satisfying his own humanity and serving humanity were not always compatible urgencies, however. As he built his career, those in his personal sphere often had less of him than they needed or wanted. It was a precarious balance. Ever adept at self-representation and unabashed self-promotion, Ximenes possessed the alacrity and integrity necessary to survive and thrive in his upwardly mobile trajectory to national prominence. His rhetorical prowess enabled him to write (and speak) effectively across academic, professional, and civic communities. He published seven volumes for the University of New Mexico Bureau of Business Research as an economist. An exemplar of the citizen scholar, Ximenes left an authorial trace in every sphere he occupied. His press for distinction in every arena—academics, the military, and politics—was counterbalanced by a strong humanitarian impulse. Unlike Johnson, Ximenes never held an elected office. He saw himself as a public servant, not a politico. Nevertheless, he admired men like Johnson who knew how to gain and hold power.

Ximenes never spoke ill of Johnson, despite the debacle of the Vietnam War that led to the nadir of LBJ's political career. Ximenes never overtly confronted Johnson for his contradictions. If he had, he would have been cast out of Johnson's small and continuously shrinking inner circle. Ximenes remained confident that the pall that darkened Johnson's legacy for decades after his presidency would be lifted as the impact of Great Society policies and programs were realized. Ximenes forgave the incessant oversights, oversteps, and slights. The scales were, in the end, balanced for Ximenes. He simply wished that history would tell the full story. And for Ximenes, the full story of Johnson and the Great Society included milestones in Mexican American civil rights reform. For Ximenes, the Great Society remained the metaphorical glass half full.

As for his own public career, Ximenes wanted to do well. He wanted to be successful. And he wanted the same for everyone. He was the middle son who just wanted everyone to get along. He looked to the intrinsic reward systems of public life, reveling in the esteem and benefits of social prominence. The differences between Ximenes and Johnson were far greater than their similarities. Beneath the veneer of shared politics and the trope of the *buen amigo*, Ximenes and Johnson shared little in common. The ethical compass directing the course of their lives moved them toward very different goals.

While Ximenes enjoyed the mobility of being a member of the professional class, in the end, he was a tourist passing through in the fast lane. Ximenes never owned the bodacious Cadillacs that were the signature status symbols of men like Johnson and his *buen amigo* Héctor García. Ximenes never adopted the messianic stance or jeremiad rhetorical posturing that characterized García's prophetic style. Ximenes's tastes were modest. His rhetorical style was direct and protean, shifting shape to accommodate his audiences and to reflect the multiple cultural rhetorical ecologies he occupied. The proverbial Hermes figure, Ximenes was willing to do business with the merchants, thieves, politicians, and power brokers. He was comfortable in many different environments. And yet, for his entire married life, Ximenes only ever owned one home, the small adobe house that he and María built on Monroe Street in Albuquerque. He could have demanded more, but he was satisfied with the thrill of the journey (and less interested in the status symbols of success).

These three Texas men converged and diverged in a number of ways: styles, tastes, and personalities. However, Ximenes, García, and Johnson had one thing in common: they thrived in the political limelight. The erotics of politics enchanted them: the energy, the tension, the contact, the pursuit, the drama. They loved the public attention that politics offered them. All three men shared a passion for the public sphere with all its entanglements and associations. And they loved the political process, engaging with others toward constituting a communion of minds. In other words, they reveled in rhetoric.

Few insiders survived the political maelstroms of Johnson's career. Known for withering the souls of countless men, Johnson was an unrelenting force of nature. He was known across circles for rhetorically mowing down every-thing in his path.[5] In a mythic universe, Ximenes was Hermes to Johnson's Zeus: the crafty network operator to the overbearing political god; a master of relationship building to Johnson's mastery of domination.[6] The political forces that ultimately claimed Johnson and ran him out of office did not consume Ximenes. In the end, Ximenes outlived Johnson by more than forty years. Johnson raged all the way to the grave; Ximenes's wry, hermetic smile graced his journey to the end. Rhetorical resilience was both a gift and a practice Ximenes cultivated in every sphere of belonging—from small-town Texas to the White House.

The Art of Memory: Testimony and Told Story

The remote outposts of south central Texas represented a rich geohistorical site of competing visions and conflicting histories that inflected Ximenes's notions of self. Manuel Castells's *Power of Identity* contends that identity represents complex constructions of meaning forged through social roles and cultural attributes that individuals internalize, value, and prioritize. The act of self-construction, or self-fashioning, is a dynamic process using the raw materials of history, geography, biology, and collective memory.[7] The internal mapping of cultural encounters, the confluences and disso-nances of lived experience within the contested spaces of Texas (the region of Greater Mexico), constituted the multilayered ethos (social positions) and the *nomos* (normative values) metonymically marking Ximenes's identity as a self-ascribed "Mexican American."[8]

The cultural rhetorical ecologies that shaped Ximenes's identity include the broad dimensions of linguistic, cultural, educational, ideological, economic, and political features of his primary, secondary, and tertiary relationships. Spanish was his first language. Ximenes learned English when he entered the public schools of Floresville at the age of five. Unlike many of his peers, Ximenes was literate in both Spanish and English. He was one of the few Mexican Americans who completed high school and was academically suc-cessful enough to be admitted to and attend the University of Texas at Aus-tin. He spoke and wrote English with few orthographic or phonological influences from Spanish as his first language. Ximenes acquired the formal registers of professional discourse beginning with his stint as a clerk with the Civilian Conservation Corps (CCC) immediately following his high school graduation. Fluent and eloquent in spoken and written Spanish and English, Ximenes was able to exercise growing authority in his circles of belonging throughout his rhetorical career.

His military service as an officer in the U.S. Air Force during World War II further enhanced his communicative repertoire. He served as an aviation cadet and then an officer in the Air Force, eventually teaching new cadets in the training command. His record of overseas military service and distinguished leadership as an Army Air Corps officer gave him strong authority in both military and civilian circles. Ximenes's acquisition of the discourses of military culture and its emblems of distinction further enhanced his social cachet.

Over the course of his rhetorical career, Ximenes's expanding spheres of agency afforded him access to four types of social power: the *ascribed power* of being a sixth-generation descendant of a Tejano colonial family and son of Floresville's political *patrón*; the *acquired power* of a distinguished military career and a graduate-level college education; the *transgressive power* of serving as a community organizer and activist; and the *transformative power* of acting as an advocate for Mexican Americans through his role as a White House–level administrator.

Joe's Boy: From Floresville to Washington, D.C.

Vicente Treviño Ximenes was born on December 5, 1919, in Floresville, about forty miles from the landmark Spanish colonial city of San Antonio, Texas. Situated in the south central section of the state, which geographers call the shatter belt, this region once served as hunting grounds for nomadic tribes such as the Tonkawas, Kawankawa, Comanches, and Lipan Apaches. In the wake of Spanish colonization of the eighteenth century, the sprawling hacienda of Francisco Flores de Abreyo was donated to its Spanish-heritage inhabitants and became the township of Floresville. This farming village eventually formed the center of rural Wilson County's political and economic life, a small oasis of stability in the crosscurrents of a contested frontier. The surrounding territory of Texas, however, remained embattled throughout most of the nineteenth century.

The U.S.-Mexican War raged only miles from the El Paso–Juarez border from 1846 to 1848, following the annexation of Texas to the United States. The long-term geopolitical battle between Mexico and the United States over boundaries and territory, most famously mythologized with the stories of the 1836 Battle of the Alamo, permanently recalibrated social relations between Anglo and Mexican/Spanish-origin residents of the region. As descendants of the early Spanish colonists as well as indigenous inhabitants of the region, the Ximenes family was uniquely positioned in the contestations over land ownership.

Moreover, the Ximenes family claimed ancestry with one of the fallen heroes of the Battle of the Alamo, Damacio Jiménez. These histories of belonging and stories of entitlement influenced the Ximenes family's sense of place as first peoples predating the arrival of other Anglo-European immigrant populations including German, Polish, and Irish newcomers. The constitutive nature of family lore helped to coalesce the attributes of identity that Vicente Ximenes embraced as his own. He was proud of the paradoxical histories of his own family legacy: Spanish, Tejano, Mexican, and Indian. He was all of these, but not without the unresolvable contradictions that seemed to motivate his unrelenting urge toward social justice. The cultural and racial *mestizaje* of Ximenes family history, informed by notions of white privilege and the pigmentocracy of Texas social stratification, was embedded with the unresolvable dilemma of a genealogy descended from both the colonized and colonizer.[9] Uneven enforcement of the Treaty of Guadalupe Hidalgo left many Mexican-origin citizens landless, destitute, and with subordinate status. These inequities and injustices would endure for generations. The Ximenes family held onto their colonial claims of belonging as Tejanos as well as their identification with Spanish and Mexicano culture.

The region continued to develop steadily throughout the nineteenth century with the growth of ranching and plantation farming. The incorporation of Wilson County (Floresville served as the county seat) was officially recognized at the onset of the Civil War. It was also the moment when the good citizens of the region sent their soldiers to support the Confederacy. Public records of the area indicate that a number of slaveholders resided in the region. Like the rest of the state of Texas, slavery in Wilson County had helped to enhance the wealth and productivity of the plantation owners. Agricultural products of the area expanded to include the cultivation of cotton, corn, sugarcane, and peanuts. Participation in the war effort was motivated by the desire to protect economic and political interests in the region, which were increasingly dependent on slave labor and *mexicano* peonage.

Following the Civil War, Wilson County fell under carpetbag rule and was ultimately controlled by self-appointed judge John W. Longsworth, who "assumed authority as clerk and all other offices."[10] The ancestral Spanish colonial families of Floresville and the vicinity had already begun to lose their land and political influence in the area. By the mid-nineteenth century,

Anglos dominated the political and economic structure of the region. A record of early public officials in Wilson County (1860–64) includes only three individuals with Spanish surnames: Vicente Cantu, Rafael Herrera, and Francisco Ximenes (a possible distant relation). By the end of the nineteenth century, the majority of public officials were of non-Spanish origin with surnames such as Pickett, Sutherland, Reagen, Floyd, McAllister, Hughes, Rutter, and Morgan.

At the close of the late nineteenth century, Wilson County had evolved into an increasingly mixed demographic of white landowners, poor whites, blacks, Mexicans, tenants, sharecroppers, and farmworkers. The open grasslands and natural resources of the region (oil and natural gas) became magnets of opportunity in the era of industrialization. With the success of the ranch and farm industries, a booming commercial infrastructure followed. When the railroad reached the region in 1886, Floresville proudly claimed two hotels, two steam gristmills and cotton gins, its own newspaper known then as the *Floresville Chronicle*, a bank, dry-goods store, millinery, blacksmith shop, and restaurant. By 1890 the growing commercial life of Floresville touted over sixty business owners including a dentist, music teacher, photographer, lawyer, physician, Methodist minister, jeweler, harness maker, and bookstore owner. Five of the leading proprietors and professionals carried Spanish surnames.[11]

Regardless of the shifting political dynamics, the Hispanicization of Texas was a constant with the continuous wave of immigrants from south of the border, especially during the Mexican Revolution (1910–20). Political and economic turbulence in Mexico throughout the late nineteenth and early twentieth centuries brought refugees like Héctor P. García's family to South Texas from Mexico. Additionally, a second wave of Spanish colonists joined the scene and settled in the region. Upheaval in the sugar markets during the nineteenth century and a subsequent global recession stirred an exodus from the Canary Islands, a strand of Spanish islands off the northwest coast of mainland Africa, bringing thousands of new immigrants to the Americas. With the collapse of the sugar-based economy in the Canary Islands and growing competition with former New World colonies, this new generation of Spanish-origin immigrants eventually claimed a place on the Texas frontier. San Antonio (and the adjoining Wilson County region) became home to many of these Canary Island immigrants.

Conflicts over colonial primacy, hereditary privilege, and an emerging white-dominant pigmentocracy further complicated social dynamics within the Spanish/Mexican-origin communities of south central Texas. The historical, socioeconomic, and demographic features of the region constituted a complex political climate and rhetorical training ground for Ximenes. Negotiating the divide between "conquerors and conquered, as victors and vanquished" has been a cross-generational struggle for Mexican-origin peoples.[12]

How did Ximenes and his family fit into this situation? The complexities of race and social stratification challenged the position of the Ximenes family and other Mexican Americans of the region. In *The White Scourge: Mexicans, Blacks, and Poor Whites in Texas Cotton Culture*, Neil Foley notes:

> The fusion of cotton and cattle culture, of plantation and ranch, created a hybrid economy that mixed mostly small farmers (whether tenants or sharecroppers on plantations or owner-operated family farms) with large-scale, industrialized cotton ranches that employed hundreds of farm workers. In south-central Texas many blacks and poor whites were displaced as tenants and sharecroppers were reduced to farm workers, along with Mexicans, on corporate cotton ranches.[13]

Like many descendants of indigenous tribes and Spanish colonists, the Ximenes family became aliens in their own land. The Ximenes family came from a clan of colonists who settled the area when it was still Mexican territory. Whereas themes of displacement shape the family narrative, tropes of resignation and victimization do not, as Ximenes describes:

> My father's ancestors included an Indian mother and a German and a Spanish and Indian father. My mother's ancestors were Spanish. All spoke Spanish and with Mexico as our national origin, except my great-grandmother who was born in Alsace, France. Her parents by name of G'Sels landed in Galveston, Texas, and traveled to San Antonio to occupy a land grant. Both her parents died shortly after they arrived in San Antonio and three of their children were adopted by local families. My great grandmother was adopted by a de la Garza family of Graytown, Texas, and took on the name of de la Garza. She married my great-grandfather Estevan Ximenes, originally from Chihuahua, Mexico.[14]

The Ximenes family's colonial rights were conflicted by issues of race, class, and citizenship well before the dawn of the twentieth century. The family's claim to hereditary privilege as heirs of indigenous ancestors as well as Spanish colonizers and Tejano settlers provided cultural cachet and a measure of ascribed power that Vicente accessed throughout his rhetorical career. He was proud of his deep New World roots.

Additionally, Vicente's strong European physiognomic traits (skin color and features) afforded him the benefits of the ascribed privileges of whiteness in the pigmentocracy of U.S. and Latin American cultures (an asset as well as a source of anguish). Under certain social conditions (outside South Texas) Ximenes could pass for white. As a rhetorical countermove to ascribed whiteness, Ximenes embraced the label *Mexican American* his entire life. He neither identified with the more homogenous term *Hispanic* nor embraced the label *Latino* or *Spanish* because, in his mind, both of these terms denied the *mestizaje* of his indigenous heritage. Although he could be perceived as white, Ximenes perceived himself as brown. Sympathetic to the Chicano activists of the 1960s, Ximenes appreciated the indigenous mythos of the movement and its celebration of an off-white identity. He resisted the claims of Spanish racial purity that other Mexican-origin groups such as the League of United Latin American Citizens (LULAC) strategically espoused throughout the twentieth century (chapter 2).

Vicente was born on the edge of America's age of new imperialism and a national zeitgeist lauding nationalism and racial purity. As Frederick Pike argues in *The United States and Latin America: Myths and Stereotypes of Civilization and Nature*, at the beginning of the twentieth century, America's dominant groups consigned Mexican and Latin American immigrants to the lowest rungs of social hierarchies. Pike contends, "Like Indians, immigrants in their bulk could be incorporated only into society's bottom ranks. In this way, alien elements not up to becoming true Americans 'could serve the dominant culture without qualifying for social and political equality.'"[15] Although the Ximenes family history includes a complex mix of Spanish colonists, indigenous nomadic American Indians, and European immigrant groups, to Anglo Texans they were simply considered Mexicans. In the perception of the Anglo hegemony of Texas, the Ximenes clan belonged to a class of outsiders, the Mexican-immigrant caste. The racist attitudes that applied to blacks and Indians in early twentieth-century America applied likewise to Mexican-origin peoples regardless of birthplace, socioeconomic status, or citizenship. The issue was race—the binaries of whiteness and color. The epicenter of those attitudes rested deep in the heart of Texas in San Antonio, home of the Alamo.

Ximenes grew up in this period of anti-Mexican violence and divisive racial attitudes that relegated his people to third-class status. The threat of the notorious Texas Rangers to all *mexicano* peoples, *la gente decente* as well as *recien llegado* (the prestigious native-born class as well as the immigrant class), was endemic. The *campesinos* (farmers) lost their lives; the *rancheros* (ranchers) lost their land. As Pike describes, Texan Anglos demonstrated even stronger "antigreaser prejudices" than Californians; the Texans sometimes justif[ied] their attitudes by pointing to the bloodthirsty Mexican bandits who infested the border area. They thought little of killing a Mexican, because Mexican cutthroats along the Rio Grande allegedly regarded "the killing of a Texan as something to be proud of." In the Beadle dime novels that became best-sellers in the late nineteenth century, Texas cowboy heroes did not engage so much in cowpunching as in killing Mexicans and Indians, whom authors depicted as equally lacking in humanity.[16]

From his earliest days, Ximenes was an heir to this U.S. system of structural violence and institutionalized discrimination, both a survivor of and a witness to twentieth-century American de jure and de facto racism.[17]

Spheres of Belonging and Ecologies of Intimate Discourse

Vicente was the middle son of the eight children born to José Jesús Ximenes and Herlinda Treviño Ximenes: Hercilia, Benjamin, Edward, Waldo, Mary Magdalene, Madge, and Joe. Vicente and his siblings grew up close to the last vestiges of the original ranches of colonial Texas, an area known as Rancho de las Cabras, a site currently earmarked for national park designation. Situated near the town of Floresville, Rancho de las Cabras served as an eighteenth-century mission established by Spaniard colonists to generate wealth for the adjacent Mission Espada by raising goats, sheep, and cattle.[18]

The waves of European immigrants settling in the region throughout the eighteenth and nineteenth centuries became a part of the Ximenes family tree, adding a host of surnames indexing Old World and New World identities: Roth, Koenig, Rivera, Meyer, Zuniga, Treviño. Ximenes descendants helped to build the town and held leadership positions in city government for generations.

Ximenes's father, José, was a graduate of Draughon's Business College of San Antonio. Both of Vicente's parents maintained a strong commitment to education.[19] Ximenes remembers his mother, Herlinda, being an avid reader, literate in both English and Spanish. Although the emerging LULAC did not take root in Floresville during Ximenes's childhood, his father belonged to the Associacion Mexicana de Lodi of Texas. The main function of this *mutualista* (mutual aid) organization was to maintain a community hall for political meetings, dances, Cinco de Mayo, and Diez y Seis de Septiembre celebrations. This *mexicano* association organized these community activities for the Spanish-speaking constituency of Wilson County, providing a network of support and informal political organizing.

Although they had little socioeconomic prestige, the Ximenes family cultivated significant cultural and social capital within their community. Five of the Ximenes children attended college, a remarkable achievement for the region and the era. The Ximenes family ultimately distinguished itself in the community by producing teachers, a small-business owner, a lawyer, a physician, and an economist.[20]

José ran his own subsistence farm and then built his own general store, which he ran for years before competition forced him out of business. Educated, articulate, and literate in Spanish and English, José was an important figure in his community. As noted by Julie Leininger Pycior in *LBJ and Mexican Americans: The Paradox of Power*, José Ximenes was a political force in his own right throughout early twentieth-century South Texas. He had more formal education than most of the town leaders (Anglo or *mexicano*). José held a distinguished role in Floresville as something of a political organizer for the Democratic Party among the Spanish-speaking constituency. José was also a lifelong friend of the town's esteemed newspaper editor, Sam Fore.[21]

José also served as the court interpreter and became active in local politics. He provided both legal and business guidance for citizens of Floresville, interpreting documents for those who could not speak English, bailing out those in trouble with the law, and extending credit to those who were struggling financially. José was eventually appointed the district clerk for adjoining counties. In many respects, José functioned as the political *patrón* of Floresville, effectively negotiating between Anglo and *mexicano* as well as state and local power structures.

José kept well informed about national politics. Although José did not openly discuss politics with his children in the home, he was an avid supporter of New Deal policies and recognized the shifting political terrain along with his *compadres* in Floresville. The Ximenes family listened to President Franklin Roosevelt's fireside chats on the radio. Spanish and English radio programs were regular features of daily life in their household. Vicente was a young teenager when FDR became a regular voice in the family home. Their Floresville home cultivated rich educational and civic literacy opportunities for the children through regular participation in public activities at church, school, mercantile, and *la mutualista*. Vicente reveled in the opportunity to listen to the local citizens who came to José's mercantile to buy groceries and *platicar* about local politics.

Vicente quickly recognized the disparities between Mexican-origin students and their Anglo counterparts in the Floresville school system that began with elementary grades and extended through high school. Racial as well as language discrimination represented enduring barriers for Mexican Americans during Ximenes's formative years. Ximenes recalls:

> I attended a segregated elementary school for Mexican Americans in Floresville, Texas. After I graduated from the Mexicano elementary school where I spoke English and Spanish, the teachers at the integrated high school prohibited me from speaking Spanish. My father and mother spoke Spanish and English at home and with the rest of the community. My classroom experience, however, taught me to look upon my native language and people as bad and the English language and white people as good. I estimate that about one hundred Mexican Americans started first grade with me and five graduated in 1939 from Floresville High School.[22]

As one of the five Mexican American students to graduate, Ximenes belonged to a distinguished group within the larger community.[23] Whereas Anglo students received practical and academic training in the public schools, Mexican American students were largely tracked toward vocational and manual labor. In *Refiguring Rhetorical Education: Women Teaching African American, Native American, and Chicano/a Students, 1865–1911*, Jessica Enoch confirms the experiences Ximenes describes in the Floresville public schools. Enoch notes, "In addition to segregating Mexican students, providing them with dilapidated educational facilities, and offering them only manual and domestic education, Anglo educational officials also expected Mexican students to assimilate into American culture, and in turn, reject the Spanish language and their Mexican cultural traditions."[24] Nonetheless, the Ximenes family resisted these trends, excelling academically and retaining a strong *mexicano* identity.

The Ximenes family lived in dynamic tension within these Texan cultural rhetorical ecologies, navigating the deprivation and generativity of these cultural contact zones. Ximenes reflects:

> My grandparents and my father and mother never spoke of the transition from Mexican to Texan to U.S. citizen and the protection of civil rights of Mexican Americans. Life and the struggle for survival went on as before except that some of the white immigrant settlers of English, Polish, and German national origin considered the Mexican American a conquered people to be treated as second class citizens or worse.
>
> Jose Jesus Ximenes, my father, and other Mexican American leaders formed an association to protect themselves from the discriminatory practices of some of the white settlers. My father was a graduate of a business

college and became a patron who negotiated conflicts between the new settlers who now governed the town and the original Mexican Americans who built and managed what used to be La Villa de Flores.[25]

At each phase of Ximenes's journey, he acknowledged the accretion of power that came with each new sphere of his social experiences. He openly articulated the political as well as professional agency that followed his journey of twists and turns through South Texas. Ximenes remembers:

> My first job after high school was as a member of FDR's Civilian Conservation Corps. I never experienced discrimination in the Corps. However, when the CCC camp was moved from Floresville to Seguin, Texas, a town named after Juan Seguin, a hero of the Texas revolution, we encountered blatant discrimination against Mexican Americans from some of the owners and employees of bars, businesses and restaurants that would not serve us.
>
> As company clerk of the two hundred member camp, I learned to work with persons from all nationalities and geographic areas of the U.S. I learned discipline, human relations, leadership, and the work ethic from my father and mother, and one year with the CCC's solidified those values and made them part of the rest of my life.[26]

Vicente would become both a beneficiary and supporter of Roosevelt's New Deal programs and policies, a foreshadowing of the Great Society programs he would help to implement in the Johnson administration in 1967. Vicente vividly recalls that in José's opinion, FDR was the "savior of everything."[27] The New Deal represented promise, opportunity, and equality. Ximenes recognized what his contemporary Héctor P. García had similarly embraced. The New Deal changed the political expectations and opportunities of Mexican Americans.

Vicente's older brother, Edward, attended medical school at the University of Texas Medical School in Galveston with Héctor P. García from 1936 to 1940. Both Edward and Héctor, the sons of poor but hardworking *mexicano* merchant-class families, worked part-time to put themselves through medical school. In the privileged sphere of the University of Texas Medical School, they shared connections to a common culture, language, and socioeconomic condition. Like the Ximeneses, Héctor García came from a large, close-knit family whose educated father demanded more for his children than racist social configurations afforded them. During a visit to see his brother at the medical school in Galveston, Vicente met Héctor for the first time. They hit it off. Vicente confides, "He became my best friend outside my family."[28] Héctor maintained a close association with the Ximenes family, visiting their home in Floresville on his way back to Mercedes on the Texas-Mexico border. It would become a friendship and liaison with far-reaching implications.

As residents of the historically contested arid region of South Texas, known as the Nueces Strip, Mexican-origin families like the Garcías and Ximeneses survived through communal claims to the land and resource exchange. The Garcías and Ximeneses were merchants by trade, but they exchanged more than just dry goods. They were purveyors of cultural, social, and political knowledge valuable to the maintenance of the larger community. As agents of social cohesion, the García and Ximenes families held esteemed positions in their communities. They were highly regarded for their generosity and equanimity.

Equally important, Ximenes's and García's mothers played very influential roles in the lives of their families and communities, promoting education, civic responsibility, literacy, religious training, and cultural awareness. With large, boisterous, and noteworthy families, the Ximeneses like the Garcías distinguished themselves through church participation, educational achievements, and civic engagement. They shattered the prevailing social expectations that relegated Mexican Americans to second-class citizenship. Ximenes and García were raised through childhood with strong expectations that they would achieve social prominence in their respective spheres.

As a result of the importance their families placed on both education and on gaining social prominence through community engagement, both García and Ximenes grew to become charismatic and dynamic leaders, men in search of a rhetorical platform and a stage for the performance of leadership in some capacity. García eventually resolved these familial expectations by becoming a physician and practicing medicine to help the poor. Ximenes lived up to his family legacy of social prominence by earning a master's degree in economics, becoming an educator, and advocating on behalf of marginalized groups. Both Ximenes and García credited their fathers for their success in the public sphere.

Texas Big Boys: Mentors and Power Brokers

Because of his strong position in the community and his belief in the promise of New Deal policies, José Ximenes took an active and influential role in local politics. He knew how to build alliances with the Mexican American as well as Anglo leaders of the region. José maintained strong relations with Sam Fore, editor of the *Floresville Chronicle-Journal* and chairman of the Texas Democratic Party. Ximenes thoughtfully describes the role of cultural and political broker that his father played in Floresville:

My father used political power, much as we do today, to beg, plead, and demand jobs and community resources for our barrio. Sam Fore, Editor of the Floresville Chronicle Journal and Texas Chairman of the Democratic Party, was a friend who supported my father's efforts to improve our barrio. Wealthy King Ranch owner and Congressman Richard Kleberg and Lyndon Johnson, his office manager, dropped in to see my father at election time to ask for Mexican American votes. I attended political meetings with my father where I was introduced to Lyndon Johnson as "Joe's boy."[29]

The small-town allegiances forged in Floresville and other South Texas communities set the stage for a lasting political partnership between Vicente Ximenes and Lyndon B. Johnson. The political network with which José Ximenes was associated in Floresville included other key players from South Texas. Vicente's elder brother Edward attended high school with John Connally, who would become Johnson's congressional aide in 1938 and the governor of Texas in 1963. The other leading man in the Floresville political sphere was Sam Fore, who would coincidentally become a dedicated mentor to both Johnson and Ximenes.

The figure of Sam Fore loomed large in South Texas politics through the New Deal era, influencing not only the rhetorical career of Vicente Ximenes but the future of Lyndon B. Johnson. Fore remained a personal friend, mentor, and political supporter of Johnson beginning with Johnson's years as an aide to Richard Kleberg and lasting through LBJ's White House years. Johnson exalted the devoted Fore as the "the Saint Paul of Floresville."[30] This triangulation of political allies would prove especially productive for both Johnson and Ximenes. Throughout FDR's New Deal era, Fore had helped to launch the careers of well-known Texas political leaders like Richard Kleberg. Fore was well loved and well known across the cultural divide of the region for his great accessibility, affability, and political acumen.[31]

As a liberal Democrat and editor of the *Floresville Chronicle-Journal*, Fore advanced FDR's New Deal agenda through the Dust Bowl years and promoted sustainable farming and ranching techniques throughout Wilson County. He warned the region about overdependence on cotton and urged the county's farmers to diversify their crops. Fore helped destitute farmers secure Federal Crop Loans and published articles on the Emergency Farm Mortgage Act to help families survive the regional blight in 1933. During World War II, Fore promoted peanut production as an alternative source of rationed fats and oils. He published FDR's speeches in the *Chronicle-Journal* in support of New Deal programs and circulated announcements about the $62,000 in grants available to Wilson County residents. Fore also helped to secure Works Progress

Administration (WPA) funding for soil and water conservation projects. Additionally, he sponsored annual training field trips to Texas A&I University in Kingsville for farmers and dairymen to promote sustainable practices.[32]

Elma Fore recalls that her husband, fondly known in Floresville as "Mr. Sam," routinely "asked for thousands of jobs for boys and girls and got them, too. From his home in Floresville, he could call up these people in Washington and get them [Floresville youth] jobs up there [in Washington, D.C.]."[33] Fore also feverishly campaigned for the twenty-nine-year-old Lyndon B. Johnson when he ran for a seat in the U.S. Congress in 1937. Ximenes remembers, "I was associated with President Lyndon Johnson off and on from the time I was a teenager in the 1930's until January 1973 when Johnson died. I tagged along with my father when he campaigned for Johnson. I nailed Johnson posters to mesquite trees during the campaigns."[34] Floresville became a training ground in politics for both Ximenes and Johnson.

In 1938 Fore promoted the theme of "Peanuts on Parade" for the annual county fair and launched the annual Floresville Peanut Festival. John Connally, then a young, ambitious college student, was crowned king of the Peanut Festival. The giant peanut sculpture later mounted in the town plaza in the center of Floresville stands as a tribute to Sam Fore's agrarian reform efforts in Wilson County. Ximenes was eighteen years old in the summer of 1938 when the first Peanuts on Parade fair attracted politicians and dignitaries from across the state including Governor W. Lee O'Daniel, who led the parade. Ximenes remembers Johnson mingling with Fore and Floresville residents during annual community festivities like the Peanut Festival and local *matanzas* (pig roasts). Johnson eventually hired Connally to serve as his congressional aide, following Fore's recommendation.[35] Connally had the pedigree, the family wealth, and the political ambition. The durability of these formative alliances held for decades. Ximenes learned later in life that his father José and Sam Fore had routinely intervened on Vicente's behalf from as early as the 1940s when Vicente first appealed to Johnson for a position in the National Youth Administration (NYA). This thirty-year political triangle endured until Fore's death in 1966. The long-standing alliances forged between Johnson and Ximenes evolved out of this constellation of common allegiances and common experiences beginning in Floresville.

The Topoi of Texas

While the political association between Ximenes and Johnson began in the town square and mesquite fields of Floresville, the confluence of their professional lives began in the public school classroom. Both Ximenes and

Johnson gained entrée into the professional class through their service as educators in the Texas public school system. Both Ximenes and Johnson would serve as principals of small South Texas elementary schools before entering public life.[36] Ximenes recounts:

> Johnson obtained a teaching certificate from San Marcos State Teachers College. My sister obtained a teaching certificate at the same time Johnson attended the college. Johnson's first job was as principal of a segregated Mexican American school in Cotulla, Texas. The experience as a teacher of poor and discriminated-against Mexican Americans became a part of the rest of his life. However, his willingness to help the cause of the Mexicano was kept under wraps because his racist constituency would come down hard on him if he expressed his feelings publicly.
>
> It was not until 1965 when the civil rights movement was in full bloom and he won an overwhelming mandate in the 1964 election that he began to openly and publicly express his desire to help the Mexican American. Johnson used his Cotulla, Texas experience in his 1965 voting rights speech when he said, "It never occurred to me in my fondest dreams that I might have the chance to help the sons and daughters of those students and to help people like them all over the country. But now I do have that chance and I'll let you in on a secret—I mean to use it."[37]

Johnson's political career was launched on the heels of his brief stint as an educator with the help of Richard Kleberg. According to Robert Kleberg (Richard's brother) Johnson's father, Sam Johnson, was also one of Richard Kleberg's earliest supporters. The Kleberg-Johnson alliance was something of a whirlwind political love affair. Richard Kleberg announced his candidacy for the Fourteenth Congressional District on November 13, 1931, with Sam Johnson's endorsement, winning the election on November 25. Lyndon Johnson, Sam's politically ambitious and restless son, was promptly appointed as Richard Kleberg's congressional secretary on November 29, 1931.[38] Although Lyndon Johnson jettisoned his brief teaching career for national politics, his formative experience as a teacher in the Texas public school system would help to define him.

The discourses that both Ximenes and Johnson exchanged to affirm their alliance evolved out their shared ethos as educators and as native Texans. Moreover, these stories helped to mitigate the power differentials between them as a rich Anglo and a poor Mexican American. Johnson's brief but impressionable teaching experiences in Cotulla, Texas, forged his formative identification with Mexican Americans. Likewise, Ximenes's foundational political experiences in Floresville forged a formative identification with

Texas Democrats. Out of the shared topography of rural Texas, Ximenes and Johnson's political association evolved like prairie grass, thin and tenuous but durable enough to withstand the vicissitudes of change.

Johnson's brief stint as an educator began with his one-year appointment as school principal (September 1928 to May 1929) during a break from his college studies to pay off his debts. Johnson was immediately devoted to the task of enhancing the competitive climate of the small, underfunded "Mexican" school. He even donated part of his salary to his educational improvement projects. In *Lyndon Johnson and the American Dream*, Doris Kearns Goodwin documents Johnson's efforts at Cotulla: "Within three months, therefore, he had introduced a spectacular array of contests—spelldowns, public speaking tournaments, volleyball games, baseball games, track events, field events. Since Cotulla had no money for equipment of any kind, Johnson invested half of his first month's salary to buy softball bats and gloves, volleyballs, and basketballs."[39] As for his own academic trajectory, Johnson was a marginal student. He did not have the grades to get into the University of Texas at Austin and barely got through his studies at the teachers college in San Marcos. Goodwin observes further, "There is more than a hint of something compulsive, an unremitting drive to organize and prescribe conduct in accordance with the configurations of his own beneficent will. But Johnson never seemed aware, in Cotulla and afterward, that the benefactor might destroy his recipient's capacity to grow and find expression on his own."[40] Johnson's patronizing style became an ingrained pattern of advocacy and self-aggrandizement that both endeared Johnson to his beneficiaries and alienated them.

After graduating from Southwest Texas State Teachers College at San Marcos in August 1930, Johnson then took a job as a debate coach at Sam Houston High School in Houston, Texas (September 1930 to November 1931). Ironically, in 1928 the yearbook of the teachers college, the *Pedagog*, spoofed Johnson's capacity for being a larger-than-life figure and named him a distinguished member of the so-called "Sophistry Club: Master of the gentle art of spoofing the general public."[41] As Goodwin notes, "Even in college, Johnson did not regard, or at least did not portray, success as an end in itself. The drive for power was justified by the belief that in controlling others he was acting in their best interests."[42] Johnson's aspirations as a teacher ended as soon as he signed on as congressional secretary to Richard Kleberg on November 29, 1931.[43] Johnson saw his destiny in politics, not the classroom. Johnson needed Kleberg to go where he wanted to go politically. Apparently, Kleberg needed Johnson as well.

Kleberg relied on Johnson's irrepressible drive, political instinct, and calculating ambition. According to Elma Fore, Richard Kleberg "was not a practical man. He was an educated man. . . . [B]ut he didn't know how to manage his campaign. Well, Mr. Fore was managing it for him until he hired Lyndon Johnson."[44] Johnson took charge of every facet of Kleberg's campaign. Ximenes was only thirteen years old when he first met Johnson stumping for Kleberg. Ximenes recounts, "Representative Kleberg would come around every election year and ask for Dad's support in the primary."[45] Floresville, the seat of Wilson County, was close enough to San Antonio to merit Kleberg's political focus and rhetorical attention. Moreover, the Democratic political network and the influence of Sam Fore kept Floresville humming for the Kleberg machine. Like other small agricultural towns, Floresville needed leaders like Kleberg and Johnson, who brought home public works projects.

The Depression had taken a stranglehold on the region as well as the nation. These were desperate times for agricultural communities like Floresville. Families were losing their farms, their businesses, and their dreams. For Vicente, these were not only challenging times; they were also exciting times. He learned early in life how to find opportunity in adversity. Vicente enjoyed having a front-row seat to the discussions, debates, and deliberations. Over the next five years, Vicente cultivated a passion for politics. By 1937 Johnson was running for a congressional seat himself, and Vicente was an accomplished and ambitious high school student following his father on his rounds with local leaders and state politicians. Unlike Johnson, Vicente excelled in his studies. His grades earned him admission to the prestigious University of Texas at Austin.

But like Johnson, Ximenes enjoyed, above all else, studying the moves of the politicos. He heard the arguments and learned about the issues. He watched how big political figures (and powerful men) did business. Ximenes followed the campaign activities with the kind of enthusiasm and fascination that other children his age devoted to sports events and traveling carnivals. The public debates and speeches intrigued him. Johnson, Kleberg, and Fore stirred up votes at the barbecues, festivals, and *matanzas* throughout the Floresville community during election years. Vicente watched how votes were won, bought, and traded. He observed how Johnson's searing political determination and savvy political instincts complemented Kleberg's less-than-efficacious political acumen.

Richard Kleberg (heir of the world-famous King Ranch of South Texas) was a popular but fairly inept political figure. He was neither the effective businessman nor the powerful politician his family expected him to be. What he lacked in ethos in terms of work ethic and ambition, Kleberg made up for with a big and bold personality. A January 1932 article in the *American Business Survey* titled "A Real Cowboy Graces the Halls of Congress" paints a bold picture of the man who mentored Johnson into Congress:

> Recognized as a leader among the cowmen of the Southwest, Mr. Kleberg
> is the trustee of the largest private ranch in the world, the King Estate, a
> vast range that extends along the Gulf of Mexico, north of the Rio Grande
> for nearly 100 miles and it comprises 1,280,000 acres, an area twice that of
> the State of Rhode Island. . . . During the campaign, which was a classic
> example of psychological insight, he addressed the Mexican voters of his
> district in their own tongue, thus winning from them a wildly enthusiastic
> reception; a few days later, confronting a German audience, he again used
> the language of the people he addressed.[46]

Kleberg's lighthearted, vivacious character and his passion for singing Mexican folk songs, horseback riding, steer roping, and late-night drinking parties made him a popular figure throughout South Texas. Describing the raucous tenor of Kleberg's campaign trail, the vibrant social events that ultimately captivated young Vicente's political imagination, biographer Robert Caro writes: "Playing his accordion and singing in Spanish to San Antonio's thousands of Mexican-American voters, waving a big sombrero as he led rodeo parades (and at the Robstown Rodeo, roping and throwing a calf in a respectable fourteen seconds), telling funny stories, Kleberg won easily. But campaigning was the extent of his interest in his new job."[47] Mixing it up and meeting the locals was Kleberg's forte. Ximenes watched how Kleberg navigated cultural differences and engaged voters. Kleberg's affable style was disarming and helped to bridge the power differentials between the haves and have-nots. Ximenes remembers:

> The economic and political climate in our community was similar to that
> of Johnson's in the hill country of Fredericksburg, Johnson City, Kerrville,
> and Luchenbach. I am told that there is a bar in Luchenbach that has a
> sign that reads, "if you came here to forget, please pay in advance." We
> were all just folks, poor and struggling to make a living from the land that
> was not particularly rich and bountiful. Our part of the county was mostly
> sand and Johnson's mostly oak trees. Elected positions in the counties and
> towns were fiercely sought after and politics was a way of life.[48]

Ximenes watched how these important men operated. These South Texas political campaigns indelibly marked Ximenes's rhetorical imagination.

The CCC and the Roots of Change

After graduating from high school, Ximenes joined the CCC in October 1939. As a response to the agricultural and climate crises that gave rise to the Dust Bowl years, the CCC was instituted in March 1933 to help restore the land and the local economy of communities like Floresville devastated by drought and poverty. The ecologically inspired film *The Plough That Broke the Plains* debuted in 1936 in the Texas Panhandle, where ranchers and farmers had endured over five years of drought conditions. The mass migration of climate refugees, unemployed workers, and displaced farmers, poignantly depicted in the folk songs of Woody Guthrie and the literary works of John Steinbeck, reflected economic conditions that the Ximenes family endured firsthand.

The restoration efforts of the CCC represented the promise of reviving the devastated prairie lands of the Great Plains region extending down to South Texas. Moreover, the CCC resisted the pattern of displacement that removed families from their homes and reinvigorated the Mexican cultural concept of *querencia*, a reverence for the land and its people. This experience represented Ximenes's first direct encounter with one of FDR's New Deal initiatives. Reflecting on the social and economic impact of work programs like the CCC, Ximenes remembers, "I don't think people know how close this nation came to having a revolution."[49]

In the CCC Ximenes observed firsthand the starvation and desperation of people throughout the region. He listened to the political debates challenging the inequitable distribution of wealth and witnessed citizens questioning the government. South Texas, like most of the nation, faced the economic and environmental devastation of the Depression era with overcultivated, deforested, and depleted natural resources. With unemployment figures at 25 percent and the failure of family farms and businesses, the need for labor opportunities extended across America into communities like Floresville. The environmental and economic crises of the Dust Bowl years were inextricably intertwined with social and racial politics when Ximenes applied for his first job after completing high school. Nearly 80 percent of the applicants were young Hispanic men like Ximenes.

Ximenes remembers the conversations that circulated in town squares and community meetings. He recalls, "Maybe this whole system needed to be changed. People were angry enough. FDR saved this country."[50] With the institutionalization of the CCC, millions of young men were put to work. Each month twenty-five dollars out of every thirty-dollar paycheck was sent home to the families of the CCC workers to feed and support communities on the brink of collapse. Ximenes argues that the CCC was the most proenvironmental organization ever established, supporting an unparalleled workforce of environmentalists who planted trees to prevent rampant erosion throughout the West and Midwest, cultivated mismanaged forests, established hiking trails and visitor centers in national parks, and restored depleted soil for agriculture. Moreover, the CCC helped to establish a national ethic of service and conservation. Ximenes was part of a work-programs movement to restore the national well-being, indelibly shaped by the guiding philosophy of the CCC: "heal the land, heal the man."

The CCC camp where Ximenes helped to clear mesquite trees and work the land for agricultural development was located fifty miles from Floresville. Named the Richard Kleberg Conservation Camp in Seguin, Texas, the CCC provided Ximenes on-the-job training as well as vocational classes. When Ximenes saw an opportunity for professional advancement, he taught himself typing and was eventually hired as company clerk, a position he held for a year before enrolling at the University of Texas in Austin in 1940, seeking a degree in education. The salary and the work experience offered by the CCC prepared Ximenes for what he would encounter in his first year of college-level education and beyond. Ximenes remembers:

> In September, 1940 my father and mother drove me to Austin to attend the University of Texas. My father planned the trip so as to avoid towns known to discriminate against Mexican Americans. New Braunfels, lo-cated between Austin and Floresville, was not a good place to stop for lunch. My secondary and high school teachers always managed to pick Landa Park in New Braunfels for school picnics, even though it was well known that Mexican Americans were not allowed in the swimming pool.
>
> I lived in the University endorsed Saldivar cooperative with nineteen other Mexican Americans. Mexican Americans who lived in dorms would drop by to tell us we segregated ourselves in the cooperative and therefore should not cry discrimination against us by the white Anglo. Arguments sometimes ended with physical fights between the coop members who claimed that Mexican Americans brought the discrimination on them-selves and those of us who claimed it was imposed on us. In spite of all the rhetoric among Mexican Americans on discrimination and civil rights, I found few written materials or books and histories in the University libraries that addressed the hot button issue of discrimination against the Mexican American.[51]

Ximenes spent one year studying at the University of Texas (1940–41), earn-ing a teaching certificate that qualified him to apply for a teaching position near Floresville. Ximenes encountered the same struggles that his brother Edward and his friend Héctor García had faced at the University of Texas as one of the few Mexican American students enrolled.

The first year of college demonstrated to Ximenes the implicit and explicit inequities in higher education. Ximenes recounts:

The year I spent at that cooperative gave me some insights on how the political, economic, and social system kept us in a second class status. We debated the discrimination against us day and night. None of us could study at the Saldivar cooperative, because the debates raged on into the late night hours. The Mexican American non-members of the cooperative looked down on us for segregating ourselves. The cooperative, however, was the only way for some of us to get a college education. On the other hand we argued that the few Mexican Americans in clubs, fraternities, and sororities were tokens. There were cooperative members who were rich and about half of us were so poor we sometimes could not pay the rent. The heated debates between the rich and poor members would sometimes end with blows and the housemother would have to intervene to cool things off. The year at the co-op was my baptism into the world of race, color, discrimination, ethnic groups, and human rights.[52]

With limited financial support and few support networks available, Ximenes struggled with isolation and poverty as he worked toward his degree. Ximenes describes:

When I told my uncle Ysidro that I was accepted to attend the University of Texas he, without hesitation, dug into his pocket, and gave me a five dollar bill to help with school costs. My uncle Ysidro had no idea how far that five dollar bill would go towards my education. My dad figured I had found a way to attend the University of Texas and offered to help when the time came to pay the bills. I never bothered my dad about school costs because Ed, my older brother was at UT Medical School at Galveston and my sister Hercilia was in San Marcos State Teachers College. Waldo, another older brother was working and helping with household expenses and waiting to get his chance to enter University of St. Mary's Law School.[53]

When an opening for a teaching position became available, Ximenes left the university to join the workforce. He accepted a position as principal at a small elementary school in Picosa, Texas, in 1941. Like Johnson, Ximenes would begin his professional career teaching in a segregated elementary school in South Texas and learning to navigate the economic and educational disparities of structural discrimination.

As Texas native sons, Ximenes and Johnson occupied a common space triangulated by key points of influence, a triangulation within which they were able to cultivate and sustain a contact of minds. First, their boyhood civic imagination was stirred by the populist politics of their fathers. Second, as young professionals, their nascent sympathies were sparked by the educational lives of marginalized students. Third, as civil servants, their first assignments demanded hard labor serving vulnerable citizens and direct hands-on involvement with FDR's progressivist New Deal public work projects.

New Deal Discourses and Other Big Ideas

WPA efforts like the CCC, NYA, Farm Security Administration, and Federal Writers' Project together constituted a tapestry of democratizing discourses transmitted through the omnibus legislation and rhetoric of New Deal liberalism. Both Ximenes and Johnson received foundational professional training in FDR's work projects. Ximenes and Johnson recognized the import of these early experiences as beneficiaries of New Deal programs: Johnson in the NYA (1935–37) and Ximenes in the CCC (1939–40) and NYA (1940–41).

Johnson was appointed NYA director for the state of Texas in 1935, his first high-level administrative position after serving as secretary to Congressman Richard Kleberg. The appointment gave him direct access to FDR's New Deal programs and national visibility. The NYA was designed to mentor and support students through their education as well as supplement their academic skills with work experience. The CCC functioned more like a military boot camp promoting hard labor and offering skills training. These New Deal public works projects would prefigure Great Society programs some thirty years later such as Manpower Development and Training, the War on Poverty, and the Model Cities Program that Ximenes would help to administer through Johnson's presidency.

Johnson was just twenty-seven years old when took the state NYA director position serving twenty-five thousand Texas youth with part-time employment, high school retention programs, and college preparation.[54] A July 1935 press release describes young Johnson as an ambitious leader who was no stranger to hard work, including manual labor:

> This young South Texan is no brain truster. One degree—that of Bachelor of Science—has been enough for him, and probably will be. . . . Johnson, well above six feet in height and dark-haired has few diversions or hobbies. He has been a little busy for them, since at 18 he went to work shoveling gravel on a highway for a dollar a day in order to obtain enough money to make at least a two days start on his college career. At times in his life he has held as many as five jobs at the same time, and the great aim of his life is to simply keep busy.[55]

Johnson's political imagination was shaped by his formative experiences with New Deal programs.

However, Johnson's mixed political record on African American civil rights issues also began in the NYA. When the offices in Washington, D.C., urged Johnson to appoint a black representative to the NYA Texas State Advisory Board, Johnson resisted. In a September 22, 1935, letter to John Corson at NYA headquarters in Washington, D.C., Johnsons asserts:

> The turmoil which would result in the State Advisory Board and from the publicity that would inevitably follow, would react to the detriment of the negroes and all their projects. I feel confident that anyone who knows conditions in Texas will bear me out in the statement that both the whites and the negroes would be thrust further apart then by such a move. . . .
>
> The racial question during the last one hundred years in Texas—and particularly since Texas entered the Union in 1848, and again after the Civil War—has resolved itself into a definite system of mores and customs which cannot be upset overnight. So long as these are observed there is harmony and peace between the races in Texas. But it is exceedingly difficult to step over lines so long established and to upset customs so deep-rooted, by any act which is so shockingly against precedent as the attempt to mix negroes and whites on a common board.[56]

Johnson's conflicted record on race and institutionalized discrimination began early in his public life. Pragmatism and opportunism trumped idealism.

While both Johnson and Ximenes lauded the possibilities of liberal democracy and New Deal public works programs like the NYA, Ximenes's perceptions of discrimination and structural racism were formed from a subject position entirely different from Johnson's. Both knew the crippling impact of poverty. Both knew the challenges of manual labor. Both recognized the realities of racist social structures in Texas political life. But Johnson came to the NYA from a privileged position as a white male and former congressional secretary who had served for several years in Washington, D.C., drawn a steady salary, and lived among prosperous and powerful men.

Ximenes, in contrast, came to the CCC and NYA as a young rural Mexican American high school graduate, struggling with poverty at home and facing discrimination across the region where he served. Ximenes approached social reform as the adept networker. Johnson identified with poverty because he had escaped it. Ximenes identified deeply with the economic crises gripping the nation because he lived there. Ximenes saw his story reflected in the lives of others all around him. He never lost access to his past or the sense of his own vulnerability.

Ximenes worked briefly with the NYA in Austin while attending the University of Texas. Reflecting on his own experience as one of the few Mexican Americans employed by the NYA, Ximenes notes that access to the NYA programs were not evenly accessible to minorities or to women, and he recalls appealing directly to Richard Kleberg for a position in the NYA after serving with the CCC for a year:

> In August 1940, I wrote to Congressman Richard Kleberg and asked for a letter of recommendation to NYA for a part time job in Austin. He replied that he would do what he could. I then received a letter that advised me to report to the Health Department of the State of Texas. I arrived in Austin in the first week of September and immediately took a bus to the Health Department located in downtown Austin.[57]

Ximenes's early associations with Kleberg and his Floresville connections through Sam Fore helped him secure a position in the NYA program. Ximenes recounts:

> I had just resigned from the CCC program after a year and decided to attend the University of Texas. I had no idea where I would get the money to pay for room and board. I had the first semester tuition. I did not save any money from the CCC since twenty-two dollars of the twenty-five I was paid was sent home to my father and mother.
>
> I knew about the NYA and wrote to LBJ for help in getting an NYA job while in school. There was also the chance that my father asked Sam Fore to call LBJ about my application. My father did things like that without telling me. At any rate I received and filled out an application for an NYA job and was approved. I worked for the Texas Health Department in downtown Austin. I did mostly record keeping and was paid something like fifteen or twenty dollars a week. Anyway it was enough to keep me in school for a year and one summer at the University of Texas.
>
> I supplemented my NYA pay with work at the Saldivar Cooperative by serving tables and at times dishwashing. From time to time I would, when desperate, call Hercilia my sister for help to get enough to pay the monthly rent at the cooperative.
>
> I do not recall that any of the nineteen Mexican Americans at the Saldivar Coop worked for the NYA. I suspect that any one of them would qualify or could get in if they wanted. I do know that the University work force had a large number of people who were on NYA pay. But then not too many Mexican Americans applied for University or college training. The preponderant majority of Mexican Americans that needed help applied

for the CCC work program. Eighty percent or more of the CCC members in my camp were Mexican Americans. Not too many Mexican American women sought NYA jobs of any kind in the government sector. The large number of NYA jobs were made possible by political favors asked for and received from Johnson's NYA whose objective was to get the economy moving again by the pump priming method. Mexican American fathers looked after their sons and got them into the CCC and the daughters were to stay home and help with the daily household chores.[58]

The WPA programs were vital to Ximenes as an aspiring college student. As a direct beneficiary of both the NYA and CCC, Ximenes became an avid proponent of FDR's progressive social democratic agenda even before he reached voting age. Ximenes was part of FDR's growing national audience, reading and responding to the rhetoric of the New Deal presidency.

Emma Tenayuca and South Texas Dissent

Depression-era South Texas represented a raucous and robust political environment including an active labor movement led by Mexican Americans. While Ximenes was mesmerized by the political prowess of figures like Kleberg and Johnson—and was mentored by figures like newspaper editor Sam Fore; his father, José Ximenes; and his friend Héctor García—he also identified deeply with the issues of the disenfranchised classes. Concomitant with the growing political career of Johnson, other social and political influences were shaping the rhetorical sphere of South Texas. Labor activists in San Antonio in the late 1920s and through the 1930s were gaining strength among Mexican-origin workers. The presence of vocal Mexican labor activists in the region shaped Ximenes's political imagination and social sphere.

Emma Tenayuca, a young Mexican American activist growing up in San Antonio, help to coordinate the emerging San Antonio Workers' Alliance by mobilizing strikes, protests, and demonstrations in the 1930s on behalf of workers displaced by WPA cutbacks that ultimately discriminated against Mexican-origin peoples. Tenayuca, a contemporary of Ximenes, was born in 1916 and came of age as an activist at the same time Ximenes began working with his father. Tenayuca quickly took a leading role in mobilizing workers and Mexican-origin women in San Antonio.

During Ximenes's high school years, the young Tenayuca dramatically illustrated the power of direct action protest. Tenayuca led the walkout of six to eight thousand workers from 170 San Antonio pecan-shelling plants on January 38, 1938.[59] It was a spontaneous protest, yet widely publicized throughout the region. Tenayuca was unanimously elected honorary strike leader. She was also promptly arrested on charges of leading Communist agitation. The events surrounding Tenayuca's labor advocacy on behalf of pecan workers demonstrated the possibilities of moral protest in changing inequitable labor conditions. Ximenes would imitate Tenayuca's act of public dissent a year later in June 1939 when he led a walkout of Mexican American students during the Floresville High School graduation ceremony to protest inequitable educational practices. Ximenes recounts: "The parent teacher association farewell banquet insulted the Mexican American graduates by seating us together in a corner of the hall. We walked out during the invocation. I and one other graduate left our caps and gowns at the principal's front door and did not attend the graduate ceremony."[60] Tenayuca went on to rally for minimum wage laws and more humane working conditions for laborers in the San Antonio pecan-shelling industry, cigar manufacturing, garment industry, and agriculture. Tenayuca understood firsthand that Mexican American women workers were targets of labor exploitation, frequently relegated to piecework labor practices that demanded the enlistment of entire families, even young children, to earn subsistence wages. Mobilizing San Antonio's west side residents, among the poorest workers in the nation, Tenayuca advanced the cause of pecan shellers, who averaged less than $1.75 per week in wages.[61]

Additionally, Tenayuca recognized that the New Deal programs in South Texas were not equitably distributed and, in some cases, actually "penalized Texas's Mexican working classes and contributed further to their impoverishment."[62] Plow-under policies of the New Deal administration eliminated up to one-third of the Texas cotton crop, reducing the cotton production jobs of Mexican-origin workers. The twenty-one-year-old Tenayuca was appointed to the National Executive Committee of the Workers' Alliance. The groundbreaking efforts of organizers such as Tenayuca established a new presence in the class struggle between subordinated Mexican-origin groups and the Anglo-dominant social structure of South Texas.

Tenayuca's legacy in San Antonio provided a powerful precedent for laborers, women, and Mexican Americans seeking social justice:

> [Tenayuca] recalled that in the women's ward of the San Antonio City Jail, as many as three dozen women and their children were placed in cells built to accommodate six people. When the incarcerated strikers protested against the overcrowded conditions, the jailors responded by turning fire hoses on them. Many of the prisoners were infected with tuberculosis, and the overcrowding contributed to the spread of the disease. Jails were

filled beyond capacity, and hundreds of strikers were driven fifteen to twenty miles out of town when finally released and had to walk back to San Antonio.[63]

Laborers' demands included full collective bargaining rights, livable wages, humane work conditions, and union recognition. Tenayuca herself was sent to jail a number of times during the strikes in which police attacked men, women, and children on the picket lines. Newspaper reports of the daily arrests that totaled over a thousand strikers represented a pivotal moment in racial divisions, class conflict, and labor relations in Texas. Details of the 1937 San Antonio labor strike and the oppression of women workers deeply affected the eighteen-year-old Ximenes. Over a decade later Ximenes would come to identify with labor movements like the one led by Tenayuca. He would ultimately support *la causa* of Mexican American laborers as a leader of the American GI Forum in New Mexico (chapter 2).

The Halo Effect: World War II and the Male Military Ethos

In December 1941, a week after the attack on Pearl Harbor, Ximenes joined the U.S. Air Corps in San Antonio. He left his job as the principal of the Picosa Elementary School. Ximenes then trained as a cadet in bombardier school at Kirtland Air Force Base in Albuquerque in 1942 before serving as an officer. He was promoted to second lieutenant in June 1942 and was then transferred overseas. Ximenes completed fifty combat flying missions in North Africa and Italy. His theater of military operations was centered in Africa in support of the British Allies. He witnessed firsthand the devastation of war and suffering of displacement. Ximenes was decorated by the Air Force with the Air Medal and the Distinguished Flying Cross for his service as lead bombardier on a B-17 Flying Fortress. The June 20, 1943, citation for the award of Distinguished Flying Cross by the Air Corps of the U.S. Army describes the events:

> For extraordinary achievement while participating in aerial flight on a large number of high altitude bombing missions in the North African Theatre of Operations, as bombardier. On 24 January 1943, while on a bombing run over the docks of Sousse, Lt. Ximenes' B-17 sustained a heavy attack from enemy fighter planes. Repeated attacks resulted in disabling the number three engine, which immediately caught fire. As the crippled plane dropped out of formation it was attacked by additional aircraft which desperately attempted to turn the bomber off course, but as bombardier, Lt. Ximenes directed the pilot over the target without evasive action and

succeeded in scoring a number of direct hits. With the bombs away, Lt. Ximens [*sic*] returned to his nose guns and aided largely in driving off the enemy fighters, enabling his aircraft to return safely to its home base. His inspiring courage and sound judgement under conditions of great peril have in this, and in many other missions, reflected great credit upon himself and the Armed Forces of the United States.[64]

The journey of war hero and decorated soldier began for Ximenes during his military service in World War II. Moreover, he found a kindred spirit throughout the war years in Héctor García.

Héctor García, who served as a major in the Army Medical Corps in Europe, likewise spent time in Africa during his military career. Both men left the military as decorated officers. At the close of his military service, Ximenes served as a flight instructor and squadron leader at the bombardier school in San Angelo, Texas, from 1943 to 1946. As for Ximenes's *buen amigo*, Héctor García also served with distinction as an army officer and a medic. García received the Bronze Star for service achievement while running operations across enemy lines. Military service remained a source of pride and a critical facet of identity for both men, personally and collectively. Through their family, cultural, regional, and military connections, Ximenes and García shared this common military male ethos.

Unlike García and other contemporaries, Ximenes did not return home with a European war bride. Ximenes found the love of his life back in Floresville, Texas. He was transferred to the training command in San Angelo, Texas, in the summer of 1943. During a thirty-day leave, he returned to Floresville to visit family and met his future wife, María Castillo, at a Floresville town hall dance. Ximenes recalls:

> It was done the way they used to do the courting. The mothers would bring their daughters to the dance, and they would sit on one side of the hall. And then, when the music started, you dashed out there to see if you could get a girl to dance with you. But it all depended on whether the mother accepted you. If she accepted you, she would kind of move her head, like saying OK.[65]

Ximenes received the nod for María's hand, immediately falling in love. Without fanfare the young lovers were wed during Vicente's leave on September 1, 1943, by the justice of the peace in San Antonio. María was only seventeen years old, and Vicente was twenty-four. María joined him in San Angelo, where they established their first home and began their family. The newlyweds rented a single room in a boardinghouse, where the good-hearted

but overzealous Baptist landlady practiced hymns on an old upright piano
into the late hours of the night. "We were so young and in love hiding away
together in our bedroom as she played 'Amazing Grace' all night long,"
Ximenes laughed, remembering.[66]

After seven years of military service Ximenes retired as an Air Force major
in 1947 before moving to Albuquerque, New Mexico, with María and their
infant son, Estevan (also called Steven). They decided to leave Texas for the
economic, educational, and cultural opportunities available to them in New
Mexico. Vicente had spent time in Albuquerque in the Air Corps during
the war. He felt at home in Albuquerque. New Mexico's legacy of Hispano
leadership was an especially attractive feature of the state. The rich historical and cultural features of the region along with the vast natural beauty of
New Mexico resonated deeply with Vicente. Pragmatically, the proximity
of Kirtland Air Force Base provided easy access to military benefits, and the
educational opportunities offered by the University of New Mexico represented promise and hope for the young family.

Vicente and María built their adobe casita on Monroe Street near the
expanding reach of downtown Albuquerque. Vicente worked to finish his
undergraduate degree at the University of New Mexico. Meanwhile, their
family grew quickly. Their children Olivia, Ricardo, and Ana were born in
Albuquerque. Vicente and María called Albuquerque home for the next six
decades. New Mexico remained their sanctuary for the rest of their lives.
The modest adobe near the historic Mother Road, old Route 66, would be
the only home they would ever own.

2. New Mexico and the Political Imagination of the American GI Forum

*O*n September 8, 1951, Ximenes penned a letter to Dr. Héctor García reflecting on his experience attending the Texas state convention of the American GI Forum (AGIF) in Austin. The AGIF state convention marked the third year of robust mobilization for this veterans' rights organization. Ximenes's letter would launch a thirty-year exchange between Ximenes and García, who together navigated the evolution of the AGIF and the future of Mexican American civil rights reform. The stream of epistolary rhetoric that flowed between these two groundbreaking activists reflects the intimate discourses of close friends, respected colleagues, and trusted partners—a communion of minds they would extend over time to include Lyndon B. Johnson. In his September 1951 letter, Ximenes writes:

> Dear Hector, Needless to say, I was very well impressed with the GI Forum State Convention. The only regret that I have is that I didn't get to talk with you a little more about the activities of the organization. However I realized that you had enough on your hands trying to get the organization's work done in a reasonable amount of time.
>
> I do wish to offer some of what I think is constructive criticism. It seems to me that you and the organization spend too much time trying to disclaim any Communist affiliation. The work which you and the organization are doing speaks loud enough in favor of capitalism and free enterprise. It does not seem to me that it is necessary to apologize for that type of work. Many a liberal organization has been deliberately led into open debates on the question of Communist affiliation. Regardless of the outcome of such debates, the fact that the organization chooses to engage in such debates tends to decrease the value of the organization in its real work which is that of improving the lot of the Latin-American. If you get a chance read Owen Lattimore's "Ordeal of Slander" and you'll get an idea of what I am trying to put across.[1]

Ximenes's letter demonstrates confidence in the durability and trust shared between them, a confidence necessary to risk offering guidance and criticism. He stands as an equal to García, a stance not all of García's followers were able to assume with the same bearing and élan. It was a quality that would serve Ximenes in the task ahead of him in Albuquerque, where established leaders in the New Mexico Hispano community were not eager to admit a young upstart organizer.

However, Ximenes, uninitiated in political organizing, offered well-intentioned but naïve rhetorical advice to García. What Ximenes did not take into account in 1951 was the extent of Republican backlash to New Deal policies, the insidious nature of the House Un-American Activities Committee, and the power of congressional investigating committees to ruin the lives of powerful and ordinary citizens alike.[2] Ximenes would soon discover just how far the scope of McCarthyism reached. The defamation of character and social stigma borne by accused Communist sympathizers were more than imaginary threats in this 1950s Cold War climate.

Ultimately, Ximenes's constructive comments to his friend and mentor would come back to haunt him. He would quickly come to realize the meaning of the commonplace "A little knowledge can be dangerous thing." With the hubris of an overachieving college student in economics at the University of New Mexico (UNM), Ximenes was steeped in textbook Keynesian economics and 1950s-era Americanist ideology. The specter of Communist red-baiting and Senator McCarthy's House Un-American Activities Committee were still too remote from Ximenes's own experience. He would soon come to appreciate the irony of his recommendations and the naïveté of his unsolicited comments.

Ximenes would come to understand why García remained ever cautious about keeping the AGIF from circulating too closely to political orbits perceived to be Communist. García's concern was not unfounded. This chapter takes into account the socioeconomic, cultural, linguistic, and political features of New Mexico as Ximenes's field of rhetorical practice. Close rhetorical analysis illustrates how the cultural rhetorical ecology of New Mexico offered an especially efficacious context for aligning the emergent strands of postwar Mexican American civil rights rhetoric in relation to other key institutions and social movements of the era and the region. Chapter 2 also illustrates the key features that distinguished New Mexico as a formative place for building Ximenes's early rhetorical career. As an ambient rhetorical space, New Mexico provided a number of striking contrasts to Ximenes's prior experience of the cultural rhetorical ecologies of Texas.

Expanding the Postwar Rhetorical Imagination

Ximenes reconnected with his good friend Héctor García in Corpus Christi, Texas, in the summer of 1951. Ximenes had completed his bachelor of arts in education at UNM in 1950 and spent a year casting about for a satisfying career path.[3] A lifetime career as a classroom teacher did not seem like the path he wanted. Ximenes spent a year as a research assistant in the Department of Economics after earning his BA degree, trying to find his intellectual niche before beginning his graduate studies program. The pragmatism of business appealed to Ximenes. It was a natural extension of his father's work as the owner and manager of the neighborhood mercantile in Floresville. Ximenes liked the social connections that a small business could cultivate. Commerce represented not only a space for exchanging the material goods of everyday life but one for circulating the news and issues of everyday rhetoric. The mercantile, with its wooden floors, dusty corners, and crowded shelves, was a critical space—a social sphere resting between *oikos* and *polis* (home and public life) that was critical to the work of citizenship. The small-town store was the soul of *el barrio*. Ximenes wanted to extend these early formative experiences into the large expanse of his new and ambitious life in New Mexico.

For Ximenes, the academy was a metaphorical mercantile, a marketplace for the circulation of ideas. He was not attracted to the insularity of the ivory tower however; he preferred the cacophony of the public sphere. The field of economics straddled both worlds. The study of economics productively aligned his interests in commerce, government, and community development and, at the same time, sharpened his skills in research and writing. The work of the research economist would take him out into the community to talk with people. This opportunity gave him an intellectual space akin to the small-town mercantile, allowing him to hear the stories of and rub elbows with everyday people. Finally, in terms of his middle-son position in his large family, Vicente found something that both distinguished him from his siblings and honored his father's legacy.

By the summer of 1951, the future seemed rich with possibility. Ximenes was well positioned to the join the professional class. He had secured a full-time research fellowship with the UNM Bureau of Business Research and admission to the MA program in economics. Ximenes was a proven performer and had earned academic distinction as a member of the Phi Delta Kappa and Phi Kappa Phi honor societies. He was just thirty-two years old and eager to forge a new social network when he met up with Héctor García again in 1951. Leveraging the acquired power of a college education, a distinguished military career, and a promising academic appointment, Ximenes was searching for a political platform to do what he enjoyed most. Since his youth in Floresville, what Ximenes loved most was the churning white-water thrill of political action. It was a precarious balance—navigating the tensions of love and desire.

The difference between love and desire that José Limón examines in *American Encounters: Greater Mexico, the United States, and the Erotics of Culture* is a useful distinction here in divining the rhetorical choices that shaped Ximenes's future life experiences and social position at this critical juncture. *Querencia,* or love for family and home, and *la patria mexicana* represented abiding and unassailable attachments for Ximenes. However, the successes Ximenes realized through his experiences as a decorated war veteran, a college student, and an emerging professional stirred a desire for something quintessentially American—and that was social mobility. The American dream was not readily available to all citizens. Without this desire for what was not equally accessible to Ximenes and Mexican Americans in the 1950s, there would not have been a seismic shift in Ximenes's narrative. Desire pressed Ximenes beyond the ascribed limits of class and social position.

Limón maintains that "the United States generates desire, a desire not only to survive but to better one's life circumstances, a desire for a different national narrative."[4] Ximenes, like his father and brothers before him, tapped into that desire for social power and mobility. The AGIF became a space where he cultivated not only his desire for a different national narrative but a collective *mexicano* desire for a different story. It was bumping up against this desire for mobility and encountering the obstructions of institutionalized discrimination and racism that moved and enraged him; his was a drive stirred by an almost congenital passion for politics. Without these antecedent conditions, the necessary internal and external exigencies for sustained action would have been insufficient for Ximenes to move through the incessant obstacles ahead of him.

In hindsight Ximenes realized that he had been at the proverbial fork in the road, personally and professionally, in the summer of 1951. The cloud of McCarthyism was gathering in 1951, and he could have found shelter in a quieter professional life. With the completion of his master's degree, a midlevel administrative career at the UNM Bureau of Business Research was nearly assured. Ximenes was a strong writer and researcher. He could have thrived in the meritocracy of the academy. Moreover, with the completion of doctoral studies, he could have achieved academic distinction in the professorate or upper administration like his contemporaries George I. Sánchez and Julian Samora.[5] Ximenes could have been the exceptional case, one of the few Mexican Americans in the nation with a PhD and a tenured faculty line or administrative position at this uniquely Hispanic land-grant institution. He could have chosen the more easygoing course and played it a little safer by limiting his sights to professional advancement and eschewing political activism, but there was a restlessness in him that the easygoing course would not satisfy. Careerism without activism seemed like a hollow professional life, and García offered Ximenes the uncertainty, the thrill, and the satisfaction of the seeker's journey.

According to Ximenes, he was passing through Corpus Christi during a visit to see his family in June of 1951. He called García to reconnect after years of silence and miles of distance between them. García invited him to drop by his medical office to chat. In quintessential García fashion, the good doctor did not inform Ximenes that he would be conducting an AGIF meeting at the same time. Ximenes remembers the visit:

> When I called to tell the doctor I was in town, I indicated that I just wanted to come by and say hello. I was in Corpus Christi to spend a couple of days at the beach and then return to Albuquerque, via Floresville. Discrimination, injustice, poverty, and the plight of the Mexican American were the furthest from my mind.
>
> I noticed a large number of vehicles parked outside the doctor's office when I arrived and assumed someone was having a community health session. As I entered the office, Dr. García was addressing the group of persons who were obviously poor and from the barrio of Corpus Christi. The doctor introduced me as a friend who came all the way from Albuquerque to visit with him. The doctor then continued to address the group he called "GI Forum members." Most of his remarks were on the need to organize and bring new members into the GI Forum.
>
> Then he launched into the grievances the Mexican American had that in effect made us second class citizens. We had fought for our country and deserved to be represented in local, state, and national government. He kept reminding everyone that organizing to demand our rights was the key to improving the condition of the *Mexicano*. The doctor was passionate in both English and Spanish and at first it appeared to me that he was talking radicalism, but as I listened to his plea it was a brand of non-violent action. He was exposing the discriminatory acts that took place daily in the lives of the *Mexicano*.
>
> This meeting was the first time that I had heard a person speak publicly for everyone to hear the discrimination lodged against the *Mexicano* and then name the organizations or officials who discriminated against us. I had been in bull sessions that discussed all the facets of discrimination, but none that expressly opened up the avenues to eliminate the hurt being placed on the *Mexicano*. After the meeting the doctor asked me to help him organize GI Forums in New Mexico.

He gave me constitutions, by-laws, and other material and thus began our drive to expand the American GI Forum of Texas into the American GI Forum of the U.S. From that day forward I gave every ounce of energy outside my work to the development of the GI Forum and the fight to gain first class citizenship for the Hispanic and Mexican American.[6]

Ximenes was swept into the current. He not only observed but also experienced how García used his persuasive influence among his followers. Directing rhetorical power toward fair and useful political outcomes was something Ximenes had watched his own father do as the political *patrón* of Floresville. He watched how García orchestrated the flow of resistance rhetoric like a *mayordomo* gauging and controlling the flow of water through an *acequía* system of interconnected channels. García knew how to operate a complex system of gates and canals to keep the flow of ideas and energy open and moving. Reflective of his experiences listening to the Floresville politicos of his youth, Ximenes jumped in with both feet.

What Ximenes did not know when he arrived at García's medical office that day was that García already had plans to invite Senator Dennis Chávez of New Mexico to affiliate with the expanding veterans' organization. Recruiting a novice community organizer like Ximenes and a senior legislator like Dennis Chávez from New Mexico to advance the goals of the AGIF would prove to be a very productive move for García. Building an alliance among liberal Democratic legislators in and beyond Texas was a savvy step toward exercising influence over national policy making. As former advocates of the League of United Latin American Citizens (LULAC), García and Chávez had this common thread to connect them, but little else.

García's vision for expanding the AGIF into New Mexico was steadily percolating when Ximenes wandered into García's medical offices in June 1951. LULAC and Senator Chávez had already shared a long and productive history in New Mexico (chapter 3). However, García and the AGIF had no presence in New Mexico yet. After Ximenes's visit to his Corpus Christi medical offices, García would promptly invite Senator Chávez to deliver an address at the 1951 AGIF state convention set for August. García's correspondence to Senator Chávez repeatedly stated how eager he and the members of the AGIF were to meet him. The tone of his letter was collegial but not overly familiar. "We are very grateful and thankful that you have accepted our invitation, and you may be sure that we are all happy and anxious to meet you," García writes.[7]

The fledgling alliance between García and Senator Chávez was finally forged during the AGIF state convention. The New Mexico connection took shape in this rhetorical moment, an open exchange of admiration and vision. As reflected in Senator Chávez's 1951 keynote address, the affiliation between the AGIF and Chávez promised to be a mutually beneficial association. However, an organizational point person in New Mexico would be necessary, and Ximenes efficaciously filled that role. In his remarks Senator Chávez expresses his admiration for García and the young and ambitious Texas AGIF:

> Now, Dr. Garcia and your associates have done a grand job, you and the people who have helped you in forming this organization, whose purposes are so noble, deserve the gratitude not only of the people whom you are trying to help, but also that of all liberal and progressive people who know that the cause of democracy and freedom can only be served by according the rights, social and economic advancement among them all people without regard to race, color, national origin or religion.
>
> When I see this assemblage, I think back to my youth, when peonage, low wages, poverty, illiteracy, disease, and political bossism prevailed in New Mexico. We have not quite overcome our problems but the enthusiasm which you and this young group of GIs are showing here today brings to mind how a few of us felt some 40 years ago in New Mexico when we set out to change what existed there then, and which to a great extent we have succeeded in doing.[8]

Ximenes was in the right place at the right time. With the zeal of the newly baptized, Ximenes left the 1951 AGIF state convention with a mission. Through García's and Chávez's mentorship, Ximenes learned how to open up channels of opportunity, allowing a new current of mobilizing energy to flow into New Mexico and beyond. Forming new discursive channels, however, demanded that Ximenes both align himself with the political currents of the Texas AGIF and distinguish himself from García's groundbreaking movement and foundational political tributaries.

Border Crossing: Expanding Rhetorical Spaces

García had established the AGIF in March 1948 by building on the organizational framework of LULAC, which had been established in Corpus Christi twenty years earlier. The AGIF was an extension of LULAC, but with a difference. Invoking the key tenets of Franklin Roosevelt's 1944 Economic Bill of Rights and companion GI Bill of Rights, García used the AGIF as a conduit for direct action on behalf of his clients denied medical support and other GI bill benefits. The GI bill was a federal promissory note to all

veterans that García expected the U.S. government to honor. According to
Arthur Schlesinger Jr., "FDR's Economic Bill of Rights represented a crys-
tallization, precipitated by the Great Depression, of 40 years of analysis and
agitation by reformers, journalists, social workers, professors, and practical
politicians"[9] The GI bill, a significant legislative piece of FDR's Economic
Bill of Rights, provided a federal umbrella of protection for veterans (education, housing, employment, and medical benefits), a constellation of public
services that García wanted to access for Mexican Americans. García, well
read and well informed, keenly coordinated his rhetorical project with the
larger social currents of the day.

Significantly, 1948 also marked the release of the widely published works
of Mexican intellectual José Vasconcelos and his visionary treatise *La Raza
Cósmica*. Originally released in 1925, this literary document inspired pride and
solidarity among Mexican-origin peoples throughout the Americas. Circulation to wider audiences throughout the Americas promoted a philosophy of
empowerment among the "brown races" of the world. Vasconcelos celebrated
New World *mestizo* identities, interrogating Eurocentric ideologies and the
vestiges of racial purity myths of medieval Spain. Delineating the rich mix of
Old and New World cultures and racial identities throughout the Americas,
Vasconcelos debunked the stigma of racial mixing. Anticipating cultural
constructions of hybridity, Vasconcelos lauded the transformative possibilities of cultural contact and racial difference. His notion of *la raza cósmica*
offered a new perspective on the consequences of conquest and colonization
and the emerging *mestizaje* of indigenous and European groups. Vasconcelos
argues, "Las circumstancias actuales favorecen, en consecuencia, el desar-
rollo de las relaciones sexuales interaciales, lo que presta apoya inseparado
a la tesis que, a falta de nombre major, titulé: de la Raza Cósmica future."[10]
(Current conditions, consequently, promote the development of interracial
sexual relationships that lend support to the theory, for lack of a better name,
of the future cosmic race.) Vasconcelos's racial theory resisted white privilege
and historical European and American pigmentocracy. Mexican-ness was
something to celebrate. The hybridity of race and language represented a
cultural strength, not a liability, for post–Mexican Revolution intellectuals
like Vasconcelos.

The U.S. civic imagination in 1948 was further conditioned by other key
public moments. By the late 1940s African American civil rights activist
Bayard Rustin initiated one of the first Freedom Rides through the South to
confront segregation, a resistance strategy reenacted in 1964 with Freedom
Summer. The year 1948 also represented the milestone moment when the
historic Freedom Train (memorialized by Langston Hughes's celebrated

poem) made whistle-stops throughout the Southwest with visits to El Paso and Albuquerque. As a metaphor of the national imagination, the Freedom Train traveled to all corners of the country carrying the most revered historical document of the United States—the Constitution. A New Mexico resident, recalling the historic moment, writes:

> On Sunday, February 15, 1948, the Freedom Train came to Santa Fe for one day. It was cold and cloudy when the train came into town from El Paso, Texas, and many of us kids were there to greet its arrival. . . . Can you believe that the original Constitution and Declaration of Independence were there for all to see? And the originals of Lincoln's Gettysburg Address and the Emancipation Proclamation?[11]

For citizens from historically excluded groups such as Mexican Americans, the confluence of events in 1948 signaled a change in expectations. Men and women across cultures refashioned their roles as citizens. The experiences of World War II permanently altered the social expectations of returning soldiers and their families in terms of race, class, and gender. By December 1948 the adoption of the Universal Declaration of Human Rights, ushered by Eleanor Roosevelt through the United Nations, further bolstered the discursive resources and available means of persuasion that García appropriated to advocate for the needs of his South Texas constituencies.

Accessing these national and international post–World War II discourses of advancing human rights, more broadly, and veterans' rights, more specifically, García conceptualized the AGIF as a veterans' rights organization that would mitigate the historical suffering and exploitation of South Texas citizens. The scope of the AGIF quickly sharpened, however, within its first year to advance Mexican American civil rights issues tenaciously. Less than a year after its formation, the watershed event of the Private Félix Longoria case, set in South Texas, catalyzed the AGIF as a civil rights organization.

García's rhetorically adroit handling of the Félix Longoria case in January 1949 put the AGIF and the plight of Mexican Americans in the national spotlight for the first time in modern history. García's media exposure of racial discrimination in South Texas and his call for national scrutiny of the small Texas town of Three Rivers opened the floodgates of disputation. Refusal to carry out the Longoria family's request for burial services for Private Félix Longoria "because the whites here wouldn't like them to use the funeral home" represented an affront to the American ideals for which the United States had fought overseas.[12] García enlisted the support of then freshman senator Lyndon B. Johnson. Johnson, in turn, arranged for Private Longoria's burial at Arlington Cemetery. The burial of Félix Longoria evolved into an international spectacle marked by military honors and media attention. The successful outcome of the case demonstrated to García and his followers that Mexican American citizens had the capacity to shape public opinion and to generate political action. The affiliation between García, Johnson, and the AGIF would last for the next two decades.

Labeled a "militant Moses," García quickly earned the reputation of an agitator, unabashedly flinging jeremiad-style rhetoric at racist Texas Anglo politicos.[13] Through the maelstrom of the Longoria incident, García and his followers discovered effective means for rallying attention to their cause.[14] The challenge of leveraging that exigence and subsequent public attention to effect permanent institutional change through legislative reform, however, required new models of activism.[15]

The problem in 1951 when Ximenes joined the organizing scene was how to maintain public attention long enough to make sustainable changes on behalf of Mexican Americans. After the collective success of the Longoria case, the AGIF needed to find new strategies for expanding its support base and incorporating its agenda for Mexican American civil rights into the fabric of national policy. García did not initially conceptualize the AGIF as a civil rights organization. His foundational vision centered on building a veterans' rights organization that promoted the interests of working-class Mexican Americans, especially with issues related to GI benefits such as health, employment, education, and housing. García's own ambivalence toward the notion of civil rights complicated his goals for the organization.

As a relatively recent New Mexico resident, Ximenes, however, quickly found himself operating within an exponentially more complex postwar situation. Ximenes had to find a way to situate himself in the constellation of discourses already in circulation. New Mexico's rich cultural history and complicated political ecology demanded that he cultivate a new range of rhetorical responses, including the formation of new alliances with prominent political figures such as Senator Chávez and other advocacy organizations such as the National Association for the Advancement of Colored People (NAACP), the Anti-Defamation League, and local labor unions (chapter 3). The social, material, and ideological dimensions conditioning Ximenes's coalition-building process not only shaped him as a leader; they helped him reimagine the scope and possibilities of the AGIF as a veterans' civil rights organization.

For García, Ximenes represented a promising new leader for the AGIF. As an economist, educator, and researcher working at UNM, Ximenes offered an important professionalizing presence for his organization. Ximenes's growing expertise—his research and scholarship in economics that would include studies of the natural gas industry, income and employment patterns, housing, wages, and construction in New Mexico—and his insights into these regional economic issues would help to inform the civic activism agenda for the AGIF in New Mexico. The academic, civic, and professional literacies Ximenes had already acquired, and would further refine through the AGIF, represented the keys to first-class citizenship.

García recognized early on the need for cultural brokers and political liaisons capable of mediating between Anglo and Mexican American social systems. Sustaining a visible and productive presence in the South Texas political landscape was a continual challenge for García. Most of the members of the AGIF belonged to the working class or were migrant laborers or immigrants with limited resources and access to established power structures. Many migrant workers followed the crops to *el norte*, returning to Texas at the close of the season as poor as when they had left. Only a small number of AGIF members had a college education; some had a high school education in segregated, underserved "Mexican" schools like the Cotulla elementary school where Lyndon Johnson had served as principal in 1929. A few AGIF members were small business owners with growing influence in local commerce. Others were laborers in the oil and ranching industries of Texas. An elite group of AGIF leaders like the loquacious Ed Idar Jr. and the mercurial Gus García (no relation to Héctor) were up-and-coming lawyers who helped to cultivate the legal imagination of the veterans' rights group by shaping the public rhetoric of equal access and organizing against discriminatory practices in private and public sectors.

Ximenes brought a different perspective to the AGIF, a new voice to the podium, a new presence at the table. The commonalities of García and Ximenes allowed them to operate in separate spheres toward shared outcomes. Their distinguished histories, however, differentiated them into a class of their own. In *The New Rhetoric: A Treatise on Argumentation*, Chaim Perelman and Lucie Olbrechts-Tyteca call this phenomenon "the contact of minds." All efficacious rhetorical action requires "an effective community of minds" and some level of agreement (assent), implicit or explicit, in the formation of an intellectual community.[16] Ximenes and García shared a "community of minds" forged through their common backgrounds in South Texas and mutual experiences in education, familial structure, military service, culture, language, religion, region, and professional positions.

Although Ximenes and García had personally experienced the limitations of poverty and racism, their personal backgrounds also set them apart from the constituencies they served. As Ximenes explains, "We knew how to do business with 'the man.'"[17] Finding ways to engage and confront the dominant discourse of white male hegemony in politics and industry would be a prolonged and necessary challenge for Ximenes and García. It was a challenge from which the two men rarely shirked. Neither Ximenes nor García were averse to political conflict. In fact, they thrived on it. Their shared traits and histories helped them to cultivate the necessary rhetorical alacrity to meet with conflicts head-on and resolve division. Linguistically, culturally, socioeconomically, and politically, Ximenes and García understood how to mediate multiple social positions. Both were well prepared for engaging in the rhetorical arts of "agonistic pluralism."[18] As Chantal Mouffe argues, "the novelty of democratic politics is not the overcoming of this us/them opposition—which is an impossibility—but the different way in which it is established. The crucial issue is to establish this us/them discrimination in a way that is compatible with pluralistic democracy."[19] Ximenes and García cultivated an ability to negotiate with adversaries, confronting, compromising, and building alliances with white power brokers.

"The Land of Entrapment"

As soon as he returned to New Mexico in the summer of 1951, Ximenes began mobilizing to establish a chapter of the AGIF in Albuquerque. It required eight people to charter a new chapter, but he had difficulty recruiting new leaders. His early attempts were frustrated by fear and racism. Points of resistance came from arguments based on denial, fear of backlash, and provincialism. Where did he fit into the cultural mosaic of New Mexico? As a veteran, a graduate student, and a professional researcher, Ximenes had access to a number of potent legitimizing identities. He used all of these cultural materials in cultivating his rhetorical resources and social identities.

Ximenes straddled the legitimizing institutions of the university, the military, the church, and the New Mexico professional class. The motivating situation for Ximenes in Cold War–era New Mexico was that he did not fit completely and comfortably into any of the available legitimizing institutions. He simply could not adopt these legitimizing identities wholesale. He also discovered he was not alone in this sense of civic alienation. Ximenes sensed the inequitable power relations among these New Mexico constituencies. Poverty, social marginalization, and economic segmentation represented a land of entitlement as well as entrapment for many groups, including newly arriving Mexico-origin immigrants.

The opportunities for socioeconomic mobility for Mexican American, Mexican national, and Hispano citizens remained severely limited. Economically, New Mexico had become increasingly dependent on the defense industry beginning in World War II with the establishment of national laboratories, the statewide infrastructure supporting the Manhattan Project, and Cold War nuclear proliferation that followed in its wake. The wealthy white elites capitalized on political and economic resources while the native-born majority (Hispano and American Indian) remained locked in poverty. Ximenes began navigating through this complex and unstable cultural rhetorical ecology. Joining a generation of post–World War II change agents, Ximenes sought to agitate New Mexico's political *disturbance ecology* through the mobilization of the AGIF.[20] His rhetorical career evolved during a historical moment profoundly invigorated by an entire generation of politically engaged and socially conscious Mexican Americans.

Other veterans came home from the war with an enhanced sense of global citizenship and social justice. Additionally, Mexican American women who served in the war effort at home and abroad came away with heightened notions of their agency. The war experience demanded that Mexican American women expand their spheres of influence within the workplace by acting as head of their household, working outside the home, and serving overseas. As Naomi Quiñonez observes in "Rosita the Riveter: Welding Traditions with Wartime Transformations," the wartime social conditions "proved to be especially significant for Mexican American women, whose new wage-earning status created a sense of self-sufficiency and intensified issues of self-identity."[21] These changes helped to generate a growing demand for gender equality within the home and the workplace. The postwar socioeconomic climate was changing political sensibilities and social configurations for many groups. Nevertheless, institutionalized discrimination and class segmentation still obstructed the full inclusion of returning Mexican American veterans.

Ximenes often heard Albuquerque's established leaders argue that "New Mexico already had good race relations."[22] Strategically constructed since the territorial period to reflect a tricultural mythos, the postwar New Mexico represented in travel guides and mass media reflected an idyllic American melting pot of harmonious Anglo, Hispano, and Indian coexistence. However, a three-hundred-year legacy of colonization, genocide, and bloody resistance waged among Anglos, Hispanos, and Native Americans churned below this placid idyllic surface. The presence of a New Mexico African American minority, a presence predating the Civil War, further complicated the racial political climate of the state.[23]

Citizenship and belonging in Albuquerque, New Mexico, for Ximenes rested with mixed communities: veterans (at the nearby Air Force base), students at the university, parishioners at the local Catholic church, and neighbors living in his middle-class housing development off Central Avenue where he and his family had built their home. In many respects he was living in what Chicana scholar Laura Gómez calls an "off-white" universe.[24] He wasn't Anglo or European; he wasn't Hispano or Spanish; he wasn't *mexicano*; he wasn't white; and he wasn't indigenous. He was all of these and none of these. The panethnic designations of Hispanic and Latino were not available categories of identification in 1951.[25] Ximenes understood intuitively his own *mestizaje*. From this heterogeneity he cultivated new spheres of belonging by aligning disparate groups and affiliations. But navigating the cultural divide and class segmentation of New Mexico remained an enduring challenge.

When Ximenes launched the AGIF in New Mexico, he was not just an un-initiated or uninformed upstart. Vicente and María had been residents of New Mexico for over four years, having established a life and family in Albuquerque in 1947. They had made the cross-country trek in a 1938 Pontiac from Texas to New Mexico with their young son, Steven, who was born in San Antonio, near their hometown, in 1946. Although Ximenes was a sixth-generation Tejano, he wanted the opportunity and cultural diversity New Mexico could offer him and his family. Moreover, his large, upwardly mobile cohort of seven siblings back in Texas had already set the family expectations and parameters for success. Ximenes needed the social elbow room to define himself on his own terms. Vicente's brother Edward was establishing a successful medical practice in San Antonio. His brother Waldo was a prominent attorney. His sister Hercilia was an established teacher. New Mexico represented a fresh start for Vicente and his young family on many fronts.

Vicente and María had built a modest adobe style home on Monroe Street near Central Avenue and not far from the major thoroughfare of Albuquerque's historic Route 66. Their son Ricardo (Rick) was born in Albuquerque in 1950, followed by Olivia in 1954 and Ana in 1961. Their son Steven attended the local Catholic school. The family was active in the local Sacred Heart Catholic Church. Ximenes had served at Kirtland Air Force Base in Albuquerque during World War II, maintaining contact with the local military community. In sum, Ximenes had formed a strong and visible presence in the Albuquerque community well before trying to initiate mobilizing efforts through the AGIF.

Despite these strong social ties, Ximenes's initial efforts at establishing the AGIF in Albuquerque were thwarted by several factors. Albuquerque's established leaders argued, "You will set us back and ruin the good work that is being done by the political party." Or they said, "New Mexico is different. New Mexico is not Texas."[26] Ximenes was both confused and frustrated as he tried to discern the complexities of the cultural rhetorical situation. He candidly expresses his frustration to García in the closing paragraph of a September 8, 1951, letter:

As I mentioned to you at the Convention, I am finding the possibilities of establishing an affiliate to the GI Forum here in Albuquerque. Such an organization is definitely needed in spite of the fact that many persons have told me that no discrimination exists in Albuquerque. Those people however are either blind or they would rather turn their back on it since some of them as individuals may not have ever met with it. Send if possible, a copy of the Constitution and by-laws of the organization and any other material which you think would be of interest.[27]

The prospects for a New Mexico chapter of AGIF offered Ximenes the leadership opportunities he wanted and the community he needed. At the same time, he struggled to understand the resistance he faced in getting this project off the ground.

Social Constructions of Place and Belonging: Race and History in New Mexico

New Mexico, reluctantly admitted to the United States in 1912, had been an official state of the union for a little over thirty years when Ximenes moved to Albuquerque. In the rural northern region of New Mexico, Hispanos represented 76 percent of the population, Indians 10 percent, and Anglos 14 percent.[28] Although Hispanos lost their majority status in the urban centers of Albuquerque and Santa Fe to the Anglos who settled there after the war, Spanish-speaking Hispanos still constituted a substantial majority in northern New Mexico. In *Occupied America: A History of Chicanos*, Rodolfo Acuña observes that racism increased with accelerated Anglo migration to New Mexico after World War II, when white Texans moved across the state line to work in the oil and mining industries. Gradually Anglos gained political and economic control of the eastern half of New Mexico, an area frequently called "Little Texas." Because of this region's strong cultural and demographic connections to Texas, many of the discriminatory labor, housing, educational, and public use practices were imported to New Mexico along with these transplanted Anglos.[29]

By the strength of their numbers in the northern and western sections of the state, however, Hispanos were still able to maintain some influence over New Mexico politics even as they were losing wealth and their claims to Spanish land-grant holdings. The dynamics of Hispano hereditary privilege, majority status, intricate kinship networks, and durable cultural traditions throughout New Mexico helped to distinguish this region from other annexed territories of Greater Mexico such as Texas, Arizona, and California. The historical struggles of Spanish colonialism and U.S. imperialism were not over by the mid-twentieth century. Moreover, the promises of the 1848 Treaty of Guadalupe Hidalgo were unevenly and unreliably realized throughout New Mexico.

These complex social, cultural, linguistic, and political legacies of the region persisted through the twentieth century and dramatically conditioned the rhetorical situation Ximenes faced in his adopted state. The cultural rhetorical ecology of New Mexico reflected a distinct ecotone, or cultural transition zone. As a contact zone of diverse linguistic, cultural, and historical backgrounds (indigenous, Spanish [including Jewish and Moorish], Mexican, and Anglo-European), New Mexico had resisted a monolithic identity for generations. Moreover, the remarkably diverse microclimates and geologies, literally and metaphorically, had conditioned the political economies and social formations of this region for centuries. Cultivating an effective presence as a leader required that Ximenes acknowledge and accommodate a wide range of regional factors: ethnolinguistic diversity, political dynamics, indigeneity, colonial history, and economic shifts. Ximenes spent the first four years as a New Mexican citizen acculturating and learning the intricacies of his new home state.

Ethnolinguistic Diversity

First, Ximenes needed to acknowledge the breadth of ethnolinguistic diversity across New Mexico's communities. Language issues shaped the spheres of possibility for Ximenes. Not only was New Mexico home to many language varieties (Spanish and English as well as over twenty indigenous linguistic codes); postwar migration patterns had also introduced Asian and Pacific Island immigrants to the region. Ximenes's own linguistic resources included Spanish (a regional variety commonly called Tex-Mex) and English (as a second language). However, Ximenes did not speak the historic Spanish of Nuevo Mexico. Spanish as a colonial language held an esteemed place in the dominant Hispano New Mexico culture. New Mexico, distinguished as the only state in the United States with a constitution written in Spanish, placed a high value on maintaining the distinct heritage language variety of the region. In *Preservation of the Village: New Mexico's Hispanics and the New Deal*, Suzanne Forrest notes:

> Through their influence of the 1910 Constitution, which went into effect in 1912 when New Mexico became a state, they effectively laid the groundwork for the protection of both their legal rights and culture. It made New Mexico officially a bilingual state, putting English and Spanish on equal basis for all state business. It provided for the training of bilingual

teachers, prohibited separate schools for Anglo and Hispano children, and specifically, provided that the rights guaranteed by the Treaty of Guadalupe-Hidalgo would remain in force in the new state.[30]

Linguistically, New Mexico is home to several varieties of Spanish, some classical variations of which are still spoken in the northern parts of the region and reflective of the cultures of sixteenth-century Spain. The Spanish that Ximenes encountered in New Mexico was not the same Texas variety of Mexican-origin Spanish spoken in South Texas. Language purity myths stigmatized the language practice of code-switching characteristic of contact varieties of Spanish such as Spanglish and Tex-Mex. Ximenes simply did not speak the archaic varieties of Castellano Spanish characteristic of New Mexican Hispano Spanish speakers. And he did not see himself as a heritage Spaniard. Ximenes identified as Mexican American, not as Spanish American or Hispano. Language attitudes and stigmatization served as markers of power and privilege.

The post–World War II shift toward adopting English and Anglo cultural practices was in progress when Ximenes moved to New Mexico. Traditional Spanish naming practices were gradually fading with the impact of assimilation and the Americanization of New Mexico culture after the war. Names such as Baudilio, Benito, Procopio, Frutoso, Tranquilino, Elicita, and Dionicia were eventually exchanged for names such as David, Michael, Debra, and Jennifer so that the new generation could more easily fit into Anglo-dominant postwar society. Interestingly, this trend toward anglicizing Spanish names was a trend reflected in the Ximenes family as well: Estevan eventually became Steven and Ricardo became Rick. The patterns of adaptation, accommodation, and resistance evidenced by Ximenes contributed to a kind of self-fashioning that both distinguished him and acculturated him within postwar New Mexico society.

Indigeneity

Second, indigenous influences in New Mexico configured the social milieu of New Mexico during the postwar era when Ximenes established himself in Albuquerque. While Ximenes had an intuitive sense of the cultural divide separating Hispanos, Anglos, and Native Americans, he would come to better understand native sovereignty and why he would never have direct access to the tribal communities of New Mexico. Narrative constructions of American Indian cultural identity reflect complex and highly contested histories of conquest, resistance, and resilience. Ximenes's indigenous familial roots, extending back to the Kawanka and the nomadic tribes of Texas, had no direct connection to New Mexico's tribal peoples. His family story did not align with the nineteen pueblos or other sovereign nations such as the Jicarilla Apache and Navajo throughout New Mexico. Ximenes did not satisfy membership requirements as a descendant of native peoples through matrilineal kinship or blood quantum documentation. In other words, access to regional tribal communities in New Mexico was not available to Ximenes as a Tejano *mestizo* with an undocumented indigenous lineage to ancient nomadic peoples. Moreover, Ximenes did not speak any of the native languages or have the insider knowledge to interpret the cultural codes. He did, however, recognize his own *mestizaje* as the descendant of Spanish and indigenous lineages.

Like the Hispanos of New Mexico, Native Americans were annexed as a people in constellations of sovereign tribal nations.[31] According to Forrest, "when the territory of New Mexico was acquired through annexation by the United States in 1848, both Indian and Hispanic land titles were guaranteed by the treaty of Guadalupe-Hidalgo."[32] Under the terms of this treaty, Native Americans, like Mexican-origin residents, were regarded as full citizens with the right to sell their land. But like their Hispano counterparts, American Indians found the treaty protections to be less binding than those promised. Hispanic and Indian land titles had become almost inextricably entangled since the Spanish colonial period. Spanish land grants and claims of native sovereignty represented embattled contests between first peoples and first colonial settlers for hundreds of years.

The exact details of pueblo land grants in relation to the dimensions, geographic location, and terms of use were often nebulous and infrequently recorded. Spanish colonists often encroached on Indian territories, establishing homes, farms, and ranches on pueblo grants. Sacred lands were increasingly violated and appropriated, displacing native peoples from the lifeblood of their cultural lives. Some pueblos permitted Hispano homesteaders in their territory to help protect their land from raiding nomadic tribes of Ute, Apache, and Comanche. A growing *mestizaje* of indigenous and Spanish cultural and familial connections gradually developed over generations. To further complicate land grant claims, Forrest notes, "Indian and Hispanic families intermarried and the lands were passed down to offspring who might claim either Indian or Hispanic allegiance."[33] Hispanic and Indian cohabitation in the region, therefore, represented a complex—sometimes interdependent and often contested—set of arrangements from the beginning. Native American cosmology and culture directly and indirectly infused the New Mexico social landscape when Ximenes first called Albuquerque home.

The Native American icon of the Zia symbol, representing the dynamic forces of birth, death, growth, and entropy, was adopted for the New Mexico state flag in 1912 when this southwest territory became a part of the United States. The Zia symbol reflects the four directions (or energy forces) of the universe: east (birth/emergence) to west (death), north (entropy/dormancy) to south (growth/regeneration). The number four is a sacred number in a Native American worldview. Hence, the Zia symbol is a sacred image representing the four quadrants of the universe. The Zia not only designates the geopolitical and rhetorical realities of New Mexico but a complex, dynamic, and sacred cosmology as well. As a bioregion in the southwest quadrant of the Zia symbol, from a Native American perspective, New Mexico citizens live in dynamic tension between death and transformation.

As the site of what native peoples claim was the "First American Revolution," New Mexico has been a contested space of conquest and reconquest for centuries. The legacy of Spanish colonizer Juan de Oñate's repressive regime eventually ignited the historic Pueblo Revolt in 1680, a defining moment in Indian and Hispano relations that continues to inflect social dynamics between these communities today. Centuries of occupation and exploitation by Spanish colonial powers left an indelible imprint on native collective memory. The warrior legacies of native peoples remain vital facets of New Mexico life and culture. Commemoration and memorials recognizing the Pueblo Revolt led by Tewa leader Po'pay signaled a critical shift in defining New Mexico race relations.[34]

New Mexico's deep and enduring legacy of Native American leadership, culture, and resistance indexes the durability and primacy of its first peoples. Unlike Texas, whose nomadic indigenous populations suffered nearly complete annihilation during Spanish and Anglo-American colonialism, New Mexico's nineteen pueblos as well as the expansive Navajo and Apache nations continued to shape the social and cultural dynamics of the region. Ethnolinguistic heterogeneity among tribal communities was critical to retaining identity, restoring solidarity, maintaining insularity, and protecting sovereignty. Native American writer Luci Tapahonso, a member of the Diné (Navajo) nation, details the loss of her native language in the Anglo-directed school systems of New Mexico: "My first memory of speaking English in school consisted of three words: 'what,' 'yes,' and 'no.' When a white adult spoke to me, I would say 'What!' not as a question, but as a loud and emphatic answer. I repeated this until I understood what was being said. Since speaking Diné was forbidden, many of us did not talk at school or in the presence of whites."[35] Native communities continued in their struggle to retain their own languages, models of governance, family configurations, cultural practices, and economic systems.

Hispano Politics

Third, social currents following World War II began reconfiguring cultural and political balances. With the incursion of Anglo industry and technology, Ximenes needed to recognize the roles and influences of his political predecessors, especially Senator Dennis Chávez, who represented a powerful source of political resistance to the Anglo *pátrones* of the state. The senior Hispano power brokers wielded considerable influence after the war and did not readily welcome an aspiring community organizer like Ximenes whose agenda risked disrupting the balance of power. From the 1930s and into the 1960s, the legacy of Dennis Chávez represented an enduring presence in the New Mexico political environment, shaping and restructuring Anglo and Hispanic power relations after World War II. With the support of Senator Chávez, LULAC eventually gained a foothold in New Mexico throughout the 1930s and 40s. This Hispano political group provided enduring support to Chávez's career and ultimately lobbied with Senator Chávez for the formation of the Federal Employment Practices Commission in 1941. Figures like Senator Chávez needed to be won over if Ximenes and the AGIF hoped to gain a legitimized presence in New Mexico.

Born near Albuquerque in the village of Los Chávez in 1888, Dionisio (Dennis) Chávez represented one of the great bootstrap narratives of Hispanic leaders. He was the descendant of farmers who established and lived in the Hispano Los Chávez village for generations. Chávez worked his way through law school at Georgetown University without the benefit of prior formal education or personal wealth. Chávez's early life growing up in a rural village paralleled Ximenes's own personal biography. Chávez worked in a mercantile as a young boy, delivering groceries across town and listening with an attentive ear to the political debates exchanged in *el zocolo*. A brief narrative biography published in the 1958 AGIF national convention program brochure relates Chávez's story. Building on his liberal Democratic political convictions, Chávez was elected to New Mexico's House of Representatives in the 1920s and eventually won New Mexico's only seat in the U.S. House of Representatives in 1930. Chávez found his way to the U.S. Senate in 1935 and held the seat until his death in 1962.[36]

Senator Chávez brought New Deal government work programs to New Mexico, helping to invigorate the local economy and the Democratic Party. Consequently, Chávez complicated the Republican stronghold in the state. Under Chávez's leadership, Depression-era politics and New Deal programs in the Southwest ushered in a number of countervailing forces. New Deal programs strongly reconfigured cultural, racial, and economic relationships in New Mexico. New Mexicans began lobbying for racial equality and political participation with the help of Senator Chávez in the New Deal era. As a cohort, Hispanos began making demands on the federal government to equalize the distribution of wealth and opportunity across social groups. In 1939 President Roosevelt responded to Senator Chávez's lobbying efforts and approved the formation of a Civil Rights Section in the U.S. Justice Department that protected not only African Americans but Mexican Americans as well. Additionally, Senator Chávez pushed for the approval of Executive Order 8802, issued in 1941, that created the Fair Employment Practices Committee, opening the doors for Mexican American participation in U.S. defense industries. Ironically, it would take nearly another decade before the Fair Employment Practices Committee gained political traction in New Mexico.

Following World War II, Senator Chávez played a leading role in introducing civil rights legislation during the Truman administration. During the Eisenhower era, Senator Chávez worked to repeal the poll tax and took a vigorous stand against the red-baiting tactics of Senator McCarthy. As Ximenes recalls, "at the time, the very mention of civil rights would be considered communist."[37] Chávez remained a political force in the state for forty years. He was a complex and much-admired political figure. As AGIF member Isabelle Tellez remembers, Senator Chávez "was very close to the people."[38] All aspiring leaders needed to check their card with Senator Dennis Chávez if they were going to be successful with his constituencies. This was a lesson Ximenes quickly learned. When he returned to Albuquerque from Austin after his first AGIF Texas state convention in 1951, a visit to the offices of Senator Chávez was his first move.

Economic Shifts

Finally, economic and political power in New Mexico remained largely concentrated among elite Anglos for more than a century. As the region became dependent on defense dollars and moved away from an agricultural economic base throughout World War II, the means of production shifted from self-sufficiency to a market economy. As Chicana environmentalist Laura Pulido observes, "Hispanos initially settled the region through a system of land grants (*mercedes*) and developed an agropastoral system based on vertical transhumance grazing and subsistence agriculture. Communities were organized to include private land for the home, garden, and feed production and collective ownership of the highlands for grazing, timber, and other resources. Water was furnished by *acequias*, a gravity-based irrigation system well suited to arid environments."[39] This agropastoral system was increasingly threatened by mining, oil, and gas industries through the war years. Furthermore, New Mexico's tourist industry, spurred by the burgeoning railroad industry through the 1900s, traded on the cultural mystique of the region by exoticizing New Mexico's geographic and cultural features. Pulido further argues that "the state has pushed tourism, based on wealthy outsiders' desire to consume the landscape, the cultural diversity, and the natural resources of the area."[40]

The rural multisource economy and Hispanic communitarian interdependence prior to the incursion of New Deal programs and policies through the 1940s had disrupted Hispano communities by making many of New Mexico's communities entirely dependent on federal programs such as the Civilian Conservation Corps, Works Progress Administration, and National Youth Administration. When these programs evaporated after World War II, entire communities found themselves in abject poverty and disarray. As Forrest concludes in *Preservation of the Village: New Mexico's Hispanics and the New Deal*, "The individualization and secularization of production, the individual acquisition of wealth, and the market regulation of land and labor delivered the coup de grace to Hispanic self-sufficiency."[41]

Economic influences shaping postwar New Mexico that moved the region from an agricultural economy to one fueled by defense and technology industries ultimately led to the establishment of nuclear and research production facilities at Los Alamos National Laboratories in Los Alamos and at Sandia National Laboratories in Albuquerque. Anglo dominance was reinforced by the multiple, interlocking facets of the military-industrial complex, New Mexico's primary source of economic power since World War II. The move toward technology and industry and away from ranching and farming strained the New Mexico socioeconomic and cultural balance. The war economy stimulated the mining industry and the rapid development of natural resources such as uranium, silver, copper, and other ores. In "World War II and the Education of Hispanos," Getz observes:

> As the state's defense and technology industries developed, a new cohort of highly educated scientists, technical people, and military personnel moved into the state for the first time. Educators had assumed they were training New Mexican children for jobs in agriculture and trades, not atomic science or technology. Without the educational background to perform highly skilled technical work, Hispanos were often relegated to service and labor jobs. It was apparent, in the postwar years, that in terms of preparing Hispanos for scientific, engineering, or technical careers, even the best-intentioned educators had failed the Hispano community.[42]

As an emerging economist, activist, and leader, Ximenes wanted to change the marginalized position of Mexican Americans and the downward socioeconomic trend facing vulnerable communities across the state of New Mexico in light of these economic shifts.

The AGIF in New Mexico

The impacts of racism and institutional discrimination ultimately locked the majority of Hispanos in a lower socioeconomic status. Hispanos, *mexicanos* (immigrant), Mexican-origin citizens as well as Native American groups were not only losing ground in the Anglo-dominant socioeconomic situation; they were being stripped of their cultural and linguistic legacies with each decade following the war. Trying to organize a resistance movement in New Mexico during this postwar period without cultural sensitivity and consideration for the disparate histories and political factions was a formula for failure. Engaging in the jeremiad rhetoric of an uninitiated outsider would have represented a doomed proposition for Ximenes, who recognized the folly of his position. He was in new and potentially hostile territory as a Mexican American veteran and Texas native recently transplanted and trying to establish himself in New Mexico. In terms of finding a place in the region's social landscape, he began to see how race, class, and history deeply inflected the terms of inclusion in New Mexico's social order. These unspoken, invisible codes of belonging began to assume shape in the first year of mobilizing for the AGIF in Albuquerque.

Nativist Hispanic ideologies in New Mexico afforded little social prestige to *mestizo* outsiders. In the social pecking order of Hispano culture, Ximenes was on the same lower rung as the *recien llegado* Mexican immigrant. Upper-class Hispanos maintained a strong sense of class status, especially in relation to lower-class New Mexican villagers and working-class *mexicanos*.[43] To further complicate issues of social position, as a descendant of nomadic Indians, Ximenes could not really claim indigenous affiliation either. As a *mestizo*, a member of a mixed racial class, he was neither white nor black. He was other. Nor could Ximenes adopt the term *Hispano*, which was reserved for persons with Spanish heritage claiming white privilege and denying *mestizo* Mexican lineage. Hereditary privilege had shaped social configurations in the region for hundreds of years before Ximenes called New Mexico home. Self-ascribed as Mexican American, Ximenes would have to find common ground with other Spanish-speaking cohorts and their collective experiences of racial discrimination.

Class identification with Hispano natives and the elite of New Mexico would prove to be an unproductive mobilizing strategy. In the Iberian-centric consciousness of New Mexico, Ximenes did not belong to the privileged group claiming prestigious European origin. Into the historically polarized world of New Mexico cultures, therefore, Ximenes did not fit neatly. He would need to learn how to negotiate the divisions separating Anglo, Hispano, and Native American groups and to mediate the enduring fault lines in the cultural geography of the region.

Altogether, the complex historical archaeology and cultural ecology of the region contributed to the subliminal resistance that newcomers like Ximenes often encountered in New Mexico, especially if they arrived with an agenda and ambition. These social and historical conditions cultivated the rhetorical situation within which the AGIF eventually took root. It was significant that Ximenes chose to center the foundation of the AGIF in the historic Hispano community of Barelas rather than in the newly expanding postwar developments throughout Albuquerque, which were invigorated by the GI bill and Federal Housing Administration benefits.

By locating the AGIF in Barelas, Ximenes built this nascent organization upon rich historical layers of collective memory, Mexican American activism, transnational commerce, New Deal optimism, and cultural exchange. The barrio of Barelas was built near the riverbed of the Rio Grande, which provided safe and accessible crossing along the path of El Camino Real, the famed Spanish colonial route connecting Mexico City to the northern frontiers of New Spain. The AGIF of New Mexico would call Barelas home beginning in the early post–World War II era.

This was a significant and symbolic site for the emergence of a Mexican American civic organization. Barelas and the Sacred Heart Catholic Church had been the historical center of Hispano activism in New Mexico throughout the twentieth century, the home neighborhood of such prominent figures as Senator Chávez and Professor George I. Sánchez. Built in 1921 by the residents of Barelas at the corner of Fourth Street and Stover, Sacred Heart provided a site for community organizing, educating the local youth, and celebrating the religious rites of the area's Catholic constituency.

After three months of struggle, Ximenes called the first AGIF meeting in New Mexico in December 1951 in the basement of the Sacred Heart Catholic Church in the barrio of Barelas. Eight people joined Ximenes at that first meeting. The charter members of the AGIF chapter were teachers, a lawyer, a college student, and a city employee. The names include Robert Esparza, Victor Gonzales, Ben Chávez, Manuel Chávez, Avelino Gutierrez, Santiago Campos, Alfonso Proo, Procopio Martinez, and Ximenes. After open discussion and debate, Ximenes was elected chairman of the first chapter of the AGIF in New Mexico. Ximenes recounts:

> The organizational meeting of the Albuquerque GI Forum was held in the basement of the Sacred Heart Church. Eight persons came together and I was elected chairman of the GI Forum in 1951. Two months after the first meeting I received a frantic call from Monsignor Garcia. The FBI had been by to ask him questions the Monsignor could not answer about the GI Forum. If word got out in public that the FBI questioned the Monsignor, the GI Forum would be doomed. I was scared because I had brought together friends to join the GI Forum and I knew the McCarthy Communist scare tactics had ruined the lives of many people. My professor of government had been literally run out of Wisconsin by the adherents of Senator McCarthy and for a few hours after the Monsignor's call I was frozen with fear of what might happen.
>
> Then I picked up the GI Forum constitution and by-laws and headed for the FBI office. I presented myself to an FBI person and told them I could answer any questions they had about the GI Forum. Our membership was open to anyone who would swear allegiance to the U.S. The FBI person listened to all I had to say without any response to my statements. I then satisfied the Monsignor as to the legitimacy of the GI Forum, but I never told the new members about my actions with the FBI. About twenty five years later when I was the main GI Forum speaker to celebrate the Federal Judgeship of Santiago Campos, one of the original members of the Albuquerque chapter of the American GI Forum, I told the Judge that in 1951 he was the subject of an FBI investigation.[44]

From the outset Ximenes needed to move forward with both vision and caution. Having an organization for catalyzing citizens in direct action tactics to confront civil rights violations against Mexican-origin peoples represented a new, but tenuous, political force in New Mexico.

In turn, the cultural rhetorical ecology of New Mexico not only shaped Ximenes's rhetorical fields of practice; it indelibly transformed the political imagination of the AGIF. In a series of public and private letters, Ximenes described the challenges he faced over the first year of organizing the AGIF in New Mexico. On December 20, 1951, Ximenes circulated one of his first acts of public rhetoric in the form of a letter to the editor of the *Albuquerque Journal*. The message embedded in his three-hundred-word statement thoughtfully identifies the major issues and Cold War themes motivating the formation of the AGIF in Albuquerque that same year. Ximenes opens his letter with this declaration: "This is a letter about death." He then constructs a contrast between "death in New Mexico" and "death in Korea." The illustrative narrative that follows describes a recent event in Loving, New Mexico:

> On November 16, the Hobbs Daily News-Sun reported the death of two Mexican children from starvation. I assume that they meant that the children were American citizens of Mexican extraction, since it was reported that their legal residence was Yoakum, Texas. It seems no welfare funds were available for these American citizens because the law prevented disposition of funds to non-state residents. Furthermore, it seems that a nurse could not help the children because the nurse could not speak Spanish. Since when does a nurse have to speak Spanish in order to detect malnutrition. I always thought malnutrition was a health condition, not a language.[45]

The deaths of these two children Ximenes blames on the welfare system and on Clinton Anderson, U.S. senator from New Mexico, for his neglect of local conditions. He contrasts the deaths of the two children in New Mexico with the deaths of 108 U.S. Hispanic soldiers in Korea who gave their lives as American citizens.

This alignment seeks to establish a moral distinction between the noble and honorable Mexican American soldiers killed in battle overseas and the disgraceful and dishonorable deaths of two innocent Mexican American children starved to death in the U.S. homeland. Ximenes deals with the particular cases, not general categories. Ximenes closes his letter of protest with a critique of New Mexico lawmakers and candidates campaigning for election and promoting various economic programs in the state. Ximenes argues, "Not one single law-maker or would-be law-maker uttered a word about solving New Mexico's situation with reference to the two children that starved in Loving, New Mexico. Perhaps silence means consent."[46] Significantly, Ximenes signs his letter as "chairman" of the newly founded AGIF in New Mexico. However, Ximenes's public rhetoric confronting Senator Anderson put him in a precarious and oppositional position against this powerful political figure with ties to UNM, where Ximenes worked. Moreover, Senator Anderson was a strong proponent of New Mexico's defense industry and the Cold War surveillance commerce growing across the state. Ximenes would find out over the next two decades just how far the reach of Senator Anderson's influence extended and the negative implications of making enemies with this politically influential legislator and businessman (chapter 5). Ximenes's letter to the editor also foreshadowed the heavy risks he would struggle to balance through the next two decades.

The Balancing Act: Risks and
Consequences of Political Activism

In personal letter to Héctor García on February 12, 1952, Ximenes described the political obstacles he had encountered trying to expand the AGIF throughout New Mexico in the months following his first meeting at the Sacred Heart Catholic Church in Albuquerque. He was facing his first big clash with the established power brokers of the state. Within the first few months of its founding, the AGIF of Albuquerque and Ximenes were already embattled with the local power brokers of politics and industry. Ximenes reports:

> We've engaged in a tough fight with the Home Builders Association with reference to low cost housing. They have sent one of their "hatchet" men to put a stop to our project. . . . We told the SOB to go to hell. There are certain principles that we do not compromise. What I am telling you now is just between you and I since I promised not to discuss the meeting or publicize it. When he found out that we were not for sale, he threatened to call us names, I suppose he meant socialism, etc. We told him to go right ahead, but only at his own risk because we believe that a court suit can be brought against him if he does.[47]

Ximenes also reveals in his letter to García the more personal agonistic struggles he had to face with his own family members. There is a shadow of foreboding woven into this personal letter.

By the following summer, Ximenes reported to García that his closest family members had begun to criticize him over his political activism. His older brothers Edward and Waldo were beginning to achieve professional and financial success back home in Texas. They were openly questioning Ximenes's devotion to community organizing and his involvement with the AGIF in New Mexico. Less than a year after attending his first AGIF state convention in the summer of 1951, Ximenes was deeply entangled in the New Mexico political scene. Moreover, the new Albuquerque chapter of the AGIF began taking on a life of its own, claiming more and more of his time and energy.

Only eight months after the inaugural meeting of the Albuquerque AGIF, Ximenes confides to García in an August 8, 1952, letter: "The family was down from San Antonio for about two or three days. They can't understand why I should be putting in a little work for the betterment of our people. Even Edward has forgotten that it wasn't long ago that we lived in a house with a dirt floor. Now I can see why it isn't so hard for a person like Gus [García] to go to pieces."[48] Ximenes was struggling to strike a balance, but the scales were tipping. The sacrifices of public service and casualties of political activism were manifested in the broken lives of figures like Gustavo "Gus" García. The evidence was already in. Ximenes knew how much Héctor García had sacrificed for the cause. Héctor had already mortgaged his medical practice, his home, and his family (literally and metaphorically) building the organizational framework of the AGIF. The demands never ceased. The long-term impact on Héctor and his family was tremendous. Consequently, Ximenes's concerns were not unfounded.

By the close of 1952, Ximenes was already feeling the pressures of community organizing after only a year of affiliation with the AGIF. He was trying to balance it all: school, work, family, and community. The social injustices he had encountered in his first year of mobilizing compelled him to stay the course. During the first year of organizing, from 1951 to 1952, Ximenes helped launch New Mexico chapters in Loving, Carlsbad, Hobbs, Silver City, Clovis, Portales, Logan, Tucumcari, Roswell, Artesia, Las Cruces, Deming, Clayton, Grant County, Belen, Bernalillo, Grant, Gallup, Santa Fe, Las Vegas, Santa Rosa, and Espanola. Over the next six years, he helped to organize twenty-three chapters in New Mexico in all. With a growing support base for the organization, Ximenes also began taking on highly visible political issues and engaging in direct action strategies to confront discrimination. In his August 17, 1952, letter to Héctor García, Ximenes details the growing political tensions:

> We have uncovered some information on what happened to 250 farm laborers that went to California to work for some fruit growers company. The New Mexico Employment Security Agency was used as the intermediary. $10–12 per day were advertised, good housing, and living conditions, and 6 months to a year of work guaranteed. Instead the workers were paid 5 dollars for the first week and fed rice with rat turds in it three times a day. The workers are back and I have already interviewed five of them and gotten written statements of the whole damn mess.[49]

In his capacity as chair of the Albuquerque AGIF, Ximenes served as a liaison for the farmworkers to seek full compensation and to litigate their broken contract with the fruit growers through the New Mexico Employment Security Agency. It was a bold move. Although Ximenes cultivated a political presence for the AGIF and met with limited success in New Mexico through his first year, he still had to face the intractable and historical dimensions of the rhetorical situation that he could not change. Ximenes reflects:

> The Mexican Americans who populated the cities in the South such as Roswell, Carlsbad, Hobbs, Clovis, and Tucumcari claimed education and employment discrimination. A small but politically powerful Spanish American group from the Northern counties wanted no part of the GI Forum's open assault on discriminatory practices against the Mexican Americans and Spanish Americans of the nation. When and where to organize American GI Forum chapters was a real problem for me.[50]

In the minds of the established Hispano community, Ximenes was a radical newcomer to the New Mexico cultural and sociopolitical scene. Although the Ximenes family had enjoyed a measure of insider status in the South Texas political situation, Ximenes was a political outsider in New Mexico. While he was able to tap into the wave of postwar GI optimism (and frustration) among Mexican American men and women who experienced the same kinds of obstacles and inequities within the legitimizing institutions of the government, industry, education, and professional fields, Ximenes was still regarded as an interloper in the New Mexico political scene.

In the anti-Communist red-baiting historical moment of the early 1950s, community organizing was a bold and risky move even for a Cold War liberal like Ximenes. The public circulation of the very term *civil rights* was instantly perceived as a code word indexing suspicious activity by Communist subversives. Under the aegis of the AGIF, this growing of alliance of Mexican Americans, unionized labor, and blacks and Jews in Albuquerque quickly sent up a red flag. Ximenes was marked for observation for suspected un-American activities. He found himself in sketchy company.[51] It was a practice that would ultimately cost Ximenes his job a decade later.

As a researcher for the UNM Bureau of Business Research, Ximenes reached out to college students, educated young professionals, and veterans who were willing to agitate to make visible the inequities within the community. They were the risk takers and visionaries. The AGIF gathered political strength by taking on statewide discrimination issues. One of its first major projects was to enact an antidiscrimination law in public places such as workplaces, restaurants, hotels, recreational facilities, and others.

A Desert of Possibility: Growing the New Mexico Narrative

The next two years were spent growing the membership of the Albuquerque chapter and seeding new chapters across the state. As Ximenes recounts, "A close knit core of Albuquerque American GI Forum men and women made it possible for me to expand the Forum into a national organization."[52] Heeding

García's guidance, Ximenes staged subsequent AGIF meetings at the Sacred Heart Catholic Church in an attempt to deflect the attention of government officials ever on the lookout for subversives and spies. Vicente recalls, "The Catholic Church meeting place would give me cover from attacks by those who thought that any human rights organization, especially one made up of Mexican Americans, must be by definition a subversive organization."[53]

The contours of the New Mexico political landscape had been irrevocably altered by an interlocking economic system that coupled the military with a burgeoning security industry during World War II. As home to the Los Alamos and Sandia National Laboratories, strategic sites of U.S. nuclear weapons research and development, New Mexico became the heart of the military-industrial complex from World War II into the Cold War era. Although this hypervigilant red-baiting climate challenged the rhetorical situation for Ximenes, it did not hinder the evolution of the AGIF. Despite being on the FBI's watch lists, Ximenes and the AGIF grew exponentially. Ximenes reflects, "Once I broke the ice in Albuquerque, Hispanics from all parts of New Mexico, especially 'little Texas,' came to see me to get Forums organized in their communities."[54] Texas-neighboring towns of New Mexico, such Clovis, Portales, and Hobbs, struggled with the domination of Anglo political bosses and looked to the AGIF as a means of organized resistance. Ximenes took on other civil rights issues and won labor battles on behalf of city garbage workers. Ultimately, he helped to organize twenty-three chapters of the AGIF in New Mexico, a branch in Arizona, three in Colorado as well as chapters in California, Kansas, Michigan, and Illinois. Ximenes recalls:

> As I expanded the organization in Albuquerque other dedicated volunteers supported and defended the GI Forum like Attorney Lorenzo Chávez, Zeke and Helen Duran, Louis and Isabelle Tellez, Clarence and Ana Gailard, Leo and Minnie Hernandez, Duven and Emma Lujan, Raul and Rose Cordova, Frank Martinez, Ray Powell, Frank Jaramillo, Jose Gonzales, Meril Esquivel, Zeke and Irma Hernandez, Atty. Felix Salinas, Vicente Jasso, Ernest Sanchez, Francis Sanchez, and Atty. Alfonso Sanchez. Senator Dennis Chávez was also my friend and helped in my efforts to organize a national GI Forum.[55]

Growing a coalition of activists through a volunteer political economy, Ximenes helped to establish a mobilizing base for Mexican American civil rights reform in the shadows of New Mexico's expanding security culture. The coalitions that Ximenes organized thrived through the 1960s, aligning community activists across social groups that included labor unions, the NAACP, and the Anti-Defamation League. Ximenes and the New Mexico

AGIF helped to enlarge the rhetorical imagination of this growing veterans' rights organization. He enacted the transgressive power of agonistic pluralism to constitute a counterpublic through the AGIF in New Mexico.

From 1951 to 1961, Vicente and María Ximenes represented the public faces of the New Mexico AGIF. Unlike Héctor and Wanda García in Texas, the Ximenes were political partners in the establishment of the AGIF in New Mexico. They spent over a decade devoting time, energy, and financial support to the AGIF community. From the outset, the AGIF was a family affair. "I couldn't have done any of this without María," Ximenes recounts.[56] Family and community members together recognized María as "a major contributor in the construction of the American GI Forum national headquarters in Albuquerque."[57] Her keen sense of hospitality, adept organizational skills, compassionate demeanor, faith, openness to possibilities, and unwavering commitment to her family and the community provided the emotional glue that held this homespun project together. They were joined by numerous families who found a way to dedicate considerable gifts of time, talent, and treasure to the organization.

Vicente and María Ximenes along with the charter members of the AGIF devoted the same energy, a spirit of *koinonia* (fellowship) that many of them evinced in their religious lives in the Catholic Church, to their public life with the AGIF.[58] The AGIF as a voluntary organization, directly informed and invigorated by its alliance with the Catholic Church, provided a mechanism of empowerment and a conduit for public life for Spanish-speaking communities in the Southwest. The establishment of the first chapter of the AGIF in New Mexico at the Sacred Heart Catholic Church reflected the Texas AGIF organizing practices implemented by Héctor García. Local parishes offered space for social and cultural events, protection from red-baiting tactics, and occasional financial support. Tamale sales after Sunday masses eventually helped the Albuquerque AGIF fund legal expenses related to the civil rights cases they were advocating. The symbiotic relationship between the AGIF and the Catholic Church extended into nearly all facets of public life—social, cultural, political, educational as well as religious. In many respects, this institutionalized alliance resembled the kind of interdependent relationship black churches cultivated with African American social reform groups such as the NAACP and Martin Luther King Jr.'s Southern Christian Leadership Conference throughout the 1950s and 1960s.

As an emerging activist and community organizer, Ximenes operated at the rhetorical crossroads of Cold War hysteria, Americanist propaganda, civil rights polemics, and postwar Mexican American patriotism. The role of labor and direct action strategies in New Mexico was gaining political and rhetorical strength when Ximenes began mobilizing for the AGIF in 1951. As exemplified by Ximenes's engagement with New Mexico's longest labor strike in 1951, finding common ground within this politically fractious regional terrain remained his most enduring challenge.

Salt of the Earth: *Cultivating the Cold War Political Imagination*

The historic Empire Zinc mine strike near Silver City, New Mexico, conditioned the rhetorical imagination of the AGIF as it gained traction in New Mexico. The Local 890 chapter of the International Union of Mine, Mill, and Smelter Workers of Hanover, New Mexico, comprising 1,400 members of predominantly Mexican origin, staged one of the nation's most effective and groundbreaking strikes in New Mexico, lasting fifteen months from October 1950 to January 1952.[59] The formation of the first chapter of the AGIF in New Mexico coincided with this historic labor strike. Ximenes and the newly established AGIF chapter demonstrated solidarity with the strikers by providing food, clothing, and supplies for the families of the mine laborers.

The grievances of the Empire Zinc mine workers included racial discrimination in job duties and pay, lack of sanitation for *mexicano* housing, no-strike contract clauses, and inequitable power sharing between labor and management. The local authorities of Silver City and Hanover asked the governor to send in the National Guard as soon as the strike began. Placing an injunction on the mine workers to shut down the strike failed to quell this historic labor incident. The wives of the mine workers took over the picket line and shut down access to the Empire Zinc mine. The dramatic showdown between the women and local law enforcement agents and the resulting incarceration of forty-five women, seventeen children, and a six-month-old baby shocked observers locally and nationally. Many of the workers, including the striking women, spent several months in jail and paid heavy fines. The nation would not again witness women and children marching on the front lines protesting discrimination until Martin Luther King Jr.'s direct action civil rights campaign in Birmingham, Alabama, over a decade later in 1963.

The actions of the men and women of the Local 890 garnered national and international attention including the notice of independent film producers Paul and Sylvia Jerrico. Sympathetic to the plight of the mine workers, the Jerricos were inspired to make the groundbreaking film *Salt of the Earth* based on the incident.[60] *Salt of the Earth* was released in theaters around the nation in 1954 and promptly banned by the U.S. government as un-American propaganda. Civil rights activists like Ximenes and the newly formed AGIF Albuquerque chapter, however, recognized the import and implications of the Empire Zinc mine strike. Ximenes and AGIF organizers promptly helped to establish chapters of the AGIF in southern New Mexico communities such as Deming and Silver City in the wake of the Empire Zinc strike.

Overstepping LULAC's reluctance to stir racial tensions or engage with *mexicano* immigrant issues, Ximenes cultivated the political imagination and rhetorical resources of the AGIF by supporting the mine strikers of the Local 890. Although northern New Mexico communities and the established Hispano communities remained relatively indifferent to the mobilizing efforts of the AGIF, Mexican American and Mexican migrant workers in the southern and eastern sections of the state strongly identified with the rhetoric of social justice promoted by Ximenes. The emerging AGIF in New Mexico offered solidarity and support to the striking men and women in Silver City and mobilized citizens throughout southern New Mexico. Ximenes recalls:

> At the time of the filming of the "Salt of the Earth," the American GI Forum of Silver City and New Mexico was fighting the Kennecot Corporation's segregated housing and school policies. We complained to the Corporation about the segregated pay lines for the workers. We were also fighting the Silver City School Board's gerrymandered school districts. Atty. Felix Salinas, GI Forum legal advisor, appeared before the school district board and demanded and was successful in getting the school districts redrawn. The GI Forum action was even before the 1965 Voting Rights Act that outlawed district lines that discriminated against Mexican Americans and other minorities. The "Salt of the Earth" controversy was strictly a union's fight for working conditions and wages. The GI Forum's part was to send food and clothing to the strikers. We did not yet have a dog in the union's fight for wages and working conditions.[61]

Ximenes and the AGIF not only helped to sustain the workers and their families through gifts of food and clothing; they promoted civic education in the everyday practices of citizenship. AGIF leaders persisted in organizing Mexican American participation in local government, cultivating civic literacy and public education.

The ultimate success and international acclaim of the Empire Zinc strike contributed to the political exigencies enhancing Mexican American identification with the civil rights agenda promoted by Ximenes and the AGIF in New Mexico. Ximenes helped to galvanize working-class Mexican Americans who could not find protection or support within the scope of LULAC as a civic organization. Furthermore, the success of the Local 890 represented a collective affirmation for all Mexican American laborers in the region who sought redress for discriminatory work conditions.

Ultimately, the labor strike and the film the *Salt of Earth* provided a clear and visible case of Mexican American political activism in New Mexico. It offered a model for direct action, organization, collective activism, and deliberative processes. *Salt of the Earth* changed the available means of persuasion for Ximenes and the AGIF. In addition to establishing AGIF chapters in the region, Ximenes later testified before the Silver City School Board to contest the discriminatory practice of dividing the school district along racial and ethnic lines. The efficacy of the Empire Zinc workers direct action strategies and the activism of the women for the Local 890 further inspired the mobilization of Albuquerque garbage workers (chapter 3), a protest supported directly by Ximenes and the AGIF. Ximenes and the AGIF remained a mobilizing force throughout New Mexico. Offering behind-the-scenes support and solidarity to the Empire Zinc mine workers, the AGIF quickly established its reputation as a politically effective and socially responsive organization.

Above: Vicente Ximenes at the Richard Kleberg Conservation Camp of the CCC in Seguin, Texas, circa 1939. Personal Papers of Vicente T. Ximenes.

Left: Ximenes during World War II with the U.S. Air Corps, circa 1942. Personal Papers of Vicente T. Ximenes.

Above: Ximenes (*bottom row, fifth from left*) with U.S. Air Corps squadron mates of a B-17 Flying Fortress, circa 1942. Personal Papers of Vicente T. Ximenes.

Right: Ximenes, lead bombardier, with B-17 aircraft *The Reluctant Dragon*, circa 1942. Personal Papers of Vicente T. Ximenes.

Vicente and María Castillo Ximenes as newlyweds in San Angelo, Texas, circa 1943. Personal Papers of Vicente T. Ximenes.

Right: Vicente and María at the Kirtland Air Force Base in Albuquerque, New Mexico, circa 1947. Personal Papers of Vicente T. Ximenes.

Below: Women of the Local 890 chapter of the International Union of Mine, Mill, and Smelter Workers during the Empire Zinc mine strike, Hanover, New Mexico, circa 1951. Jack Cargill Collection, J. Cloyd Miller Library, Western New Mexico University, Silver City, New Mexico.

AGIF Albuquerque Chapter One headquarters building project at 621 Gabaldon Road Northwest, Albuquerque, New Mexico, July 1955. Personal Papers of Vicente T. Ximenes.

Ximenes as the president of the AGIF Chapter One at a swearing-in ceremony for officers of the AGIF Ladies Auxiliary, Albuquerque, New Mexico, circa 1957. Personal Papers of Vicente T. Ximenes.

Ximenes and members of the Daughters of the American Revolution at the AGIF flag exchange ceremony in Albuquerque, New Mexico, February 1957. Personal Papers of Vicente T. Ximenes.

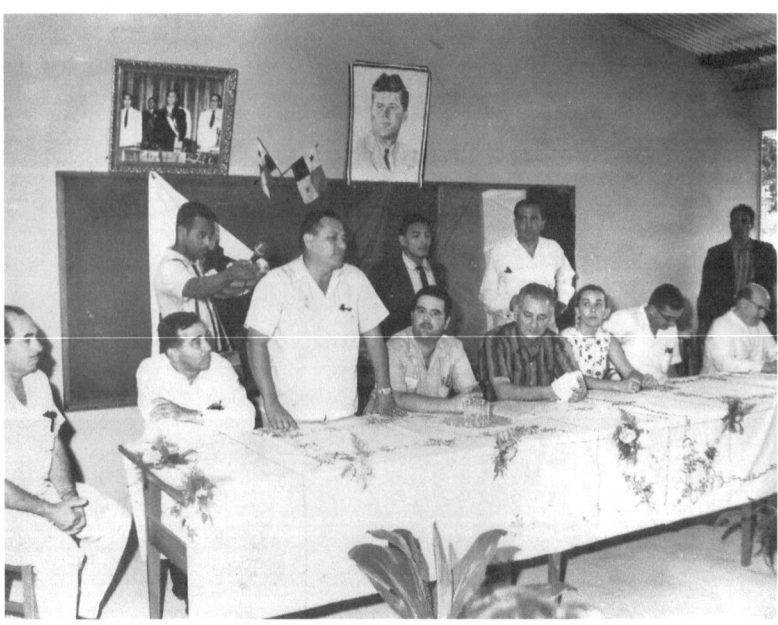

Ximenes serving in the Alliance for Progress program with USAID in Latin America, circa 1963. Personal Papers of Vicente T. Ximenes.

Ximenes with USAID project inspectors in Latin America, circa 1963. Personal
Papers of Vicente T. Ximenes.

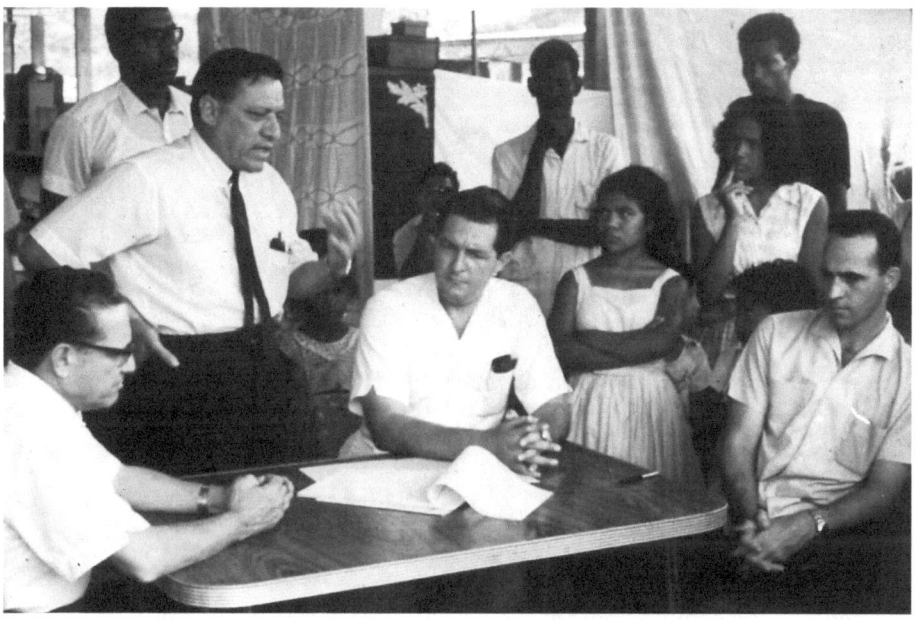

Ximenes as the assistant director of development planning for USAID in
Panama, circa 1965. Personal Papers of Vicente T. Ximenes.

Ximenes leading a USAID project planning meeting in Panama, circa 1965.
Personal Papers of Vicente T. Ximenes.

Ximenes as the commissioner at the EEOC swearing-in ceremony with
President Lyndon B. Johnson at the White House, June 9, 1967. Personal Papers
of Vicente T. Ximenes.

President Johnson with María and Vicente at the EEOC swearing-in ceremony in a reception line at the White House, June 9, 1967. Personal Papers of Vicente T. Ximenes.

Ximenes family with children (*left to right*) Ricardo, Olivia, and Ana, with President Johnson at the EEOC swearing-in ceremony at the White House, June 9, 1967. Personal Papers of Vicente T. Ximenes.

President Johnson and six-year-old Ana Ximenes at the EEOC swearing-in ceremony at the White House, June 9, 1967. Personal Papers of Vicente T. Ximenes.

President Johnson arriving for the Cabinet Committee Hearings on Mexican American Affairs in El Paso, Texas, October 26–28, 1967. Personal Papers of Vicente T. Ximenes.

President Johnson with Commissioner Ximenes and White House cabinet members at the Cabinet Committee Hearings on Mexican American Affairs in El Paso, October 26–28, 1967. Personal Papers of Vicente T. Ximenes.

Commissioner Ximenes with an AGIF member at the Cabinet Committee
Hearings on Mexican American Affairs in El Paso, October 26–28, 1967.
Personal Papers of Vicente T. Ximenes.

3. The Public Rhetoric of Vicente Ximenes: Citizen Scholars and Mexican American Civil Rights Activism

n a lecture published in the *American GI Forum News Bulletin* in January 1956, Ximenes presented a multifaceted portrait of New Mexico's uneven economic landscape to his American GI Forum (AGIF) readers. Using the epistemic rhetoric of exemplification, illustration, and narration, Ximenes enacted the role of citizen scholar to depict New Mexico's welfare program. As a research associate of the University of New Mexico's (UNM) Bureau of Business Research, Ximenes relied on a broad range of available means of persuasion. Enacting all facets of the classical Aristotelian five canons of rhetoric, Ximenes efficaciously aligned his own experiences of the New Mexico situation (shaped through memory) to construct (invent, style, and arrange) and circulate (deliver) his research to audiences throughout the region.[1]

This 1956 lecture reflects a significant shift in Ximenes's rhetorical career. This act of public rhetoric advances a complex stance demonstrating Ximenes's newly acquired professional ethos by carefully aligning his authority as an economist with his evolving civil rights agenda. Ximenes's rhetorical alacrity is displayed as he effectively synthesizes the multiple dimensions of his social identities. The lecture suggests his growing sophistication as a rhetor. Ximenes's own transformative experiences living and working in New Mexico are further evidenced in his lecture. He gives voice to the dissonances and confluences shaping his own civic consciousness, character, and public vision of what it means to live in right relationship with his community. Reading and responding to the world through the rhetoric of economics, Ximenes discovered a way to coalesce his seemingly divergent civic and professional roles.

When Ximenes published this 1956 lecture, he was in his fifth year as a research associate in economics at UNM and an organizational leader of the New Mexico AGIF. He had completed his master of arts degree in economics at UNM in 1953.[2] With the 1956 publication of his UNM Bureau of Business Research lecture on the "welfare situation" in New Mexico, Ximenes takes on the dual role of a professional writing and a writing professional. In her essay "The Ecology of Writing," Marilyn Cooper suggests that writers enacting an ecological model of writing engage in the work of writing as a social practice and activate the "dynamic interlocking systems that structure the social activity of writing."[3] In his 1956 lecture Ximenes assumes the stance of both citizen scholar and writing expert seeking to illustrate the historical consequences of institutionalized discrimination and to disrupt the material conditions of racism.

This chapter examines Ximenes's rhetorical career in mid-twentieth-century New Mexico and his emerging role as a citizen scholar. Taking a cultural rhetorical ecology approach to this analysis of Ximenes's community organizer period of civic engagement, chapter 3 situates the ethnolinguistic dimensions of communicative action and the dynamic process of discourse circulation through key rhetorical events to consider how these events shaped Ximenes as a leader. During this dynamic phase of the AGIF's expansion in New Mexico, Ximenes distinguished himself through a number of landmark moments including the 1954 Albuquerque garbage workers case and the 1957 Daughters of the American Revolution flag incident. Each of these rhetorical events represents complex community organizing projects that help to constellate Ximenes's public identity as a leader.

The Rhetorical Topoi of "Juan Garcia" and "Jack Williams"

Since the formation of the AGIF in New Mexico in December 1951, Ximenes had been experimenting with a range of resistance discourses. He learned how to press the limits of social stratification through a number of self-authorizing acts of citizenship. He began to realize how the work of public rhetoric conditions complex political environments by disturbing the social ecology. His rhetorical fields of practice continued to expand over the course of the next five years. By 1956 Ximenes was confident, successful, and established enough as a citizen of the New Mexico cultural rhetorical ecology to exercise agency through the legitimized identity of an MA-level graduate and the conferred authority of his professional position. His job as a business researcher had given him the intellectual space and resources to generate the evidence with which he could support his social justice agenda. The New Mexico public sphere had become his canvas. As illustrated by his 1956 "welfare situation" lecture, Ximenes draws a representative portrait of New Mexico. He writes:

> There are various ways of preparing a talk on population as it affects the welfare picture. One is to note that 55 per cent of the population of New Mexico was born in this State, 42 per cent in other States, and 3 per cent in foreign countries. From this base we would have to investigate, among

other things, the characteristics, habits, customs, religion, and economics of the 55 per cent born in New Mexico.

To be more specific we would have to go into the history and background of the Spanish speaking and Indian population of the State. We would have to look up the case history of Juan Garcia from Arroyo Seco who gave up his subsistence farm for a janitor's job in Albuquerque and a hitch on the welfare rolls.[4]

Ximenes demonstrates a keen understanding of the multiple dimensions of the rhetorical situation for this lecture and, at the same time, attends to the informational needs of his diverse audiences. He seeks to engage both a primary professional business audience and a secondary civic audience.

The cultural rhetorical ecology of the New Mexico situation is mapped through the genre of narrative.[5] There is a story he wants to tell with characters, events, and obstacles to overcome. He understands that his diverse audiences will take away very different messages. The *topoi* around which his argument coalesces, however, help to unify his disparate audiences. The take-away message implied but never overtly stated asserts that institutionalized discrimination is simply bad business. Ximenes embeds this assertion within a win-win-win proposition. The logos of his subliminal proposal goes something like this: better the socioeconomic conditions of Mexican Americans; then the New Mexico business environment will prosper, and the welfare situation will improve as well.

In many respects Ximenes's lecture demonstrates his growing rhetorical agency as a citizen scholar writing across communities. Ximenes provides a nuanced preview statement to his lecture to set the stage. Although he intends his primary audience to include economists, educators, and business leaders, Ximenes's secondary audience includes everyday citizens (local and national AGIF members) with whom he deeply identified. Narrative becomes the rhetorical device that allows Ximenes to accommodate these disparate stakeholders.

Ximenes adroitly represents his observations and empirical research through the narrative of description in a series of representative anecdotes. He constructs an imaginative fiction:

After Juan arrives in the urban areas, it would be necessary to find out why he becomes the victim of small loan companies, suede shoe salesmen, and reducing machine peddlers. We'd probably find out that Juan made a down payment with the last few dollars he had on a television set that barely fits in one of the two rooms he occupies in a section of town that is known for its large number of outside toilets.

Juan has no particular skills so he gets the dirtiest jobs in the community. His older daughter finds it hard to secure employment, because an
employee of an employment agency tells her "it's hard to place Spanish
people in this community." Juan's younger children are constantly ill, but
medical attention is rather expensive, besides Juan does not believe that
modern doctors know much about medicine, and he prefers to take his
family to a "*curandera.*"

Juan goes through a series of experiences in the urban areas of New
Mexico that he calls "*un monton de mala suerte.*" Finally a relative that has
just returned from California tells Juan of the many good paying jobs in
that State.

This lecture illustrates Ximenes acting on the postwar rhetorical situation,
ultimately moving himself and the New Mexico AGIF toward the desired
outcomes of civic inclusion and socioeconomic mobility.

In the cultural rhetorical ecology of mid-1950s New Mexico, Ximenes
seeks to make visible the material and social conditions impacting "Spanish
speaking" populations in New Mexico. He uses an imaginative fiction to
tell his story. The figure of Juan Garcia is a metonym representing his larger
constituency. Ximenes invokes the term *Spanish speaking* to designate the
primary stakeholders of his research. He does not use the terms *Latino,
Chicano,* or *Hispanic.* As sociologist G. Cristina Mora notes in *Making Hispanics: How Activists, Bureaucrats, and Media Constructed a New America,* the
historical shift toward Hispanic panethnicity did not begin until the early
1970s.[6] None of these categories were available to Ximenes in 1956, so he
constructs fictive categories through a series of representative anecdotes.

The pathos of Ximenes's argument rests in the strategic use of the vernacular in both English and Spanish. Through the act of code-switching with
the phrase "*un monton de mala suerte*" (a mountain of bad luck), Ximenes
projects an emotional appeal by representing the sociolinguistic identity
of his subject, his audience, and himself. Interestingly, Ximenes does not
translate this phrase for his English-speaking audience members. Nor does
he not translate "*curandera*" (a spiritual healer or cultural broker of traditional
medicine).[7] Ximenes allows these Spanish discourse markers to signal that he
is an outsider speaking to other outsiders (Spanish speakers among English
speakers). Paradoxically these idiomatic expressions also signal Ximenes as
an insider speaking to other insiders (Spanish speakers among other Spanish
speakers). Code-switching functions as a rhetorical twist, a trope, *un chiste,* a
trickster turn. This shape-shifting discourse operates as a solidarity marker
at multiple levels. This is an emblematic rhetorical move. Ximenes, a master

of the enthymeme, understood the power of the suppressed premise and the efficacy of shape-shifting discourses.

Ximenes's first rhetorical task in this lecture is to define his population. *Spanish-speaking people* in the United States, as a linguistically constructed minority during the 1950s and 1960s, generally referred to Mexican Americans, Cuban Americans, and Puerto Rican Americans. Ximenes signals the problem of linguistic racism facing Spanish-speaking groups in his reference to "Juan Garcia's daughter," who is denied employment because of her ethnolinguistic identity. Juan's younger children, reflective of the Spanish-speaking children about whose deaths in Loving, New Mexico, Ximenes wrote in 1951 (chapter 2), index the inequitable access to health care and social goods facing Spanish-speaking groups.

Ximenes understood inductively and deductively that Spanish speakers and nonnative speakers of English face significant discrimination in the workplace. The empirical research necessary to make this claim would need to be gathered across the state to make his case statistically significant. Ximenes knew intimately the struggles of what it meant to be a Spanish-speaking American and to belong to an economically vulnerable community. Intellectually, he knew the kind of data he still needed to acquire to make a quantitatively compelling argument. Morally and emotionally, he also knew that advocacy on behalf of these vulnerable communities demanded immediate action even with incomplete information. This representative anecdote acts as both a container for social action and a lacuna for unfinished research (a research program that Ximenes ultimately would take up some ten years later in his roles as commissioner of the Equal Employment Opportunity Commission and chair of the Inter-Agency Committee on Mexican American Affairs).

Discrimination against Spanish-speaking citizens as a civil rights issue was gaining traction through the mid-twentieth century. The three major Spanish-speaking groups (Mexican, Puerto Rican, and Cuban) made up the vast majority of the "Latin America diaspora" in the mid-twentieth-century United States.[8] These key Latino groups lived in very distinct worlds at all corners of the country.[9] While Ximenes had no authority or experience to represent the latter two groups, he had a deep understanding of the Mexican American experience in the United States.

In the 1950s Mexican Americans represented the largest group of Spanish-speaking citizens, more than twice the number of Puerto Rican citizens. Concentrated largely in the Southwest, Mexican Americans lived largely in rural political economies such as those Ximenes was studying in New Mexico. Puerto Ricans, in contrast, resided in urban centers such as New York and New Jersey and mobilized through the mid-twentieth century. Puerto Rican Americans established civic organizations throughout northeastern urban communities. Cuban Americans through the 1950s and early 1960s represented a small diaspora centered in Miami, focused on political resistance to Castro's Cuban Revolution.[10] These sociolinguistic distinctions and related civil rights issues became increasingly visible as the AGIF developed a national profile through the 1950s and 1960s.

In terms of the regional New Mexico situation, Ximenes had already gained nearly ten years of direct experience navigating the New Mexico landscape. He soon discovered that belonging also meant entanglement. Not only had New Mexico environed or encircled Ximenes; he had environed New Mexico through language, literacy, and inquiry. By 1956 he was deeply entangled in the New Mexico rhetorical landscape, politically, personally, and professionally. His BA degree in education and his brief stint as a school principal in South Texas had helped Ximenes understand the inextricable connections among language, literacy, and citizenship. Socioeconomic prosperity represented the fruit of full citizenship.

Over the course of his professional and civic life, Ximenes practiced the rhetorical arts of the citizen scholar by paying attention to his social environments, bearing witness to his own experiences, and describing what he learned. His depiction of economic marginalization through the rhetorical device of "Juan Garcia from Arroyo Seco" (a pseudo–case study) reflects Ximenes's own immersion experience in the cultural rhetorical ecology and political economy of New Mexico. Transculturation into the New Mexico socioeconomic and ethnolinguistic situation over the previous decade had challenged him at every level. As previously examined in chapter 2, Ximenes had learned to recognize the regional and generational variations within the Spanish-speaking communities of New Mexico. He had learned to consider the distinct cultural ecologies of New Mexico's native-born groups, indigenous as well as Hispano. He recognized the socioeconomic and cultural impact of Anglo migration patterns into New Mexico in the decade following World War II.

While struggling to correct inequities in the New Mexico situation, Ximenes also took on new opportunities to leverage his growing social privilege, position, and power. He was awarded a prestigious fellowship by the John Hay Whitney Foundation to attend the Twelfth Annual Institute of Race Relations at Fisk University in July 1955. This professionalization experience and training helped to legitimize his authority as an economist and a civil rights activist. Ximenes's growing rhetorical alacrity, as evidenced in his UMN Bureau of Business Research "welfare situation" lecture, indicates the constellation of his various social roles. The creative alignment of his disparate identities through the exercise of acquired, transgressive, and transformative powers helped to distinguish Ximenes as a professional researcher and citizen scholar.

Ximenes's trajectory reveals that as an emergent leader constellates a public self, shifting from a resistance identity toward a legitimizing identity, the leader adopts a project identity, which seeks to generate a just society and transform its organizations and institutions. Rhetorical imagination must become grounded in structural change in order for individual and social transformation to occur. There is a kind of consubstantiation involved in the journey, as the emergent leader co-constitutes himself as the subject in relation to his own social universe. Nevertheless, there is never a perfect correspondence between the objectives of the social actor and the outcomes of his projects. Even as the desired changes evolve, unintended consequences emerge within the leader's public and the private spheres. Ximenes was wildly successful, sometimes even at his own peril.

Cultivating Citizen Scholars and Postwar Liberal Democracy

In his roles as economist, activist, and citizen, Ximenes unequivocally advanced the liberal democratic project in each of his spheres of influence. Ximenes embraced the democratic values of equal rights, political access, and social mobility as he understood them through his participation in New Mexico's educational, business, political, and religious spheres. Throughout his tenure as a researcher at UNM and his leadership with the AGIF, Ximenes's shift from a resistance identity toward a legitimized identity was directly tied to his capacity to demonstrate how he was enacting these democratic principles and venerable American ideals. The national tenor was shifting away from the New Deal liberalism of Roosevelt and Truman. President Eisenhower, who had been elected to his first term in office in 1952, was reelected in 1956, the same year that Ximenes presented his lecture on the welfare situation in New Mexico. Although Ximenes had acquired his political instincts through New Deal liberalism, he established his professional and rhetorical bona fides during the Eisenhower period. Ximenes's social justice agenda was necessarily multivalent, advancing New Deal liberalism in Cold War rhetoric. Throughout the duration of Ximenes's AGIF activist period, there was a Republican president in the White House, a military icon—a five-star general—presiding over Cold War America. Ximenes's local and national available means of persuasion took a sharp right turn as Eisenhower took office.

National and global Cold War tensions continued to condition the rhetorical climate with direct implications for New Mexico as home base for U.S. nuclear research and industry through the 1950s. The structure of feeling and ambient national rhetorics to which Ximenes was able to align his own authority remained precarious. Postwar optimism, social democracy, and New Deal liberalism were receding by 1952. McCarthyism was firmly entrenched.

Eisenhower had delivered his "Atoms for Peace" speech to the United Nations General Assembly on December 8, 1953. The costs of dissent were high. The security clearance of Robert Oppenheimer, the Manhattan Project physicist, had been revoked in 1953 after he renounced the nuclear arms industry. Julius and Ethel Rosenberg were executed in June 1953 on charges of treason and espionage. Escalation of Cold War rhetoric was evidenced across the nation, but nowhere more directly than in New Mexico. The push-pull dynamic between global powers over nuclear proliferation claimed the region's natural resources, educational system, and economic structure. As Cold War rhetoric scholar Martin Medhurst observes, "planned at the highest levels of government, shrouded in secrecy, aided by the military-industrial complex, and executed over the course of two decades, the campaign to promote the peaceful use of the atom was conceived in pragmatism, dedicated to realism, and promoted in the spirit of idealism."[11] Ximenes adopted many of the same rhetorical tactics of pragmatism, realism, and idealism, but for different purposes.

Nuclear proliferation throughout the 1950s remained hidden in the dark ecology of New Mexico. The political scope of the nuclear industry (controlled by federal-level forces with the highest degree of security clearance) was well beyond Ximenes's sphere of influence. The military-industrial complex was bigger than any single entity or political figure. UNM increasingly provided resources for the nuclear industry brain trust in terms of training engineers, technicians, and administrative personnel who staffed the national laboratories in Los Alamos and Albuquerque.

The economy of the state prospered while the regional environment realized the irreversible impact of serving as ground zero for uranium mining and nuclear testing. The Cold War marriage of deep capitalism to military proliferation was consummated in New Mexico. Ximenes, nonetheless, discovered ways to accommodate these complex political conditions through research and strategic action at the grassroots level. He found an approach to civil rights activism that somehow worked in the political climate of his time.

Ximenes's political activism exercised through the expansion of the New Mexico AGIF received the support of a number of legitimized organizational entities. The Diocese of Santa Fe voiced support for the emergent AGIF in New Mexico. As reported in the *American GI Forum News Bulletin* of June

15, 1953, Archbishop Edwin Bryne of Santa Fe presided at the first annual state convention of the New Mexico AGIF, which included representation from fifteen new organizational chapters and over two hundred delegates.[12] Within eighteen months of the first AGIF meeting in the basement of Sacred Heart Catholic Church in Albuquerque, Ximenes had witnessed the exponential growth of this Mexican American civic organization throughout New Mexico. The following year Senator Dennis Chávez extended his political aegis to the AGIF at the second annual convention of the New Mexico AGIF in June 1954 with three hundred delegates in attendance.[13] Basking in his success beneath the political halo of Senator Chávez, Ximenes delivered the keynote address for the 1954 state convention.[14] The legitimized authority of key public figures (and their offices) helped to affirm Ximenes's own emerging public authority.

By cultivating a strong network of alliances with important social organizations and public figures, Ximenes's own legitimized identity was enhanced and recognized. He was no longer considered an unknown and an upstart. He could no longer be dismissed as a maverick Tejano agitator. By 1956, Ximenes was a *nuevo mexicano*, a citizen, a leader. He had earned the privileges of inclusion and the benefits of citizenship through tireless public service. Ximenes was nominated for the Outstanding Citizen of Albuquerque Award in 1956 and was awarded the Albuquerque United Nations Human Rights Award three years later in 1959. The constellation of these honors and these key rhetorical moments suggests that not only was Ximenes's public ethos becoming widely recognized but that he was deeply confident acting through that ethos. His ethos was sufficiently consistent with his character and moral convictions to be authentic and efficacious. These measures of integrity and ethical congruence were very important to Ximenes. Taking on the classical virtues of the proverbial "good man speaking well" sat well with him. He had cultivated an ethos that embodied the social values of his place and time while simultaneously finding ways to agitate the inequitable political and economic system. Ximenes reflects:

> For some reason, the GI Forum was expected to jump into any controversy that happened to come along. We had our hands full in fighting for human rights in our schools and communities of the State and nation. The GI Forum by 1954 had enough experience to know when to take on an issue and fight until we prevailed. By 1954 we were a strong statewide organization that made decisions by a governing board and had the strength to prevail in any fight with the opposition. In short we had to pick and choose the issues that best suited our ability to carry the projects to conclusion.[15]

Ximenes cultivated a growing sense of *kairos*, or right timing. He learned to listen to the needs and issues around him, connecting them to a structure of feeling. Ximenes developed the gift of *phronesis* (practical wisdom) as he learned to attend to the *kairotic* dimensions of his rhetorical moment. Echoing the tenor of the era, Ximenes's used pragmatic approaches toward realistic goals with idealist values.

How did Ximenes navigate the identity nexus between agitator and academic? Using the rhetorical arts of the citizen scholar, Ximenes legitimized his stance of resistance to institutionalized discrimination by contributing to the epistemic process of knowledge construction. In other words, he engaged with democracy as a way of governing and a way of knowing. The social construction of knowledge became a powerful rhetorical tool. He not only learned how to pay attention to his environments, give witness to his own experiences, and describe what he learned; Ximenes systematically modeled these rhetorical arts to others. Moreover, he used the conduit of professional writing to circulate his findings through reports, monographs, and the AGIF *News Bulletin*. Finally, Ximenes was a skilled orator. He knew how to tell a good story. He knew how to expose the villain and, at the same time, give the villain the opportunity for right action. Ximenes let the story drive the discourse of economics. He dispensed with theory, pared down the evidence, and let the story speak for itself.

As illustrated in his 1956 "welfare situation" lecture, Ximenes understood how to mediate the specialist discourses of economics as an academic discipline for a nonspecialist audience. He effectively navigated the cultural rhetorical ecotones, or discursive transition zones, of academic, professional, and civic communities. Ximenes adapted not only his use of genres, tropes, and registers but his types of epistemic evidence as well. Rather than employing qualitative indexes of racial inequalities in New Mexico's socioeconomic conditions, Ximenes relied on narrative. In his lecture he constructs two imaginative fictions, the rhetorical personas of "Juan Garcia" and "Jack Williams," to illustrate the disparate experiences of institutionalized discrimination in New Mexico. Ostensibly the figure of "Juan Garcia of Arroyo Seco, New Mexico" represents the Mexican American experience and the figure of "Jack Williams of Jackson County, Texas" represents the Anglo experience. Ximenes describes their disparate points of view and social conditions:

> Then there are 42 per cent of the population that were born in other states and are now living in New Mexico. This large percentage of people certainly affect the welfare picture in New Mexico. People from other states bring along, in addition to their household belongings, ideas on how to

handle the welfare problem in New Mexico. Their discussions on welfare usually begin with "now back in Cedar Rapids we have lien and relative responsibility laws" or perhaps some other method of handling the problem.

Jack Williams from Jackson County, Texas has very definite ideas about Mexicans, Negroes, and Indians. Back in his county, an American of Mexican descent has not served on a jury for over 50 years. Jack thinks it's alright for Negroes and Mexicans to share the same swimming pools and be neighbors, but these two groups should stay on their side of town. Jack used to work hard as an oil field worker and he wants his representatives to get some of these lazy people off the welfare rolls and make them go to work just like he used to.

Jack's representatives in the legislature can be counted on to oppose welfare legislation that will put teeth in the Fair Employment Practices Act and the Anti-Discrimination law. Jack knows that this is the right thing to do, because back in Jackson County they never had any welfare problems. And now with the reapportionment of the legislature, Jack is confident that his views will predominate. Jack is only one of the approximately 90,000 persons born in Texas now living in New Mexico. Here we leave Jack.[16]

Ximenes constructs an archetypal Janus-type figure, representing the two faces of the New Mexico citizen as halves of the whole. By contrasting the civic consciousness of "Juan" and "Jack," Ximenes demonstrates the disparities in citizen wisdom among Mexican American and Anglo populations. Unlike Jack, Juan is unaware of his civil rights and the institutional mechanisms available to protect him and his family from discriminatory employment practices. Jack, in contrast, understands his rights and his privileges. He exploits his growing majority status and uses the legislative process to protect his privileged political and economic position.

There is an enthymeme constructed within this representative anecdote and a suppressed premise to which Ximenes's primary audience members in academic and business spheres do not have access. The tertiary audience members constructed through this lecture include the AGIF constituency, who would have been well positioned to decode the embedded message. Here Ximenes infuses an ironic twist: AGIF members know that the purpose of the AGIF is to fill the gaps in citizen wisdom that the fictional figure of Juan Garcia represents. For them, Juan Garcia is a metonymic device for the uninitiated citizen, the exploited and uneducated Mexican American. Cultivating *phronesis*, the practical wisdom of citizenship, rests at the very heart of the AGIF mission. The motto of the AGIF is not stated but implied simply by illustration: "Education is our freedom and freedom should be everybody's business."[17]

Ximenes, the rhetorical shape shifter, explicitly advances a lecture on the problem of the welfare situation that, at the same time, implicitly legitimizes the mission and goals of AGIF civil rights activism. Cultivating educated and engaged citizens is the solution to marginalization and exploitation. These *topoi* allow Ximenes to construct a multivalent text that reaches across audiences. These are signature features of Ximenes's public rhetoric. The alacrity of Ximenes's rhetorical style, cultivated through his direct experience in diverse contexts across generational, cultural, and class lines, distinguishes him both as a writer and a speaker.

Over the course of his career as an associate with the UNM Bureau of Business Research, Ximenes wrote and published seven monographs between 1954 and 1958: *Natural Gas in New Mexico; Housing in New Mexico; Income by Counties in New Mexico; Demand for Dentists in New Mexico; 1957 Income by Counties in New Mexico; 1958 Directory of New Mexico Manufacturing and Mining; Wages in the Construction Industry of New Mexico.*[18] Ximenes served as the principal researcher for all of these projects. He understood how to engage in the intellectual life cycle of knowledge making: conducting field observations, gathering data, analyzing evidence, constructing arguments about his findings, and circulating his ideas. He learned to write effectively across communities—academic, civic, and professional discourse communities. Additionally, Ximenes knew how to use the AGIF *News Bulletin* as a means for circulating his research to broader audiences. He was a regular contributor to the *News Bulletin*, beginning in 1952, the inaugural year of the AGIF in New Mexico, and continuing throughout his AGIF tenure of more than ten years. His effective use of epistemic rhetoric enhanced his authority in professional, academic, and civic spheres. These formative literacy experiences would also inform his approach to national and international leadership (chapter 4).

The Tropes of Cold War Mexican American Activism

Ximenes's model of leadership resonated with working-class Mexican American communities, a quality that eventually helped him bridge the generational divide between the World War II generation of Mexican American reformers of the 1950s and the Chicano activists of the 1960s. His political impulse and rhetorical imagination rested on four dimensions of democratic practice, values inculcated in his youth growing up in South Texas. Dissent, deliberation, dissonance, and disputation were the discursive undergirding of Ximenes's earliest activist work as an organizer for the AGIF. Ximenes's application of *phronesis*, his pragmatic engagement with the major issues of the Cold War rhetorical situation, teleologically aligned his rhetorical career over the next two decades.

From a classical rhetorical perspective, the effective leader must cultivate what Aristotle termed prudence, or *phronesis*. The good citizen evolves with maturation, experience, and reverence for the *polis* (fellow citizens). *Phronesis* as a virtue of citizenship is concerned with how to act appropriately and circulate effectively across social situations. The negotiation of disparate rhetorical contexts requires both breadth in experience and depth in ethical conviction. The citizen scholar must learn to live in a paradox between deep conviction and deep doubt.[19] The power of the rhetor rests in the adept and ethical use of information, acting as a reliable witness. Bearing witness, in these respects, is not only a rhetorical act but a historical and epistemic act of knowledge making. Ximenes had an intuitive understanding of the *phronesis* of citizenship and the power of testifying to one's own experience.

In her essay "Lying in Politics" Hannah Arendt observes, "Facts need testimony to be remembered and trustworthy witnesses to be established in order to find a secure dwelling place in the domain of human affairs."[20] The rhetor, as such, plays a powerful role within the community, as arbiter of facts and knowledge (logos), model of credibility (ethos), and conduit of emotion (pathos). Prudence, or practical wisdom, is the quality that permits these three rhetorical forces to cohere. This virtue represents a critical feature of the good speaker according to classical rhetorical theory.

The transformation from a resistance identity to a legitimized identity entails a maturation process that includes the acquisition of perspective, balance, and insight through experience. Ximenes had evidenced these dimensions of *phronesis* by 1956. His strategic use of Cold War rhetoric demonstrated the development of these legitimizing traits. Ximenes generally took the long view, eschewing the dramatic appeals of the rhetorical jeremiad such as the imminent-danger thesis frequently used to fend off the threat of Communism.

Negotiating these polarizing positions represented an enduring challenge for Ximenes through this decade of professional and civic development. He found a way to embody conservative citizen virtue through the rhetoric of *phronesis* at the same time as he advanced the liberal democratic agenda to protect individual civil rights. Resisting the tyranny of the majority, secured by the nation's white, conservative, and wealthy political structure, demanded the formation of a counterpublic that was vocal, visible, and viable. The cultural, political, and ideological pluralism of the rhetorical situation of New Mexico in the Cold War era provided the political resources necessary for instigating and invigorating an emerging counterpublic capable of generating new deliberative forces.

The protection of the individual rights of the nation's minorities, as argued by Mexican American advocates like Ximenes, represented a cornerstone of the liberal political agenda throughout the twentieth century. Cold War liberal reformers representing diverse constituencies needed to straddle both conservative and liberal discourses. Activists needed to assert their concerns for public virtue and the common good and, at the same time, resist corruption. The peculiar problem facing Ximenes in 1956 was how to structure his arguments for Mexican American civil rights reform out of the dissonant strands of rhetoric available within the Cold War cultural milieu.

For Mexican Americans, issues concerning citizenship and border identity established the parameters of Cold War liberal discourse, nationalist politics, and civil rights rhetoric of the 1950s. Plumbing the deepest anxieties of Mexican-origin groups, questions about belonging (cultural, national, linguistic, and political) were then, as they are today, the most potent. As *topoi*, these themes framed the available means of persuasion for the major postwar Mexican American reformers.

In New Mexico these themes of social progress were magnified through the lens of cultural deficiency. The intellectual architect of this argument, George I. Sánchez, built a civic and educational agenda around the interlocking constructs of imminent danger and cultural deprivation. Sánchez was one of the most successful native sons of New Mexico. Controlling the dominant discourse in education and public policy on Mexican issues such as bilingual education and immigration, George I. Sánchez had a far-reaching rhetorical influence.

"The Grand Old Man" of Mexican American Civil Rights Rhetoric

George I. Sánchez, professor of history at the University of Texas at Austin, was among the strongest voices in the mid-twentieth century on behalf of Mexican Americans. An ardent supporter of New Deal liberalism, Sánchez advanced a doctrine of social advancement and a rubric of Americanist principles. He served as a mentor to many emerging leaders through the League of United Latin American Citizens (LULAC). Sánchez and Héctor García had maintained a close association beginning in the 1940s during their shared association with the University of Texas. García and Sánchez's partnership grew over the next two decades through their mutual affiliation with LULAC. In an October 27, 1951, letter to García, Sánchez writes:

The Spanish-speaking people constitute the least sponsored, least vocal, and the least understood of the large minority groups in the United States. As regards [to] special government concern, philanthropic support, or effective group organization and leadership, this is virtually an orphan group. Because of this orphan or step-child status, the Spanish-speaking people are in a particularly difficult position when it comes to solving some of the major problems which confront them.[21]

Written on letterhead of the American Council of Spanish-Speaking People, an organization that Sánchez himself had established, Sánchez's letter advances a series of metaphors to reflect the social position of Mexican Americans within the racial hierarchy of the United States.

The implicit meanings of *orphan* and *stepchild* suggest a broad range of inequitable national relations. To extend Sánchez's metaphor, Mexican Americans as binational stepchildren represented the collateral damage of divorce and remarriage. Mexican Americans, the birth children of Mexico, were reluctantly acquired through divorce custody arrangements delineated by the Treaty of Guadalupe Hidalgo.[22] In contrast to the privileges of blood heirs, national stepchildren suffer from their questionable status and contested claims of lineage and inheritance. Denied hereditary privilege, Mexican Americans had been relegated to second-class citizenship for over a hundred years. This trope represents an enduring symbolic figure for Mexican-origin peoples, an emblem of the complexities of *mestizaje* and border identity shaping immigrant and nationalist rhetorics throughout the twentieth century and into the twenty-first century. It was not the first time Sánchez deployed this metaphor in reference to Mexican Americans.

As a native of the Barelas barrio in Albuquerque and author of *Forgotten People* released in 1940, Sánchez was a regionally and nationally, if not internationally, recognized authority on Mexican American issues in 1951 when Vicente Ximenes first began mobilizing for the AGIF in Albuquerque. Sánchez, a descendant of the earliest Spanish colonists of Nuevo Mexico, remained a complex figure throughout his long and controversial professional life. He fancied himself as something of *un hidalgo*, the great-great-grandson of Spanish aristocrats. As Carlos Blanton observes in *George I. Sánchez: The Long Fight for Mexican American Integration*, Sánchez "made multiple, contradictory claims to larger identities such as whiteness, Mexican-ness, and *mestizaje*."[23] Although Sánchez had already left New Mexico in 1940 to teach at the University of Texas, he sustained strong intellectual, professional, and familial connections to Albuquerque.

Fondly described as the "grand old man of the Mexican American civil rights struggle," George I. Sánchez had an intellectual and political scope to his reputation that cannot be overstated.[24] His professional influence helped to win the day with the landmark 1947 case of *Méndez et al. v. Westminster School District* in Orange County, California. This Mexican American desegregation case set a precedent seven years ahead of the 1954 landmark Supreme Court ruling in *Brown v. the Board of Education*.[25] The *Méndez* case was the first time that a federal court ruled against public school segregation of Mexican American children based on language and other pedagogical needs. Sánchez's influence helped to sway the court on behalf of Spanish-speaking children in the U.S. Southwest.

As Ximenes gained recognition over a decade as organizer for the AGIF and economics researcher at UNM, a new voice of authority countered and complicated the previously uncontested position of George I. Sánchez. Sánchez had served as the national president of LULAC through the 1940s. He had served as a researcher at UNM from 1930 to 1935, eventually accepting an appointment as an associate professor of education at UNM for several years before moving to the University of Texas.

Sánchez's depiction of *nuevo mexicanos* in *Forgotten People* was not universally celebrated, however. During a lecture by Sánchez in Albuquerque, sponsored by the Southwest Council on Education of Spanish-Speaking People in January 1950, Ximenes noted that audience members expressed outrage and objection to the illustrations of New Mexicans in his research. Ximenes recalls, "New Mexicans did not see themselves as 'forgotten' at all; they felt exposed and demoralized by Sánchez's report. They didn't like being called poor and ignorant. In many respects, they reacted like the subjects of the Saunders-Leonard immigrant report in South Texas did. Sánchez used many of the same terms for New Mexicans as he used for *mexicanos* in Texas. It was a real eye-opener for me."[26] Some of the more inflammatory adjectives that Sánchez deployed to describe *nuevo mexicanos* in *Forgotten People* include "pathetic," "helpless," "handicapped," "fatalistic," "uneducated," and "superstitious."[27] He cast New Mexicans as "stepchildren of a nation," living in medieval antiquity and battling "their own cultural inadequacy." The subjects of Sánchez's study lack agency, choice, and the capacity to shape their own lives. As victims of conquest, geography, climate, and cultural isolation, Sánchez argues, "The New Mexican is not yet an American culturally."[28] Sánchez's rhetoric did not always play well with the people for whom he advocated.

Ximenes rejected the disabling victim narrative that dominated the reactionary rhetorics of the era and promoted a dialectic of dissent to recast the national narrative of Mexican American presence. Ximenes possessed a quality that Sánchez lacked: *phronesis*, or practical wisdom. And unlike Héctor García, who relied heavily on George I. Sánchez for funding, guidance, and political support, Ximenes did not fall under the spell of Sánchez's intellectual power or political prowess. As former LULAC leaders, García and Sánchez carried the rhetorical and ideological baggage of LULAC anchored in the class politics, elitism, and pigmentocracy of the era.

LULAC: The Rhetorics of Race and Class

Founded in 1929 in Corpus Christi, Texas, LULAC represented the pre–World War II generation of Mexican American reformers. These foundational organizers had successfully established chapters throughout the nation for over twenty years before the formation of AGIF.[29] LULAC had realized rapid expansion throughout the 1930s with chapters established throughout Texas and into New Mexico, Arizona, California, and Kansas.

The LULAC chapter in New Mexico was already fully institutionalized by the time Ximenes began mobilizing for the AGIF in Albuquerque in 1951. According to Cynthia Orozco, the Albuquerque LULAC Council No. 34 proved to be the most successful chapter of the state. Orozco notes that between 1934 and 1943 the Albuquerque chapter focused on a number of issues: the establishment of Barelas Community Center, the formation of the Hispano/Latin American Studies Program at UNM, the appointment of Hispano leaders as diplomats to Latin America, and the advancement of federal appropriations bills on behalf of New Mexico.[30] LULAC successfully aligned forces with Roosevelt's Works Progress Administration as early as 1939, lobbying for the establishment of the new community center and sponsorship of the National Youth Administration in Albuquerque.[31]

Significantly, Albuquerque was also the site of the 1942 LULAC national convention, a euphoric occasion that marked the dedication of the city's new community center located in the historic neighborhood of Barelas. The LULAC ceremonies featured former Barelas residents and dignitaries, Professor George I. Sánchez, and New Mexico's own Senator Dennis Chávez.[32] The visibility and political efficacy of LULAC's leadership were clearly established when Ximenes began mobilizing for the AGIF in Albuquerque in the early 1950s.

Issues of race, class, and ethnolinguistic discrimination had been problematic for Mexican-origin groups in New Mexico well before Ximenes attempted to introduce the AGIF in Albuquerque. LULAC had been engaging with the problem of racism in New Mexico for more than a decade before

Ximenes arrived on the scene. However, LULAC sought a conciliatory approach to racist laws and social practices. Rather than confront the color line directly, LULAC demanded that Latin Americans be recognized as "white" in the bifurcated system of racial privilege. If there was one dimension of the LULAC ideology Ximenes wanted to dismantle, it was the presumptive hereditary privilege of whiteness.[33]

As long as LULAC constituents enjoyed white status and privilege within the community, they did not agitate against the discriminatory status quo. By aspiring to an assimilationist white middle-class social position and dissociating themselves as a caste apart from Mexican nationals and *recien llegados*, LULAC picked its battles carefully. Mexican nationals were strictly barred from membership in LULAC. Acting as an advocacy organization for all *mexicanos* and people of color was not their calling; joining America as first-class and "pure" citizens was the primary aim of LULAC. As LULAC's constitution states, its aims were "to develop within the members of our race the best, purest, and most perfect type of true citizen of the United States of America."[34]

In brief, LULAC did not seek to dismantle white privilege. Instead LULAC sought to distance Mexican Americans as an ethnic group from historical designations as a people of color. LULAC leaders reasoned that first-class citizenship in the racial hierarchy of U.S. society would be best achieved by claiming whiteness. As Craig Kaplowitz argues in *LULAC: Mexican Americans and National Policy*, the early LULAC founders steered away from identifying with their Mexican-origin roots and emphasized "Anglo middle class values as prerequisite to joining the American mainstream."[35] LULAC leaders, in sum, actively resisted the government practice of racial labeling Mexican-origin groups as nonwhite. Toward their assimilationist aims, LULAC lobbied for the U.S. Census Bureau throughout the 1930s to classify persons of Mexican descent as white, a change eventually reflected in the 1940 U.S. census. This act of identification represented a nettlesome compromise with enduring consequences for postwar Mexican Americans. Ximenes became the principal leader pressing the AGIF to fill this gap left open by LULAC by providing a collective outlet for the underrepresented Mexican American working class and engaging with African Americans in civil rights efforts.

Breaking with the Past: New Directions and the AGIF

While Ximenes and the New Mexico AGIF wanted the social mobility and economic access that LULAC had fought to achieve over the past twenty years, their platform for social justice was far more capacious than LULAC's.

To realize this shift, the New Mexico AGIF carefully crafted a project identity distinguishing itself from LULAC. By the mid-1950s the New Mexico AGIF found itself leaning more radically toward nation-reforming discourses as LULAC found itself maintaining its more conservatively established position toward nation-maintaining discourses. The old goals of first-class citizenship and social access remained, but the ways in which emergent activists pursued these goals changed.

Ximenes was part of this new cohort of radical leaders who would use the platform of the AGIF in Albuquerque in new ways to actively engage with issues of class and to confront racial discrimination and economic disparity. He would build connections with the National Association for the Advancement of Colored People (NAACP), the Anti-Defamation League (ADL), and labor unions in New Mexico, breaking new ground on behalf of the AGIF. Ximenes provided a counterdiscourse to the dominant discourse of LULAC and filled the racial gap in New Mexico through forging alliances between the AGIF and the NAACP. Ximenes tells the story:

> My first action as leader of the GI Forum was to join the NAACP and the Jewish Anti-defamation League in their effort to create a Fair Employment Practices Act in New Mexico. There were no African Americans and probably no Jews in the legislature. About one third of the legislators were Hispanic or Mexican American and I took it upon myself to lobby all the lawmakers on behalf of the FEPC. Representative Albert Amador from Rio Arriba County in the House and Fabian Chávez from Santa Fe in the Senate sponsored the bill. Every Hispanic and Mexican American and Anglo Democrat from Albuquerque voted for the bill. Every Anglo from Little Texas voted against the bill. The bill tied in the Senate and Hispanic Lt. Governor Tibo Chávez broke the tie and passed the bill. We exposed all kinds of myths about Hispanics and Mexican Americans on the day the FEPC became law. We exposed the racial discriminatory beliefs of the Little Texas legislators. We proved to the critics of the GI Forum that we could work with Anglos, African Americans and Jews on common issues. Today the law functions as the Human Rights Commission of New Mexico.[36]

Inspired by the rhetorical possibilities of direct action, Ximenes would establish new alliances with other activists and leverage his position within academia to expose the inequitable social order.

One of the first community advocacy projects that came to Ximenes and the Albuquerque AGIF during their early phases of mobilization was brought to them by local NAACP activists. Ximenes did not find the issues. The issues found him. As early as 1952, during the inaugural year of the AGIF in New Mexico, Hobart La Grone, president of the Albuquerque chapter of the NAACP, reached out to establish a partnership with Ximenes. The Albuquerque NAACP had been active for nearly as long as New Mexico had been a state. The first chapter of the NAACP was founded in New Mexico on January 5, 1915, aligning forces with the grassroots civil rights organization the Independent Society of New Mexico. With a growing but small African American minority presence, building coalitions with other minority groups represented a productive strategy for the NAACP in New Mexico.[37]

Hobart La Grone first contacted Ximenes in 1952 with a request for his assistance in an effort to pass a bill in the state legislature on behalf of the state-level Fair Employment Practices Commission (FEPC). Senator Dennis Chávez, the NAACP, and Mexican American leaders throughout the Southwest had played a pivotal role in the formation of a national-level FEPC in 1941. The efficacy of the FEPC in New Mexico, however, had been severely limited, if not designed for structured failure, in the decade that followed.[38]

In *Labor Rights Are Civil Rights: Mexican American Workers in Twentieth-Century America*, Zaragosa Vargas delineates the exigences leading up to the rise and fall of the FEPC in the Southwest in 1941.[39] With the onset of U.S. involvement in World War II, the defense industry began its rapid pace of war production. Mexican American and African American civil rights leaders rallied together for the formation of a government watchdog organization to ensure an equitable distribution of jobs and benefits. However, Mexican American blue-collar laborers remained underrepresented in the federally sponsored defense labor force. Senator Chávez was among the most vocal legislative proponents of the FEPC, with hopes of leveling the industry playing field. Chávez stood in good company. The formation of the FEPC promised a new level of solidarity between African American and Mexican American leaders. Senator Chávez considered the milestone a hopeful symbol of future cooperation.

The accomplishments of Senator Chávez on behalf of the FEPC in New Mexico were significant but incomplete. The enduring inequities in the distribution of opportunities and resources for Mexican Americans remained largely ignored by the federal government. Mexican American leaders continued to agitate to have their plight recognized by the FEPC, calling for FEPC hearings in the Southwest in 1942. The FEPC had been tasked with examining discrimination claims by Mexican American mine laborers in West Texas and New Mexico. However, President Roosevelt summarily canceled the 1942 FEPC hearings scheduled to convene in El Paso, Texas, in fear that the exposure of workers' grievances documenting unfair labor practices toward Mexican Americans would ultimately endanger the fragile Good Neighbor policy with Mexico and Latin America.

Although efforts continued to be advanced by Senator Dennis Chávez and other FEPC proponents to hold the hearings in the Southwest, they were never convened.[40] Throughout the following decade, the FEPC consistently failed to protect the civil rights of Spanish-speaking peoples despite the continued efforts of prominent leaders such as Senator Dennis Chávez, George I. Sánchez, and Carlos Casteñeda (University of Texas history professor). Eight years after the ill-fated southwestern FEPC hearings, a state-level office of the FEPC was finally established in New Mexico in 1950. However, this frail legislative entity was never funded.

The FEPC remained an inactive and largely impotent entity within the New Mexico political structure, lacking the necessary funding or political clout. Senator Chávez tasked Ximenes with stirring up grassroots support for funding the FEPC. With Chávez's guidance, the expanding New Mexico AGIF mobilized to urge the state legislature to pass a $25,000 FEPC appropriations bill in 1953.[41] Although the first attempt at these legislative initiatives failed, Ximenes persisted and eventually prevailed over the next few years.

While Ximenes mobilized to help Senator Chávez get political traction for the FEPC, Ximenes in turn enlisted the senator's help to repeal the poll tax. The poll tax and other pernicious mechanisms like literacy tests and English-only policies prevented historically excluded groups, especially the poor and people of color, from voting in many states, including Texas. Ximenes extended an invitation to Senator Chávez to speak at a Texas rally sponsored by Héctor García and the AGIF to oppose to the poll tax. Over the next few years, Senator Chávez regularly attended local and national AGIF events and conventions as a participant and guest speaker. Ximenes recounts:

> The poll tax throughout Texas and the South was not ended until the Johnson administration. Beginning in 1948, Dr. García and the GI Forum were heavily involved in the fight to end the poll tax. The GI Forum fought to encourage people to pay their poll taxes when they were in effect, and then fought just as hard to end them. I participated in the campaign to end the poll tax by getting Senator Chávez, the first senator to push for the end of the poll tax. Senator Chávez was vehemently against the poll tax in Texas, even though New Mexico had no poll tax.[42]

Ximenes succeeded in constructing an alliance between the old and new guard, bridging the established political career of Senator Chávez with the emerging profile of the AGIF. Although the poll tax did not end until the

Lyndon B. Johnson administration in 1964 with the ratification of Twenty-Fourth Amendment, Ximenes had the support of Senator Chávez to help move the landmark legislation forward.

Ximenes took a more interracial and interdenominational approach to coalition building in New Mexico than the AGIF in Texas had used in its initial three-year mobilization period under García. From the outset Ximenes established alliances with both the NAACP and the ADL as he built the foundation for the AGIF in New Mexico. He learned how to cross class, racial, cultural, and religious boundaries to forge stronger alliances among marginalized groups and to promote civil rights advocacy in new ways. Joining forces with the ADL, a Jewish advocacy organization established in 1913, was an especially important shift in the historic anti-Semitic legacy of post-colonial New Mexico. Building an ecumenical bridge, a connection initiated and sustained by a predominantly Catholic-affiliated group like the AGIF, on behalf of the civil rights of all peoples of color was an unprecedented move not only for New Mexico but for the nation.

The NAACP and ADL of Albuquerque had been mobilizing together to pass legislation to fund a state-level FEPC to protect the rights of workers, especially those of minority groups in New Mexico. The leaders of the local NAACP and ADL looked to Ximenes to carry the bill through the legislative process. They needed the aegis of a Hispanic leader to pass the legislation. The African American and Jewish minorities were not significant enough in size or political clout to merit notice in the state capital. The irony of the situation was not lost on Ximenes.

The NAACP and the ADL were looking to Ximenes to coalesce the political sway they needed. Although Hispanos historically represented the majority of the state's population, Anglo hegemony in the urban regions of Albuquerque and Santa Fe effectively sustained inequitable employment practices for Hispanos as well as Native Americans and African Americans. Additionally, anti-Semitism, entrenched throughout New Mexico since colonial New Spain and the era of Mexican Inquisition, endured in the Cold War era. The complex, dynamic, and conflicted history of Jewish presence in New Mexico, a number of whom lived undercover as crypto-Jews in fear of persecution, informed the role of the ADL in promoting legislative protection through the formation of a state FEPC.[43]

Nevertheless, there was no precedent in the short history of the AGIF for forming a public alliance with the ADL. LULAC had carefully eschewed political entanglements with other historically excluded groups over its twenty-year history. In this Cold War moment, the potential for political backlash, if not complete censure by local and national-level security institutions such as the FBI, was a real threat. Ximenes had a number of challenges to weigh and roles to balance in this decision. The social stigma of aligning forces with African American and Jewish groups was an initial concern for him. He was a novice leader of an emerging organization that was not readily welcomed by the established Hispano community in New Mexico. Moreover, as a newly hired researcher at UNM, he was a staff (nontenured) state employee. Agitators risked being labeled and sanctioned for un-American activities by their employers.

To join forces with the NAACP, labor organizations, and the ADL to confront the historical undercurrent of discrimination and racism in the state would without question throw the red flag around the AGIF that drew McCarthyist suspicion. Additionally, as the sole income provider for a growing family, Ximenes had to consider the implications of losing his job by cultivating a public profile and leading role in this government fight. By going after the State of New Mexico, Ximenes was quite literally "biting the hand that fed him." The personal stakes were high and the potential for political fallout, enormous. Ximenes recounts:

> The New Mexico Fair Employment Practices Commission was the first major issue that I undertook as the leader of the GI Forum. Hobart La Grone of the NAACP was fighting a lonely battle to get an FEPC in New Mexico and he came to me for support of the legislation. I was not sure if I should get involved with a black and the Jewish ADL as my first issue to throw the GI Forum into the fight.
>
> Once I heard from Mr. La Grone that they needed the Hispanic legislators to support the idea and a bill, I brushed away any thoughts of backlash and fear of reprisals. I led the GI Forum into the battle with a passion to succeed in my first battle for human rights. Representative Albert Amador of Rio Arriba County and Senator Fabian Chavez wrote up identical bills in each house of the legislature and the fight was on. I lobbied hard to get all the Hispanic and Albuquerque legislators to support the bill.
>
> There was scuttlebutt that some Hispanic legislators would not support the bill. We thought we could get some of the Anglo legislators from the South and East Little Texas counties to support the bill. As it turned out every Anglo legislator from the Little Texas counties voted against the bill. Every legislator from the historic Northern Hispanic counties voted for the bill and the Anglo and Hispanic legislators from Albuquerque supported the bill. The House passed the bill with a big majority. The Senate legislators tied and Lt. Governor Tibo Chavez of Valencia county cast the deciding vote and we won our first GI Forum attempt to get into the battle for civil rights.

I learned a number of lessons. The Hispanics will come together to support civil rights legislation contrary to community talk. The Little Texas Anglos who always talked about their friendship for Hispanics when it came to civil rights could now be counted to vote against civil rights. Finally, on a major issue like civil rights, the liberal Anglos, blacks, and Jews could come together with Hispanics as a group to achieve a common goal.[44]

In the end, the state FEPC project was a risk worth taking. The successful passage of the bill in 1954 represented a win for all stakeholders involved. Significantly, minorities and women in New Mexico won the protections they needed in the workplace. Ximenes's willingness to play public advocate for the legislation hinged on two hopes: first, that the legislation would succeed; second, that the AGIF would gain statewide recognition for its role in the initiative. Both of his hopes were realized.

Ximenes's success not only pleased and surprised him; it pleased and surprised his friend and mentor back in Texas. Ximenes recounts, "Dr. Garcia and the Texas GI Forum cheered on this upstart GI Forum of New Mexico who was victorious at the highest levels of New Mexico government." This was not a project, however, he could have launched and won single-handedly. "It was just a lot of good luck that the NAACP and ADL trusted me to do the job for them," Ximenes openly admits.[45] He would never have succeeded had he launched the initiative from scratch. The NAACP and the ADL had done the formative groundwork before approaching Ximenes. The legislation demanded the support and synergy of the NAACP, ADL, and AGIF together to achieve its final success.

The Albuquerque NAACP had initiated the bill, trading on the reputation and strength of its national organization. The ADL had provided the legal background and procedural knowledge necessary for legislative action to draft and circulate the bill. Finally, the AGIF gave the legislative traction, building consensus and cross-cultural endorsement. Neither the NAACP nor the ADL had a large enough constituency to sway the vote. With the backing of the AGIF and the Hispanic electorate, however, the bill was able to achieve the critical mass necessary to pass. The 1954 AGIF New Mexico state convention passed a resolution to support the New Mexico FEPC appropriations bill.[46]

Following the success of the state FEPC legislation, Ximenes and the AGIF acquired the reputation as a "go-to" organization for civil rights problems in the state. Ximenes's political alliance with senior statesman Senator Chávez was now secured. Issues continued to come to Ximenes for support and action on the part of the AGIF. Keeping the momentum going, the New

Mexico AGIF eventually coordinated efforts with the American Federation of Labor, NAACP, LULAC, and B'nai B'rith for the successful passage of a New Mexico antidiscrimination bill through the state legislature in 1955.[47]

City Politics and the New Mexico Patrón System

Pressing issues of class, race, and ethnolinguistic identity, Ximenes's advocacy efforts on behalf of Albuquerque's garbage workers represent another landmark activist moment. Ximenes reflects:

> By 1954 the GI Forum was strong enough to take on the City of Albuquerque patron system. The Hispano and Mexican American garbage workers were being abused, but no one dared to expose the injustices. It was a political arrangement that kept elected officials in power and anyone who dared intervene would find themselves out of business or out of a job.
>
> All the garbage workers were Hispanos and Mexican Americans, except the superintendent. The second in command was a fellow named "El Chicote." The Democratic precinct chairmen were the supervisors and reported on how the workers voted. We broke the entire system up by organizing a GI Forum of City garbage workers. Many times the supervisors planted people to disrupt our meetings and we had to physically throw them out. Finally, an election was held in which the administration was replaced. The new mayor and city council adopted a merit system and that ended the patron system.[48]
>
> From 1951 through 1954 garbage workers would come to our meetings at the invitation of Alfonso Proo, a City water engineer.[49] Alfonso was interested in getting me to hear the complaints the workers had against the Superintendent and his assistant Sonny Aragon. In 1953, I decided to represent workers who had complaints of abuse in regard to wages, working conditions, injuries, political pressure to vote for or against a candidate for office. The entire garbage department was rife with rumors, chistes and cuentos. I heard of plots to sack some person because of personal matters that should concern no one except the worker. Benefits of a better route for some workers and the worst ones for others. The health condition of the workers and their families was poor and the Superintendent and his foreman played political favoritism as to who gets off for illness and who does not.
>
> The garbage department was a miserable hellhole. The workers were not issued work shoes or clothes. The workers at that time lifted garbage cans full of every kind of filth one can imagine and at the end of the day

the City did not provide a place to wash their hands. The workers needed a place to change their clothes before going home to their wives and children in the filthy clothes. What was happening to the garbage workers was a crime and the City Council headed by Clyde Tingley, City Manager Edmund Engel, and Superintendent Robertson knew it.

I began representing garbage workers who complained against the Superintendent. I was always turned down by the Superintendent and the City Manager and then I appealed to the City Personnel Board for relief. There I found Ray Powell, a concerned member, who argued my side of the complaint. I kept taking complaints to the board and getting workers reinstated with back pay. My time was limited and I had to find a better way to help the garbage workers. I decided to organize them as a separate American GI Forum with their own officers and a system to take up complaints against the Superintendent. Our first meeting to organize included persons who came to disrupt the meeting. As soon as I opened the meeting a person stood up and started heckling me. I tried to respond from the podium and ask the person to take his seat. We were prepared for the confrontation and I asked Alfonso Proo, a powerfully built person, to stand by in case of trouble. Alfonso Proo then went up to the troublemaker and took him by the scruff of the neck and hurled him out of the Sacred Heart Gym where we were meeting.

There were others who came for the same purpose of disrupting the meeting, but after they saw what happened to the first heckler, slowly slinked out of the meeting hall. The Sacred Heart meeting confrontation was only the beginning of the harassment that followed against the officers of the GI Forum. The Mexican American foremen doubled their efforts to make life miserable for the GI Forum officers. The breaking point came when GI Forum member Jose Gonzales was injured on the job. The foreman and the Superintendent fired Gonzales while he was in the hospital fighting for his life. We took this issue before the City Council and not only won the case, but Gonzales was awarded workmen's compensation on account of the injury.

The old patron system worked real well to control the votes of the two hundred garbage workers and their families. It was a dream come true for any patron who could deliver two hundred votes and their families for a Hispano candidate in a national, state and local office. The Mexican American foremen who worked for the garbage department Superintendent were the leaders of our communities. These foremen were also political precinct chairmen who controlled the votes of hundreds of people in the Albuquerque valley area.

I thought that what was happening to the Mexican American and Hispano people in the valley was a crime. Mexican American and Hispanic
candidates for office thought it was necessary to control the votes, in spite
of the abuse, to fight the Anglo newcomer who threatened the power of
the Mexican American and Hispanic throughout New Mexico. When I
took it upon myself to fight the patron system in Albuquerque and New
Mexico, I was considered a traitor. I was attacking a system the Mexican
American and Hispano candidates thought was the best way to hold on
to political power.

I, on the other hand, thought it best to tear it down, fight discrimination
openly, and told our Mexican American and Hispano candidates to ask
for the votes of everyone. Therefore, at least in theory, the candidate answered to the needs of the voter and not some patron who abused garbage
workers to the point of what I thought was a crime. The fight between the
GI Forum and the City of Albuquerque and the garbage department was
nasty and at times violent.[50]

Ximenes maps out the working-class political structure and caste system
in New Mexico. He also represents the heterogeneity among New Mexico
latinidad, indexing dimensions of class and race.

In terms of New Mexico's pigmentocracy, Ximenes uses the term *Hispano*
to signify the native-born, Spanish-identified New Mexican citizens, who
generally considered themselves white. He uses the term *Mexican American*
for native- and nonnative-born, *mexicano*-identified New Mexican citizens
(like himself), who generally considered themselves *mestizo* (Spanish and indigenous). The distinctions are significant. Organizing working-class laborers
necessitated recognition of the often invisible and intractable divisions between groups. In many respects, Ximenes's activism shifted the AGIF from a
deliberative democratic model of mobilizing to an agonistic pluralist approach
to political participation in New Mexico. He pressed the limits of the legal
imagination, destabilized the entrenched caste system between Hispano and
Mexican American workers, and helped to dismantle the old *patrón* system.

As a newcomer to New Mexico political life, Ximenes was willing to
expose both the pigmentocracy and the *patrón* system. Ximenes brought his
own understanding of how the system worked by observing his own father
navigate the South Texas *patrón* system in Floresville during his youth. But it
was more than just passion for a good fight that kept him in the fray. Ximenes
knew that initiatives like the FEPC and civil rights organizations like the
AGIF would remain impotent in New Mexico if he failed to break through
the old *patrón* system of buying and selling votes to the highest bidder.

Ximenes and the AGIF needed to establish their political clout. His willingness to confront the local political bosses (Mexican American, Hispano, and Anglo), to press the limits of established practices, and to stir the democratic process toward agonistic pluralism earned the kind of "street cred" Ximenes needed. He successfully pushed his reform agenda on behalf of the garbage workers through the city council to prevent wrongful termination, establish a merit system, and improve work conditions.[51] Ximenes disrupted the formal and informal political structure of the *patrón* system, taking the issue from the streets to city hall. Stirring up political passions in the public sphere, however, had exceeded the tolerance of the good Monsignor García and brought an end to the Sacred Heart Catholic Church as the regular meeting space for the Albuquerque AGIF. The growing success and recognition of the AGIF throughout New Mexico called for a gathering place of its own.

"Buy a Brick"

The first efforts toward establishing a permanent AGIF building were launched in 1953. The site for the New Mexico AGIF headquarters was in the Old Town district of Albuquerque. The formation and ownership of a collective space represented the value and necessity of the *agora*, a gathering place for community action. The AGIF had used the basement of the Sacred Heart Catholic Church in Barelas for the first two years. The Albuquerque AGIF found political protection under the aegis of the pastor, Monsignor García, who protected Ximenes when the FBI suspected him of un-American activities and launched its investigation of the new organization. As the reputation of the AGIF grew, so did its size and respectability. The new veterans' rights group needed more space than the basement could afford them and more permanence than this transient arrangement could provide.

The AGIF building in Albuquerque gave the organization a new level of legitimacy locally and nationally. Héctor García never established a permanent and stand-alone headquarters in Corpus Christi. In contrast to Ximenes, García directed AGIF activities by conducting meetings and writing correspondence at his own doctor's office in between patient visits. Other AGIF chapters established homes in churches and temporary settings. None of the other chapters throughout the 1950s were able to acquire the capital and collective will to own land and build a permanent meeting space. The decision to build a New Mexico AGIF headquarters was reached in August 1953.[52] Organizers launched a building fund, the "Buy a Brick" campaign, to sponsor the construction of the new headquarters for $1.00 per adobe brick.[53] The AGIF building in Albuquerque enhanced the professionalism and profile of the organization. Within the next three years Albuquerque would become the national headquarters of the AGIF when Ximenes was elected national chairman in 1956. Ximenes recounts:

> It was my idea to build a headquarters for the GI Forum. I was tired of begging for a place to meet and conduct the business of the Forum. It also provided us with a cause to produce something to keep the Forum members interested in something other than civil rights and community activity. It really was a build it and they will come project. The building was a source of pride in that we could invite dignitaries to speak and politicians to state their case in our own territory.[54]

The project of building the AGIF structure was both a family endeavor and a social event. The AGIF eventually acquired the land at 621 Gabaldon Road Northwest near Old Town Albuquerque from the family of Isabelle and Louis Tellez, charter members of the Albuquerque AGIF.

The New Mexico AGIF celebrated a number of milestones as plans for the new building were under way, including the wedding of Louis and Isabelle. The young Isabelle Ogaz Tellez served as the secretary of the New Mexico AGIF, and Louis was the state director of the New Mexico AGIF. In his honored role as a *padrino* for their upcoming nuptials, Ximenes delivered an affectionate tribute for the betrothed couple. Ximenes's witty comments were later published in the *American GI Forum News Bulletin*, underscoring the good-humored rivalry brewing between the New Mexico and Texas AGIF state conventions. The March 1955 *News Bulletin* reported, "It was a lucky break for the New Mexico Forum that a New Mexico bachelor was the winner,' Chente said. 'At times we were afraid that at one of the state conventions somebody would try to cross the Rio Grande into New Mexico and woo our secretary away.'"[55] In the following years, charter members Isabelle and Louis Tellez assumed local and national leadership roles and helped to establish and manage the national office in Albuquerque.[56] They were especially instrumental in advancing AGIF processes of governance and organizing conferences, board meetings, and programs throughout the 1960s. In a December 15, 1957, letter to Héctor García, Ximenes praises the organizing work of Louis Tellez and recounts recent accomplishments in New Mexico:

> Louis Tellez is doing an excellent job. This past week two Forums were organized in New Mexico: Espanola and Deming. I attended both organization meetings. . . . All Forums are definitely active and planning for expansion. . . .

The GI Forum in New Mexico has definitely shown that it must be recognized by all groups and individuals. Every aspirant to the governorship in New Mexico has made personal calls to talk to me about their program for New Mexico. I have laid our programs on the line and pulled no punches.[57]

Ximenes and Tellez helped to launch new chapters across the state. Within a few years the Albuquerque AGIF was able to purchase a plot of undeveloped land near Old Town through several thousand-dollar loans from three lenders: prominent Albuquerque attorney Lorenzo Chávez; Ximenes's brother Dr. Eduardo Ximenes of San Antonio; and Shirley Driggs, a statistician who was Ximenes's colleague at the UNM Bureau of Business Research. This plot of land became the building site for the future AGIF headquarters in New Mexico.

The building materials for the new headquarters were obtained by Procopio Martinez and Zeke Duran. They also helped to coordinate the labor of other AGIF members. The men hauled and set the adobe bricks for the building. The vigas for the roof of the building were cut and carried down by permission of the Cibola National Forest from the drought-stricken piñon trees in the Sandia Mountains. They needed over one hundred vigas of fifty feet in length. AGIF member Ernest Sanchez and his construction company provided the truck for hauling the lumber. Every member and friend of the AGIF contributed skills, labor, and cost-saving input.

Ximenes and his young family joined members of the AGIF on weekend picnics in the Sandia Mountain forest gathering and hauling lumber for the building. The men did the cutting and hauling; the women prepared meals and watched over the children who accompanied families on the regular excursions into the pine-covered mountains. To help repay the loans for the land, María Ximenes and members of the AGIF Ladies Auxiliary conducted weekly tamale sales. As the building became a reality, local banks were willing to loan additional funds to finish the construction.

The final structure was a capacious meeting hall with space large enough to accommodate over two hundred occupants. It became a gathering place for AGIF meetings and events as well as banquets, wedding receptions, tamale sales, and other community functions. Ximenes poignantly recalls:

We proved that Mexicanos can get together and finish what to me was a war we had to win, because the Anglos were waiting to hear us walk away from the project we started. It was much like the role we as Mexican Americans played in the war, the sweat and tears on the beach in Normandy or

Iwo Jima. We had to win and now we had to come home and show how discipline and tenacity can accomplish any worthwhile project.[58]

The process of building the AGIF headquarters enacted an expansive energy system of relationships. The economies of labor required to accomplish this organizational goal invoked all four dimensions of the classical notion of *oikos* (the home, the community, the soul, and the family). The New Mexico AGIF distributed these economies of labor largely along traditional gender roles. Women clearly contributed all the forms of labor related to the work of home building, or *oikos*. The men contributed to the labor of community building as well as to the labor of political activism in the *polis*.

The synergy evolving out of this energy system, organized around traditional male and female roles, proved to be successful even if highly circumscribed along gender lines. The women of the New Mexico AGIF were vital and visible members of the organization at every stage of its development. The AGIF women were not, however, directly involved in the front-stage power struggle of the *polis*, fighting the political threshing machine beyond the parameters of the organization itself. The risks to life and limb assumed by labor activists like the women of the Empire Zinc mine strike in 1951 New Mexico were not part of the mobilizing tactics of the AGIF.

Going National

Ximenes was elected national chairman of the AGIF in 1956 at the national convention held in Pueblo, Colorado.[59] He had helped to plan the convention in Pueblo and organized a New Mexico delegation to travel together to participate in the beginnings of the national organization.[60] José Ontiveros coordinated the hotel arrangements. Zeke Duran designed and published the program brochure for the convention. Ximenes drove his New Mexico delegation to the first national convention of the AGIF in the same 1938 blue Pontiac that had transported his young family a decade earlier from San Angelo, Texas, to Albuquerque, New Mexico, in 1947.

The rapid national expansion of the AGIF indexed the rhetorical import and exponential impact of Ximenes's vision. The collective success of this grassroots organization was the direct outcome of the generous donations of time, energy, and financial commitment from countless individuals. In less than a decade after its historic first meeting at Lamar School in Corpus Christi, Texas, in 1948, the AGIF had grown substantial enough to set up a national headquarters in Albuquerque in the hand-built pink adobe building. By 1957 the AGIF headquarters in Albuquerque became the site of both the

1957 AGIF national convention and the symbolic Daughters of the American Revolution (DAR) flag exchange. This historic flag ceremony with DAR was held in front of the AGIF building in Albuquerque in February 1957, a significant moment in the national life of the organization and U.S. civil rights history. The ceremony signaled a moment of resistance and reconciliation.

In February 1957 Art Tafoya, chairman of the Denver AGIF, along with José Ontiveros and Molly Galvan of the Pueblo chapter reported a racist incident in Colorado to Ximenes. Their reports indicated that the local chapter of DAR had refused to allow a Mexican-origin boy to carry the American flag at a ceremony for the Colorado Industrial School for Boys in Golden, Colorado, scheduled for February 12. The correctional institution was populated largely by Mexican-origin boys (many of whom were born in the United States to parents who were immigrant Mexican nationals). Questions of race, national identity, and cultural belonging were at the center of the controversy.

As national chairman of the AGIF, Ximenes took the lead on the issue and expressed outrage to the local and national press. He immediately fired off a wire to DAR national president Mrs. Frederic Groves and all chapters of the AGIF.[61] Within twenty-four hours, thousands of responses poured out in protest. Senator Dennis Chávez of New Mexico sent a telegram in rebuke, reminding public officials in Colorado that Mexican Americans had carried the U.S. flag in Bataan in World War II.[62] Governor McNichols of Colorado, in response, suspended all pending DAR activities in the state.

The rhetorical efficacy of this incident was clear to Ximenes. As delineated by Héctor P. García in his statement "A Brief History of the American GI Forum in the US," this veterans' organization vigorously promoted itself as an "anti-communist" and "patriotic" civic organization.[63] The American flag was a powerful symbol for this civic group; the colors were woven into the official emblem of the AGIF. The metonymic conceptual overlay of the U.S. flag onto the ethos of the AGIF was strategic. The rapid expansion of the AGIF over the past decade had been the direct result of its adroit alignment of the dominant Americanist discourse with civil rights reformist rhetoric. Having DAR deny a Mexican-origin child the opportunity to carry the U.S. flag was a civil rights violation in Ximenes's mind, one potentially as incendiary as the refusal of a funeral director to bury Mexican American soldier Private Félix Longoria in 1949. Ximenes did not waste any time reacting to the infraction. He stirred public debate and demanded immediate redress, transforming the conflict into dramaturgical crisis.

The *Denver Star* and *Amarillo Globe-Times* noted that the Lincoln Day flag-carrying pageant had been immediately canceled following Ximenes's complaint. Charlotte C. Bush, chair of the Denver chapter of DAR's Patriotic

Education Committee, publicly defended her position: "I wouldn't want a Mexican to carry 'Old Glory,' would you?"[64] This enthymeme, framed as a rhetorical question, was advanced by Charlotte Bush in her capacity as a DAR official. Her statement not only revealed the ethos of the speaker but the expressed goals of the organization. The suppressed premises of Bush's assertion are that, first, Mexican-origin people are not American citizens and that, second, only American citizens are entitled to carry the flag. This brief assertion was sufficiently damaging to DAR that it called for immediate action from the national headquarters. The rationalization for the act of discrimination by Charlotte Bush cast a pall over DAR leaders and their entire organization. The infraction deeply affected both the AGIF and DAR as prominent civic organizations.

DAR national president Mrs. Frederic Groves responded immediately by pulling the charter from the local DAR chapter and offering to travel to Albuquerque to exchange flags with the AGIF as an act of reconciliation. The consequent dialogue between Ximenes and Groves focused on finding a solution for all offended and offending parties. The flag incident that brought the AGIF and DAR into conflict can be analyzed with Aristotle's *Poetics*, a treatise on the events of staged human drama. Tragic *hamartia* involves agency and the choices of actors. The *hamartia*, or mistakes, of the DAR flag incident contained all the elements for stirring tragic drama: the motivating offense, the inflammatory rhetoric, the public outrage, and the polarization of embroiled parties. Ximenes, however, disarmed the tragic drama through *phronesis* and deliberation. The crisis became a turning point in an otherwise tragic process. Ximenes responded as an agent exercising choice, not as a victim. He expanded his local and national ethos through this highly contentious controversy by relying on both *dianoia* and *phronesis*. As Mary Whitlock Blundell argues in "Ethos and Dianoia Reconsidered," "this kind of rhetorical *dianoia* will contribute significantly to the expression of personal ethos."[65] *Dianoia*, according to Plato, is the capacity for reflection, discursive engagement, and higher-order critical thinking. *Dianoia*, as Ximenes aptly illustrated in his response to DAR, is integral to the cultivation of *phronesis*, or citizen wisdom.

The flag exchange ceremony was promptly staged in front of the Albuquerque AGIF building. This represented the first national-level rhetorical event for the AGIF since the 1949 Longoria incident (chapter 1). The participants included representatives of the AGIF and DAR, who presented the AGIF with a gift of a U.S. flag. The flag was carried and honored by Roberto Duran, son of New Mexico AGIF leader Zeke Duran. Through this event, the AGIF and DAR established common ground through the symbol of the U.S. flag.

The event enacted both dramatic ethos and *dianoia*, restoring the dignity of Mexican-origin citizens and affirming the moral and intellectual qualities of the actors. Through the exercise of *praxis* (purposeful action), the leaders of the AGIF and DAR demonstrated together the virtues of good citizenship.

The flag itself provided a symbolic and common focal point, a set of values that all participants could honor. As a veterans' rights organization, the AGIF represented and advanced the virtues of citizenship and patriotism. Echoing the rhetoric of atonement, members of the AGIF demonstrated through performance the collective sacrifice of Mexican American veterans for U.S. citizenship. The structure of the event carefully reflected military ceremonial protocol, aligning the ethos of Revolution-era America with postwar America. It was a quiet and solemn event, evocative of a ceremony honoring a fallen soldier. Reverence and ceremony replaced discord and drama. The casualties of the DAR incident were metaphorical. The victim narrative of Mexican Americans was laid to rest. Another narrative emerged in its place. Mexican American citizens assumed the role of arbiters of the legacy of American history. By resisting political escalation, Ximenes demonstrated good thinking (*dianoia*) as well as good character (ethos). The flag exchange in a public performance spoke louder than words. Paul Woodruff observes, "Ceremony joins leaders and followers in a common reverence and reminds them that they hold certain ideals in awe together."[66]

President Groves and one other DAR representative attended the ceremony. The event did not receive press coverage, much to Ximenes's disappointment. Because the offending incident had occurred in Colorado, outside the purview of the local press, the resolving action lacked the necessary urgency to make the headlines. Besides, as Ximenes knew, the New Mexico press consistently avoided giving coverage to any event that suggested racial discord existed in the state. The offense had not happened on New Mexico turf; hence the public act of reconciliation was considered irrelevant, at best, and potentially incendiary, at worst. An event that ceremoniously represented Mexican Americans (through the AGIF) exercising authority over a staunchly conservative Anglo institution (through DAR) could open a Pandora's box of political retaliation. The city of Albuquerque was deeply invested in a myth of *convivenica*, mutual and peaceful tricultural coexistence. In 1957, Cold War sentiments extended broadly and deeply throughout the city of Albuquerque, a community economically dependent on the defense industry, agriculture, and a growing tourist industry. The last thing the press and local officials wanted was an event highlighting the regional and national heritage of institutionalized discrimination.

Although ignored by the local press, the DAR flag exchange was a landmark event nonetheless. President Groves delivered a statement expressing regret for the incident and delineated the action she took to punish the DAR chapter and person who had refused to allow a Mexican American boy to carry the American flag. Ximenes formally accepted the apology and national DAR's presentation of the American flag. Symbolically, the AGIF raised the presented flag in front of the newly constructed national headquarters of the AGIF in Albuquerque.[67] Equally significant, the event signaled the authority of Ximenes as an emerging national leader, demonstrated his prudent exercise of *phronesis*, and publicly resisted the stepchild status of Mexican Americans in Cold War America. In effect, Ximenes disrupted the disabling narratives advanced by the early reformers and asserted a new rhetorical trajectory for Mexican American civil rights activism.

Héctor García recognized and applauded the moves by Ximenes with the press and with DAR. In his February 23, 1957, letter to Ximenes, García remarks, "I am glad you will accept the offer. . . . I believe that we have gained a lot of ground and command and respect of a lot of organizations."[68] García understood the range of responses Ximenes could have enacted in retaliation for DAR's violation. The AGIF had been rhetorically flogged in public over the racist and reactionary tactics of the anti-"wetback" campaigns promoted by George I. Sánchez and Ed Idar in the early 1950s. Through his exercise of *phronesis*, clearheaded practical wisdom, Ximenes exploited the flag exchange for a more productive outcome. He promoted an act of resolution through which both parties could recover esteem. The flag exchange ceremony in Albuquerque, New Mexico, provided a public occasion within which the AGIF (representative of Mexican American citizens) and DAR (representative of Constitution-era Anglo-American citizens) could regain honor.

Ximenes and the AGIF created an occasion that was open, inclusive, and transparent to the public. Ximenes took a proactive stance with DAR, not a passive position. The flag exchange ceremony and the symbol of the American flag provided a common and contextualized language of inclusion. Moreover, Ximenes gained credibility with the larger AGIF organization as well as with DAR and the general public through his exercise of tolerance, forgiveness, and acceptance by inviting the offending party into the protected space of the AGIF.

Significantly, Ximenes's resolution of the DAR incident reflected one of the major ideological currents informing the activities and agendas of the AGIF. As a system of social practice, the AGIF not only explicitly modeled its ceremony and structure closely on military culture; it also implicitly embodied the values of the Catholic Church. Most of the reformers of the AGIF (in New Mexico and Texas) were active members of the Catholic Church. The aims of the AGIF's reform agenda closely adhered to the principles and espoused beliefs of Catholicism.[69] Ximenes's resolution, in effect, enacted the basic tenets of the Judeo-Christian model of social justice, mercy, and reconciliation embedded in the implicit foundational Catholicism of the AGIF.

Ximenes's model of deliberation sought to promote the inclusion of the stranger and the outsider, the practice of hospitality, the acceptance of difference, the exercise of good and appropriate timing, and the empathic and respectful regard for others (even antagonists and enemies). Did Ximenes "turn the other cheek" rather than exact "an eye for an eye" from DAR? The evidence suggests that he did more than just turn the other cheek; he demanded that DAR turn the other cheek as well to reset the terms of inclusion within that organization and the national imagination. Ximenes offered two measures of practical wisdom as illustrated by the DAR flag exchange ceremony: forgiveness and the willingness to move forward to restore dignity.

In sum, 1957 proved to be a banner year for Ximenes and the New Mexico AGIF. It was also a watershed moment nationally, as 1957 marked the year that President Eisenhower signed new civil rights protections into law. In the weeks leading up to the historic passage of the 1957 Civil Rights Bill, Ximenes and the New Mexico AGIF hosted the national AGIF convention in Albuquerque. The optimism was palpable. Ximenes presided over the convention as the national AGIF chairman. Since its formation in 1951, the New Mexico AGIF's civil rights report card was stunning. Ximenes had catalyzed a growing inter-ethnic coalition of activists, advanced the labor rights of city workers, helped fund the previously impotent New Mexico FEPC, supported the passage of statewide civil rights legislation, expanded the AGIF throughout New Mexico, and established the first and only AGIF organizational office building in the nation. All told, Ximenes helped to organize twenty-three chapters of the AGIF in New Mexico, a branch in Arizona, three in Colorado, as well as chapters in California, Kansas, Michigan, and Illinois.

At the 1957 AGIF national convention, the thirty-eight-year-old Ximenes proudly showcased the new AGIF headquarters in Albuquerque, a space legitimizing the AGIF locally and nationally. Moreover, the successful resolution of the DAR flag incident enhanced not only his ethos, as the founder of the New Mexico AGIF, but offered the ambitious organization a heuristic for restorative justice. As far as Héctor García was concerned, Ximenes's organizing credentials had no equal. Within weeks of the national AGIF convention in Albuquerque, President Eisenhower signed the Civil Rights Act on September 9, 1957. The AGIF found itself in growing alignment with the national tenor. Although the 1957 Civil Rights Act failed to repeal the poll tax or universally protect the voting rights of historically excluded groups, the national discourse on civil rights had expanded the legal imagination of the postwar generation.

4. Latinidad: *The Question of Democracy and the Americas*

*I*f there was a moment that foreshadowed the next decade of Ximenes's public life, it was the 1958 American GI Forum (AGIF) national convention marking the tenth anniversary of the veterans' organization. In his opening remarks for the 1958 convention in Chicago, Ximenes called attention to the Cold War *kairotic* moment and set the stage emotionally and intellectually for the future of the AGIF as a national organization. Equally significant, his reflections indexed the tenor and tensions of the global situation. He knitted together the rhetorical strands of his message by reasserting the first principles of the AGIF organizational charter. In his remarks Ximenes reflects:

> Ten years have elapsed since the first GI Forum was organized in Corpus Christi, Texas. Its motto: "Education is our freedom and freedom should be everyone's business." With this motto and the philosophy of St. Francis of Assisi, "where there is hatred, let me sow love; where there is doubt, faith; where there is despair, hope; where there is darkness, light; where there is sadness, joy": the American GI Forum was able to attract people into our organization who had never been members of a civic and veterans charitable organization.[1]

From Ximenes's rhetorical vantage point, Mexican Americans did not represent a forgotten people. In his bold counternarrative, Mexican Americans were an irrepressible people, a gathering force moving through history. Ximenes shifted the Mexican American civic narrative from a passive victim position to an active rhetorical stance at a pivotal moment in Cold War politics. Chapter 4 focuses on the evolution of Ximenes's national and international rhetorical career through pivotal moments spanning the six-year period from 1958 to 1964, including his Alliance for Progress program appointments in Latin America.

Hemispheric Anxieties and the AGIF in 1958

Poised on a national stage in America's heartland, Ximenes delivered a convention address that carefully wove itself into the tapestry of the U.S. rhetorical imagination. The primary aim of Ximenes's message was to validate

138

the AGIF's achievements and to collectively claim first-class citizenship for Mexican Americans. His secondary aim was to catalyze sustained Mexican American activism. According to Ximenes's 1958 remarks, the AGIF and its members represented victors in the battle for social justice and exemplars of American democracy. His act of public rhetoric demonstrated, among other things, his newly established national authority and his recognition of the historical value of the occasion.

As national chairman of the AGIF, Ximenes found himself standing at the forefront of a robust and ambitious civic organization. He had succeeded his mentor and friend, AGIF founder Héctor García, as national chairman. Relying on his own self-styled public ethos and the gravitas of acquired power, Ximenes's public identity had progressively evolved alongside the national profile of the AGIF. His probationary period as apprentice organizer had finally come to a close. He had served the AGIF in both regional- and national-level offices. In his 1958 address Ximenes reveled in his tenure as the national chairman of the AGIF.

While he took stock of their collective achievements, Ximenes did not directly defer to his friend and mentor Héctor García. Ximenes demonstrated reverence and respect for García's legacy, but his opening remarks refrain from directly mentioning García by name. Ximenes acted through his own rhetorical agency, employing all the necessary moves of ceremonial discourse. His public address evidences the virtues of epideictic rhetoric, enacting both praise and blame as he reflected on the past and projected into the future. With this brief act of public rhetoric, Ximenes set the terms of Mexican American civil rights discourse and, at the same time, expanded the vision of this civic organization. Ximenes asserts:

> Time and again it was necessary to prove to many people including our American people of Mexican descent that the GI Forum meant what it said in the [AGIF] constitution. Time and again it was necessary to prove to our people that the principle of equal opportunity and the right and privilege to vote was an idea worth working for and worth every sacrifice necessary. Time and again it was necessary to prove that a first class education for the low income groups, especially the American of Mexican descent was a necessity and the GI Forum was ready to work for these ends. All these things were and are part of the principles and ideas of the American GI Forum.[2]

Ximenes invoked U.S. Constitution discourses, aligning the foundational tenets of self-governance with the practices and principles of the AGIF. He also lauded his AGIF colleagues and fellow citizens. Ximenes praised the

AGIF for its tenacity and reiterated the pragmatic imperatives of democratic practice. American democracy is more than an idea, he contends; it is action:

> Still we know that the mere act of writing these principles into our constitution or saying them does not make them so. Perhaps the one thing that has distinguished the American GI Forum from many other organizations that also have these same principles is the fact that we have acted on them. We believed what we wrote and said the GI Forum stood for. We sacrificed and worked and argued and defended our program before all people.[3]

In this bold move of self-authorization, Ximenes distinguished the AGIF from other U.S. civic organizations of the Cold War era. He emphasized the gritty work of democratic engagement, chastising the empty gestures of charity groups that fail to make structural changes to inequitable socioeconomic systems. Finally, Ximenes laid blame on the political detractors and self-interested opportunists who disrupt the democratic process, while at the same time separating himself and the AGIF from the political sellouts, the perpetrators of oppression at home and abroad. He foregrounded the revolutionary work of the AGIF and aligned its mission with the democratizing vision of the nation's founding leaders. Ximenes summarizes:

> Ours has been an organization without fear of speaking up for the Truth. Ours has been an organization unafraid to defend the rights of people irrespective of their race, color, or creed. Ours has been an organization with the courage to defend and espouse the cause of those less fortunate people who find themselves without economic resources. Ours has been an organization with the guts to stand up to the political prostitutes or "coyotes" as we call them in the Southwest and prevent them from selling us out to the highest bidder.

Rather than name white hegemony as the enemy of democracy directly, Ximenes uses the metaphor of the coyote, the wily trickster, to signify the adversary among them. In his characteristically coy manner, Ximenes deploys this loaded term to call out his adversaries: Anglo power brokers and the other political factions implicated by the term *coyotes*, which suggests a number of shadow figures in Ximenes's narrative—the political *patrón*, the self-serving border crosser, the pimp, and the smuggler.

Addressing this gathering in the urban center of Middle America, Ximenes could not rely on the New Mexico cultural rhetorical ecology to define the terms of engagement. He also had to be careful not to stir Anglo acrimony and racial hatred. So he offers "coyote" as a metonym to signal the historical power differentials between Anglo-Americans and Mexican Americans, rich and poor, educated and uneducated, privileged and underprivileged. Using the rhetorical device of *anaphora*, repetition of the phrase "ours has been" to emphasize their collective journey, Ximenes builds tension. By repeating the phrase again and again, he creates a litany of resistance. Ximenes concludes by emphasizing the need for continued resistance and action:

> We do not want these "coyotes" to get paid off on the basis of votes delivered while our children remain without a first class education, our streets remain unpaved, our people continue to go without medical aid, and our homes barely holding together. These are a few things we have worked on and must continue to push for if the GI Forum is to be known as an organization that performs the job it set out to do.
>
> The path of the GI Forum depends on our ability to continue along the path of working for those people who want so badly to find honest and intelligent leadership.[4]

It was a significant moment in the life of the AGIF. The organization had evolved from a strictly local veterans' rights civic group into a national clearinghouse for Mexican American issues. The ten-year anniversary in 1958 was a tipping point in the history of the AGIF. Within the span of a decade it had garnered support and recognition as the go-to organization for all matters affecting the U.S. Spanish-speaking constituency, eventually eclipsing the League of United Latin American Citizens in political visibility and national profile. Ximenes engaged the *kairotic* moment of the organization and the nation.

El Duende: *The Shadow Ecology of 1958*

The year 1958 began and ended with a bang.[5] The major themes stirring the national imagination revolved around key *topoi*: the urgency of the space race, the threat of the Soviet Union, and the instability of Latin America. Cold War anxiety remained high. The United States was in second place in the space race; Communism was gaining traction in Cuba; the political and economic volatility in Latin America destabilized U.S. interests. To make matters worse, by 1958 the United States was in an economic recession with more than seven million Americans unemployed. Tracing the trajectory of the postwar civil rights movement begins in the year 1958, as the western hemisphere simmered with Cold War anxieties and political repressions below the halcyon surface of the Eisenhower administration. C. G. Jung's *The Undiscovered Self* was released in 1958, tapping into the shadow of collective unconscious. Jung cautioned an anxious generation, "The spiritual transformation of mankind follows the slow tread of the centuries and cannot be hurried or held up by any rational process of reflection, let alone brought to fruition in one generation."[6]

The year began with a brief burst of optimism when, on January 31, the United States launched *Explorer I* in response to the 1957 wake-up call that was the shocking success of the Soviet Union's *Sputnik*. Senator Lyndon B. Johnson was scrambling to redeem the U.S. space program, putting forward a resolution on February 8 for the formation of the Subcommittee on Aeronautical and Space Science, a measure that would help to establish NASA in July.[7] By the end of the year, however, national confidence was badly shaken by a series of worrisome international events.

Fidel Castro stirred U.S. fears of a Communist threat offshore by fomenting revolution in Cuba. The Cold War was now in America's own backyard. Castro began broadcasting Radio Rebelde in February 1958 as U.S. industrialists and political analysts shuddered at the implications. America's capitalist playground was no more. A Communist Cuba was inevitable when Castro launched attacks on Havana in April. After more than one hundred years of U.S. imperialism in Latin America, the United States wanted to own and control more of the region than it could have.

When Vice President Nixon made a diplomatic trip to Venezuela in May, he was jeered and pummeled with tomatoes through the streets of Caracas. On May 18, 1958, *Life* published a six-page spread of the riotous reception of Richard and Pat Nixon throughout Latin America.[8] The limousine carrying Richard and Pat Nixon was attacked by angry protesters and nearly overturned. Secret Service agents drew guns against the crowds. Visibly shaken and enraged by the violent reception, Nixon declared that the agitation was "Communist-planned, Communist-led, and Communist-controlled."[9] Left-wing demonstrations broke out everywhere in South America, gaining worldwide attention.[10]

Nixon's ill-fated trip, envisioned as a White House diplomatic tour through seven Latin American countries, instead resulted in international criticism of failed U.S. economic policies and political practices. Anti-U.S. attitudes spread throughout the western hemisphere, as it become abundantly clear that the citizens of Latin America were growing deeply disenchanted with all things *norteamericano*, especially the Eisenhower administration.

Relations between the United States and Latin America in 1958 were a feverish dance, an oddly choreographed push-pull performance of awkward missteps, marked by both political events and cultural shifts. The year saw the birth of bossa nova in Rio de Janeiro with the release of João Gilberto's recording of *Chega de Saudade*. This overnight cultural phenomenon moved

America's body and soul, filling living rooms and lounges across the United States. The cultural, political, and rhetorical tensions pressing the U.S. public imagination in 1958 were symbolically reflected in the vibrant notes and pulsing beat of Latin music captivating audiences throughout the Americas—a rhythmic fusion both disruptive and seductive.

Latinidad (a Spanish term indexing both constant states of being as well as shifting notions of cultural identification) was something both exoticized and demonized in U.S. public culture. The racial, linguistic, ideological, and cultural mixing reflective of Latin American societies violated cherished Anglo-American norms and notions of purity. *Latinidad* was a dynamic and disruptive process of identity formation shaped by shifting geopolitical spaces, new and innovative cultural productions, flexible notions of citizenship, linguistic contact, transnational migration patterns, and the porosity of national borders.

The permeability of the border separating the Americas was never more palpable. As 1958 came to a close, the historical complexities of Latin America–U.S. relations were surfacing as Latin America resisted U.S. hegemonic and expansionist designs. On December 29, 1958, revolutionary leader and Argentine physician Ernesto "Che" Guevara led rebel troops in the invasion of Santa Clara, Cuba. By December 31, Cuban dictator Fulgencio Batista had resigned the presidency and boarded an airplane with his family for the Dominican Republic. Counterterrorist attacks against Castro's revolution had failed, and the U.S-sponsored puppet regime had collapsed.[11] On that note, the year 1958 ended with an ominous boom. The position of the United States as a global superpower was in serious question.

Latin America: Counterrhetorics and "Russo-Imperialist Communism"

As the celebrated keynote speaker of the 1958 AGIF convention, Senator Dennis Chávez spoke on May 17, applauding AGIF milestones and forecasting into the future. The AGIF extended a hero's welcome to Chávez at the 1958 AGIF convention in Chicago. Seven years had elapsed since his first speech to the AGIF in Austin, Texas, in 1951. In the intervening years, the center of power for the AGIF had shifted from Texas to Chávez's state of New Mexico. In those seven years the organization had transformed itself from a primarily regional, working-class veterans' organization into a nationally recognized coalition of highly accomplished Mexican American activists and leaders.

Responding directly to the present political turmoil in U.S.–Latin America relations, Chávez voiced national anxieties about Latin America and

Communism. He also helped to set the stage for the rhetorical platform of John F. Kennedy's 1960 presidential campaign. Following on the themes advanced in his speech to the 1951 AGIF Texas state convention in Austin (chapter 2), Chávez commended the AGIF for its landmark achievements and charged the civic organization with democratizing not only the U.S. Southwest but the nation as a whole. The global advancement of American exceptionalism would become a major theme for Kennedy's campaign platform two years later. As a native New Mexican, Senator Chávez had a stake in the issues pressing the nation's southern borders. The scope of Chávez's keynote address reached beyond the geopolitical boundaries of the United States, however. He not only set the stage for future U.S.–Latin America relations; Chávez prefigured the future career of his New Mexican political compatriot and AGIF convention host, Vicente Ximenes.

As Chávez described the volatile political conditions in Latin America, he carved out a rhetorical space on the international stage for AGIF leadership. Chávez first extends these words of praise to his audience: "You have, as American Veterans, labored to obtain equality of opportunity without special privilege by focusing public attention on discrimination in education, housing, work, business, and politics locally."[12] Chávez invoked the bootstraps mythos, a narrative with which he himself deeply identified and often advanced through his own story of the self-made man. Chávez used the discourse of commerce to frame his agenda for the democratization of Latin America. He proposed the marriage of market capitalism to social democracy, a partnership first formed against the expansion of Communism in Europe during the postwar period through the Marshall Plan.

Building on the democratization of Latin America as a common vision, Chávez then sought to expand the political imagination of his audience. His timely and provocative oratory reached out to his listeners to move them to action and assent. The convergence of Americanist ideology, the resurgence of political power within the Democratic Party, and the game-changing potential of the U.S. Spanish-speaking electorate were key themes ignited in Chávez's 1958 AGIF keynote address. These *topoi* would become key themes in the upcoming 1960 presidential race and in Kennedy's presidential administration. Mapping the situation, Chávez describes the recent events in Latin America: "We are all aware of Vice President Nixon's unfortunate experience in South America. A mission of friendship was received by indignities and abuse. I am sure you feel indignant, as I do, at the discourteous, insultive [*sic*], and reprehensible attacks visited upon the persons of two Americans, Richard Nixon and his wife, Pat, and upon the office of the Vice President of the United States."[13]

Chávez keenly understood the history of U.S. empire building throughout Latin America. Moreover, he understood the political and socioeconomic implications for colonized groups, drawing from his own experience repairing the social wreckage and restoring civic access in the historical aftermath of U.S. appropriation of Greater Mexico (a drama played out in his own backyard of the U.S. Southwest for more than a century). The violent turn of events in 1958 was yet another chapter in the story of U.S. occupation throughout the Americas, a story over one hundred years old. Chávez asserts, "On the surface, Nixon's trips seemed timely and in order, but the State Department either overlooked or probably discounted the mounting anti-American feeling in all of South America. They forgot that there is some reason for distrust and even hatred of the United States. . . . They are indelibly imprinted in the political consciences of all Latin Americans. They are alive today."[14] Chávez painted the picture of a common history and a common enemy for his AGIF audience. Additionally, he interrogated the knee-jerk U.S. military response in Latin America and called for a reversal of the Eisenhower administration's political tunnel vision and laissez-faire diplomacy. In his closing remarks, Chávez portends:

> The fate of Latin America, whether we like it or not, is irrevocably linked with ours! We can't afford under any circumstances for Russo-imperialist communism to take over Latin America. We are absolutely dependent upon them: their markets, raw materials, manpower, their political influences in world opinion and international organizations such as the U.N. etc. are absolutely indispensable! We can't just write them off! Unfortunately, that is what we have been doing since World War II.[15]

Within eighteen months of Senator Chávez's keynote address, the 1960 presidential election campaign season would move the nation toward Kennedy's imagined "New Frontier." Literally and metaphorically, *latinidad* was a part of Kennedy's ambiguous frontier. For the next eighteen months, Ximenes would work alongside Senator Chávez, Héctor García, and the AGIF to guide Kennedy toward a democratic vision of hemispheric *latinidad*. The 1960 Viva Kennedy campaign offered the platform to shape Cold War U.S.–Latin America relations.

Shifting the National Narrative:
The 1960 Viva Kennedy Campaign

Ximenes became a strong supporter of the Viva Kennedy Clubs through the 1960 presidential campaign, ultimately sponsoring a Kennedy rally with Senator Chávez in New Mexico. Ximenes along with Senator Chávez helped to deliver what the Democratic National Committee (DNC) labeled the "Spanish-speaking vote." John F. Kennedy accepted the Democratic nomination on July 15, 1960, in Los Angeles, constituting his candidacy around the trope of the "New Frontier." In his acceptance speech, Kennedy constructs the extended metaphor that would become his signature phrase throughout his administration:

> For I stand here tonight facing West on what was once the last frontier. From the lands that stretch 3000 miles behind me, the pioneers of old gave up their safety, their comfort, and sometimes their lives to build a new world here in the West. They were not captives of their own doubts, the prisoners of their own price tags. Their motto was not "every man for himself"—but "all for the common cause." . . .
>
> [A]nd we stand today on the edge of a New Frontier—the frontier of the 1960's—a frontier of unknown opportunities and perils—a frontier of unfulfilled hopes and threats.[16]

Using the topography of the U.S. Southwest as the geographical and metaphorical platform for his presidential bid, Kennedy cast the national gaze toward what would become a tumultuous decade of change.

Populations in Texas and other states of the region were not generally receptive to Kennedy or the Kennedy-Johnson ticket. The Democratic hopefuls made a sweep through the Southwest in the final months of the presidential campaign, scraping up every last necessary vote. During a rally at the Alamo in San Antonio, Texas, on September 12, 1960, candidates John F. Kennedy and Lyndon B. Johnson were openly heckled by picketers with signs emblazoned, "We don't want the Kremlin and the Vatican."[17] Johnson, a native son, was unabashedly jeered. The tall, Anglo, Texan, and Protestant vice presidential candidate was caustically labeled "Lyndon Benedict Johnson," an epithet that stemmed from his support and passage of the 1957 Civil Rights Act, which guaranteed voting rights for every American, something anathema in many southern states.

The issue of Communist expansion in Latin America figured prominently in Kennedy's remarks throughout the Southwest. In his September 12 campaign speech at the Alamo, Kennedy raised many of the same points that Senator Chávez had advanced in his 1958 AGIF national convention keynote address. Reflecting on the failures of the Eisenhower administration to implement the vision of Franklin D. Roosevelt's Good Neighbor policy in Latin America, Kennedy asserts:

> I don't want to see the United States do anything in Latin America at the point of Castro's pistol. I want us to do it because we believe in it. . . .

The New Frontier of which I speak does not consist of things which we promise we will do for you. It consists of the things which you can do for your country, the opportunity for service, the opportunity to help this country realize its great potential, here and around the world. In the American Revolution, Thomas Paine said, "The cause of America is the cause of all mankind."

I think in 1960, the cause of all mankind is the cause of America. If we succeed here, if we are strong in this country, if we are carrying out policies of assistance to our people, if we hold out the hand of friendship abroad, if we present an image of vitality and strength, then the people around the world will determine that the future belongs to freedom. But if we stand still, if we look back, if we mark time while the Communists move ahead, then people in Latin America, Africa, and Asia will determine that the future belongs to the East and not to the West.[18]

The intertwining *topoi* of American exceptionalism and Communist expansion in the Western hemisphere set the parameters of the 1960 Kennedy campaign.

There is little doubt that the well-seasoned, self-made Senator Chávez tutored the young, bon vivant, Ivy League Senator Kennedy on talking points for the campaign trail throughout the Southwest. Chávez, deeply concerned about his constituency in New Mexico and the turbulence in Latin America, wanted an end to the Eisenhower-Nixon regime. To help assure that outcome, Chávez played an especially strong role in promoting the Kennedy-Johnson ticket. The hectic campaign schedule of the seventy-two-year-old veteran senator included rallies throughout New Mexico, Arizona, California, and Texas. Chávez's efforts were unrelenting, and he delivered two speeches at every political rally, one in English and the second in Spanish. He recirculated the themes advanced in his 1958 AGIF national convention keynote address in Chicago, further criticizing the Eisenhower-Nixon administration "as relics of the past and as anti-working people."[19] Kennedy's campaign remarks echoed Chávez's well-rehearsed arguments in almost every way.

Chávez boldly called for a return to New Deal programs and policies. Additionally, Chávez forcefully attacked the Republican administration's foreign relations policies in Latin America, lauding Franklin D. Roosevelt's Good Neighbor policies. He again called attention to Venezuela's violent reception of Vice President Nixon in 1958, reminding voters how the highly unpopular U.S. public official had been pelted with tomatoes by angry citizens throughout Latin American. Chávez claimed that U.S. military and industrial intervention in Latin America had backfired. These policies, asserts

Chávez, were "imperialistic and responsible for keeping dictators and military leaders across Latin America."[20]

Ximenes joined Chávez in the push to get *nuevo mexicanos* to the polls, invigorating the Viva Kennedy Clubs through the dense regional network of the New Mexico AGIF. Together Chávez and Ximenes worked tirelessly to get voters out for the young and relatively unknown presidential candidate. Because of their efforts, Kennedy was generally well received by the large Hispano Catholic population in New Mexico. Lyndon B. Johnson, however, did not evoke the same warm response.

Mexican American leaders like Senator Chávez, Héctor García, and Ximenes knew from the outset of the 1960 presidential campaign that Spanish-speaking voters favored the young Catholic candidate. Moreover, Kennedy's wife Jacqueline, a glamorous brunette evocative of the screen stars of the Mexican cinema, spoke Spanish fluently. Johnson's drawbacks, however, were many for Spanish-speaking voters. He was Texan; he was an Anglo; he was rich; he was a Protestant. Johnson, with his Texas drawl and his demure and self-effacing Southern belle wife, Lady Bird, was simply no match from a Mexican American voter perspective. "You are not selling it down to the level of the little people," García once reported to Johnson in June 1960.[21]

The formation and expansion of Viva Kennedy Clubs in the wake of the Democratic National Convention stirred Spanish-speaking voters in unprecedented numbers. Moreover, the Viva Kennedy Clubs sparked heightened awareness within the U.S. public imagination of Latin America and the U.S. Southwest. More than any other political figure stumping for Kennedy, Senator Chávez was the one who successfully cultivated the romance between Mexican Americans and the would-be president. He presented Kennedy to Spanish-speaking voters as *un amigo*, a good friend, someone they could trust. The political courtship represented a powerful rhetorical sleight of hand, one that obscured some of the more difficult aspects of *la raza*'s relationship to U.S. expansionist tendencies.

Héctor García was initially reticent about supporting Kennedy's candidacy over Johnson in the primaries because of his long-term association with Johnson beginning with the 1949 Longoria case (chapter 2). Nevertheless, García enthusiastically climbed on the Kennedy bandwagon immediately after the 1960 Democratic National Convention and stepped up to direct the wildly successful Viva Kennedy Clubs. García once described the collective infatuation among the Spanish-speaking voters with Kennedy as a kind of "enchantment."[22] The metonymic alignment of Kennedy with *latinidad*— Latin American identity and politics—was initially formed in the alchemy of the 1960 campaign and the political crucible of the Viva Kennedy campaign.

This metonymic relationship endured throughout Kennedy's administration and even after his death. Viva Kennedy campaign materials exploited Mexican American stereotypes with visual images representing Kennedy with a sombrero jauntily perched in larger-than-life proportions on a small, docile burro (a symbol invoking the traditional donkey emblem of the Democratic Party as well as exploiting entrenched *mexicano* stereotypes).

In the end, the Kennedy-Johnson ticket won by a thin margin with 49.7 percent of the vote compared to Nixon's 49.6 percent. The Spanish-speaking vote helped make the difference. Over the course of the 1960 campaign, the AGIF had enhanced its national profile, claiming over one hundred thousand members by the end of year.[23] The AGIF had demonstrated to the DNC the scope of its influence and the verity of its political power. García, Ximenes, and the AGIF achieved broad recognition as the premier Mexican American civic group and advocacy organization.[24] In sum, through the Viva Kennedy Clubs the AGIF fulfilled the civic vision Ximenes had advanced in his 1958 AGIF national convention remarks by mobilizing Spanish-speaking citizens nationwide in a march toward expanded democratic participation.

Ximenes was no longer on the sidelines of national politics. Through the mentorship of Senator Chávez and the sustained advocacy of García, Ximenes was ready and willing to take a larger role in national public life. He had helped get Kennedy and Johnson into the White House. Ximenes, García, and their AGIF *compadres* at last saw themselves as political insiders when they received invitations to Kennedy's inaugural ball. The thrills and disappointments of political activism that Ximenes had first experienced organizing the AGIF in New Mexico would continue through the next decade.

The Kennedy Administration: Payback, Backlash, and Unpaid Debts

The mobilization of the AGIF through its establishment of the national Viva Kennedy campaign had successfully brought out the Spanish-speaking vote for Kennedy. The political alliance came with an unspoken Faustian pact: deliver the Mexican American electorate and, in turn, receive high-level appointments for Mexican Americans. García's and AGIF leaders' expectations of political payback from a grateful President Kennedy proved both naïve and unachievable. Although the AGIF had developed a national network of Viva Kennedy Clubs throughout the country at an unprecedented rate, their relative political clout was still not significant enough for the Kennedy administration's serious attention. Héctor García was both demoralized and enraged by the repeated dismissals of his recommendations by the Kennedy administration.

By January 1961 it was clear that very few Mexican Americans were designated for the highly coveted government appointments that the AGIF had struggled to secure through its tireless campaigning for Kennedy. In March 1961 Senator Dennis Chávez was publicly criticizing President Kennedy's failure to deliver high-level appointments for Mexican Americans. Subsequently questioned by a journalist during a televised press conference about his failed promises to Spanish-speaking Americans, President Kennedy replied, "I quite agree with you that we ought to use what I consider to be a great reservoir of talent, and I think this is particularly true in our relations with Latin America. So I will just say to you that it is a matter of interest and that we will continue to see if we can provide—if we can associate them with our administration more closely."[25]

Meanwhile the gathering clouds of political retaliation were stirring in New Mexico, where Ximenes had been mobilizing for over a decade. His growing reputation as an agitator and activist continued to rile New Mexico's Anglo elites and Republican politicos—some of the "coyotes" he had been speaking out against since the 1958 AGIF national convention and continuing to mobilize against through the Viva Kennedy movement. With the success of the Kennedy campaign, New Mexico conservatives became increasingly aware of the fact that Ximenes had not only helped to get New Mexican Spanish-speaking voters for Kennedy; he had stirred the mobilization of organized labor and aligned forces with other civil rights entities. The exhilaration in the AGIF and the Mexican American electorate at the outcome of the 1960 election was not shared by everyone on the New Mexico political scene.

By the beginning of 1961, Ximenes began to realize that New Mexico political forces wanted to remove him from his position at the University of New Mexico (UNM) and shut down his political platform. In January 1961 Senator Clinton Anderson alerted the university's president, Thomas Popejoy, of his displeasure with Ximenes, who had run afoul of the U.S. senator beginning with AGIF mobilizing efforts in the early 1950s that exposed New Mexico's political bosses and *patrón* politics. Ximenes's high-profile role with the Viva Kennedy Clubs further disturbed Senator Anderson. As a wealthy and well-established Albuquerque businessman and Democratic Party political figure for more than two decades, Senator Anderson was one of the Anglo elites benefiting from *patrón* politics.

Senator Anderson increasingly regarded Ximenes as a threat to his political stronghold in New Mexico. Additionally, Anderson had served as chair of the Joint Committee on Atomic Energy for the Eighty-Fourth and Eighty-Sixth Congresses through the Eisenhower administration. The State of New Mexico and UNM were principal beneficiaries of the nuclear research laboratories. As an employee of UNM troubling the established political economy of the state, Ximenes was treading on dangerous terrain. The ill-fated Bay of Pigs invasion in April 1961, only three months after President Kennedy's inauguration, stirred anxieties across the nation, especially among New Mexico politicos. As home base to an expanding nuclear arms industry, New Mexico was ground zero. Agitators like Ximenes became political scapegoats for heightened Cold War anxieties.

Ximenes's growing regional and national profile as an agitator and civil rights activist raised concerns with New Mexico legislators, public figures, and government leaders. The success of his civil rights activism through the AGIF ultimately jeopardized Ximenes's job at UNM. Complaints about Ximenes's civil rights activism were sent from Senator Anderson to President Popejoy.[26] Senator Anderson had not forgotten Ximenes's first public confrontation with him ten years prior in Ximenes's December 1951 letter to the editor of the *Albuquerque Journal* holding Anderson accountable for the death of Mexican immigrant children in Loving, New Mexico (chapter 2). Ximenes's bold public rhetoric attacking "coyote" politics and the racist Anglo hegemony had gone too far. The political climate in Cuba and Latin America further aggravated the situation. Ximenes's social justice agenda and rhetorical platform appeared perilously close to Fidel Castro and Che Guevara's jeremiads against U.S. imperialism.

In light of these threats to the New Mexico political establishment, Anderson's message to UNM president Popejoy after the 1960 election was unequivocal: Ximenes had to go. Interestingly, President Popejoy, a member of the Anglo elite and a widely respected public figure, remains distinguished as the longest-standing president in the history of the university. Popejoy held office at UNM for some twenty years, a formidable force known to tamp down dissent and political disruption. Carefully guarding the reputation of the institution, Popejoy routinely dismissed UNM faculty and staff suspected of un-American activities. By January 1961 Ximenes was being pressured to leave his post. Within the next few months, he was instructed to resign his position at the UNM Bureau of Business Research or be fired. The full extent of Senator Anderson's animosity toward Ximenes would not be known to Ximenes until 1967 with his nomination for commissioner of the Equal Employment Opportunity Commission during Johnson's presidential administration (chapter 5).

As the honeymoon of the Kennedy election faded for those involved with Viva Kennedy organizing, the realization struck that no Mexican Americans had made Kennedy's short list for appointments in high-level administration in the federal government. Héctor García pelted the new administration with letters, memos, reports, and telegrams to no avail.[27] He put forward his personal recommendation for an appointment for Ximenes at the same time that Ximenes's professional situation at UNM was rapidly deteriorating. García's telegram directed to Attorney General Robert Kennedy reads: "Respectivefully [*sic*] request appointment of Vicente Ximenez [*sic*] University of New Mexico as sub secretary of state for Latin American Affairs. Mr. Ximenez is highly qualified and believe he will help improve understanding and relations between us and our Latin American brothers. Dr. Hector G. [*sic*] Garcia Founder American GI Forum Co Chairman Viva Kennedy Club." In a letter to President Kennedy in support of Ximenes's nomination, Zeke Duran, chairman of the Albuquerque AGIF, delineated Ximenes's character and accomplishments. Duran asserts:

> It is well-nigh impossible to measure the high esteem in which Mr. Xi- menes is held among the Spanish speaking people of the United States. He has contributed immensely toward the betterment of their lot in many areas where they were considered as second-class citizens and has won for them the recognition they deserve.
>
> In New Mexico, his spare moments are all devoted to projects which have for their goal the betterment of the community. To those of us who have observed him in action, it is like witnessing the realization of de- mocracy in action, since it is only within a democracy that such refined talent can be cultivated. He is indeed a credit to our democratic ideals and possesses the courage to struggle for their ultimate fruition. He does not cringe when the honor of our democracy is at stake.[28]

Ximenes's eventual appointment to serve in Quito, Ecuador, as an economist for the Alliance for Progress program of the U.S. Agency for International Development (USAID) represented one of the many firsts he would achieve over the next decade of his public life.

Mexican American leaders across the nation began conducting a letter-writing campaign calling for additional Hispanic appointments. The White House remained silent. Senator Chávez was the first public figure to finally step forward and publicly criticize President Kennedy for neglecting the Hispanic electorate. He lambasted the new administration for ignoring the Spanish-speaking constituency, which had helped to put Kennedy in the White House. Kennedy did not want to risk bringing unknown, unproven performers into his administration, preferring only the most promising and highly credentialed appointees. According to Ignacio García, "Undoubtedly, the White House had a different perspective on the matter of appointments. The president wanted to surround himself with bright, successful, well-placed individuals who had experience in economics, business, the academy, and foreign policy."[29] Herein Mexican Americans found themselves in a catch-22: they could not get appointments because they did not already have appointments. Privilege engenders privilege.

By February 1961, political oversights and disappointments fueled national discontent among Mexican Americans and Latinos. When pressured by the press to respond to this public criticism, President Kennedy alluded to a small list of nominees under his consideration. Ximenes found himself among a select few advanced for a federal appointment. Others on Kennedy's cursory short list included El Paso mayor Raymond L. Telles Jr. and Los Angeles city councilman Edward R. Roybal.[30] Arturo Morales Carrion, a Latino with Puerto Rican heritage, received the appointment of assistant secretary of state to Latin America.

Problematically, there were very few names on the White House rosters of Mexican Americans with any federal government experience. Few Mexican Americans had access to the political power structure that provided the credentials necessary to distinguish an individual for high-level positions. The short list was very short indeed. Senator Chávez was one of the few Hispanics to claim membership among the elite Washington insiders, distinguished by his East Coast university degree and his record of election to a federal office. Moreover, few Mexican Americans acquired the educational, political, economic, cultural, and social markers of promise and success necessary to belong to the inner circle of the White House and the federal administration.

In 1961 Ximenes was appointed program officer and economist for USAID in Quito, Ecuador. This was not the high-level appointment that García had proposed, but it distinguished Ximenes as a recipient of one of the first presidentially appointed international posts ever awarded to a Mexican American. Ximenes's nomination for the post was supported by New Mexico legislators, U.S. senator Dennis Chávez, and U.S. representative Joseph Montoya.[31] His starting annual salary for this federal position was $11,000.00. Ximenes turned forty-two years old when he took the appointment for USAID in Quito. It was huge leap for Ximenes and his family. María and their four children (Steven, fourteen years old; Ricardo, eleven; Olivia, seven; Ana Maria, eight months) all joined him overseas.

Ximenes and the Latin American Alliance for Progress

Kennedy's Alliance for Progress was largely a reaction to Castro and the Cuban Revolution, aligning the fears and concerns of U.S. military strategists, Cold War liberals, religious groups, and progressive intellectuals. In the new spirit of volunteerism inspired by Kennedy's call to public service, numerous church organizations such as the Young Christian Workers and Young Christian Students began responding to the plight and poverty in Latin America. Ximenes reflects, "By the time Kennedy became president in 1960, the churches had already established a large number of organizations dedicated to the idea of liberation theology in Central and South America. The churches preached a heavy handed and emergency type of assistance to the poor. The ultimate objective for the church and the government was to help the poor and stop communists from taking over the weak regimes."[32] Motivated primarily by growing Cold War anti-Communism, Kennedy's emerging U.S.–Latin American Alliance for Progress put Ximenes in a new and tenuous political landscape. Ximenes's appointment to Latin America came only months after President Kennedy's invasion of Cuba's Bay of Pigs in April 1961, an ill-conceived and poorly executed military debacle. Ximenes was in Quito when the Cuban Missile Crisis rocked the western hemisphere in October 1962. Ximenes remembers:

> I carried out programs that cost millions of dollars in direct assistance to the poor of Ecuador and Panama. We built schools, medical clinics, roads, bridges, and even direct funds to shore up the budgets of the countries. We organized some projects that blew up in our faces; for example, the Civic Action program that funded the military to do economic develop-ment projects. Ultimately, the Civic Action projects served to empower the military and did nothing to help the poor.[33]

Ximenes found himself in the vortex of international ambiguity during his service in Latin America. The Cold War rhetoric generated by the Kennedy administration revealed a Communist-centered hypervigilance that perme-ated Kennedy's foreign policy in Latin American as well as Southeast Asia. In his capacity as attorney general, Robert Kennedy's Cold War seminar address on May 17, 1963, articulated the administration's Cold War stance. Robert Kennedy asserts:

> The Communist purpose, now as in 1917, is to remake the work in the Communist image. The Communist faith, now as ever, is that history inevitably will sweep all other forms of society, democracy, into obscurity.
>
> The Communist conviction is that any means is justified to undermine and capture free governments and free peoples.
>
> The enormous global struggle which we call the cold war is being fought at every level. Moscow remains energetic and alert, and its challenge to our freedom is dangerous—and enduring.[34]

The jeremiad rhetoric circulated by the Kennedy administration indelibly shaped the available means of persuasion. Ximenes took on the mantle of Kennedy's New Frontier vision.

In a June 21, 1963, letter to Héctor García, Ximenes described his own perceptions and experiences of culture shock as a political outsider traveling through Ecuador. Ximenes writes:

> It has been my good fortune to travel rather extensively throughout the country of Ecuador and look over the economic conditions and possibilities for development in the various regions. There were some places where I asked myself, what in the hell am I doing here? But at the same time it was most interesting and not many people get the chance to see parts of Ecuador the way I did and that includes even Ecuadoreans who have never gone into the remote areas of the country.
>
> I visited places where the people are truly primitive and are not too far removed from the stone age man. But even these people want a change and a better way of life since they have come in contact with the civilization of modern man. Tu Amigo, Vicente.[35]

Correspondence between Ximenes and García was relatively scant over the four years that Ximenes served in Ecuador. Nonetheless, the AGIF answered the call to service in Latin America. The Albuquerque chapter of the AGIF offered support to Ximenes while he was in Ecuador by organizing fund-raisers for educational supplies for the Quito Civic Action project. An initiative called "Operation Amigo" organized by AGIF officer Zeke Duran in 1962 sought to generate citywide support in Albuquerque for the Garcia-Moreno Elementary School in Quito. A promotional flyer titled "Your Contribution to Operation Amigo Is a Strike against Communism" was circulated by the Albuquerque AGIF. In describing the social conditions of Quito, the flyer exploits Cold War rhetoric to advance the cause:

> OPERATION AMIGO, is a project sponsored by the American GI Forum, a Veterans family organization, to help give the school the essential educational facilities. . . . Mr. Ximenes will coordinate all aid through the School-Parents [*sic*] Association. The plea is being made to all citizens of Albuquerque, all businessmen, laborers, housewives, school teachers, and children.
>
> Your help is needed—NOW! These conditions, this poverty as it exists now, is the breeding ground for communism. Sooner or later, all believers in our Democracy, will have to make a stand against the evils of communism. Communism is like a cancer, and it has many roots in South America. The time to up-root this cancer is NOW.[36]

The military ethos implied by the name of the project, Operation Amigo, advances a host of mixed metaphors suggesting both battle and friendship. The promotional flyer foregrounds the name of Ximenes to enhance the ethos of the initiative, trading on Ximenes's reputation as a community organizer and human rights activist in New Mexico. The rhetorical construction of the audience as "businessmen, laborers, housewives, school teachers, and children" invokes gender and class differences as well as establishes a common identity as citizens of Albuquerque. A letter of support from García to Ximenes dated April 6, 1962, reports on the progress of Operation Amigo:

> I was very pleased to have been able to go to Albuquerque, New Mexico, in trying to set out your project, Operation Amigos [*sic*]. . . . I want to compliment you on the fine work that you are doing and hope that you will be able to continue on your fine type of work that is doing so much for our country. Believe it or not, I do envy you and sincerely wish that we were organized well enough on every level so that I could go and help out.[37]

García closes by expressing his regret that he has not had time to write more often or to launch a stronger fund-raising campaign for the Quito project. Interestingly, García also underscores the fact that the primary concern of the Alliance for Progress in Latin America was not for Latin America itself but for securing U.S. national interests and borders from Communism. As Ximenes would come to realize, the international altruism in South and Central America extended only as far as U.S. interests and investments.

An article dated April 26, 1962, in the Quito newspaper *El Comercio*, reporting on the ceremony where the proceeds of Operation Amigo were presented to the local school, describes the efforts of Ximenes and the AGIF:

> El señor Vicente Ximenez agradecío por haber invitado a esta ceremonia, mencionando que la cooperación de la ciudadania de Albuquerque tiene un sentido particular, brindado con sinceridad y de todo corazón. Esta es una señal que las gentes de la América Latina se identifican con el afán de educar a los niños, dijó. [Mr. Vicente Ximenez [*sic*] is thankful for the invitation to this ceremony, noting that the cooperation of the citizenship of Albuquerque is particularly meaningful, given sincerely and whole-heartedly. This is a sign that the peoples of Latin America identify with one another in the effort to educate children, he said.][38]

Ximenes's fund-raising efforts achieved little more than political goodwill with local leaders. Ximenes struggled with the limits of his office. He began to recognize how unflagging dedication can narrow perception and lead to intellectual myopia and the loss of critical consciousness.

Although Ximenes's performance met and exceeded the expectations for his job description, he began feeling restless and distressed by the nebulous nature of the U.S. objectives in Latin America. Political unrest was fomenting not only in Cuba but throughout Central and South America through the 1960s. The political exigences, material conditions, and social injustices creating those tensions became increasingly apparent to Ximenes as he worked and traveled throughout South America. His contributions to alleviate the suffering and deprivation of Ecuador's *campesinos* seemed negligible beside the immensity of the need.

The historical and material conditions that eventually inspired the evolution of liberation theology through 1960s were evidenced to Ximenes during the tenure of his public service in Latin America. The interlocking system of unequal development of countries in the western hemisphere was a pernicious outcome of colonization and imperialism.[39] Problematically, the vested interests of the United States politically, economically, and militarily exploited rather than liberated Latin American peoples from historically rooted oppressions.

"Babaloo": Latinidad *and Icons of Disruption*

Anti-Communist hysteria, anti-Castro politics, and anti-immigrant (so-called wetback) policies conditioned public sentiments toward Latino populations throughout the Kennedy-Johnson years. The cultural stereotypes of the Southwest and *latinidad* that circulated throughout Cold War American popular culture spanned a broad spectrum of representation, exoticizing, romanticizing, as well as demonizing the Latino as Other. Characters such as the hot-tempered Cuban band leader Ricky Ricardo, the shiftless Frito Bandito, and bumbling José Jiménez (the homespun spaceman) indexed the negative, racist tropes of the era.

The Mercury astronaut skit, performed by comic Bill Dana, which popularized the cliché "my name . . . José Jiménez," first appeared on national television on the wildly successful *Steve Allen Show* in 1959. The skit was a lampoon of the Mercury space program at the dawn of the U.S.-Russia space race, historically coinciding with Castro's Communist revolution in Cuba. The inept astronaut who spoke with a heavy Spanish accent represented the antithesis of the robust, competent, and articulate American astronaut, an icon upon which the United States rested its desires and anxieties over questions of global dominance. The clumsy Spanish-speaking caricature took on a life of its own over the following decades. The figure of José Jiménez was later popularized in the 1980s film *The Right Stuff*, as well as the 1990s HBO series *From the Earth to the Moon*.[40]

The attitude of the Cold War mythos toward *la raza* covered a host of conflicting anxieties and desires. The collective ethos constructed by popular culture of *latinidad* (inept, inarticulate, irrational) stood in dialectical opposition to the constructed ethos of the white Anglo-Saxon Protestant majority (temperate, competent, rational, articulate). If not laughable, icons of popularized Latino culture were cast as something dark and exotic such as the black cartoon character known as Memin Pinguin from the comic books published in Mexico since the 1940s.[41]

Racial ambivalence circulated across both sides of the border. The stigmatization of dark-skinned peoples in the pigmentocracy of New World social structures was not limited to the United States. The twentieth-century racist attitudes toward *mestizo*, indigenous, and African-origin peoples in the United States were equally entrenched in Latin American and Mexico. Whiteness as a trope of inclusion was not restricted to Anglo-European New World cultures, and these racial hierarchies endure into the twenty-first century, as well.

Kennedy's Alliance for Progress launched a countervailing force against the perceived threats of Communism and the shadow ecology creeping into U.S. society across the country's southernmost borders. President Kennedy proposed the Alliance for Progress in March 1961 to enhance the political, social, and economic framework of Latin American communities. On March 13, 1961, before the ambassadors of Latin American in the East Room of the White House, President Kennedy delivered these remarks: "Therefore I have called all people of the hemisphere to join in a new Alliance for Progress—*Alianza para Progreso*—a vast cooperative effort, unparalleled in magnitude and nobility of purpose to satisfy the basic needs of the American people for homes, work and land, health and schools—*techo, trabajo y tierra, salud y escuela*."[42] His speech was broadcast throughout the western hemisphere in English, Spanish, Portuguese, and French. Kennedy's new initiative promoted land and tax reform throughout Latin America as well as democratic government and the free market. Enhanced by the star appeal of the First Lady, Kennedy sought to stir a new level of commitment within the American public for his Alliance for Progress initiatives. With Jackie at his side, charming audiences with her fluency in Spanish, Kennedy tried to undo the political damage to the presidency and U.S. international authority that had resulted from Nixon's strained relations with Latin America during the Eisenhower administration.

Over the next few months, President Kennedy and Jackie visited Puerto Rico, Mexico, Venezuela, and Colombia, retracing the ill-fated diplomatic trip of former vice president Richard Nixon and his wife, Pat, three years earlier. Kennedy convened a meeting with all six presidents of the Central American governments in Costa Rica. Further extending pan-American goodwill and a spirit of international exchange, the Kennedys hosted dignitaries from Brazil, Panama, Colombia, Honduras, Chile, and Bolivia. The opulent gift exchanges between various Latin American countries and the White House included priceless relics such as a silver chest from Peru, a fifteenth- century pre-Columbian bowl from Panama, a triptych from Chile, an 1832 bronze relief of Simón Bolívar from Venezuela, and gold jewelry from Mexico. The bold vision and rhetorical scope of Kennedy's Alliance for Progress program, however, foundered after the regal ceremonies and public displays. While it promoted a heightened national interest in Latin America, the program ultimately proved unsustainable through the regime changes that occurred within and outside the United States. The Alliance for Progress in Latin America lost rhetorical momentum after the assassination of John F. Kennedy.

Héctor García's November 29, 1963, letter to Ximenes, stationed in Ecuador with the USAID program, disclosed the news of the president's death. García laments:

> Dear Chente, At this time there is nothing much more than I can say concerning the assassination of our President. I will say, though, that the people from Texas are generally to blame. Personally, I even feel a great amount of guilt since I believe that we could have gotten this state to be a liberal state and that the racial discrimination, hatred, and prejudice, would have never created the favorable climate in this state for the assassination of our beloved friend and president. However, I have tried very hard as any human could, but you know the results. Right now we are not thinking of anything else, but mourn his death. Everybody in sadden [sic]. I am angry and bitter that this state contributed to his death.[43]

If Ximenes was restless to return to the United States during the honeymoon period of the Kennedy administration, he was even more determined to get home in the dark days following the president's death. Caught in the cross fire of a failed mission to protect the country from Communism, Ximenes wanted more than a midlevel overseas administrative appointment. Helping Lyndon Johnson secure a legitimate claim to the presidency would become Ximenes's ticket home.

"Shotgun Wedding": The (Illegitimate)
Presidency of Lyndon B. Johnson

The rage and rancor that had greeted Kennedy and Johnson in Dallas on their southwestern campaign trail on November 4, 1960, hung like a shadow, an omen over the swearing-in ceremony of Lyndon Baines Johnson on November 22, 1963. Just three years before Kennedy's assassination, Johnson had faced the bitter resistance within his home state. Conservative Democrats had stormed the lobby of the Adolphus Hotel, where Johnson was scheduled to deliver his campaign speech in November 1960.

Johnson's fellow Texas Democrats and Republican counterparts had greeted him during the final days of the 1960 campaign carrying placards reading, "LBJ Sold Out to Yankee Socialists," "Let's Beat Judas," and "LBJ—Counterfeit Confederate."[44] Even Lady Bird Johnson had been physically attacked by one of the women protesters while the angry crowd spit on both Johnson and his wife. A police escort was dispatched to the Dallas hotel as television cameras recorded the violent reception. The hostility that Johnson had encountered in November 1960 resurfaced in 1963 immediately before and after the assassination of President Kennedy, challenging his legitimacy and loyalty to the Dixiecrats who had supported his ascent to power over the previous two decades.

The November 1963 trip to Texas by Kennedy and Johnson was intended to mend growing rivalries between the Texas Democratic Party and the national party and assuage the rancor that had been dramatically demonstrated in Dallas in 1960. Kennedy wanted to be sure of reelection in 1964, and the Kennedy-Johnson ticket would need to carry Texas. The Texas Democratic liberals and conservatives were still feuding when Kennedy and Johnson arrived in Dallas on November 22. The violent rampage Johnson had encountered three years before was still fresh in their memories. When a White House aide expressed concern their about plans for a procession by presidential motorcade through downtown Dallas in light of the hostile Texas political climate, Kennedy remarked, "if somebody wanted to shoot me from a window with a rifle, nobody can stop it, so why worry about it?"[45]

Johnson was very careful to establish the legitimacy of his new office immediately after the assassination. Later criticized as insensitive to Kennedy's widow and brother, Attorney General Robert F. Kennedy, Johnson decided to return immediately to Washington, D.C., with the body of the fallen president. Taking the oath was Johnson's first priority as soon as official word of Kennedy's death was released. Johnson was sworn in aboard *Air Force One* as thirty-sixth president of the United States at 2:38 P.M. CST in

Dallas with Lady Bird and Jackie at his side in her blood-splattered pink suit.[46] He took his oath not on the Bible but on Kennedy's missal that was found on Kennedy's bedside table on *Air Force One*. Johnson delivered his first presidential statement at 6:10 P.M. at Andrews Air Force Base upon his arrival in Washington, D.C. He later regretted his brief remarks for their overly formal and impersonal tone. Unger and Unger summarize the events of that day:

> Fate had suddenly made him the world's most powerful man, with no chance to adjust, to plan, to consider. Other presidents had succeeded through their predecessor's death, but none, since Theodore Roosevelt sixty-two years before, after his assassination. But one thing could not be gainsaid: plagued by doubt until the end that he would even retain second place for four more years, Lyndon B. Johnson was now president of the United States.[47]

Becoming president by a tragic turn of fate distressed and haunted Johnson from the moment he took the oath of office. According to Unger and Unger, he was so concerned about how Kennedy's death would affect the outcome of the 1964 presidential election that the deeply troubled new president called the treasurer of the DNC, Richard Maguire, upon his return to Washington, D.C., on the night of November 22 to discuss "what we need to do and how we need to do it."[48] Just as he feared, Johnson would struggle beneath the weight of Kennedy's shadow and the mythos of Camelot throughout his new administration.

The need for some vision, some imaginary fiction equal to or greater than Kennedy's New Frontier was the principal rhetorical imperative for rebranding and reconstructing Johnson's administration, which was widely regarded as illegitimate. Reflecting on his contested place in history, Johnson later confided to his biographer Doris Kearns Goodwin:

> I took the oath. I became President. But for millions of Americans I was still illegitimate, a naked man with no presidential covering, a pretender to the throne, an illegal usurper. And then there was Texas, my home, the home of both the murder and the murder of the murderer. And then there were the bigots and the dividers and the Eastern intellectuals who were waiting to knock me down before I could even stand up. The whole thing was almost unbearable.[49]

Johnson's designs on the presidency and his carefully constructed political career over the previous thirty years, the calculations of the same savvy politician that had been inducted into the facetious Sophistry Club at Southwest

Texas State Teachers College in 1930 (chapter 1), simply did not include this tainted place in history. If anything fueled the grandiosity of what would become the rhetorical construction of the "Great Society," it was this desire and this unrelenting drive to secure his place in history and to replace the fleeting utopian fiction of Kennedy's unrealized vision. Kennedy's New Frontier would never be enacted and tested in the many ways that Johnson's Great Society would be extended and critiqued.

"¡Seguro Que Sí! ¡Lyndon Johnson es Mi Buen Amigo!"

The new administration under Lyndon B. Johnson ushered in a shift of priorities and political focus, from a preoccupation with the New Frontier toward a reaffirmation of New Deal policies through Great Society programs and policies. Ximenes and his constituency would be direct beneficiaries of Johnson's new administration. By early 1964 Ximenes, who had stayed on as a program economist with USAID in Quito, Ecuador, after the Kennedy assassination, was becoming increasingly disenchanted with his middle-management position, unable to bring about significant change in the program. He was on the front lines facing the desperate conditions of communities throughout Latin America. Ximenes began recognizing firsthand the limits of Kennedy's Alliance for Progress program.

In the wake of Kennedy's assassination, Ximenes expressed his professional restlessness and personal frustration to Héctor García in a series of letters resulting in García's attempt to intervene on Ximenes's behalf with the new Johnson administration. As an eyewitness to U.S. programs in Latin America, Ximenes wanted more influence over policy-making functions. Ximenes's desire to leave the USAID program and join the Johnson administration was eventually heard by key decision makers through García. The mechanism for obtaining a position with more national influence came six months later in June 1964 with a summons to Ximenes from Washington, D.C., to lead the Viva Johnson campaign.

Ximenes's key role in this political landscape of 1964 was to bring out the Latino vote that would keep Johnson in the White House. Johnson wanted an overwhelming victory over Goldwater to repair the legacy of his ill-gotten presidency and secure his place in history. However, the New Left was becoming increasingly disenchanted with Johnson. African American voters did not trust him after his mixed reception of the Mississippi Freedom Party delegates at the 1964 Democratic National Convention. The youth voters rallying for free speech in universities across the nation and protesting against the Vietnam War did not trust him. Burdened by the almost beatified shadow of the young and promising fallen president, Johnson could not exploit the halo effect of the Kennedy administration or leverage his incumbent status to win the bid. A DNC fact sheet, reporting on campaign organization, warned Johnson and his campaign managers of overconfidence.[50]

Johnson needed the support of the Latino electorate to win the presidential campaign. Even more importantly, he wanted to legitimize his presidency. As in the 1960 campaign, Johnson once again relied on Héctor García to deliver. Along with other key leaders, Héctor García had forged a political climate and a national agenda for Mexican Americans through the Viva Kennedy Clubs. Many of their goals for policy changes and high-level appointments had not been realized in the Kennedy administration. As a result, Johnson faced a disappointed and disengaged Latino public going into the campaign.

Moreover, Johnson's successful passage of the 1964 Civil Rights Act responded, in part, to the demands of African American constituencies but still had not addressed some of most pressing civil rights issue for Mexican Americans. The poll tax and other infringements on voting rights such as literacy tests remained intact, impairing full civic participation by U.S. minority groups. Poor and working-class Mexican Americans, like African Americans, were negatively affected by poll taxes and literacy tests. In the minds of many Mexican Americans, the promises made during the 1960 Kennedy-Johnson campaign had been overlooked, if not altogether dismissed.

As the campaign season fired up in the summer 1964, Johnson faced an election about which Latino voters (especially those outside Texas) were politically indifferent, if not divided and ambivalent. Johnson needed some unifying theme and organizing force to keep Mexican Americans as voting Democrats. "Late Organization, Overconfidence Feared" was the summary opinion of a subhead on the DNC fact sheet. Johnson was informed on all sides of the need for mobilization and coordination to guarantee the victory of the Johnson-Humphrey ticket in November.

The call for Ximenes came in June 1964 from the U.S. ambassador in Ecuador. The U.S. embassy in Quito had received a message dispatched from President Johnson through DNC director Craig Raupe.[51] Ximenes was flown to Washington, D.C., from Quito to meet with Raupe. Ximenes did not know why he had been called. Unknown to Ximenes, Héctor García and other prominent leaders had been lobbying Johnson to revive the Viva Kennedy Clubs for the 1964 election. Rudy Ramos had served as the point person for the AGIF's lobbying efforts and was less than enthusiastic to learn that Ximenes was recruited for the post. By the summer of 1964, the presidential campaign was off to a rocky start. The Democratic National Convention in Atlantic City had been a mixed success for Johnson with the Freedom Summer demonstrations of the growing African American civil rights movement in the South and the fractious events surrounding the Mississippi Freedom Party delegates.[52] Johnson did not support the Freedom Party, steering clear of endorsing the strategies of the black civil rights activists.

Héctor García warned Johnson that Goldwater was capturing Mexican American voters who had become disenchanted with the Kennedy-Johnson administration's failure to make substantial appointments and support programs benefiting Mexican Americans. García's warnings about the growing discontent of the Mexican American electorate in the wake of the Viva Kennedy campaign had been steadily directed to the DNC and the White House as early as 1961. García and the AGIF reminded Johnson that continued failure to recognize and support the contributions of Mexican Americans within the DNC would have negative consequences in the 1964 election.[53] Ximenes recounts:

> I was in Ecuador doing the job I had been trained to do at the University of New Mexico. My economic development and political science training made the assignment an enjoyable and productive one. The call for me to come to Washington came from the White House to the American Ambassador in Ecuador. I did not apply for the Viva Johnson campaign directorship. Dr. García placed my name in nomination and worked to get the appointment.[54]

Characteristically optimistic, Ximenes minimized his growing discontent with his USAID appointment in Ecuador. Emphasizing the positive outcomes of his efforts in Quito, Ximenes nevertheless wasted no time relocating himself and his family back to Washington, D.C. The constellation of experiences and spheres of influence that Ximenes brought to Johnson's presidential campaign would continue to grow as Ximenes leveraged his expanding political alacrity with the national profile of the AGIF.

¡Viva Johnson!: Selling the Dream

Ximenes came on board with the Johnson campaign in September 1964, arriving in Washington, D.C., after the volatile and dramatic events of Fannie Lou Hamer and the delegates of the Mississippi Freedom Party during the 1964 Democratic National Convention in Atlantic City.[55] Freedom Summer represented a searing indictment of Johnson's vacillating civil rights record. In his nomination acceptance speech, Johnson called for a mandate from the American people, advancing the vision of the Great Society as an imaginative fiction and counternarrative to the growing restlessness of the nation. Setting himself apart from Kennedy's 1960 campaign and the *topos* of the New Frontier Johnson charged, "This nation, this generation, in this hour, can begin to build the Great Society—a place where the meaning of man's life matches the marvels of man's labor."[56] The framing statement of Johnson's presidency and vision for his legitimized administration was launched in Atlantic City amid the cacophony of competing voices. In speaking to the convention, Johnson extended the Great Society vision that he had mapped out just months before in the University of Michigan commencement address (chapter 5). It was Ximenes's task to bring the voices of the Mexican American electorate to Johnson's turbulent campaign and to give witness to Johnson's Great Society vision.

Ximenes had been out of the country for three years and following national events through Quito newspapers, State Department communiqués, and letters from Héctor García. Ximenes was eager to join the political fray; but only after assuring that his family was safely relocated with him to Washington, D.C., did he hit the campaign trail for Johnson. Ximenes was willing to negotiate the ambiguities of working for the DNC after leaving his State Department position, but he was not willing to leave his family behind in Quito. Stumping for Johnson would demand that he be on the road in every corner of the nation for the next four months. Ximenes recalls, "I knew enough by then how the government works. If I didn't make sure my family made it back to the states before the election, the government might not have ever gotten around to helping us make the move home. There was no way I was going to leave them behind on just the word of the DNC or Craig Raupe."[57] International relocations were costly in terms of both time and money. As he demanded, however, the government arranged the Ximeneses' move back to the States. As soon as he had settled his family into their new home in Washington, D.C., Ximenes was on the road organizing Viva Johnson Clubs all over the country.

Ximenes realized immediately that there was no template or master plan for establishing the Viva Johnson Clubs. Whereas Héctor García, Carlos McCormick, and the AGIF leaders had provided the time, energy, and imagination for the organization of the Viva Kennedy Clubs for the 1960 presidential campaign, none of these political efforts were codified for future campaigns. Ximenes quickly discovered that the Viva Kennedy Clubs had lacked any real formal structure. García had simply grafted the Viva Kennedy Clubs onto the AGIF organization across the county and let the clubs sprawl like wild vines. The DNC had nothing concrete to offer Ximenes in terms of direction. Johnson and Raupe gave no specific instructions or guidance.

Furthermore, no records had been kept of the 1960 Viva Kennedy Clubs by the DNC. Other than the enduring goodwill of García and the national AGIF, Ximenes was starting from square one. Ximenes set up an office in Washington, D.C., and went to work.

Over the next three months, Ximenes implemented a highly coordinated organizational structure for the Viva Johnson Clubs.[58] As noted by the October 9, 1964, *Congressional Quarterly Fact Sheet*, there were a number of significant contrasts between the 1960 and 1964 Democratic campaigns. One of the most striking differences of the 1964 campaign was the formalization of the minority subcommittees. The 1964 Democratic campaign enhanced the professionalism and coordination of the organization and, at the same time, institutionalized the mobilization of a number of ethnic interest groups.[59]

The DNC eventually constructed an elaborate organizational plan with intricate reporting lines across national regions and interest groups. Ximenes reported to Craig Raupe, coordinator of the DNC's "Nationalities" division. Louis Martin, DNC deputy chairman and editor of the *Chicago Daily Defender*, provided oversight for what the DNC labeled the "Negroes and Nationalities" (an umbrella term for all non-WASP groups). According to the DNC there were seventeen nationality groups: Italian, Polish, Mexican, Greek, German, and Puerto Rican were the most prominent. Ximenes remembers:

> Louis Martin was considered black. But Louis Martin was really Luis Martín. He was also Hispanic. He had a Spanish surname. His family was from Cuba. We both had a good laugh about the DNC and their ethnic labels. Louis Martin was the most powerful black in the nation at that time, the Deputy of the Democratic Party Committee. It just never occurred to anyone to recognize his full cultural heritage.[60]

Louis Martin became Ximenes's strongest ally within the DNC, helping him navigate the national organization and Washington, D.C., insider politics. Whereas the DNC had squarely dismissed the Mexican American electorate during the 1960 campaign, leaders like Louis Martin helped to bring Ximenes and Mexican American voters into the organizational structure.

Ximenes began mobilizing the Spanish-speaking electorate by recruiting prominent leaders as cochairs of the Viva Johnson Clubs including Congressmen Edward Roybal (California) and Henry B. González (Texas) as well as Senator Montoya (New Mexico). Héctor García helped to manage the grassroots efforts in Texas while Bert Corona organized in California.[61] Ximenes organized Viva Johnson Clubs from coast to coast, distributing over two million pieces of literature.[62] The November 1964 AGIF *News Bulletin* provides this portrait of the Viva Johnson campaign: "Through the VIVA JOHNSON Clubs, the campaign will be taken to big and small communities. The Spanish-speaking women will be asked to canvass their neighborhoods on behalf of the Johnson-Humphrey ticket. Viva Johnson materials have been sent to all parts of the country. Posters, pins and bumper stickers are evident in political rallies throughout the country. Large Viva Johnson posters have been evident in nation-wide news photo releases."[63] Ximenes offered additional reports to Raupe over the course of the campaign indicating that he had distributed three hundred thousand Johnson-Humphrey brochures in Spanish.

The *Johnson y Humphrey* brochure relies on a mixture of genre meshing and code-mixing. The cover images include a photo of former president John F. Kennedy with these single Spanish words: *Continuemos. Adelante. Viva.* (We continue onward and alive.) Below the portrait of the fallen president in his prime, presumably seated in the White House, are photos of Johnson and Humphrey on the campaign trail with the words "Johnson y Humphrey" in one column and the words "Vote por Johnson para Presidente" in another. The inside contents of the brochure include a listing of Johnson's appointments of over fifty Spanish-speaking leaders in the Department of State, the Agency of International Development, the White House, the Department of Justice, federal courts, the U.S. Postal Service, and the Department of the Interior.[64] This Viva Johnson brochure relies largely on enthymeme, exploiting the halo effect of the beloved President Kennedy, an almost beatified martyr for many Latino voters, and at the same time advancing the suppressed premise that distinguishes Johnson's presidency from Kennedy's disappointing track record for awarding high-level Mexican American appointments.

Ximenes also issued daily news releases and launched promotional announcements on radio stations across the nation on Spanish and English programs. Volunteers made phone calls and canvassed door to door. Ximenes informed Raupe in his memo report that the Viva Johnson Club network comprised "few prima donnas" and many "real workers."[65] Ximenes was especially adept at adapting to diverse ethnolinguistic contexts. He was capable of employing a wide repertoire of discursive strategies, code-switching between English and Spanish as well as Tex-Mex as a third linguistic code, depending on his audiences. On the campaign trail throughout the Southwest in cities such as Las Cruces (New Mexico), Tucson (Arizona), Stockton (California), and Del Rio (Texas), Ximenes unabashedly employed regional varieties of Spanish commonly called Tex-Mex or Spanglish as a solidarity marker between himself and the Mexican American constituency. His adept use of Tex-Mex and Spanglish signaled to voters that he was an insider, a member of *la raza*. However, had he employed either of these registers in his official capacity as program economist in Quito or as director of the Viva Johnson campaign, Ximenes's political cachet and social influence would have been significantly diminished since these linguistic varieties carry little prestige outside the border regions of the United States. Understanding which linguistic codes to use in which contexts reflected Ximenes's exceptional communicative competence and keen sense of the rhetorical situation and sociolinguistic constraints.

Ximenes understood the range of linguistic choices he needed to employ to reach diverse stakeholders because of his experiences mobilizing for the AGIF in New Mexico. Ximenes reflects:

> I sometimes wrote my speeches to the GI Forum convention audience in correct English and switched to Tex Mex for my extemporaneous and humorous comments. In Ecuador when speaking before high level officials I sometimes wrote my speech in Spanish and switched to English for extemporaneous and humorous comments. In Panama where everyone spoke English I always spoke and made presentations in Spanish with Tex Mex for extemporaneous comments. The Panamanians were well versed in Tex Mex.
>
> I organized Viva Johnson Clubs in all states except the South and Northeast. New York was the exception. I was involved in most of the GI Forum organization efforts outside of Texas. I followed up with the Viva Johnson Clubs in all the GI Forum states plus some non-GI Forum states. I adopted the same method of proper English to the mixed audiences and a good dose of Tex Mex to remind the brothers where they came from. I enjoyed the many speeches I made. I was always at ease before any audience and felt that I could win a preponderant percentage of the persons to my point of view. It never occurred to me that I was using language to promote the ideas and programs I convinced people to adopt.
>
> I do not recall that I intentionally studied the effects on the audience I addressed. It sort of came naturally. I know of some Hispanics that worked in South and Central America that claimed that they encountered prejudice against the Tex Mex language and avoided the use in their activities. I was always up front that I was a Mexican American representing the United States of North America. Once I cleared that hurdle, the Latinos of South and Central America allowed me into their inner circle.
>
> When I addressed the poor people of the barrios or the campesinos, a good Tex Mex joke that involved English and Spanish would open doors to a dialogue with them. In fact some of the Tex Mex jokes and stories had

their origin in the Aztec and Maya civilization. I was familiar with the loss of the land and land grants and so were the campesinos [people from the countryside]. I used to tell a story about a couple of rich ranchers having drinks at a bar when a campesino walks in with a goat. One rancher says to the other I bet I can buy that goat for little or nothing. The rancher says to the campesino, "I will give you five dollars for the goat" The campesino says, "No la vendo." The rancher says to the bartender give the campesino a drink. The rancher now says I will give you ten dollars for the goat. The campesino says, "No la vendo." The rancher says give the campesino a drink. The rancher says, "I will give you twelve dollars for the goat." The campesino says, "No la vendo." And he walks out with his goat, saying, "Thanks I just came in for a drink." That campesino joke was a standard one for me in Tex Mex country and the poor in any country.[66]

Exercising the strategy of "transcultural citizenship," Ximenes effectively found ways to represent himself to Spanish-speaking working-class constituencies including Latin American Spanish-speaking officials as well to Anglo English-speaking audiences.[67] As Juan Guerra notes in his essay "Emerging Representations, Situated Literacies, and the Practice of Transcultural Repositioning," this strategy must be both consciously and intuitively practiced in order to move comfortably and with authority "between and among different languages and dialects, different social classes, different cultural and artistic forms."[68]

As illustrated by Ximenes's use of *el chiste* (the joke) as a solidarity marker, this communicative act functions as an enthymeme, relying on the audience as insiders to supply the suppressed premises. In the aforementioned joke, the audience expects the *campesino* to outwit the wealthy *rancheros* because they know that *los ricos* (the rich) underestimate his savvy command of the rhetorical situation. The suppressed premise of this enthymeme is the unspoken dominant stereotypes that characterize the poor as unsophisticated and socially inept. In the end, however, it is the *campesino* who gets the better of *los ricos* and walks away with the proverbial goat. By telling this tale, Ximenes enhances his ethos with his target audience, demonstrating identification and leveling of the political playing field. Ximenes uses humor in ways highly reminiscent of one of Mexico's most celebrated film icons, Cantínflas (Mario Moreno), by poking fun at the rich and powerful without their knowledge and masterfully manipulating the art of subtle irony.

Ximenes and his campaign leaders established over three hundred Viva Johnson Clubs throughout the country in just four months. Significantly, Latina organizers contributed as much to the campaign efforts as male leaders by launching Viva Johnson Girls' Clubs around the nation. In addition to distributing thousands of pieces of campaign literature, Viva Johnson workers stumped for LBJ by delivering thousands of speeches.[69] In a report to Raupe on the Viva Johnson Clubs, Ximenes indicated that his organization had circulated over 2 million pieces of campaign literature; coordinated over 300 different speaking engagements; issued daily news releases through 25 radio stations and 20 newspapers; and distributed 200,000 bumper stickers, 260,000 campaign buttons, 300,000 Spanish brochures, and 150,000 posters.[70]

In East Los Angeles, Ximenes featured film star Cantínflas, who attracted over fifteen thousand participants to the Viva Johnson rally. Mexican Americans came out just to see the beloved icon of Mexico's 1940s and 50s cinema. Cantínflas, considered a combination of Charlie Chaplin and Groucho Marx, played roles that lampooned the wealthy and powerful, especially the police and the government. In *Cantínflas and the Chaos of Mexican Modernity*, Jeffrey Pilcher contends that Cantínflas reflected the archetypal underdog who consistently prevails over his more powerful adversaries using trickery and a playful wit. Pilcher argues that Cantínflas represents an iconic image of a transitional Mexico, a potent emblem for the poor and disenfranchised. Cantínflas portrayed someone able to exercise a voice against oppression. For example, in the film *El Analfabeto (The Illiterate)*, Cantínflas played the role of an illiterate peasant who finds a way to exercise authority over language by whatever means possible. Cantínflas was a hero to the dispossessed.[71] His last movie, *Pepe*, was filmed in 1960 with a star of American popular culture, Bing Crosby. Although his career was on the decline by 1964 in Mexico, Cantínflas was still revered by Mexican Americans and represented a powerful symbol of resistance.

When Ximenes called Cantínflas by phone to invite him to stump for Johnson in Los Angeles, Cantínflas responded without reservation, "¡Seguro que sí! ¡Lyndon Johnson *es mi buen amigo!*"[72] Cantínflas believed that there was something authentic and trustworthy in Johnson. His enduring affection for Johnson extended back some fifteen years, a fraternal bond stemming from Johnson's advocacy on behalf of the fallen Mexican American soldier Félix Longoria (chapter 2). The poignancy of that event still tugged at Cantínflas's heartstrings and moved him to lend his voice to the Viva Johnson campaign. Cantínflas received no speaker fees, only airfare and hotel accommodations for making an appearance on behalf of Johnson. Reflecting on the moment, Ximenes remembers, "Cantínflas's rally was the biggest one Johnson had during the campaign. It was economical and targeted the Mexican Americans of Los Angeles. The Democratic National Committee could not be more surprised at how quickly we could move to obtain a goal."[73]

Other celebrities who stumped for Johnson included Vikki Carr and Ricardo Montalban, who delivered radio spots for the Viva Johnson campaign. Ximenes, acting as a cultural broker and insider, knew exactly which Latino figures in popular culture would resonate with the Mexican American electorate. Moreover, he discovered the various effective means of persuasion as he grew the Viva Johnson Clubs. Ximenes himself delivered over one hundred speeches in less than two months in Texas, Arizona, Colorado, New Mexico, California, Kansas, and Illinois.[74] The results of his rapid voter mobilization plans were staggering. Ximenes opened the eyes of the DNC and demonstrated the power of the Mexican American electorate. He remembers, "The second most effective campaign effort was a message from Ricardo Montalban in support of Johnson/Humphrey. English and Spanish records were distributed to all the Hispanic radio stations. We bought radio time from both the English and Spanish radio stations. It was economical and targeted to the Mexican Americans. It required only myself to put on this campaign program."[75]

The Goldwater campaign managers stood up and took notice of the power of Latino voters as well. They established countercampaigns targeting Mexican American voters called "Amigos de Goldwater" and "Arriba Goldwater." The Republican camp even advanced the fact that Goldwater's vice presidential candidate, William Miller, was Catholic in hopes of luring devout Spanish-speaking constituents to vote for their candidates. Amigos de Goldwater cast the Johnson camp as radical Communist sympathizers. The Johnson campaign, in turn, played on Goldwater's conservative civil rights and labor rights record, "characterizing the Arizona senator as a right-wing extremist bent on eliminating Social Security and unleashing the atomic bomb."[76] Ximenes recognized Johnson's persistent struggle to break free of the enduring enchantment with Kennedy among Mexican American voters. According to Ximenes, Johnson courted the Spanish-speaking electorate in 1964 more vigorously and passionately than Kennedy did in 1960. Ximenes reflects:

> About one million newspapers were printed by *La Opinion de New York* in Spanish. On the weekend before the election I had a chartered plane to deliver the newspapers to all the Viva Johnson Clubs. The entire newspaper was devoted to Johnson and what he had done for the Mexican American and Hispanics. All the newspapers were delivered by mostly GI Forum volunteers. Johnson had passed the 1964 Civil Rights Bill before the election and promised all of the war on poverty programs that appealed to the poor of the nation that caused the election to be a Johnson campaign.

Kennedy never really recognized the Mexican American like Johnson did. He was never able to mount programs that dealt directly with the Mexican American and he never recognized the existence of the large pool of voters. He seemed to, like most politicians from the Northeast, turn their attention to Mexico, South and Central America. So Kennedy did not directly help the Mexican American or recognize him, but he remained a hero after his death and Johnson who did everything possible for the Mexican American got stuck with the Viet Nam war. History, however, will eventually be kind to Lyndon Johnson when the accomplishments that changed America forever are recognized.[77]

As Ximenes later noted, Johnson's intervention with the AGIF in 1949 on behalf of the World War II soldier Private Félix Longoria, who was denied burial in Three Rivers, Texas, had helped to secure his reputation as a friend and ally of *mexicanos*; collective memory of Johnson's role in that incident endured north as well as south of the border more than ten years after the historic event.

Continuemos, Adelante, Viva: La Raza *Carries On*

Mexican American voters cast their ballots for Johnson in unprecedented numbers. Robert Canino, a Viva Johnson Club organizer in Austin, Texas, detailed the results of his organizational headquarters in a report to the DNC. Canino notes, "This headquarters, located in the heart of East Austin, is conveniently situated for out-of-town, county, and state visitors. It is the first ever to be located where most work is needed. Negros, Anglos, and Latin Americans have come by to pick up all kind of Spanish and English campaign material and literature available. It had its doors opened from 8:00 A.M. to 11:00 P.M. daily."[78] Ximenes likewise provided a detailed report on his activities as national coordinator of the Viva Johnson campaign. According to Ximenes, in precincts across the nation that were predominantly Mexican American, voters came out "from 10 to 1, to 20 to 1 in favor of Johnson."[79] Ximenes tried to impress upon DNC officials the importance of maintaining the Viva Johnson organization. In a memo to Raupe, he argues his case emphatically:

Perhaps more important was the fact that more Mexican-Americans voted this time than in 1960. For this reason it is important that we keep the Viva Johnson clubs supplied with material and a once a month newsletter to the members. As soon as the tabulations are in, I will prove that the Mexican-Americans have a better voting record as a percentage of registration than any other group in the nation.[80]

Ximenes urged the DNC to continue making media contact with the Mexican American electorate through national newspapers and radio promotional advertisements. He encouraged the incorporation of Mexican American women leaders into the DNC organizational structure. He asked for recognition of the AGIF and the League of United Latin American Citizens in the Viva Johnson efforts. And finally, Ximenes called for the establishment of a cabinet-level position for a Mexican American representative as well as the appointment of Mexican Americans to the emerging War on Poverty programs.

However, Ximenes's recommendations to Raupe and the DNC for ways to institutionalize the Viva Johnson structure and mobilize Mexican Americans for future campaigns were ultimately ignored. Ximenes recalls: "After the November election, it was just business as usual in Washington. For me, it was all a waiting game. I took my family on a vacation after the election, and then waited around for word from the Johnson people about an appointment. I didn't hear anything for over three months. But I was still on the DNC payroll so I didn't worry too much."[81] The DNC had matched Ximenes's civil service salary as a program economist in Ecuador. He felt confident that Johnson would not forget him or the Mexican American constituency that had helped to keep him in the White House.

Political payback for leading the successful Viva Johnson Clubs was not assured, however. Vicente and María did receive invitations to the inaugural ball at the Mayflower Hotel, a thrilling star-studded event for both of them. "I kept thinking of my father that night and wishing he had lived to share that moment with me," Ximenes recounts.[82] Ximenes considered the occasion not only a landmark for his own life but one for the Mexican American communities he had served for over a decade. The luster would quickly fade, however. There were no contracts advanced or agreements in place for job placement at the close of the election. There were no more phone calls from the White House asking for his assistance. There was just a lot of waiting. "It was a gentleman's agreement, you could say. I didn't ask for an appointment up front. I just trusted and hoped that a job would be waiting for me on the other end of the line. That's just how things are done in Washington," Ximenes explains.[83]

Without a doubt, the promise of advancing his career with a cabinet-level position had been a motivating reason for taking the Viva Johnson position. Ximenes hoped that a White House appointment would be forthcoming. He was retained on the payroll of the DNC through January 1965, waiting. Like with the Kennedy administration, however, Johnson did not make good on his promises to the Mexican American electorate. Once again, all of the prestigious appointments went to the established insiders. "Johnson just kept all the people he already had in place after taking over the Kennedy administration," observes Ximenes.[84] Ximenes and García were disappointed that the president failed once again to appoint any Mexican Americans to prominent cabinet positions.

Ximenes remained hopeful in spite of the fact he had no official purpose or duties after the ballots had been counted in November. The months passed, and by January Ximenes was doing what he disliked the most—nothing. He and his family were just sitting and waiting in Washington, D.C., for news. Ximenes turned to Louis Martin, the president's DNC campaign manager and White House aide. Never one to wait patiently for opportunity to come his way, Ximenes tried knocking on the president's door. He had similarly penned a letter on November 11, 1960, to then president-elect John F. Kennedy in the wake of the highly successful Viva Kennedy campaign. He had angled for a position with the Federal Housing Administration without success in 1960.[85] Instead, Ximenes had been offered an appointment by the Kennedy administration in the USAID program in Ecuador. It was déjà vu in 1965. In a February 15 memo to Louis Martin, Ximenes writes:

> The Mexican-American leadership needs to confer with President Johnson on the war on poverty program. . . . It is not my intention to ask for preferential treatment, although actually that is what is needed since the Mexican-American is the main problem in large areas of the United States. . . . The meeting with the President could be organized along the lines of a briefing. I can be the coordinator and brief the participants. . . . It would not be a speech session, but rather an intensive report to the President on the Mexican-American—where he is and where he wants to go. . . . The one thing I wish to avoid is to have a meeting to shake hands and take pictures and allow that to be the end result.
>
> There is no need for me to tell you of the political importance of such a proposed meeting with the President. The President who taught school to the Mexican-Americans of Cotulla, Texas is expected by those same people to call us in for consultation on our problems.[86]

Appealing to their shared experiences as former teachers in the "Mexican" schools of South Texas, Ximenes hoped to stir Johnson's sympathies. Seeking to move the president toward a stronger advocacy stance on behalf of Mexican Americans, Ximenes sought to invoke the power of deliberative rhetoric.

Given strong evidence and a reasonable proposal of action items, Ximenes felt certain that Johnson would deliver on his unmet promises to Mexican Americans. Ximenes's February 15, 1965, memo tries to carve out that deliberative space. However, the plight of the Mexican American constituency was not at the top of the president's list of civil rights priorities.

Ultimately Ximenes would not be given the opportunity to convene the proposed meeting with the president as suggested in his memo. His audacious act of instrumental rhetoric failed, but not completely. With the support of Louis Martin, Ximenes would chair the White House "Great Society Conference" four months later in Washington, D.C., in June 1965, opening the doors to a small group of Mexican American leaders from across the nation. As he postured for high-level appointments, Ximenes coordinated the Great Society Conference, staged on June 1, 1965, in Washington, D.C. Seeking to establish visibility and credibility nationally, Ximenes used the Viva Johnson platform to leverage the political clout of Mexican Americans in the new Great Society. Ximenes recounts:

> After the inauguration the jockeying for jobs and appointments starts in earnest. I relied on Louis Martin to get my resume before the committees reviewing bios. In the meantime I was asked to join Sargent Shriver in setting up the War on Poverty programs. Part of my job was to visit community action programs and make sure that maximum feasibility is employed in the jobs for minorities.
>
> I was embarrassed by the fact I could not help others get some decent appointments in the Johnson administration. I had a telephone and a desk at Shriver's office and in a fit of frustration I asked Louis Martin of the DNC to help me get a conference of the Viva Johnson leaders to meet and question the Cabinet members of the administration. Within a couple of weeks I got the answer from Louis that the President agreed. It was a two day conference. The President invited about 200 of the Mexican American and Hispanic leaders and I submitted a list of the Viva Johnson leaders I wanted at the conference. Dr. Garcia did not attend. The Cabinet members filed in one or two at a time and spoke and answered questions from the audience.
>
> The newspapers did not give an inch of ink in D.C. and nothing reached the general population. It was up to the DNC to publicize the event, but as it turned out they did not do it. I gathered that the persons that attended like Albert Peña and Fran Flores and others were pleased with the conference. The final part of the agenda included a visit with President Johnson in the rose garden. We all congregated in the rose garden. I introduced the President and he then made a speech to the conferees. That too was not well publicized.[87]

Ximenes, who was working in the Office of Economic Opportunity under Sargent Shriver at the time, served as chair of the 1965 Great Society Conference. The guest list of two hundred names included leaders of the Viva Johnson Clubs and many of Ximenes's former alliances in the AGIF.[88] A brief report and photograph of the event featured in the *Democrat* reflects that the Mexican American participants from seven states attended the Great Society Conference to "hear top Administration officials discuss Federal programs that can help their areas."[89]

Carlos Rivera, special assistant to the executive director of the Equal Employment Opportunity Commission, noted in a follow-up letter to the White House that the Mexican American delegation to the Great Society Conference had submitted a series of resolutions to President Johnson. Rivera indicates that these resolutions represented "the thinking of the leaders of the Mexican-American community who are urging a fuller utilization of the talent resources of qualified Mexican-Americans in Government service today, in addition to tapping the wealth of potentially qualified individuals who have not previously been afforded the opportunity to serve their country."[90]

The AGIF news bulletin the *Forumeer* reported that the conference was held at the Mayflower Hotel in Washington, D.C., with an estimated sixty participants and representatives from both the League of United Latin American Citizens and the AGIF. Featured speakers included Vice President Hubert Humphrey, Secretary Willard Wirtz of the Department of Labor, Sargent Shriver of the Office of Economic Opportunity, and several other Johnson administration figures. President Johnson did not attend the event, but he greeted the delegates at the White House. In his remarks Johnson invoked a recurring trope of identification, reflecting on his memories of teaching at the Mexican school in Cotulla, Texas.[91] He had used this same rhetorical device in his January 1965 State of the Union address and in his historic Voting Rights Act speech in March.

The 1965 Great Society Conference represented something close to a consolation prize for the Viva Johnson leaders in the absence of substantive programs and appointments on behalf of the Spanish-speaking citizens who had voted Johnson back into the office of the presidency. It was not the watershed moment that Ximenes hoped it would be. The list of resolutions would be unceremoniously delivered and dismissed. In sum, the 1965 Great Society Conference served as not only a precursor for the 1967 White House Cabinet Committee Hearings in El Paso but as a cautionary tale for everything Ximenes did not want to repeat. The passive, top-down lecture format had proven ineffectual. The Mexican American representatives went away with little more than they had brought to the table. They had not changed the conversation of civil rights reform as they had hoped.

Once again, the White House cabinet-level appointments for Mexican Americans would not be delivered. The exasperation that Ximenes, Héctor P. García, and the AGIF leaders had felt in 1961, when Kennedy similarly overlooked them, was felt again in 1965. Little seemed to have changed. Token appointments to a few Mexican Americans were all that followed their herculean efforts. Ximenes soon realized that the key players put in place during the Kennedy administration would remain in power in Johnson's administration. Kennedy officials, as such, became Johnson's right-hand men because they knew how to enact the president's ambitious domestic programs and audacious foreign policies.[92] The rewards for the Viva Johnson campaign for Ximenes and his constituency would not follow, at least not yet.

Ximenes realized once again that the risks, ambiguities, and compromises of public life are great. There is no secure career path in politics. Ximenes knew the risks when he signed on for the Viva Johnson campaign, but he relied on what he believed was a secure and reliable connection to Johnson. As a peripheral supporter of the Johnson campaign, however, Ximenes was still not among Johnson's most intimate inner circle. Ximenes did not circulate with the powerful and elite Washington insiders. Moreover, Ximenes had been on the fringes of U.S. life and politics for over three years, placed in a remote and relatively impotent overseas appointment. There were many others in a more direct line of access to Johnson's favors. The big power brokers were white, rich, and politically proven. Nevertheless, Ximenes had the assurance, even if implicit, that his long-term association with Johnson since his Floresville days would resolve into a mutually beneficial alliance. How those intricate grassroots connections might evolve would remain unclear to Ximenes for another two years. Ximenes relied on his association with Louis Martin for support through the uncertainties of those postelection days. Ximenes recounts:

> Louis Martin turned out to be my best friend at the Democratic Party Headquarters. I was with Sargent Shriver and nothing had happened to recognize the Viva Johnson campaign leaders. I asked Louis to help me convene a meeting in Washington with the President and members of his Cabinet Committee and he followed up on my request and we had the first ever meeting of that type. The President invited about 200 of the Viva Johnson leaders. I conducted the two day conference that ended with a meeting with the President in the rose garden. First ever.[93]

The White House cabinet appointment that Ximenes and García hoped would follow did not come as expected. It was not only a blow to Ximenes's ego; the omission of any Mexican American leader in the Johnson cabinet was a political slap in the face for the entire AGIF constituency that had rallied so fervently for Johnson's reelection.

Disappointed that no definitive space would be given to Mexican American issues in the new administration, Ximenes accepted the position of an assistant inspector of the racially divided urban neighborhoods in the Bedford-Stuyvesant section of Brooklyn. Ximenes would report to cabinet official Sargent Shriver, chair of the Office of Economic Opportunity and director of Johnson's War on Poverty program. Ximenes managed the arrangements for Shriver's inspection trips to the various program sites and found himself living in conditions much like those of the constituencies he served. Shriver also sent him to checkpoints to inspect poverty programs in San Marcos, Texas, in advance of President Johnson and his high-profile public relations team.

The position provided Ximenes with a ground-floor view of Johnson's War on Poverty programs. All the glitter and glamor of the Viva Johnson campaign—rubbing elbows with Ricardo Montalban, hosting Cantínflas at the Los Angeles auditorium, chartering overnight jets across the nation to deliver campaign materials—were clearly over. It was not the plum job he was hoping for, and he would promptly apply to serve as assistant director of development planning for USAID in Panama only six months later. Ximenes recounts:

> I hung on with Shriver until August [1965] when I was convinced that the Mexican American and Hispanic political clout was no match for the powerful interests that dominated Washington politics and decided who received appointments, even though we had a friend in the White House. . . . I told Sargent Shriver that I had accepted a position with the Agency for International Development. Haddad, the Inspector General, was with me and Shriver threw us out of his office and claimed nobody had told him about my plans to leave the Poverty Program.
>
> The next day Shriver asked me to ride with him to the airport. Shriver apologized for the outburst and said he had just been too busy with the problems of the War on Poverty. I told him I had made a commitment to AID and he wished me well and we parted friends. In August 13, 1965 I was sworn in as Director for Program and Planning of the Agency for International Development's mission in Panama. Jack Vaughn was the chief of the Latin American Bureau and he put on a rather elaborate ceremony

at the State Department. He sent out press releases and made much of the fact I was returning to AID.[94]

The front page of the September 1965 issue of the *Forumeer* prominently featured the iconic photograph of President Johnson jauntily walking beside a smiling Ximenes, intimately positioned at LBJ's right hand, as they proceed through the colonnade of the White House portico. Reminiscent of the brothers-in-arms rhetoric of the past, Johnson's photo on page 1 of the *Forumeer* was followed by a statement from the president recounting the key moments in his history with Mexican American citizens. A message to the AGIF constituency on page 2 titled "LBJ's Message to National Convention" reads:

> The American GI Forum is an example of the best traditions of a free people to organize and contribute toward the goals of the Great Society. You have demonstrated that the Mexican Americans can join together and with malice toward none work hand in hand with the best of American society in search of a better life for all irrespective of race, color, creed, or national origin. I remember the long and hard road we have travelled together from the time of the Three Rivers Case and the Longoria family to my speech on voting rights. My good friend Dr. Hector Garcia and the GI Forum were in my thoughts when I spoke of my school teaching days in Cotulla, Texas. As long as I am president, I pledge to continue the efforts to help the sons and daughters of those parents who [*sic*] I taught and others like them. My best wishes for a successful convention. Lyndon B. Johnson.[95]

The rhetorical romance between the AGIF and Johnson was short lived, however (chapter 5). Ximenes and his family spent the next two years in Panama as he extended his service with the USAID program as deputy director in Panama City. Eventually, however, Ximenes's success with the Viva Johnson campaign would translate into the formation of the highest-level committee appointment for a Mexican American in the LBJ presidential administration and implementation of the first Cabinet Committee Hearings on Mexican American Affairs in the U.S. Southwest.

5. Constructing the "Great Society":
The Topoi of the 1967 El Paso Hearings

hroughout the three years he served in the U.S. Agency for International Development (USAID) in Ecuador, Ximenes struggled to promote a social democratic agenda. He was a middle-management bureaucrat teetering between two politically fractured nations. Ximenes found himself navigating rapidly changing political situations. The perennial problem of Latin American systems of governance, destabilized by countless incidents of military coup and ubiquitous government overthrows, was also strangely reflected in the violent transfer of power from the Kennedy to the Johnson administration. The disturbance ecologies sweeping through North and South America had translated into uncertain regime changes for both Latin America and the United States. In a 1964 USAID report titled "The Alliance for Progress in Ecuador," Ximenes represents the shape-shifting rhetorical situation; he argues:

> The Governments must utilize their resources in the best possible way. Ecuador must participate in a series of reforms which will give a sound name to the Alliance for Progress program. The country must carry out an agrarian reform plan which will alleviate the problem of the rural inhabitants. Fiscal and administrative reforms must be made in order to establish a system of efficient government service. Tax reforms must be enacted giving the country a fair and equitable system which at the same time will contribute to Alliance for Progress programs. The country must eliminate illiteracy and extend, in the shortest possible term, the benefits of elementary and primary instruction to everyone as well as increase the opportunity for secondary, technical, and superior education. . . . Each and every one of the Alliance for Progress programs receives resources from the United States as well as Latin American countries. The programs have been designed so that with the sacrifices of both nations a better way of life can be maintained and advanced.[1]

Drawing on traces of the presidential rhetoric of the late John F. Kennedy, Ximenes echoes the words of Kennedy regarding his new Latin American foreign policy. Ximenes's reiteration charges, "Let's get together in an Alliance for Progress, in a vast effort of cooperation without parallel in its magnitude and in the nobleness of its purposes in order to fulfill the fundamental needs of the people of America, the fundamental needs of home, work, health, and education."[2]

Echoing Kennedy's New Frontier epideictic discourse, Ximenes seeks to align the foundering USAID program in Latin America with Johnson's evolving domestic policy. Although Johnson had not yet delivered his Great Society speech when Ximenes penned this USAID report, Ximenes draws on the available means of persuasion of New Deal liberalism. The *topoi* of the city, the countryside, and the classroom are central organizing constructs or places for Ximenes's framing arguments. Ximenes describes Ecuador as a nation in crisis, struggling for self-rule under the shadow of a military regime.

Suffering from a downturn in the international demand for cacao and other export products such as bananas, the vicissitudes of the Ecuadorian economy over the previous decade had left the nation especially vulnerable to political unrest. Workforce strikes by the national labor federation and the subsequent military coup that ousted Ecuador's president Vélasco Ibarra in the early 1960s had placed Ximenes on treacherous international political terrain. The Ecuadorian military maintained control of the government and initiated structural reforms guided by the U.S. government through the Alliance for Progress programs through 1965.[3]

The shape-shifting rhetoric evidenced in Ximenes's 1964 Alliance for Progress report aligns liberal Democratic discourses with the strands of revolutionary discourse in circulation throughout the Americas during this period. Ximenes efficaciously seeks to align confluent U.S.–Latin American discourses across divergent political and ideological systems. Ximenes's report responds to these changing political currents within Latin America and the United States. The $4.7 million USAID budget cited for fiscal years June 1962 through June 1963 was under scrutiny following Kennedy's assassination in November 1963. Alliance for Progress programs were up for renewed funding under the Johnson administration in the upcoming 1964 fiscal year. This report was compiled and delivered in the first half of 1964 during the early phase of Johnson's new presidential administration. The changing of the guard in the White House demanded a rhetoric of justification. Evidence suggests that Ximenes wrote and delivered this report in the spring of 1964 in the formative months of Johnson's presidency leading up to the historic Great Society speech in May 1964.

In justifying the work of the Alliance for Progress, Ximenes bears witness to the needs, goals, and efforts of his office. Ximenes's economic program profile represents, among other things, a description of social democracy in practice. It responds to the turbulence in the political ecology of Latin American governance. In many respects, Ximenes's Alliance for Progress efforts in Ecuador prefigured certain features of the broad domestic program proposals advanced by Johnson in his University of Michigan address.

Like Johnson's May 1964 Great Society speech, Ximenes's Alliance for Progress report advances an imaginative fiction of the future. Invoking historical visions of the "great society" originally conceived in Adam Smith's *Wealth of Nations* of 1776 "as a global economic community, knit together by bonds of international trade," Ximenes and Johnson unwittingly and independently extend Constitution-era economic principles and nation-building aspirations to their respective rhetorical situations.[4] Ximenes was on Johnson's wavelength even as he was going about trying to fulfill the mission of USAID in Ecuador. In sum, both Ximenes's act of instrumental rhetoric and Johnson's act of epideictic rhetoric reflect the capacious yet conflicted aims of social democracy—a robust network of social programs managed by the state, an executive office empowered to control the flow of political will, and an invigorated body of citizens capable of engaging in participatory democracy.

This chapter spans the three-year period between 1964 and 1967 leading up to Ximenes's eventual appointments as commissioner of the Equal Employment Opportunity Commission (EEOC) and chair of the Inter-Agency Committee on Mexican American Affairs. Chapter 5 extends to include an examination of Ximenes's role in the historic White House Cabinet Committee Hearings on Mexican American Affairs (El Paso Hearings). Ximenes strategically constructed the 1967 El Paso Hearings as a model of agonistic pluralism and the social democratic values of the Great Society.

The Imaginative Fiction of the "Great Society"

The rhetorical construction of the Great Society, cast on May 22, 1964, during the University of Michigan's commencement ceremonies, carried the ghosts and dreams of many, including LBJ's most prodigious predecessors, John F. Kennedy and Franklin D. Roosevelt. To an audience of over seventy thousand under a glaring sun radiating over the University of Michigan graduating class of 1964, President Johnson declared, "For a century we labored to settle and to subdue a continent. For half a century we called upon unbounded invention and untiring industry to create an order of plenty for all our people." Johnson charged these freshly minted college graduates to join a fractured nation in enacting a new vision: "The challenge of the next half century is whether we have the wisdom to use that wealth to enrich and elevate our national life, and to advance the quality of our American civilization."[5]

The invitation for the University of Michigan commencement had initially been extended to President John F. Kennedy in October 1963, only thirty days before his assassination. It was reissued to President Johnson soon after his stealthy swearing-in ceremony on *Air Force One* in the wake of the assassination on November 22, 1963. The occasion of the Great Society speech was overshadowed by the mythos of the young martyred president and an American dream unrealized. Kennedy had launched his own vision for the institution of the Peace Corps and his new foreign policy priorities that set the groundwork for the Alliance for Progress programs in an address at the University of Michigan in the previous year. The rhetorical situation of the Great Society speech in May 1964 was already inscribed by a number of conditioning influences that Johnson not only had to accommodate but also had to disrupt if he was going to achieve the level of presidential distinction he so deeply desired.

The text of the Great Society speech, therefore, was unavoidably infused with the confluences and dissonances of the moment—the pathos of the occasion, the ethos of the orator, and the logos of the message. Contributors to the theme and content of the Great Society speech included Fred Ricci, executive secretary of the Young Democratic Clubs; Jim Fitzpatrick, chairman of the Young Citizens for Johnson Clubs; and Johnson's own advisors Horace Busby, Bill Moyers, and Richard Goodwin.[6] Additionally, the April 18, 1964, commencement address to the University of Rhode Island delivered by the secretary of the Interior Department, Stewart Udall, served as a conceptual springboard for Johnson's speechwriters. Udall, an ardent conservationist and progressivist, had advanced the construct of the "great society" in his speech just thirty days before Johnson delivered his University of Michigan commencement address. Johnson's Great Society speech resonated because it was the product of so many sources.

In truth, the *topos* of the "great society" had been in circulation since Johnson's own father, Sam Johnson, an intellectual idealistic, political populist, Teddy Roosevelt–style progressivist, and quixotic vision maker, had served two terms in the Texas House of Representatives through the early 1900s. For Lyndon Johnson the *topos* of the great society represented the unrealized dreams between a nation and a president, and perhaps, between a father and a son. In many respects Sam Johnson had been chasing after the great society for a lifetime. "By the time his first child Lyndon was born, on August 27, 1908, Sam Johnson had lugged his dreams and ideals back to the Hill Country," observes biographer Robert Caro.[7] Lyndon Johnson picked up where his father left off, carrying his father's dreams longer and farther than Sam Johnson ever could. Poignantly, Lyndon ultimately carried the senior Sam Johnson home from the hospital to die—what remained at the end was but a shell of the man—an alcoholic, bankrupt dirt farmer.[8] Lyndon's Great

Society was not only political; it was personal. It is safe to say that Johnson spent a lifetime trying to fulfill what his father was never able to do. The Great Society narrative Johnson cultivated suffered a similar demise in the end with Johnson's 1968 renunciation speech and shadowed legacy.

Nevertheless, the moment of the Great Society speech set the parameters of LBJ's rhetorical presidency, publicly and personally. Johnson grounded his notion of the Great Society on liberal Democratic principles and New Deal politics, enacting a constellation of progressivist and humanistic values sharply reflective of early twentieth-century British social psychologist Graham Wallas's monograph *The Great Society*.[9] Johnson's speech resonated the central tenet of Wallas's treatise, advancing a vision of "a society consciously organized for the welfare of all its members."[10]

Echoing the vaulting hopes of twentieth-century liberalism, Johnson charged this graduating class of baby boomers with these words: "Your imagination, your initiative, and your indignation will determine whether we build a society where old values and new visions are buried under unbridled growth."[11] Finding traces of Wallas's social theory in Johnson's Great Society speech, swimming in the alphabet soup of ideas from which Johnson constructed his many domestic policies, is not unreasonable.[12] The Great Society was a big idea, and no one appreciated the possibilities and impossibilities of a big idea like Johnson.

Even if not a singular authorial contribution or original idea, Johnson's concept of the Great Society was both bold and capacious. The intertextuality of the speech and the polyvocal sources of its vision aligned Johnson with the leaders he most admired and most wanted to emulate. Johnson's political instincts and rhetorical savvy were, for this *kairotic* moment, in tune with the nation. Speaking to a nation at war and a generation of youth facing the draft, Johnson's description of the democratic state curiously reverberates with *topoi* evidenced in the classical Athenian epideictic rhetoric of Pericles's funeral oration.[13] For Johnson, the Great Society was more than a prosperous society; it was a flourishing community. Like Pericles's funeral oration, Johnson used the ceremonial occasion to articulate the shining qualities of democracy and showcase the nation as an exemplar of civic virtue.

The Great Society as the last gasp of twentieth-century liberalism was the biggest and the best of everything. Building on foundational New Deal rhetoric, Johnson also wanted his presidential legacy to exceed the achievements of his predecessors.[14] Johnson offered a vision of hope to a nation stripped of hope. The glimpse of Camelot and the Kennedy vision was something of the past. Johnson needed to offer something even more inclusive and inspiring. Furthermore, Johnson needed to both distinguish and align his legacy with that of his predecessors. He wanted to connect his administration with the youthful vigor of Kennedy's short-lived presidency as well as anchor it to the stabilizing force of Roosevelt's New Deal policies. In turn, he gave the nation the imaginative fiction of the Great Society, "a place where the city of man not only serves the needs of the body and demands of commerce but the desire for beauty and the hunger for community."[15] The Great Society was an invention device, a heuristic for a generative and wildly experimental domestic agenda.

Johnson was a protean character, a political chameleon. He was both a New Deal and Cold War liberal, but Johnson's "passion lay with the former."[16] As such, the Great Society speech focuses only on domestic concerns. The omission of international affairs in the Great Society speech is darkly enthymematic. Foreign affairs and diplomacy were shadow issues for Johnson. The absence of the Vietnam War from Johnson's Great Society vision represents a disturbing suppressed premise, an omission that would ultimately become the dark conclusion of the Great Society. The Cuban Missile Crisis and the Bay of Pigs that had entangled Kennedy's presidency represented failures in Kennedy's own liberal Democratic leadership, a harbinger of the presidential missteps in Vietnam that would ultimately swamp Johnson's administration. It was the unavoidable conclusion to the Great Society that Johnson would eventually proffer to the nation four years later in his April 1968 renunciation speech.

Johnson's arrogance of power that launched the vision for the Great Society domestic policy was inseparable from the hubris with which he overstepped the limits of U.S. national welfare in Southeast Asia. In "Great Societies and Great Empires: Lyndon Johnson and Vietnam" Wilson Carey MacWilliams contends, "In general, the logic of the effort to create and secure a Great Society points toward imperium. At a minimum, it prompts a quest to control whatever might threaten the project of social greatness, and it inches toward the attempt to dominate."[17] Throughout his political life, Johnson remained wedded to the vision of the great republic advanced by the framers of the U.S. Constitution and the "modern goal of mastery, abundance, and command over nature."[18]

Like the vision of democratic society advanced by Pericles in Athenian antiquity to justify expansionist goals through the Peloponnesian War, it could be argued that Johnson's Great Society speech sketches a portrait of American democratic society to justify the blood sacrifice of Vietnam. As MacWilliams argues, "America, in fact and in Johnson's vision, is a regime that dwarfs even Athenian restlessness and drive for 'growth,' its dynamism a constant intrusion on the life and culture of others."[19]

In his 1964 speech, Johnson paints a vision of a perfected nation, extending across urban and rural contexts. He describes in vivid detail his construction of the Great Society. Johnson imagines:

> The Great Society is a place where every child can find knowledge to enrich his mind and to enlarge his talents. It is a place where leisure is a welcome chance to build and reflect, not a feared cause of boredom and restlessness. . . .
>
> It is a place where many can renew contact with nature. It is a place which honors creation for its own sake and for what it adds to the understanding of the race. It is a place where men are more concerned with the quality of their goals than the quantity of their goods.[20]

Johnson constructs the metaphor of "place" as a container of the Good Society: the city, the countryside, and the classroom. These three *topoi* represent metaphorical spaces for the cultivation of nature, culture, and humanity. The metaphorical depiction of Johnson's vision of America in terms of urban and natural places builds an imaginative fiction reflective of Americanist conservative values as well as his own liberal progressive agenda. It is a vision that no reasonable citizen could reject.[21]

Johnson's Great Society speech relies on conceptual metaphors for its rhetorical impact. He exploits the power of the rhetorical presidency by establishing metaphors of place as containers for his political agenda. As he develops this association, Johnson carefully ties these conceptual frames to his vision for social change as he defines the places of the Great Society. Johnson asserts, "So I want to talk to you today about three places where we begin to build the Great Society—in our cities, in our countryside, and in our classrooms."[22]

The utopian possibilities harken back to Constitution-era values and invoke the vision of inclusion and national unity of the Gettysburg Address. The three metaphorical places of Johnson's Great Society ultimately translated into sweeping public policies: the 1965 Voting Rights Act, the War on Poverty programs, Model City urban renewal, educational reform programs like Head Start, the 1964 Wilderness Act, and the 1965 Immigration and Nationality Act.

In an interesting twist, Johnson mixes the metaphorical structure of his address. At the close of the speech, Johnson shifts conceptual systems and like Pericles's panegyric advances the metaphor of war to call the audience to action: "So will you join in the battle to give every citizen the full quality which God enjoins and the law requires, whatever his belief, or race, or the color of his skin?" Using repetition, the president echoes the call three times:

"Will you join the battle?"[23] Johnson continued to circulate these military symbols throughout the escalation of the Vietnam War.

The Great Society speech was delivered just weeks before the Democratic National Committee began ramping up for the 1964 election. As discussed, Ximenes would be summoned from his USAID post in Ecuador to spearhead the Viva Johnson campaign only months after the University of Michigan address (chapter 4). Johnson needed to set forth an ambitious plan that would catalyze voters for his reelection. The Great Society speech represented a call to action, not the least of which was a call to vote Johnson back into office.

Johnson read the sweeping election results six months later in November 1964 as a statement of consensus from the American people to enact the promises of the Great Society. "I was just elected President by the biggest popular margin in the history of the country—16 million votes," Johnson purportedly declared to his aides and liaisons soon after the election.[24] Johnson interpreted the election results as both an opportunity and a mandate.[25] He had crafted this ceremonial event and act of public oratory to be a defining moment in his presidential legacy. He wanted the Great Society speech to be inscribed in history as an exemplar of his rhetorical presidency. The Great Society speech and the programs that carried out Johnson's vision were not the products of the singular authorial effort that Johnson projected. Moreover, the implementation of the Great Society vision was not equitably enacted.

La Raza Se Junta: *The Albuquerque Walkout*

By the autumn of 1965, the glaring omission of Mexican Americans from Johnson's administration remained a sore reminder of President Kennedy's failure to deliver on his 1960 election promises to the Spanish-speaking electorate (chapter 4). Patience and confidence in the White House was wearing increasingly thin among Spanish-speaking citizens. The American GI Forum (AGIF) remained vigilant in its demands for Mexican American representation in the Johnson administration. In an AGIF statement delivered publicly to President Johnson, Héctor García directly confronted Johnson's glaring omission of Mexican American leaders from the White House EEOC Conference organized by EEOC chair Franklin Roosevelt Jr., in August 1965.[26]

Following on the heels of the September 1965 issue of the AGIF newsletter celebrating Ximenes's appointment to the USAID program in Panama, the October issue of the *Forumeer* published García's statement rebuking President Johnson's oversights in Mexican American appointments at high levels of his administration. Signed by prominent AGIF leaders including

Ximenes, the statement reads: "Because Mexican-Americans have been excluded from positions in the Executive Branch of the Federal Government, we urge the placing of Mexican-Americans in policy making positions in all departments of the Executive Branch."[27] However, Johnson did not give García and the AGIF the hearing they expected. Ximenes, in turn, was promptly dispatched to his USAID appointment in Panama after a brief White House swearing-in ceremony on August 13, 1965.

Problematically, the plight of Mexican Americans did not merit attention from the White House equal to the long overdue affirmative action measures accorded to African American citizens through the newly established EEOC. In his August 20, 1965, remarks for the inaugural EEOC conference, President Johnson described the desperate conditions and challenges of bringing the "Negro American into an equal role in our society."[28] Johnson focused national attention on the growing violence in America's cities and the widening division of the binaries of race. The mandate for civil rights reform remained limited to the social justice issues affecting African American citizens, not Mexican Americans.

Until 1965, Johnson's role in postwar civil rights reform had been inconsistent at best, beginning with his first national-level appointment as director of the Texas state National Youth Administration (NYA) in 1935 (chapter 1). African American and Mexican American constituencies had been clamoring for more than three decades for legislative measures to address the disparities while Johnson had danced around the issues in order to hold onto his political advantage as a southern Democrat. The 1949 Longoria case was the first and only high-profile civil rights issue for which Johnson had ever personally and politically advocated (chapter 2). The decided shift in Johnson's public civil rights record came in 1965, most dramatically expressed in his poignant landmark Voting Rights Act speech on March 15, 1965. The Civil Rights Act of 1964 was largely attributed to Kennedy's presidential administration. But the Voting Rights Act of 1965 and the establishment of the EEOC were cast by Johnson as the great legacies of his presidency.

The Civil Rights Act of 1964 did not go into effect until July 2, 1965.[29] The landmark Senate Bill 1750, first introduced into the Senate on June 10, 1963, initiated legislation to establish a commission on equal employment opportunity.[30] However, the new law had taken two years to go into effect after the administrative turmoil in the wake of Kennedy's assassination.[31] The launching of the 1965 White House EEOC Conference celebrated the passage of Senate Bill 1750 and signaled to the nation that African American citizens would be the primary beneficiaries of the new federal policies and programs. It was a source of great disappointment for Ximenes and García, however, that the 1964 Civil Rights Act was not more broadly conceived to protect Spanish-speaking citizens. Moreover, they were deeply discouraged to discover that the White House EEOC Conference program scheduled for August 1965 did not include a single panel or workshop on the social inequalities of Mexican American or Spanish-speaking constituencies.[32] Mexican American citizens wanted equal protection and representation under the new legislation.[33]

Resistance among Mexican Americans continued to mount against Johnson's cold-shoulder response to their demands. The next two years were spent struggling to expand the limits of the legal imagination of the Johnson administration into new civil rights legislation for the benefit Spanish-speaking constituencies. By the end of the year, EEOC chair Franklin Roosevelt Jr. openly recognized that Spanish-speaking citizens "suffered from the some of the most severe problems of employment, housing, and education in the nation," publicly committing the commission to finding better ways of implementing Title VII of the Civil Rights Act of 1964.[34] In response to enduring patterns of discrimination, EEOC chair Franklin Roosevelt Jr. announced plans to hold a conference in Albuquerque to listen to the demands of Mexican American leaders. Roosevelt sent out invitations for the Albuquerque EEOC conference scheduled for March 1966 to established Mexican American civic organizations such as the AGIF and the League of United Latin American Citizens (LULAC) and to emerging activist organizations such as the Mexican American Political Association (MAPA) and the Political Association of Spanish-Speaking Organizations (PASSO).

However, convinced that the Albuquerque EEOC conference scheduled for March 28, 1966, would prove to be yet another diversionary tactic of the Johnson administration, Mexican American leaders across these four major groups coordinated a highly publicized walkout. When the Albuquerque EEOC conference convened, elected representatives of the AGIF, LULAC, MAPA, and PASSO voiced their complaints and walked out with the fifty Mexican American delegates. The group then gathered in another room on the University of New Mexico campus to put forward a set of resolutions to send to President Johnson. The first resolution called for the appointment of a Mexican American to the EEOC.

In *LULAC: Mexican Americans and National Policy*, Craig Kaplowitz chronicles the push-pull dynamic between Mexican American activists and the Johnson administration over EEOC agendas and appointments. Describing Mexican Americans as the "step children of the Great Society," Kaplowitz argues that the EEOC walkout helped set the stage for the subsequent appointment of Ximenes to the EEOC the following year.[35] The cross-organizational solidarity demonstrated at the Albuquerque EEOC conference was a landmark moment in Mexican American civil rights activism. It is true that the resistance tactics of civil disobedience that were capturing the attention of the Johnson administration had not been part of the general mobilizing strategies of LULAC and the AGIF. Although Ximenes had routinely practiced the art of moral protest in Albuquerque throughout the early stages of AGIF organizing in the 1950s, the AGIF, by and large, had resisted using direct action tactics (chapter 3).

The Albuquerque EEOC walkout won Johnson's attention. Rodolfo "Corky" Gonzáles, a member of the Denver AGIF, organizer and author of the epic Chicano movement poem "Soy Joaquín," participated in the Albuquerque walkout and sent the list of resolutions via telegram to President Johnson.[36] Gonzáles asserts:

> As a member of the Equal Employment Opportunities Commission Conference Ad Hoc Committee which was organized March 28, 1966 in Albuquerque I would like to express my deep concern over the lack of understanding and concern by federal agencies and programs about the problems of Mexican Americans in the Southwest. Also as president of Los Voluntarios a political and social action organization I am notifying you of our unanimous indorsement [*sic*] of the following resolutions submitted to you by our committee March 28, 1966 from Albuquerque New Mexico.[37]

In a follow-up letter to Corky Gonzáles dated May 25, 1966, from Harry McPherson Jr., special counsel to the president, the White House offers this response:

> On several recent occasions members of the White House staff and other government officials have met to discuss the economic, educational, housing, and health problems of Spanish-speaking Americans and the Federal programs that were designed to meet those problems. We found that we have much to learn before we can present concrete proposals, but we have every intention of pursuing the study to its satisfactory conclusion. . . .
>
> Within the coming week we expect to discuss, with several leaders of the Mexican-American community, the possibility of having a national conference on the problems of Spanish-speaking Americans.[38]

Gestures from the White House immediately followed, but substantive results were still slow in coming. EEOC assistant Carlos Rivera sent a full report to the White House noting the scope of the national press coverage for the Albuquerque walkout that extended coast to coast from the *San Francisco Examiner* to the *New York Times* and *Washington Post*.[39] In his April 7, 1966, follow-up letter to President Johnson, EEOC chair Franklin Roosevelt Jr. describes the events at the Albuquerque walkout:

> The last of the four speakers, Albert Peña of San Antonio gave the signal for the walkout. He said they would hold their own meeting and formulate a joint program. They retired to a room in the same building, which they previously arranged. The press release, prepared beforehand, was issued shortly thereafter. It closed with this sentence, "The delegates added that if a Mexican-American Commissioner were hired, they would be willing to meet with the EEOC again."[40]

Among the resolutions sent to President Johnson were demands for Mexican American inclusion in the White House Civil Rights Conference set for June 1, 1966. The scope of the 1964 Civil Rights Act and the limited legal imagination of Johnson's cabinet had failed to examine the full spectrum of institutionalized discrimination. Mexican Americans found themselves in the ambiguous gap between the binaries of race.

Neither Johnson's nor Kennedy's legislative and programmatic responses had been extended to include Spanish-speaking groups. In order to recognize the problems facing Spanish-speaking citizens, the issues had to be named. The complexities of ethnic labeling and ethnolinguistic identity further complicated recognition of Spanish-speaking citizens as a protected class within the new civil rights legislation. The ambiguities of social identity within the U.S. ethnic landscape are evidenced in the multiplicity of terms the federal government routinely employed to categorize and identify this growing minority population: Spanish-speaking Americans, Spanish-Americans, Spanish surname Americans, and Mexican Americans represent a few of the most common labels.[41] The construction of this minority in linguistic terms meant that the effects of structural racism and the insidious nature of institutional discrimination were not interrogated in the national examination of political access and social justice.[42]

Civil rights reform measures tended to perpetuate a zero-sum game. It was an all-or-nothing model of federal equalization and reparation. Hence, the 1966 White House Civil Rights Conference, like the 1965 White House EEOC Conference, was designed exclusively to address African American issues. The Mexican American leaders who orchestrated the Albuquerque EEOC walkout wanted to register their objections with the federal government. Spanish-speaking groups, more broadly, and Mexican Americans, more specifically, felt largely excluded and alienated by the Johnson administration.[43] Under these exclusionary terms, interracial resentments and hostilities were becoming exacerbated rather than mitigated among the minority populations.

In this volatile climate, Johnson and his cabinet members were not willing to take up the growing alienation among Latino groups under the same
political framework as for African American minorities. Race, class, and ethnolinguistic identity issues further complicated the social divisions between
black and Latino populations. Martin Luther King Jr., alongside Corky
Gonzáles, ultimately responded to the growing divisions among minorities
by organizing the 1968 Poor People's March to Washington, D.C., at which
time Corky Gonzáles put forward the historic *Plan del Barrio* extending the
demands for Chicano activists.[44] The Albuquerque EEOC walkout represented a watershed moment for both the old and new guard of Mexican
American leaders. Johnson, however, continued with his stall tactics.

Other exigences conditioning the rhetorical situation of the EEOC
walkout included the 1966 Easter Sunday farmworkers pilgrimage from
Delano to Sacramento, California, led by César Chávez. The six-month-
old grape workers strike and national boycott launched by César Chávez
had received broad endorsements from the AGIF, the Student Nonviolent
Coordinating Committee, the Congress of Racial Equality, and other civil
rights organizations and political leaders, including the support of Senator
Robert Kennedy.[45] The multiday three-hundred-mile Easter Sunday March
drew over eight thousand participants, including representatives from the
California AGIF, the state chairman, and members from AGIF chapters in
Merced, Oakland, San Jose, and Richmond. In an act of interorganizational
solidarity, César Chávez had secured the support of the AGIF to provide
traffic and crowd control along the route from Delano to Sacramento. The
event marked the dramatic climax to the grape workers strike that had begun
in September 1965.[46] The May 1966 issue of the *Forumeer* depicts the key
scenes of the event:

> It was the biggest demonstration of farm workers in American history.
> Thousands of Mexican-Americans jammed the Capitol after marching
> the last four miles from a church in Sacramento. Governor Edmund G.
> Brown chose to spend Easter with his family in Palm Springs, much to
> the displeasure of the multitude.
>
> Along the way the grape pickers saw their first sign of victory in the
> strike that started last September. Schenley Industries, one of the largest
> grape growers in the Delano area, agreed to bargain with the National
> Farm Workers' Association [NFWA], the pickers' union headed by Cesar
> Chavez.
>
> Dolores Huerta, a militant leader of the NFWA, drew resounding
> cheers from the large gathering in front of the Capitol when she demanded

a special session of the Legislature to deal with better wages, improved working conditions, and union bargaining guarantees.[47]

The image of Dolores Huerta in her role as a labor rights leader was poignantly resonant of the women labor activists of the Empire Zinc strike in the 1950s, made famous in the film *Salt of the Earth* (chapter 2). A vocal Mexican American woman leading the charge for social justice stirred the rhetorical imagination of a new generation of Chicanas and Latinas.

Nevertheless, Governor Brown's cold shoulder to *la huelga* and the demands of the marchers reflected a general trend of national indifference toward Mexican American issues. In matters related to farm labor, Johnson himself had played on both sides of the fence for more than two decades. Throughout his Senate period, Johnson repeatedly placated Mexican American voters calling for the end of the *bracero* program because it exploited Mexican immigrant workers and displaced Mexican American laborers. At the same time, Johnson supported farmers and their dependency on cheap migrant labor.[48] Johnson's refusal to act on behalf *la raza* remained entrenched.

The May 1966 issue of the *Forumeer* reported that members of the Mexican American Ad Hoc National Joint Committee, the cross-organizational entity formed by the fifty delegates who participated in the Albuquerque EEOC walkout, had convened in Los Angeles on April 28, one month after the walkout, at what they called the "Unity Banquet" to draft action plans as follow-up to the resolutions sent to the president.[49] The list of Mexican American organization leaders present at the April 28 Unity Banquet included representation from the AGIF, LULAC, PASSO, the Foundation of Mexican American Studies, MAPA, and more than a dozen organizations and entities.[50] Their litany of demands once again fell on deaf ears.[51]

Instead of directly answering to the resolutions of the Albuquerque EEOC walkout telegram or the demands that emerged from the Unity Banquet, President Johnson extended an invitation to select Mexican American leaders to meet with him at the White House in a historic special meeting. The most vocal activist, Corky Gonzáles, was omitted from the guest list. Simultaneously, invitations to African American leaders for the highly publicized Civil Rights Conference called "To Fulfill These Rights," set for May 31, were sent from the White House on May 23, 1966. It was an invitation-only affair. None of the Mexican American leaders were included in the White House Civil Rights Conference.

To placate Mexican American resistance to this omission, Johnson offered a consolation prize in the form of a private White House meeting with the select group of politically friendly Mexican American leaders. White House aide Joseph Califano sent an invitation to six Mexican American leaders to attend a White House dinner on May 26, 1966. There were no representatives from Colorado, Arizona, or New Mexico included on the guest list for the intimate White House dinner. The invitation was sent to Héctor García (Texas), Bert Corona (California), Alfred Hernandez (Texas), Agustin Flores (California), Roy Elizondo (Texas), and Roberto Ornelas (Texas). Sent in his capacity as special assistant to the president, Califano's invitation reads:

> On President Johnson's behalf, I cordially invite you to a dinner meeting at the White House at 7:30 P.M. on Thursday, May 26, 1966.
>
> We hope to discuss and obtain your views on the problems of the Mexican-American and the other Spanish-speaking peoples in our country. We are looking forward to seeing you then.[52]

The intimate gathering on May 26, 1966, at the White House offered grand displays of generosity characteristic of Johnson's bodacious political style, which were, in the end, more showmanship than substance. Ximenes, serving as deputy director of USAID in Panama, did not attend the White House gathering.

Historical accounts of the White House visit with President Johnson visit vary, but all descriptions give a common portrait of Johnson acting the role of the *buen amigo* in giving his Mexican American guests a close-up tour of the White House in his coarse but folksy manner. Califano depicts Johnson's guests whooping it up, shouting out "Viva Johnson" and bouncing on the bed in the Lincoln Bedroom like a scene from a slapstick comedy.[53] MAPA president, Bert Corona, later described Johnson as "a sort of cornball type."[54]

When confronted about the absence of Mexican Americans in his administration, Johnson pointed to his office clerical assistant Mrs. Yolanda Boozer, declaring that she was a Mexican American and that she opened his mail for him every day. Her presence at the meeting was offered as clear evidence that, contrary to their complaints, he kept a Mexican American in his employment.[55] Indisputably, however, all accounts reflect a common tenor of the meeting between the president and the Mexican American leaders. In a May 26 news conference, White House officials announced the guest list for the meeting but declined requests from the press to cover the event.[56] All accounts, however, depict the informality and relative insignificance of the moment in terms of White House protocols and politics. Johnson's guests were not treated with the deference of dignitaries or the respect of equals. They were entertained as peripheral figures who could be easily placated and dismissed.

The Mexican American representatives walked away from the White House meeting with funding for the SER–Jobs for Progress package for cities in the Southwest, but they left without getting presidential approval for their EEOC walkout demands for a Mexican American appointment on the EEOC or representation at the upcoming White House Civil Rights Conference. The cat-and-mouse gamesmanship that characterized the Johnson style of baiting, batting, and tossing aside his political critics and inferiors was exhibited once again with the Mexican American constituency, which had worked so hard to elect him to office. No invitations for the White House Civil Rights Conference or EEOC appointments followed. The White House Conference "To Fulfill These Rights" on June 1, 1966, made national headlines.

"An Embattled Conference," as described by the *New York Times*, the White House Civil Rights Conference was reported to have been "disowned by an extremist minority."[57] The *Council's Report and Recommendations to the Conference* included the intellectual contributions of the august leaders of the African American civil rights movement such as A. Philip Randolph, president of the Brotherhood of Sleeping Car Porters; Dorothy Height, president of the National Council of Negro Women; Vernon Jordan Jr., representative of the Southern Regional Council; Roy Wilkins, executive director of the National Association for the Advancement of Colored People; and Dr. Martin Luther King Jr., president of the Southern Christian Leadership Conference.[58]

Johnson's tendency to "freeze out" dissenters and exclude radical voices from the national conversation was reflected in both the official guest list for the White House Civil Rights Conference as well as the short list for the May 26 Mexican American White House dinner meeting. The failure to engage the political tensions of agonistic pluralism, among other factors, limited the effectiveness of the White House Civil Rights Conference. The press and the politicos, including Johnson's White House cabinet members and staff, lamented that the event more likely evidenced the division and turmoil within the African American civil rights movement than facilitated consensus building and collective problem solving.

In this tumultuous political climate, Johnson and his aides resolved not to host another White House civil rights conference ever again. The White House was pelted with queries and criticism. *Los Angeles Times* correspondent Jack Jones published an article in April 1967 titled "Answer Is Silence: How about That White House Conference? Latins Wonder."[59] The flurry of White House internal correspondence reacting to demands by Mexican American leaders for a White House conference on issues affecting Spanish-speaking citizens reflected consistent resistance and ambivalence.[60] In a memo to Johnson from his assistant Marvin Watson, informing the president about California congressman Edward Roybal's February 1967 phone call reporting that his district was "boiling up" and pleading for a "Mexican-American White House Conference," the official hand-scribbled reply from Johnson reads, "I'll have no conference."[61]

Offering Mexican Americans peripheral and symbolic appointments of little political import and limited rhetorical power was common practice for both Johnson and Kennedy. Both presidents were pressured into acknowledging the oversight amid public criticism for ignoring the U.S. Spanish-speaking constituency. In turn, both presidents responded by awarding relatively low-impact appointments to Mexican American leaders. After mobilizing the Spanish-speaking vote for both Kennedy and Johnson, Ximenes experienced the same dismissive treatment. He was briefly recognized for his efforts and then promptly dispatched to USAID Alliance for Progress projects in Latin America by both Kennedy and Johnson.

Pulling the Floresville Heartstrings

Political expediency informed Johnson's decisions in every sphere, but the loss of his beloved mentor and friend Sam Fore on December 24, 1966, was a serious blow to Johnson's personal sphere. If there is one measure of Johnson's humanity and sincerity, it was his enduring devotion to Sam Fore, a loyal and durable relationship that uniquely revealed Johnson's largely inaccessible vulnerability. Johnson's devotion to his lifelong mentor and father figure, the editor of the *Floresville Chronicle-Journal*, demonstrated how deep Johnson's heartstrings could go. Sam Fore's presence and loss constituted part of the *telos* of the shifting rhetorical situation of Johnson's Great Society. Sam Fore's noble and humble character inspired and sustained Johnson throughout his entire political career. There were few people in Johnson's political sphere who understood the depth and significance of Sam Fore to Johnson. One of those people was Vicente Ximenes (chapter 1).

Johnson and Ximenes shared a common debt to the beloved patron of Floresville, Texas. President Johnson had flown the ailing Sam and his wife, Elma Fore, aboard *Air Force One* to Washington, D.C., for his 1965 presidential inauguration. Ximenes was there for the inaugural ball at the Mayflower Hotel in his capacity as the director of the Viva Johnson campaign. The Floresville contingent reveled together in Johnson's victory. For Johnson, the presence of Sam Fore at his inauguration offered the validation that his own father, Sam Johnson, could not. Similarly, Ximenes frequently wished that his father, José Ximenes, the political *patrón* of Floresville, had been alive to join the revelry. Johnson's adoration for his Floresville mentor did not stop there.

Following his inauguration, Johnson advanced plans for the dedication of the new Sam Fore Jr. Hall at Texas A&I University in Kingsville on March 26, 1966, only eight months before Fore's death. Johnson wanted to recognize the achievements of a man who dropped out of school in the eighth grade to earn a living and then pursued a lifetime of public service that began as a newspaper apprentice. Fore had been an ardent supporter of the agricultural university Texas A&I and had served on the first board of regents in 1929 for the fledgling institution when it was first called the Texas College of Arts and Industries. Fore's generosity to the citizens of the state of Texas was immeasurable. Johnson's gratitude to Fore went deeper than just a personal debt. His respect for Sam Fore approached reverence, something Johnson gave to no one else. It is difficult to ascertain whom and what Lyndon Johnson loved authentically. The ambivalences and machinations that shadowed most of his personal and professional relationships fill volumes. But there are two things he loved unabashedly: the state of Texas and Sam Fore.

When Fore died, President Johnson and the First Lady along with Texas governor John Connally and his wife attended his funeral at the Floresville Methodist Church on December 26, 1966. *Air Force One* was dispatched twice to the tiny rural town of Floresville by President Johnson after his election: once to bring his beloved mentor to his January 1965 inauguration and a second time to take Johnson to Fore's funeral. Over thirty years had passed since Sam Fore summoned politicos like Richard Kleberg and Lyndon B. Johnson from across the state of Texas for the first Floresville "Peanuts on Parade" celebration (chapter 1).

Enduring emotional ties and a need for a stable connection informed Johnson's fondness for Fore. An equally compelling factor influencing Johnson's selection of Ximenes for appointment to the EEOC was Johnson's growing determination to forge his own legacy that began on the mesquite prairies of South Texas and took hold on the inauspicious campus of the teachers college in San Marcos, Texas. The personal loss of Sam Fore and the sustained political pressure from the Mexican American constituency ultimately helped to tip the scales. The landmark Albuquerque walkout had happened only two days after the dedication of Sam Fore Jr. Hall, reminding Johnson of the lessons learned from his mentor. With the death of Fore, Johnson was pressed to remember the fragilities of his own power and the durability of good faith. After months of sustained protest and lobbying, the president ultimately made good on his promises to the Mexican American community.

Finally responding to the barrage of letters and telegrams from Héctor García recommending the appointment of Ximenes to the EEOC, Johnson made a decisive move on behalf of the Mexican American constituency that had helped him win the White House.

On April 4, 1967, President Johnson summoned Ximenes from his current position as deputy director of the USAID Alliance for Progress program in Panama and announced that he was putting forward Ximenes's nomination for the position of commissioner of the EEOC. Ximenes was finally invited to join the cast of lead actors during the final act of LBJ's Great Society. Ximenes was sworn in almost two years to the day after he had chaired the seemingly inconsequential 1965 Civil Rights Conference in Washington, D.C., prior to his USAID assignment sending him back to Latin American (chapter 4). The nomination for the EEOC commissioner appointment came as no less a surprise to Ximenes than had his nomination in 1964 as director of the Viva Johnson Clubs. The complexity and irony of the cultural rhetorical ecology of this historical moment was not lost on Ximenes.

The source for his nomination, once again, was Héctor García. Ximenes recalls, "As it turned out two senators from New Mexico, Anderson and Montoya, had recommended other persons. And Senator Yarborough had recommended Dr. George Sanchez. It was Dr. García who had enough clout with the President that made it possible for me to get the appointment."[62] García's lobbying for a Mexican American EEOC appointment had begun with a letter-writing campaign in the months immediately following the infamous Mexican American White House dinner meeting.[63]

As García boldly states in his September 22, 1966, letter to President Johnson, "the feeling, nationally, is that we are being ignored and treated poorly by your administration.... At times I have written to you advising you that the situation is becoming more tense. Today the administration is losing many Mexican American leaders throught [*sic*] the nation and specially [*sic*] Texas."[64] Assuming a stance of brotherly familiarity and good faith, García also prophetically warns Johnson, "I am sorry in having to advise you that the Democratic Party statewide and nationally will never again have the solid backing of the Mexican Americans that it has had in the past."[65] When Aileen Hernandez's resignation left a vacancy on the EEOC, García issued an all-points bulletin to the AGIF membership and launched a "write-in" letter campaign recommending Ximenes's nomination for commissioner.[66] The AGIF pummeled the White House with letters from every corner of the nation. In December 1966 García sent a telegram asking to meet with Johnson at the ranch and naming Ximenes for the vacant slot on the EEOC.[67]

The appointment of Ximenes, while timely and significant, did not go uncontested. Ximenes had alienated New Mexico senator Clint Anderson and University of New Mexico president Popejoy during his AGIF mobilizing years in Albuquerque (chapter 4). Based on his personal history of dogged determinism and willingness to throw himself into the fray, Ximenes would almost certainly have joined in the Albuquerque EEOC walkout both out of principle and in solidarity with *la raza*, had he been in the country and physically present to lend his support.

However, had Ximenes participated in the Albuquerque EEOC conference in March 1966, it is highly unlikely that Johnson would have approved his appointment as EEOC commissioner in March 1967. Johnson's demand for complete loyalty and his ironclad memory for perceived betrayals certainly informed Johnson's decision not include any leaders from New Mexico for his conciliatory Mexican American White House dinner in May 1966. Direct action tactics of resistance during the EEOC conference would have certainly disqualified Ximenes for the EEOC appointment. His fate as persona non gratis would have been sealed along with vocal Albuquerque walkout protestor Corky Gonzáles, whom Johnson summarily disregarded. From Johnson's point of view, Ximenes was a proven performer. He was a fellow Texan. Ximenes was faithful. He was a Floresville insider. Ximenes had been a direct beneficiary of their common mentor Sam Fore. Ximenes had helped Johnson get into the White House and to stay in the White House. In brief, Ximenes was someone Johnson could trust.

For the Mexican American constituency, Ximenes's aegis as a·community organizer for over ten years in Albuquerque made him an acceptable choice. It was a difficulty balance to strike. Ximenes was radical enough, but not too radical. Indeed, Ximenes's physical absence combined with his symbolic presence played in his favor and made him an acceptable candidate for the White House as well as a celebrated candidate for the Mexican American community. Once again, he was in the right place at the right time (or more accurately, was not in the wrong place at the wrong time).

Quelling the cross-racial tensions between Latino and black constituencies also factored into Johnson's decision to appoint Ximenes. In *The Civil Rights Era*, Hugh Davis Graham argues that President Johnson responded to "stirrings of discontent among the restive Hispanic leaders . . . voicing their resentment at being generally ignored" and addressed complaints that he had overlooked Mexican American leaders for high-level appointments in his administration.[68] Aileen Hernandez, whom Ximenes replaced on the EEOC, was born Aileen Clark in New York City to Jamaican immigrants. She graduated with a BA from Howard University in 1947 and an MA from Los Angeles State College in 1959,[69] and she served as assistant chief of the

Fair Employment Practices Commission in California before being appointed to the EEOC. Her embattled position on the EEOC illustrated, in many respects, the struggle navigating the "black-brown" political division.

Although Hernández had been active with trade union organizations in Latin America during her employment with the State Department as a labor education specialist and was an active Democrat, she was not regarded by the Mexican American community as an appropriate choice to represent Latino issues because she had acquired her Spanish surname by marriage.[70] She was a contemporary of Ximenes, with equivalent credentials and employment experience. But she lacked the backing of Mexican American constituencies as well as that of her African American male counterparts.

"When Hernandez found herself blocked by acting chairman [Luther] Holcomb, whose vote was required to produce a working majority of the three remaining commissioners" to pass EEOC policy concerning feminist issues, she signaled her decision to resign.[71] Hernandez resigned as commissioner on October 10, 1966, leaving a vacancy on the EEOC effective November 10, 1966. Hernandez went on to succeed Betty Friedan as the first black president of the National Organization of Women in 1970.

Mexican Americans wanted Hernandez's vacant spot on the commission filled by someone with the cultural and sociolinguistic background necessary to truly understand the needs and issues of Spanish-speaking citizens.[72] Through a six-month vetting process, the political efficacy of Ximenes's nomination became increasingly evident to the Johnson administration. Ximenes's appointment would help address the growing complaints from Johnson's Mexican American critics. Congressman Edward Roybal applauded the appointment in the April 27, 1967, *Congressional Record*.[73] In a telegram sent to President Johnson, MAPA president Bert Corona wrote, "I wish to commend most highly and evoke to you rejoicing for your most timely appointment of one of the finest human beings from the Mexican American community as chairman of the new cabinet level committee on Mexican Americans, Mr. Vicente Ximenes."[74] The public response to the announcement of Ximenes's nomination was overwhelmingly positive. Supporters far outweighed detractors in the flood of correspondence that poured into the White House. But not everyone supported Johnson's choice.

The objections to Ximenes's appointment, however, proved largely vague and inconsequential. Governor Connally, the former king of the 1938 Floresville "Peanuts on Parade," refused to endorse Ximenes's nomination when queried by Johnson's aides. "I've got more to do than engage in useless exercises," the Texas governor was reported saying in response to Ximenes's appointment.[75] New Mexico senator Clinton Anderson was the most vociferous opponent to the Ximenes nomination, pointing to a large file of complaints surrounding Ximenes's AGIF activities in Albuquerque and subsequent dismissal from the University of New Mexico in 1961 (chapter 4). In White House correspondence concerning the background investigation for Ximenes, James Falcon's memo to John Macy about Ximenes quotes Senator Anderson calling Ximenes a "radical" and charging that Ximenes had "made trouble for Anderson over the years."[76] Although FBI background checks on Ximenes failed to uncover anything substantive in Anderson's claims, Johnson insisted that Anderson's ruffled feathers be smoothed. Senator Anderson and Johnson's association extended back more than thirty years to 1935 when Johnson served as the director of the NYA in Texas and Anderson was the acting administrator for the NYA in New Mexico. Both men entered the U.S. Senate after the 1948 election, running as New Deal liberal Democrats and holding onto their respective seats in the legislature for decades.[77] Johnson did not want to stir up a political dust storm between his newly appointed EEOC commissioner and his longtime legislative ally. Johnson informed Ximenes of Anderson's objections, advising Ximenes to mend fences with the senior legislator before the swearing-in ceremony.

Ximenes took the meeting with Senator Anderson at the White House on June 9, 1967, in advance of the scheduled swearing-in ceremony. Demonstrating the necessary degree of deference to his old adversary, Ximenes met with Senator Anderson under very strained conditions. "It was one of the most difficult meetings I've ever had to face," Ximenes later recalled.[78] There were so many issues on the line with Ximenes's EEOC appointment, concerns both personal and political. The EEOC appointment was the culmination of many collective dreams. Ximenes did not want to disappointment Johnson, but even more, he did not want to disappoint his longtime friend Héctor García. Ximenes respectfully assured the senior statesman from New Mexico that despite their shared past as political sparring partners, he was now a seasoned administrator worthy of Johnson's confidence as the new EEOC commissioner. Senator Anderson's objections were sufficiently assuaged. Ximenes's appointment as commissioner of the EEOC went through as planned. The flurry of attention surrounding Ximenes's EEOC appointment was quickly followed by the surprising announcement by President Johnson of the formation of a cabinet committee on Mexican American affairs. Ximenes remembers:

> When I returned to the Oval Office the President then called in Califano and asked him to draw up an executive order to create the Cabinet Committee and told him to place my name as chairman. I asked the President

how was I going to get the Cabinet members to meet and he said hold your meetings here in the fish room next to my office and indicate that I will look into the progress of the committee.[79]

Ximenes's dual appointment as EEOC commissioner and chair of the Inter-Agency Committee on Mexican American Affairs was as much a surprise for Ximenes as it was for everyone else that day. In Ximenes's mind, Héctor García had once again prevailed on Johnson to make good on his campaign promises to the Mexican American constituency. Ximenes recounts: "On this appointment, Johnson went against tradition and senator prerogatives. It was time to pay political debts owed to my father, Dr. Héctor García, the American GI Forum, the grassroots Hispanics, and myself as the director of the Viva Johnson campaign."[80] Johnson promptly issued his June 9, 1967, memo to committee members Willard Wirtz (secretary of the Department of Labor), Orval Freeman (secretary of the Department of Agriculture), John Gardner (secretary of Health, Education, and Welfare), Robert Weaver (secretary of Housing and Urban Development), and Sargent Shriver (Office of Economic Opportunity) to formalize the Inter-Agency Committee on Mexican American Affairs. Johnson declares:

> Over the past three years, many members of my Administration have had discussions with Mexican American leaders and others interested in their problems. They have discussed the value of our programs to Mexican Americans in the search for equal opportunity and first-class American citizenship. The time has come to focus our efforts more intensely on the Mexican Americans of our nation. . . .
>
> The purpose of this committee is to: assure that the Federal programs are reaching the Mexican Americans and providing the assistance they need and seek out new programs that may be necessary to handle problems that are unique to the Mexican American community.
>
> I am also asking this committee to meet with Mexican Americans, to review their problems and to hear from them what their needs are, and how the Federal Government can best work with state and local governments, with private industry and with the Mexican Americans themselves in solving those problems.[81]

News of the formation of the Inter-Agency Committee on Mexican American Affairs was made public during the June 9th swearing-in ceremony. Ximenes reflects: "I believe the President kept it a secret in order to avoid the criticism that might come from others who had been asking for recognition. There is a possibility that if he had announced the creation of the Committee at the same time as the EEOC appointment the critics would have stopped the Committee appointment."[82] To mark the occasion, Johnson staged an elaborate swearing-in ceremony at the White House with a distinguished guest list that included cabinet committee members, senators, congressmen, friends, family, as well as their mutual friend and ally, Héctor García.

Invoking the trope of the Great Society, Johnson's swearing-in ceremony remarks focused on the previous three years of his presidency. Johnson sketched the trajectory of his presidential administration leading up to Ximenes's appointment as the logical conclusion of a long narrative of progress. Indirectly recognizing the oversights of the past, the president openly mused that America "is not great yet, but it has improved a lot. . . . and it is going to improve a lot more."[83] Ximenes later described the swearing-in ceremony as one of the most extravagant ceremonies he had ever attended at the White House. Following the event, Johnson took Ximenes aside and reminded him that there was not much time left in his presidency and to make the most of his new appointments. According to Ximenes, rumors of Bobby Kennedy's run for office were in circulation, and Johnson knew his White House days were numbered. Ximenes remembers, "I had to dispense with celebrations and instead hit the ground running because the 1968 elections were just around the corner."[84]

With his dual appointments secured, Ximenes exercised agency over the national narrative on Mexican American civil rights through multiple acts of authorship. He had been preparing for this moment for more than twenty years, and he adroitly used the rhetorical platform of his office not only to tell his story but to create a deliberative space for others to tell their stories. Because Mexican Americans represented a linguistically constructed minority, Ximenes immediately addressed the issue of ethnolinguistic heterogeneity and citizenship. In a July 3, 1967, *Corpus Christi Caller* newspaper article, speaking in his capacity as chair of the Inter-Agency Committee on Mexican American Affairs, Ximenes takes a bold stance promoting bilingual education: "I would like to say I am for bilingual education but not just for Mexican Americans. I think bilingual education should begin in the first grade for all Texans. I do not favor a bilingual education program which tends to segregate the Mexican American. It is my belief that the Anglo and Mexican American should both share in the cultural advantage one can get from knowing two languages."[85] Ximenes's position on bilingual education was not only progressive; it was radical. He argued for multilingual literacy education across communities. His experiences as a Mexican American growing up in the segregated schools of South Texas, a civil rights activist and economist in New Mexico, a program director in Latin America's

Alliance for Progress, and finally an administrator for the EEOC solidified his ethos as an advocate for educational reform on behalf of Spanish-speaking (and linguistically diverse) populations. Even in direct advocacy, however, Ximenes did not attempt to create a single grand narrative to represent the diverse identities of Mexican American citizens. Instead, he constructed numerous occasions for Mexican Americans to speak, beginning with the October 1967 El Paso Hearings and then continuing through the next three years with EEOC hearings in communities across the nation.

Ximenes, who had been sent out of the country by two presidents he helped put into office (first to Ecuador by Kennedy and then to Panama by Johnson), had finally joined the custodians of the "new American administrative state."[86] In truth, he belonged to a large and growing cadre of bureaucrats and civil rights caretakers.[87] Ximenes brought Mexican Americans to that expanding edge. He vectored the power of the White House to organize and prioritize the issues facing the Spanish-speaking citizens of the nation. Moreover, Ximenes disrupted the persistent neglect by White House insiders of Mexican American issues.

Ximenes's role in the EEOC and Inter-Agency Committee on Mexican American Affairs ultimately reconfigured the rhetorical landscape for Spanish-speaking citizens in the United States. Ximenes's experiences in Ecuador and Panama had broadened his notions of *latinidad*, countering, in many respects, the ethnocentrism of the AGIF. Ximenes's growing understanding of Latin American heterogeneity and cultural diversity within the Spanish-speaking communities in and beyond the United States helped shift the national consciousness and expand the consciousness of the leaders of the Mexican American civil rights movement.

As Ignacio García notes in *Viva Kennedy*, Héctor García and the leaders of the AGIF advanced a strong *mexicano* bias in terms of gaining attention and favors from the White House for Latinos.[88] For Ximenes, *latinidad* was a more capacious construct that included a broad range of peoples (indigenous, Iberian, and *mestizo*) and a rich tapestry of cultural and linguistic heritages. His own *mestizaje* complicated the ethnocentric biases he inherited and acquired. Moreover, his own experiences in the politics of compromise reaffirmed the pitfalls of ideological rigidity and cultural chauvinism.

In the end, Ximenes (and the cadre of AGIF leaders) were willing to make the necessary compromises to gain access to the White House and sustain relations with the president. As a metonymic emblem, the White House was a symbol of white power. The repeated failure of pragmatic solidarity to alleviate structural violence, nationally and internationally, ultimately closed down collaborative relations and truncated deliberative processes between

African American activists and the White House. Nowhere was this fact more evident than in the volatile and unresolvable impasses of the 1966 White House Conference on Civil Rights. The results were so disastrous in Johnson's mind that he refused to hold an equivalent White House conference on Mexican American affairs.

Ximenes and the Mexican American constituency, nevertheless, continued to do business with Johnson. Compromise comes with costs, however. Chicano nationalists perceived Ximenes and the AGIF leaders as *tio tacos* (a derogatory term equivalent to "Uncle Toms") and *vendidos* (sellouts). Such political trade-offs between Johnson and an increasingly fragmented Mexican American leadership played out throughout the period of the Great Society, which expanded and subsided in a giant mass of social programs, gliding over the turbulent terrain for the next few years like a huge, untethered hot-air balloon. Ximenes recognized the polyvocal nature of his constituency. He invited the cacophony of vernacular voices into the national narrative.

Soon after the 1967 appointment of Ximenes to the EEOC, Johnson asked Ximenes to suggest Spanish-speaking individuals for potential nomination to high-level offices. In the wake of the landmark confirmation of Thurgood Marshall in 1967 to the U.S. Supreme Court, Johnson wanted to place a Mexican American on the federal bench. "Vicente," Johnson charged, "if you can find me somebody of the caliber of Thurgood Marshall, I will appoint him."[89] Unfortunately, Hispanics as a cohort had not reached equal national levels of professional or educational preparation.

It would take over forty years, until the presidency of Barack Obama, before the name of a Hispanic judge would be put forward for U.S. Supreme Court confirmation, an occasion celebrated heartily by Ximenes in his June 3, 2009, letter to the editor published in the *Albuquerque Journal*. Remembering the four decades leading up to the historic nomination of Sonia Sotomayor, Ximenes writes:

> I congratulate President Obama for his nomination of Sonia Sotomayor to the US Supreme Court. . . . The journey to get a Hispanic on the Supreme Court began to intensify when President Kennedy was elected. . . . In 1967, President Johnson appointed me to the federal Equal Employment Opportunity Commission and the Cabinet Committee on Mexican American Affairs. My job was to find qualified persons to serve in all aspects of the federal government. . . . At that time there were only two Hispanic federal judges on the bench, but neither one had any civil rights experience that would qualify them to be a Supreme Court justice.[90]

Through the hermeneutic project of the Inter-Agency Committee on Mexican American Affairs, Ximenes helped to institutionalize a deliberative space for constituting knowledge about the conditions of Mexican Americans in the United States and to mobilize national-level initiatives toward confronting racism and discrimination embedded within national social structures: business, government, education, and judiciary.

"Let's Go to El Paso"

Ximenes wasted no time getting plans for the White House Conference on Mexican American Affairs under way. In a June 19, 1967, internal memo, only ten days after Ximenes's swearing-in ceremony, White House aide Larry Levinson noted that "Ximenes felt strongly that a Conference in Washington would be non-productive because the problems were in the Southwest and that is where the conference would be held if there was one."[91] Ximenes details the sequence of events leading up to the El Paso Hearings:

> One of the first assignments of the Committee was to organize a conference of Hispanics similar to the ones known as White House Conferences. President Johnson had made a promise to Dr. García during the 1964 election to convene such a conference. Three years had elapsed when I was given the assignment and the Hispanics were disillusioned and disappointed that the blacks had a conference and there were no plans for a Hispanic conference.[92]

After the mixed results of the Johnson's 1966 Civil Rights Conference "To Fulfill These Rights," which focused exclusively on African American issues, the White House had consistently declined to support further events of this kind on behalf of Spanish-speaking groups. The conference he was tasked with creating represented a transitional moment for Mexican Americans crossing over the ideological and symbolic threshold into the national civil rights discussion.

Ximenes contemplated how to go about organizing a White House Conference, and decided to organize a localized hearing instead of a Washington meeting, "where the usual results were some high sounding resolutions."[93] Ximenes reflects, "I wanted to bring the government to the people. A Washington conference would have brought only a few grassroots people to attend . . . The hearing format, in contrast, would give a relatively large number of our most articulate grassroots people a chance to speak from conviction and not political necessity."[94] He was also aware that he had to find a way to bring otherwise uninformed cabinet committee members into the conversation: "I had five Cabinet Committee members that I had to, not only educate, but to get the message from the horse's mouth so to speak."[95] In sum, Ximenes believed that the "best way to get them to listen to our cause was through a hearing from people most concerned with the Hispanic and Mexican American problems and solutions."[96]

Ximenes sought to provide a forum that would bring together a wide range of voices from Mexican American communities throughout the nation, not just the privileged few who had White House connections. He summoned Felix Salinas, an attorney and former Albuquerque AGIF leader, to serve on his staff as a special legal advisor and administrative assistant.[97] While scrambling to fund and staff the office for the Inter-Agency Committee on Mexican American Affairs, Ximenes requested an additional $15,000 from the Budget Bureau in his capacity as chairman to go toward the proposed White House Conference on Mexican American Affairs.[98] Ximenes's new office had no hard money to fund start-up operations and no budget line to sustain them. As a result, Ximenes relied on the goodwill and financial contributions of other departments and his cabinet committee members, such as the Department of Labor and its secretary Willard Wirtz, to fund operations for the Inter-Agency Committee on Mexican American Affairs.[99]

Ximenes immediately launched a national communications blitz using "short-hard-hitting" radio spots featuring celebrities Ricardo Montalban and Vikki Carr to improve White House public relations with Spanish-speaking citizens and to celebrate the formation of the Inter-Agency Committee on Mexican American Affairs.[100] An informational brochure was created and circulated with photos of Ximenes with María at his side at his swearing-in ceremony beside the president. The caption code-switches in Spanish and English: "Bien Hecho, Señor Presidente! Because . . . you have done more, and you are still doing more for the Mexican-Americans—Puerto Ricans and Hispanos."[101] Inside, the brochure included a short list of twenty "notable appointments of Spanish-speaking Americans."

Ximenes traveled throughout the U.S. Southwest to meet with Mexican American leaders, attend community gatherings, and deliver public addresses. He was the featured speaker for the AGIF national convention in Denver, Colorado, in August 1967. In his address Ximenes quoted the beloved martyred President Kennedy in Spanish: "Si la sociedad libre no puede ayudar a los muchos que son pobres, no podra salvar nunca a los que son ricos."[102] (If the free society can't help the many who are poor, it can't save any of those who are rich.) His address received a standing ovation, reminiscent of his early AGIF mobilizing experiences. Ximenes returned to his grassroots organizing strategies to generate community support for the proposed conference. He needed to mitigate growing frustrations and hostilities toward the Johnson administration, reduce skepticism among the White House cabinet committee members, and, at the same time, build momentum within the American press for the event.

Ximenes scouted three cites: Albuquerque, San Antonio, and Los Angeles as potential sites that would accommodate two thousand delegates, five cabinet members, President Johnson, Vice President Humphrey, Civil Service commissioner John Macy, as well as corporate and labor union officials. He met with the mayors of all three cities under consideration. All welcomed the conference. The date for the meetings was set for October 26–28, 1967.[103] In mid-September Ximenes called a meeting with the president to make the final decision about the location.

Ximenes recounts, "The President said 'let's go to El Paso.' You will get two Presidents to attend and address your conference since I will be meeting with President Gustavo Díaz Ordaz to sign a treaty."[104] With little more than a month before the hearings were to be held, Ximenes was very unsettled by the president's recommendation. Ximenes recounts:

> I swallowed hard and said, "Mr. President, I have not even talked to the Mayor or made arrangements for the five major hotels we will need." The President said, "Pick up that White House phone and tell the Chamber of Commerce we are coming to El Paso." I did and the Chamber of Commerce said something to the effect that if we don't have the hotels, we will build them. I then took a flight to El Paso to meet with the mayor. I explained our reason for the hearing to which the mayor replied, "Listen, I do not want the hearing in my town. You Mexicans will tear up El Paso." At the same time, the State Department was sending messages to our staff that they did not like the idea of a hearing on Mexican Americans since the Chamizal Treaty was going to be signed in El Paso. I reported both responses to the President and he just said, "Pay no attention. We are going to El Paso."[105]

As a liminal political place, El Paso and Chamizal represented a one-hundred-year-old border dispute between the United States and Mexico, defying the terms of the 1848 Treaty of Guadalupe Hidalgo when the Rio Grande shifted course. The dispute over the Chamizal territory had recently come to a close through diplomatic negotiations between the United States and Mexico. In brief, the United States had officially recognized Mexico's sovereignty over the Chamizal strip with the passage of the American-Mexican Chamizal Convention Act of 1964 and was scheduled to return the contested strip of land to Mexico in the fall of 1967. This landmark event signaled a symbolic political windfall for Mexico with the recovery of a very small slice of their national patrimony. The official transfer of the 630-acre Chamizal tract from the United States to Mexico was scheduled to be ceremoniously marked by President Johnson and President Díaz Ordaz in October 1967 in El Paso.

The location of the Cabinet Committee Hearings on Mexican American Affairs in El Paso alongside the Chamizal treaty signing ceremony added another layer of meaning and significance worthy of consideration. These deliberative and ceremonial rhetorics situated on the U.S.-Mexico border in El Paso performed the symbolic act of restorative justice at the Chamizal ceremony. The celebration of the diplomatic process that resulted in the return of the contested Chamizal section of the Rio Grande to Mexico constructed a powerful trope. For stakeholders south of the border, the Chamizal treaty represented an important win for diplomatic relations with the United States. And for some, it was but a feeble display of U.S. imperialism. Too little too late. For stakeholders north of the border, the Chamizal treaty was a sign of weakness and resignation.

Chamizal ultimately helped to invigorate and define the Mexican American civil rights movement by recognizing the ancestral ties and geographical/human ecologies that extend across this geopolitical border. These rhetorical acts elevated this historical moment to the realm of the poetic, signifying a binational public imagination and the transitory conflation of the outside and the inside. To memorialize this rhetorical event, the Chamizal National Monument was established in 1974 with the construction of a museum to document this historical moment of binational cooperation, diplomacy, and cultural exchange.[106] Here diplomacy is lauded as the critical rhetorical means to conflict resolution.

The El Paso Hearings enacted the deliberative democratic values and agonistic pluralism of the Great Society that LBJ's highly centralized administration failed to advance. The deliberative testimonials represented the kind of participatory democracy that Freedom Summer delegates had called for in Atlantic City during the 1964 Democratic National Convention and that the Students for a Democratic Society and the Free Speech Movement had rallied for in the fall of 1964 as the Johnson and Goldwater campaigns battled it out for the presidency. As Milkis and Mileur contend, "the idea of participatory democracy did not play a large part in LBJ's Great Society programs, but it found its way into some of them, such as community action programs, where it served as an important prelude to the emergence of participatory democracy as a leading principle of reformers of the late 1960s and 1970s."[107] The deliberative democratic impulse, occluded in Johnson's new administrative state, found its way into LBJ's Great Society through the rhetorical imagination of Vicente Ximenes and the organizers of the El Paso Hearings.

In advance of the hearings, Ximenes issued invitations to Mexican American leaders throughout the country. MAYO (Mexican American Youth Organization), which had already been protesting on behalf of Mexican American youth in the city of El Paso before the site for the hearings was announced, complained that its members had been omitted from the guest list. Ximenes met with the MAYO delegation in El Paso in advance of the conference to hear their complaints and to offer them a place on the agenda. MAYO sent five delegates to the hearings. Ximenes reports, "They did well in their presentations and then they invited me to speak to them on the Sunday after the conference at the Sacred Heart Church hall. I did. This was the same place I heard that a demonstration was being held. I was the main speaker, but no one demonstrated."[108]

Ximenes was supportive of the growing mobilization of Chicano youth. As a former community organizer, he sympathized with the counterdiscourse of this sector of marginalized citizens. Ximenes legitimized the MAYO meetings as "an attempt . . . whereby an organization could be established. And that's fine."[109] Ximenes welcomed the dissent and disputation circulating at the border nexus of the nation during the El Paso Hearings.

The hundreds of presentations by community organizers, elected officials, and local leaders promoted vision making and social critique. The conference enacted agonistic pluralism at every level of participation. Vocal activists who presented papers and served as monitors for the hearings included Ernesto Garlaza, Ralph Guzmán, the Reverend Henry Casso, Roberto Ornelas, Roy Elizondo, Albert Peña, Carlos Truan, Mario Vasquez, Louis Tellez, and James De Anda.[110] Mexican American women leaders Priscilla Mares, Delia Villegas, Dominga Coronado, and Patricia Jaquez gave testimonies on poverty, labor, and migration issues. Over one thousand people attended the El Paso Hearings and together generated over two thousand pages of testimony.

Ralph Guzmán, an assistant professor of government at California State University, delivered a robust and eloquent presentation of over five pages of recommendations about the role of scholarly research in the work of social justice for Mexican American citizens. Guzmán issues a challenge:

> Five and one-half million Americans of Mexican descent provide living testimony to repeated failures of the American conscience. The destiny of these people is inextricably entwined in the resolution of internal moral crisis. The challenge posed by these people to American scholars and American political institutions has been largely unmet. The response has been

ineffective, irrelevant, and miserly, both in material and spiritual assistance. The consequences to the Mexican-American people echo like a medieval petition to a benevolent despot.[111]

The published proceedings of the El Paso Hearings collected over fifty testimonies foregrounding labor, immigration, housing, education, and public access issues (chapter 6).[112]

Not all those who were invited deigned to come, citing different reasons for their nonparticipation. LULAC and the AGIF were represented. Although Ignacio García, in his book *Héctor P. García: In Relentless Pursuit of Justice*, charges that Dr. Héctor García did not attend, archival evidence and video footage of the hearings indicate that García was among those present at the hearings.[113] Roy Elizondo, representing a group of former Viva Kennedy organizers who established the nucleus of the new national-level organization PASSO, gave testimony. However, labor activist César Chávez declined the invitation. Chávez boycotted the event with these words in a September 27, 1967, letter to Ximenes: "Your and the President's concern for *most* Mexican-American problems is commendable. We have not participated in any such meetings and are reluctant to do so as we do not want to embarrass the administration. It is our considered opinion that the administration is not ready to deal with specific problems affecting farm workers."[114] George I. Sánchez also declined an invitation, saying, "I cannot accept the El Paso Conference as a sort of 'consolation prize,' with all due respect to the White House."[115]

Not all those working in the arena of Chicano civil rights were invited, either. Prominent Chicano activists such as Reies López Tijerina, who was under federal indictment for leading a raid on a New Mexico courthouse, were omitted from the guest list.[116] According to Ximenes, "Tijerina was supposed to come with a caravan to demonstrate. Tijerina did not attend nor did he have a caravan."[117] Tijerina's group, Alianza Federal de Mercedes, asserted that large areas throughout the Southwest "awarded as land grants by Mexican and Spanish governments had been wrongfully taken" after the region became part of the United States.[118] Problematically, Tijerina and the Alianza never directly addressed conflicting claims discrediting these colonial Mexican and Spanish land grants made by New Mexico's nineteen pueblos and other tribal communities seeking to restore native sovereignty during this same period. The question of whose claims came first remained a thorny issue that Tijerina never resolved.

Tijerina's notorious courthouse raid occurred on June 5, 1967, just days before Ximenes was sworn in as EEOC commissioner in Washington, D.C. If a single event pushed President Johnson to establish the Inter-Agency

Committee on Mexican American Affairs, it was likely the well-publicized violence that broke out in Ximenes's home state of New Mexico on the eve of Ximenes's swearing-in ceremony. State police with shotguns scoured the mountains of northern New Mexico by helicopter. National Guard troops with tanks were sent to Rio Arriba County. Tijerina and two dozen Alianza members invaded the Rio Arriba County courthouse in Tierra Amarilla in northern New Mexico to stage a land grant recovery protest. Two courthouse officials were shot and seriously injured in Tijerina's raid, one person was murdered, and a journalist and sheriff's deputy were taken hostage.

The violent tactics, anti-Semitic ideology, and polarizing discourses that became Tijerina's signature rhetorical moves throughout the 1960s and 1970s ultimately resulted in many civil rights activists of the period disavowing and distancing themselves from Tijerina's extremist measures.[119] Ximenes considered Tijerina something of a snake oil salesman, a "coyote." He believed that Tijerina's unilateral leadership style was no more effective in advancing democratic participation than the political bosses and *pátrones* of the past. "The Alianza never recovered a single land grant," Ximenes critically observed.[120] After Tijerina's death at the age of eighty-eight on January 19, 2015, little evidence remains of his legacy in Tierra Amarilla but the hand-painted words fading for nearly fifty years on the side of an abandoned and dilapidated grocery store reading, "The Dynamite Kid June 5, 1967."

In terms of historical impact and cult of personality, Tijerina and the courthouse raid have been indelibly imprinted in the Chicano memory. The El Paso Hearings, by contrast, were never woven into the grand narrative or collective memory of the Mexican American civil rights movement. The one thousand Mexican Americans gathered in El Paso have remained largely dismissed by Chicano scholarship. Effacing this deliberative event from the story of Mexican American civil rights history represents both significant memory loss and a tragic gap in the historical record. The absence has deprived generations of Mexican American scholars, public leaders, and political activists of productive models of resistance and civic engagement. The unprecedented success of the El Paso Hearings offered a valuable training ground for democratic participation and a springboard for future national-level elected officials and policy makers.

Ximenes and the El Paso Hearings represented a deliberative moment of everyday citizens giving witness to their own experience of institutionalized discrimination and civic marginalization. Furthermore, the occasion offered the opportunity to express those grievances directly to the administration.

The El Paso Hearings provided a platform for ideologically diverse voices, leaders both well known and relatively unknown. Farmworker organizers like Lauro García Jr., director of the Guadalupe Organization of Guadalupe, Arizona, openly challenged the Johnson administration. Lauro García Jr. boldly calls on the administration for action:

> In the factories, in the fields, and at this conference, scores of Mexican Americans have taken courage from [César Chávez's] lone battle with the war on poverty. . . . Yes, Mr. Secretary [Orville Freeman], unless we are ready to fight the Barry Goldwaters in my state of Arizona who talk of damming the Colorado River whose water flows into Mexico and which action will result in serious future consequences; unless we are ready to fight the Ronald Reagans in California who speak of peace but who put prisoners into the farm labor force (as of October 25, 1967 approximately 400 prisoners are in the fields, confirmed by Mr. Cesar Chavez), we are masquerading.[121]

The voices and perspectives represented at the El Paso Hearings pressed the limits of the U.S. legal imagination.

In his January 25, 1968, memo to President Johnson, Ximenes delineated action items derived from the two thousand pages of testimony.[122] These action items were framed as viable solutions in such areas as education, health and welfare, civil service problems, rural problems, manpower problems, and housing (chapter 6). All of the action items that Ximenes presented in his memo were unanimously approved by the committee members: Secretary Orville Freeman (Department of Agriculture), Secretary Willard Wirtz (Department of Labor), Secretary John Gardner (Health, Education, and Welfare), Secretary Robert Weaver (Housing and Urban Development), and Sargent Shriver (Office of Economic Opportunity). Remarkably, Ximenes had achieved consensus among these initially reluctant cabinet committee members. Ximenes recounts:

> There were many accomplishments that can be attributed to the conference. John Gardner came away from the program determined to start a bilingual program in the U.S. It was John Gardner, a member of my committee, who came up with the money in his budget to start the programs . . . I can rightfully claim that as EEOC Commissioner, affirmative action was made a part of the national agenda. I was the only Commissioner that fought and achieved the goal of affirmative action plans in the area of employment and the idea spread to almost every segment of our society.

Civil Service Commissioner John Macy, at my insistence and as a result of his attendance at the conference, started an affirmative action plan in the Civil Service. Willard Wirtz agreed to continue funding the SER Program. The Mexican American Legal Defense organization was funded by the Ford Foundation upon my recommendation to the Foundation representative who came to the conference to make a decision. Finally, Secretary Freeman started funding farm worker programs for health and housing.[123]

Other outcomes included a change in census-taking methods, the creation of bank charters for Latinos, and Hispanic inclusion in the Democratic National Committee.[124] Additionally, during his administrative tenure as chair of the Inter-Agency Committee on Mexican American Affairs, Ximenes provided oversight for the appointment of over four thousand Mexican Americans to federal positions.[125] If we consider the implementation of these afore-mentioned programs and policies, the El Paso Hearings seeded exponential change affecting not only Mexican Americans but the entire nation.

Ximenes's approach to the El Paso Hearings offered a valuable and effective model for negotiating national policy making within U.S. political structures. Moreover, the effectiveness of the policy changes enacted by Ximenes through the Inter-Agency Committee on Mexican American Affairs merits their inclusion in the historical record of major U.S. civil rights achievements. Ximenes and the participants at the 1967 White House Cabinet Committee Hearings on Mexican American Affairs in El Paso demonstrated productive models of democratic practice and civic literacy that effectively promoted dissent, engaged difference, cultivated debate, and negotiated the noise of disparate positions.

6. *Public Memory and the Reconstruction of History: The 1972 Civil Rights Symposium*

ive years after the 1967 White House Cabinet Committee Hearings on Mexican American Affairs in El Paso, Ximenes took a seat beside the luminaries of the civil rights era to preside over the rhetorical work of shaping public memory and constructing history. For the first time in U.S. history, representatives of the Mexican American community were included along with African American leaders in the intellectual work of making meaning out of the fragments of the nation's past. The 1972 Civil Rights Symposium was set inside the sanctioned intellectual sphere of the American academy, strategically situated in the physical space of the university and library at the University of Texas. In and among the vast cultural artifacts and archives of the Great Society era—the memories and stories of the key actors in the struggle for civil rights reform—Ximenes joined with a former U.S. president and vice president, a former chief justice of the Supreme Court, legislators, professors, and scholars to weave the fabric of history. Addressing this august gathering of dignitaries, Ximenes boldly reflects:

> Yesterday, while we were reminiscing about the Civil Rights Movement, we left out a significant group of people. In the fifties and sixties in Texas, one of the panelists here today, Henry [B. González] was taking the lead in the Texas Legislature on the issue of civil rights for everyone. In New Mexico, it was Senator Chavez taking the lead on these issues. In Albuquerque—one of the first cities to pass the Public Accommodations Act and an FEPC—it was Senator Chavez and Senator Montoya. In California, it was Congressman Edward Roy Ball [*sic*].
>
> There were others like Dr. Hector P. Garcia and the distinguished lawyer Gus Garcia, who took his case on jury discrimination, the *Hernandez* case, to the Supreme Court and won. Unfortunately, Gus was never recognized for his efforts: the Chicanos at the time did not understand what he had done and the rest of society hated him for it. These are some of the individuals in this part of the country that were part of the Civil Rights Movement, and they should be included in any symposium or panel or library that we may create throughout this Nation insofar as Civil Rights Movements are concerned.[1]

Ximenes played a supporting role in this landmark event as a speaker for the 1972 Civil Rights Symposium. He delivered his public address to this elite group of civil rights leaders, expanding the national discussion to include the role of Mexican Americans in the civil rights movements of the postwar era. Although they had been excluded from Johnson's first White House Conference on Civil Rights held in June 1966, called "To Fulfill These Rights" (chapter 5), the presence of Ximenes and other representatives of the Mexican American community at the 1972 Civil Rights Symposium was historically significant. Lifting the black-white binary that had overshadowed the conference of 1966, the 1972 Symposium on Civil Rights sought to represent, in good measure, the discursive pluralism and cultural diversity that had shaped the era.

This chapter foregrounds Ximenes's rhetorical role through the closing years of the Great Society from 1968 through 1972. It explores the historical significance of the 1972 Civil Rights Symposium as the capstone event of Johnson's Great Society, an occasion marked by the claim Ximenes placed on the national narrative of civil rights reform on behalf of Mexican American citizens. Chapter 6 also chronicles the downward spiral of the Inter-Agency Committee on Mexican American Affairs and examines Ximenes's relentless interrogation of institutionalized discrimination in the public and private sectors of U.S. society through the Equal Employment Opportunity Commission (EEOC). Finally, this chapter traces the efficacy of Ximenes's rhetorical career extending beyond the Johnson administration in his role as EEOC commissioner, an appointment that continued through July 1, 1971.[2]

"I Have Never Been Prouder of Anyone from Floresville"

On a bitter cold December day in 1972, the ailing former president invited civil rights leaders, scholars, and government policy makers to the ten-story white limestone Lyndon B. Johnson Presidential Library on the campus of the University of Texas in Austin for the stated purpose of reflecting on post–World War II civil rights reforms and projecting toward the future of social justice in the United States. Dedicated on May 22, 1971, the LBJ Presidential Library began releasing the Johnson presidential papers within two and a half years after his administration left office. Truncating the standard five-year waiting period, Johnson wanted his papers opened to the public as soon as possible and began opening his presidential files only six months after the library's dedication. Coordinating efforts with the LBJ Presidential Library and the LBJ School of Public Administration, the 1972 Symposium on Civil Rights was held on December 11 to mark the opening to the public of a million pages of papers on civil rights.[3]

The 1972 Symposium on Civil Rights was one of the groundbreaking events for the LBJ Presidential Library. Johnson was joined by a host of dignitaries including Chief Justice Earl Warren; Vernon Jordan Jr., director of the National Urban League; Senator Hubert Humphrey; Reynaldo G. Garza, U.S. district judge; Henry B. González, U.S. representative from Texas; and Ximenes, as well as numerous national leaders, educators, and community members. It would be the final public performance of Johnson's life. He died thirty days later.

Ximenes used the occasion both to celebrate this pluralism as well as to admonish the still much-too-limited frame of U.S. civil rights history. Ximenes was painfully aware that Héctor García had been omitted as a guest speaker for the event and had declined to attend the conference. Speaking on behalf of his *compadre* García and other AGIF colleagues, Ximenes attended to the unfinished business of the Mexican American civil rights movement. Ximenes unabashedly asserts:

> There are other matters that must be considered in our attempt to reevaluate the situation. The drive for women's rights is developing a full head of steam, and I realize that this situation must be brought to the Civil Rights Movement in some fashion, as other ethnic minorities must be brought in at this time. . . .
>
> Finally, language is to the Chicano what color is to the black in the field of civil rights and equal opportunity. Most of the national organizations engaged in the Civil Rights Movement have never given proper consideration to the subject of language as it affects the civil rights of the Spanish-speaking people; and what little has been done, has been carried out without their participation. The time has come to fish or cut bait on the language issue.
>
> There is widening division between the blacks and the Chicanos. I, like many others here, have fought for many years to preserve unity among all peoples. But the burden is getting heavier and local Chicano and white ethnic leaders will no longer support strictly white-black priority issues. Perhaps if the white-black leadership will include in their plans the top Chicano priorities, we might be able to bring together the forces that opened so many doors for people of all races, colors, national origins, and religions.[4]

Ximenes's act of epideictic rhetoric for the 1972 Civil Rights Symposium invokes both praise and blame. He honors his predecessors in the struggle for civic inclusion and confronts the selective memory of history. His public oratory openly problematizes the binaries of race, the hegemony of English monolingualism, the insidiousness of institutionalized discrimination, the postwar generational divide, and the expanding political fissures in black-brown solidarity.

The address also indexes Ximenes's own political evolution over time. By presenting a litany of Mexican American voices erased and ignored by history, figures such as the often-maligned attorney Gus García, the tenacious Dr. Héctor García, and the stalwart Senator Dennis Chávez, Ximenes gives tribute to his contemporaries and mentors, the old-guard leaders of the World War II generation. Ximenes refrains from personally laying claim to any of the advancements made on behalf of Mexican American civil rights. He says nothing about his own contributions to the story of U.S. civil rights reform. There are no audacious acts of self-promotion here. Instead, Ximenes demonstrates the confidence and gravitas of an established leader and senior statesman whose political biography had achieved a life of its own.

Ximenes limits his tribute to the past and his predecessors, but he also makes a turn toward the present and the future of Mexican American civil rights reform. He embraces the ascendancy of the younger generation by alluding to the Chicano movement in his remarks. As he sketches the story of the Mexican American civil rights movement, Ximenes also openly acknowledges the new guard of activists taking the lead in the historical narrative. Although in the opinion of some social critics, 1972 marked the downward arc of *el movimiento*, Ximenes nevertheless respectfully acknowledges the cultural and political significance of the Chicano generation and its role in the course of history.

Significantly, Ximenes adopts the mobilizing term *Chicano* to identify with the radical Mexican American constituency. He demonstrates identification with the youth counterculture and Chicano ideology as both an intellectual and rhetorical project. Ximenes, a World War II veteran, a federal-level administrator, and a former leader of the American GI Forum (AGIF) is remarkably in step with his times. Curiously, Ximenes makes no mention of the AGIF or the League of Unified Latin American Citizens (LULAC) in his 1972 Civil Rights Symposium remarks. Instead, he implicitly acknowledges that the torch of Mexican American social activism has been passed to the emerging generation of Chicano leaders. Ximenes, who had frequently been labeled a *vendido* and *tio taco* by the new wave of reformers, demonstrates respect for his successors in the movement, as well as his predecessors.

Ximenes, at some level, had found himself identifying with the Chicano student protests and public school walkouts, acts of public dissent reminiscent of his first moment of political resistance during his 1939 Floresville High

School graduation (chapter 1). The radical rhetorics of the Chicano youth generation resonated with Ximenes. Moreover, Ximenes and Chicano organizer Corky Gonzáles, who was a former AGIF member, were longtime friends. There were a number of facets of *el movimiento* that appealed to Ximenes. The liberatory impulse and Third World sympathies of *el movimiento* aligned with Ximenes's own experiences in Latin America and his understanding of the value of transgressive power when dealing with entrenched and unjust power structures. A tribute by an anonymous Chicano activist featured in the July 1, 1971, EEOC program brochure was published by the national committee in honor of Commissioner Ximenes. Acknowledging common Chicano sympathies, the writer lauds Ximenes at the close of his four-year EEOC appointment; the tribute reads, in part, "I know Commissioner Ximenes as a Chicano who believes in equality for all Americans regardless of origin, race, color, creed or sex. He struggles against injustices toward Indians, Blacks, Orientals, Spanish Speaking Americans, and women regardless of personal consequences, so that equality for all of us will come to pass."[5] Ximenes's identification with the Chicano movement was more than perfunctory. By the time of the 1972 Civil Rights Symposium, Ximenes was steeped in Chicano rhetoric. He would eventually pen essays on Chicano issues throughout the 1970s, such as his 1974 essay "Seeking a Path Out of Poverty for Chicanos" published in *Agenda*, the official newsletter of the National Council of La Raza.[6] Above all else, Chicano discourse plumbed deeply into Ximenes's own experience and understanding of *mestizaje*.

In these respects, Ximenes represented a bridge connecting the World War II generation of Mexican Americans to Vietnam War–era Chicanos. The Mexican American generation pressed the limits of the legal imagination of U.S. society toward the ascribed and acquired powers of citizenship. The Chicano generation agitated against the imperialist impulses of U.S. society and the military-industrial complex driving the war by calling for the transgressive and transformative powers of what Paolo Freire described as *conscientização* in his 1970 release of *Pedagogy of the Oppressed*.[7] Unlike Héctor García, Ximenes could not argue against the social justice principles for which Chicano activists were calling. Ascribed and acquired powers of U.S. citizenship were not sufficient for social justice nationally or internationally. Ximenes realized, at some deep level, the need for enacting all four forms of social power on behalf of his people: transgressive and transformative powers as well as ascribed and acquired powers were necessary for achieving full social inclusion.

Even if intellectually he could not condone or support some of the misguided direct action tactics advanced in the name of the Chicano movements, such as the ill-fated attempted takeover of Santa Catalina Island off the coast of Southern California in September 1972 by the Brown Berets, Ximenes could appreciate the rhetorical value of their political gestures.[8] He enjoyed the irony. But Ximenes drew the line. For him the violent June 1967 Rio Arriba courthouse raid led by Reies López Tijerina was inexcusable, on the one hand, while the quixotic Santa Catalina Island occupation by the Brown Berets, on the other hand, was amusing, harmless, and utterly ridiculous. The antics of the Chicano movement spoke to Ximenes—his appreciation for political spectacle and whimsy were all part of his own Hermes-like character. He understood the radicalism of the Chicano movement in light of the ebbing tide of liberalism and social democracy. Even decades later at the age of ninety-four, Ximenes wore his silver hair in a ponytail, *un viejito y chicano* to the very end.

With the collapse of the Great Society and his own political margin-alization from the Nixon administration, Ximenes increasingly identified with Chicano sensibilities, as evidenced in his 1972 Civil Rights Sympo-sium address, in solidarity with the energetic youth movement. Ximenes began sympathizing with a Chicano political sensibility as early as 1967. He had listened to their stories, inviting representatives of the Mexican American Youth Organization (MAYO) to give testimony at the 1967 El Paso Hearings (chapter 5). He had included Mexican American Political Association (MAPA) protestors in the 1970 Los Angeles EEOC hearings that interrogated movie industry executives about the proliferation of negative stereotypes in film and television. Ximenes could hear the same complaints coming from the impassioned voices of Chicano activists in 1967 that he himself had advanced ten years earlier in 1957.

Cognizant of the expanding generational divide separating the World War II Mexican American leadership from the Vietnam War Chicano activists, Ximenes boldly affirmed the ideological underpinnings of the emergent Chicano movement on several levels. Ximenes's adoption of the term *Chicano* signaled his own political consciousness that appreciated *chicanismo* for its advocacy role toward the political inclusion of *la raza*; the promotion of Chicano cultural arts; the endorsement of linguistic pluralism in public in-stitutions and the advancement of bilingual education; and the celebration of indigenous *mexicano* heritage and *mestizo* identity. In these respects, Ximenes parted ways with his *compadre* García, who largely dismissed Chicano ac-tivists as *malcriados* or misguided hotheads.

Although Ximenes acknowledged Héctor García in his address, he made no direct reference to the AGIF or to LULAC. By 1972 the AGIF and LULAC were no longer the exclusive arbiters of Mexican American civil rights discourses. The fracturing within the Mexican American civil rights movement through the late 1960s and early 1970s, on a parallel course with the African American civil rights movement that splintered along similar ideological lines, had led to an increasingly fragmented public discourse on race. The ideology of separatism had taken hold in both the African American movement and the Chicano movement. As a result, by 1972 there was no longer a unified public discourse about Mexican American civil rights issues. Furthermore, the Inter-Agency Committee on Mexican American Affairs had been shut down in 1969 and, along with it, a direct line to the White House. As a person of color, Ximenes, like Louis Martin, had been among the few White House insiders.

Ximenes continued to hold onto his EEOC appointment for two more years after the collapse of the Great Society, while his aspirations for the Inter-Agency Committee were jettisoned by the Nixon administration along with the other ambitious social programs of the Johnson administration. The continued absence of Mexican American political representation in the Nixon administration was a huge setback for the movement in Ximenes's opinion. With these changes on the national political landscape, by 1972 Ximenes had taken a broader view of Mexican American civil rights activism. Ximenes came to accept that the AGIF and LULAC had achieved as much as these politically right-shifting organizations could reasonably achieve in this social climate. He also understood that the issues were bigger than his own story, more capacious than any single civic group or political organization, and reached far deeper into history than any one generation.

Ximenes closed his 1972 Civil Rights Symposium remarks by calling attention to the "widening division between blacks and Chicanos." According to Ximenes, the nation's future depended not only on the resolution of black-white disparities but on the bridging of the black-brown cultural divide. Ximenes also reiterated the issue of Spanish and linguistic identity, issues first raised in 1951 with his letter to the editor about the dead Spanish-speaking children denied medical care in Loving, New Mexico (chapter 2). Very little had changed in the previous two decades. For Ximenes, linguistic discrimination was as pernicious to the health and well-being of the Mexican American community as racial discrimination was for people of color. In these ways, Ximenes's address also reaffirmed the key themes advanced in his 1956 University of New Mexico Bureau of Business Research lecture on economic insecurity among Spanish-speaking citizens (chapter 3).

In the twenty years since Ximenes first stirred the conversation on race and class in Albuquerque, New Mexico, he had come full circle. By 1972 he found himself standing among the prominent leaders of his generation and advancing many of the same issues around which he had mobilized people as a young community activist throughout New Mexico in 1951. The arguments were the much same; only the speakers and the available means of persuasion had changed. Ximenes responded to the rhetorical moment, shucking off the Cold War rhetorics and dispensing with the scapegoating discourses exemplified in his 1958 AGIF national convention remarks (chapter 4). He no longer relied on the specter of Communism to advance his rhetorical aims, forgoing the foreign policy tropes illustrated by his 1964 Alliance for Progress report (chapter 5). For Ximenes, the threat to democracy and the nation's progress was no longer external. The national backlash against the growing wave of cultural diversity and linguistic pluralism within U.S. society, evidenced by the oppressive tactics of the Nixon administration, was now the troubling impediment to full civic inclusion for Mexican American citizens. The contagious optimism of the Kennedy administration and quixotic progressivism of the LBJ administration had died with the decade.

Ximenes as a leader had exchanged his own bold determination and enthusiasm for a broader perspective and deeper wisdom. The *phronesis*, or practical citizen wisdom, which he exercised in the 1957 Daughters of the American Revolution flag-raising incident in Albuquerque (chapter 3), had constellated into something close to humility and compassion for his adversaries. He had circulated a broad array of discourses about Mexican American civil rights within and alongside the communities he served for more than twenty years. He knew firsthand the fact of institutionalized discrimination. He knew that the challenge of civil rights reform was a mountain larger than any single moment or movement or man. In this landmark moment of the 1972 Civil Rights Symposium address, Ximenes resisted positioning himself in a class separate from or above his people. Ximenes also eschewed the stance of the "militant Moses," knowing full well that the mountain he had been climbing for the half century of his own lifetime would continue standing long after he was gone.[9]

The problem of entropy had taken hold of every political and professional endeavor Ximenes pursued—from his forced resignation in 1960 from the University of New Mexico, in retaliation for his community organizing work in Albuquerque, to the 1969 collapse of the Inter-Agency Committee on Mexican American Affairs, following Nixon's election to the presidency. The inevitability of deterioration and death was palpable to him now in midlife at the age of fifty-three. Moreover, coming from the cultural rhetorical ecology of the Southwest and a New Mexican indigenous cosmology (chapter 2), Ximenes understood intuitively that the destructive forces of entropy and decline intersect with the regenerative forces of transformation and growth, often dramatically, as with the violent summer monsoon thunderstorms that sate the thirsty desert. Ximenes looked to the generations ahead that would be tasked with navigating this same treacherous terrain. His remarks remained grounded in his abiding value of *querencia*, his love for the connections and the communities he had served with dedication for more than two decades.

As Johnson receded from the political sphere and public memory, Ximenes remained an engaged presence troubling the conversation and the national status quo. Like Johnson, Ximenes would never have a national platform as capacious and influential as the Great Society plank again. The Inter-Agency Committee on Mexican American Affairs, the only cabinet-level committee representing the political interests of Mexican Americans in the LBJ administration, would fade into oblivion with the Great Society policies and programs that first established it. Arguably, Ximenes's White House tenure was too short lived for him to achieve the stature of his contemporaries at the 1972 Civil Rights Symposium such as Vernon Jordan Jr. and Roy Wilkins. Although the scope of Ximenes's political influence reached its apex in 1972, his politically engaged presence would endure for another four decades. Ximenes's brief stint in the Johnson administration would be his defining hour. Every experience henceforth would be measured against the shining moment that almost was. Ximenes was a survivor, above all else. Unlike many of his contemporaries, Ximenes endured and persisted through the turbulent four years leading up to the 1972 Civil Rights Symposium. That Ximenes navigated the most violent and riotous periods in twentieth-century U.S. history and retained his integrity as well as his social position attests not only to his keen survival instinct but to his tremendous rhetorical alacrity.

1968: "The Year That Rocked the World"

The year 1968 pulled the lid off the rolling boil of Cold War tensions that had been mounting through the previous decade.[10] The major themes stirring the national imagination in 1968, eerily echoing those of 1958, revolved around all too similar *topoi*: the ambitions of the U.S. space race, the fear of Communism prompting the escalation of the Vietnam War, and the growing incidence of social instability erupting in American cities. The violence and revolution that had held Cuba and Latin America in a perpetual state of turbulence through the previous decade were now a daily reality in the United States, with bombs, arsenals, and armed law enforcement officials storming the streets in Los Angeles, New York, Chicago, and Memphis. Not since the Civil War had the nation seen such self-inflicted violence. No longer was the attack cast as the work of a foreign threat; America was attacking itself. Revolution was bubbling up from inside the nation among students, people of color, women, and marginalized groups everywhere. The televised image of the small blue orb, transmitted by the *Apollo 8* mission in December 1968 back to a weary and war-torn world, has been heralded as the moment of saving grace in a year that defined and destabilized an entire generation.

The groundbreaking achievements of the 1967 White House Cabinet Committee Hearings on Mexican American Affairs in El Paso were promptly eclipsed by a year of national turbulence and transformation unlike any moment before or since. The disturbance ecology of 1968 radically changed the national climate and the rhetorical situation influencing the future direction of the Mexican American civil rights movement. In other words, the shape of the Mexican American civil rights movement in 1968 through 1972 flowed in syncopated rhythm with the larger social currents reconfiguring the nation. Ximenes not only recognized the shift; he was transformed by it.

The vibrancy of the Chicano movement was beginning to take hold in the U.S. Southwest in the very cities and communities in which Ximenes had once mobilized the AGIF. This new generation of reformers adopted many of the direct action strategies that the post–World War II Mexican American activists fundamentally eschewed.[11] The generational divide between World War II Mexican American reformers and the growing Chicano movement, resistance to the Vietnam War among Chicano youth, and the availability of new media and new modes of cultural production in art, theater, film, and literature represented developments that were profoundly reconfiguring the rhetorical situation of the era. The frequency of political protests in every corner of the nation and across the world recalibrated activists' available means of persuasion. The decade of Cold War anxieties and tensions that had been mounting nationally and internationally fueled an explosion of civic resistance.

By 1968 American casualties in Vietnam were mounting at alarming rates in the tens of thousands. The Vietnam War, costing an estimated at $2 to $3 billion a month, was severely draining the national economy and depleting funding sources for Johnson's ambitious Great Society programs. Johnson had built a national debt and written a promissory note he could not pay. The January 1968 approval ratings for Johnson's presidency spiraled downward as the year erupted with race riots, assassinations, war casualties, youth protests, public massacres, economic crisis, political strife, and an unleashed media frenzy.

Television news reporters, radio, magazines, and newspapers sustained a discourse of national and international disputation. The incinerating volume

Great Society Reader: The Failure of American Liberalism hit bookstores in 1968 like a harbinger of gloom forecasting the collapse of Johnson's quixotic social spending programs along with American liberalism.[12] Examining the discursive energy system igniting the nation in 1968, Ximenes needed once again to navigate an uncertain course.

Taking a rhetorical stance toward healing division, Ximenes responded to the disintegration of Johnson's administration by promoting new opportunities for change and the robust social justice initiatives evolving out of the 1967 El Paso Hearings. He was not derailed by the unrest. Ximenes understood the arc of transgressive power and the necessity of political resistance dating back to his own New Mexico community organizing experiences. He himself had gone to battle on behalf of Albuquerque garbage workers just a decade earlier. He had been dismissed from his job for agitating the local political system and confronting the business-political establishment. Furthermore, Ximenes recognized that the disturbance ecology of democracy involves public dissent evolving out of a dynamic process of emergence, growth, decline, and transformation.

"Califano Wetbacks": Navigating the Press and the White House

Against this social tapestry of national discontent, Ximenes needed to find a way to advance the goals of his own small, underfunded, and foundering office of the Inter-Agency Committee on Mexican American Affairs. He needed to tap into the spirit of the social justice movements and, at the same time, comply with the administrative constraints of his position as commissioner of the EEOC and chair of the Inter-Agency Committee. With the success of the 1967 White House Cabinet Committee Hearings in El Paso, a resounding and widely recognized professional achievement distinguishing his first year on the job, Ximenes launched January 1968 by submitting a detailed report on the recommendations from the 1967 El Paso Hearings to President Johnson. On January 25, 1968, Ximenes articulated the problems and listed the recommendations gathered from the hundreds of testimonies at the El Paso Hearings. Official attendance records for the hearings vary, but estimates range from 1,200 to 2,000 participants. In a previous November 7, 1967, memo to President Johnson, Ximenes had reported: "We sent 1,000 invitations and an additional 1,000 persons came who wanted to participate. We accommodated about 600 more than previously planned."[13] All told, it appears that some 1,200 official guests attended the El Paso Hearings and an additional 500 participants came to El Paso from both sides of the border,

either for the Chamizal treaty ceremony or for the concurrent Chicano political meetings hosted by MAPA and MAYO.

The press along the U.S.-Mexico border had reported on the developments of Ximenes's leadership of the Inter-Agency Committee on Mexican American Affairs. The October 30, 1967, issue of the Spanish-language
newspaper *El Continental* included front page photos of Ximenes and other
key participants in the El Paso Hearings including Mario Vasquez, Héctor
García, Roberto Ornelas, and Louis Tellez.[14] The *El Paso Times* published
an October 30, 1967, editorial praising Ximenes with headlines declaring,
"Job Well Done."[15] Cross-organizational relations among Mexican American groups, from moderate groups such as LULAC and the AGIF to more
militant organizations such as MAPA and MAYO, had solidified relations
through the deliberative opportunities of the hearings. The issues of migrant
workers and the challenges of transnational citizenship had also found an
open forum during the hearings. Binational relations between Mexico and
the United States were ultimately enhanced by the White House Cabinet
Committee Hearings and the Chamizal ceremony in El Paso.

Ximenes and his embattled office of the Inter-Agency Committee on
Mexican American Affairs finally seemed to be gaining the rhetorical traction and political legitimacy necessary to affect substantive change. He enlisted the advisory assistance of cross-organizational community leaders who
had served as monitors for the El Paso Hearings including Louis Tellez (the
AGIF), Roy Elizondo (Political Association of Spanish-Speaking Organizations), Roberto Ornelas (LULAC), Mario Vasquez (Unity Council), and
Felix Salinas, special assistant to the office of the Inter-Agency Committee
on Mexican American Affairs. Ximenes's final report to the president on
the progress of the Inter-Agency Committee won Johnson's resounding support. In follow-up, President Johnson called on his White House staff and
speechwriters to prepare a presidential statement to inform the nation of the
recent developments on behalf of Mexican American citizens. Not all of his
staff members were enthusiastic about Ximenes's report or the president's
forthcoming statement on the status of the Inter-Agency Committee on
Mexican American Affairs.

Drafts of the presidential statement on Spanish-speaking Americans were
circulated among White House advisors over the next few weeks. A cover
memo attached to the February 19, 1968, draft of the president's forthcoming
statement sent from one White House aide to another reveals the enduring
antipathy toward Ximenes and his office. The internal memo comments
read, "The attached draft statement on Mexican-Americans has been re-
viewed by the Califano wetbacks. They are still unhappy with the style and

ask for editing assistance."[16] The acerbic racist comments by White House staff members, pejoratively referring to Ximenes and the Mexican American leaders who helped compile the January 25 report as "wetbacks," index the kind of backlash Ximenes continued to encounter.[17]

Nevertheless the president's statement on the El Paso Hearings and the White House press conference with Ximenes proceeded as planned on February 23, 1968. Ximenes was flown to Johnson's ranch in the Texas Hill Country to consult with the president in advance of his press conference.[18] The press conference was conducted in Austin, Texas, as scheduled. The national platform Ximenes had for so long sought seemed finally close at hand.

"A Conference of High Purpose"

During the February 23, 1968, press conference, Ximenes succinctly delineated his goals for the Inter-Agency Committee on Mexican American Affairs for a national audience. He described his role in the El Paso Hearings to the cadre of journalists summoned to report on new developments. Most significantly, Ximenes publicized the broad spectrum of the Spanish-speaking population to the nation. Ximenes not only addressed the presence of Mexican Americans in U.S. society, but he acknowledged the Puerto Rican community within and outside the United States. Ximenes reports:

> There are approximately 6 million Mexican-Americans in the five southwestern states of Texas, New Mexico, Colorado, Arizona, and California. There are probably another million in various other states such as Kansas, Illinois, and other states of the Union. There are approximately 1 million Puerto Ricans in New York City, who are Spanish-speaking, although not Mexican Americans, then, whatever, number there are in the Commonwealth of Puerto Rico.
>
> Spanish-speaking in the nation as a whole, I would estimate to be approximately 10 million. That would include all the Mexican Americans, as well as the others that I mentioned.[19]

The absence of a broad cover term to describe the different Spanish-speaking ethnolinguistic groups such as Mexican Americans, Puerto Ricans, and Cuban Americans ultimately sets the terms of Ximenes's available means of persuasion. As a national-level administrator attending to the issues of Spanish-speaking citizens, the scope of Ximenes's advocacy necessarily broadens. Because Spanish-speaking Americans did not exist as a cohort within the public imagination, there was no prior federal discourse on Spanish-speaking Americans to invoke. It had to be invented.

In sum, Ximenes had successfully garnered President Johnson's support for these capacious advocacy efforts on behalf of all Spanish-speaking populations during his critical first six months as chair of the Inter-Agency Committee on Mexican American Affairs. Even more importantly, he not only had the president's ear; he had President Johnson's voice. Aligning his public rhetoric with the Inter-Agency Committee on Mexican American Affairs, Johnson issued his presidential statement at the press conference, delineating the major issues addressed at the previous October's White House Cabinet Committee Hearings on Mexican American Affairs in El Paso. The laundry list of action items Johnson set before the American public was the most comprehensive set of executive measures on behalf of Spanish-speaking citizens in U.S. history. Even Ximenes's most ardent critics could not refute the efficacy of Johnson's action items and the significance of his remarks. Johnson asserts:

> Last October, in El Paso, I attended a conference of high purpose. There with the Vice President and members of the Cabinet, I met with 1,200 Spanish-speaking Americans.
>
> This was the first time that the Mexican-American community had an opportunity to discuss matters of direct concern—ranging from education to economic opportunity, housing to health—with the highest officials of government. . . .
>
> Ideas and suggestions flowed to a Cabinet-level committee on Mexican-American Affairs which I appointed last June. Based on the recommendations of the committee—many of which stemmed from the El Paso conference—I have taken the following actions:
>
> In education: I have signed into law the first federal bilingual education program. It will help Spanish-speaking children overcome the barriers of language which have prevented them from receiving the fullest benefits of education.
>
> I have asked Congress to provide funds to expand and improve adult and vocation educational programs aimed particularly at those Americans who have no high school diplomas. About 20 percent of them are Spanish-speaking.
>
> I have instructed the Secretary of Health, Education, and Welfare to: Accelerate the training of specially-trained teachers to work with Mexican-American school children and migrant workers; insure compliance with Title VI of the 1964 Civil Rights Act. This forbids discrimination in school district boundaries and in quality education, wherever the schools receive federal financial assistance.[20]

The litany of action items that Johnson supported included Medicare support for Mexican American communities and migrant workers; access to $1 billion in funding from the Model Cities Program for housing throughout the Southwest and Puerto Rico for Spanish-speaking communities; and the Fair Housing Act to end housing discrimination. The list also addressed wages, job discrimination, recruitment, and training for Spanish-speaking workers. It was the most comprehensive presidential statement and declaration of support for Spanish-speaking populations ever issued by a U.S. president. Not since his March 1965 Voting Rights Act speech had Johnson directed as much national attention to the condition of Mexican Americans in U.S. society.[21]

Then, the music stopped.

Johnson's groundbreaking statement was quickly overshadowed four days later by Walter Cronkite's field report from Vietnam. The February 23 presidential statement addressed to the press was a remarkable moment in the Mexican American civil rights struggle. However, the rhetorical valence of the moment was quickly dampened by the staggering images and sobering words broadcast across the world through Cronkite's February 27 televised message about the tragic state of affairs in Vietnam.[22] The February 1968 "Report from Vietnam by Walter Cronkite," which aired on the *CBS Evening News*, shocked the nation with the staggering news: "To say that we are mired in a stalemate seems the only realistic, but unsatisfactory conclusion. . . . But it is increasingly clear to this reporter that the only rational way out then will be to negotiate, not as victors but as an honorable people who lived up to their pledge to defend democracy, and did the best they could."[23] The credibility of Johnson's presidency and the Great Society were crumbling. Johnson, the White House, and the American public were thrown into a seemingly endless tailspin.

"I Shall Not Seek"

On March 31, 1968, Johnson announced to the nation that he would not seek reelection. Ximenes vividly recalls the occasion he learned of Johnson's decision: "We knew the party was over the day Johnson renounced his candidacy for re-election. In March 1968, President Johnson asked me and Dr. Héctor García to travel to Mexico City with Vice President Humphrey to witness the nuclear non-proliferation treaty signing with Mexican President Díaz Ordaz. On the return flight to Washington, D.C., Humphrey told us that President Johnson announced he would not run for the presidency."[24] In a televised speech to the nation reporting on the war in Vietnam and reflecting on the achievements of his Great Society policies of the previous four years, Johnson declared:

> What we won when all our people united must not now be lost in suspicion, distrust, and selfishness among any of our peoples.
>
> Believing this as I do, I have concluded that I should not permit the Presidency to become involved in partisan divisions that are developing in this political year. With America's sons in the field far away, with America's future under challenge here at home, with our hopes—and the world's hopes—for peace in the balance every day, I do not believe that I should devote an hour of my time to any personal partisan causes or to any duties other than the awesome duties of this office.
>
> Accordingly, I shall not seek—and will not accept—the nomination of my party for another term as our President.[25]

Johnson stunned not only the nation but his closest cabinet members and staff with his announcement. Comments from the president's cabinet and staff rang with disbelief. Robert Weaver, secretary of Housing and Urban Development, described himself as "speechless." Jake Jacobsen, special assistant to the president, reflected, "We have heavy hearts—some tears here." Stewart Udall, secretary of the Interior Department, exclaimed, "Knocks me flat." Willard Wirtz, secretary of the Labor Department, was flabbergasted with the news and commented, "Good heavens!" Orville Freeman, secretary of the Agriculture Department, summed up his reaction with "Good Lord! I'm astounded."[26] Ximenes felt tremendous despair over the news. After nearly a decade of tentative relations with the White House, he had finally begun to receive federal attention on behalf of Mexican American issues. With Johnson's surprising announcement on national television, Ximenes knew that presidential support would be short lived.

Just one week after the president's renunciation speech, funding for the office of the Inter-Agency Committee on Mexican American Affairs began drying up. An April 3, 1968, memo from Joseph Califano to White House assistant James Gaither reported: "Commissioner Ximenes concerned about funds for the Interagency [*sic*] committee on Mexican-American Affairs. He desperately needs funds before the end of the week in order to maintain his 26 man staff."[27] Among the action plans proposed by Califano to respond to Ximenes's fiscal crisis was the following recommendation: "I can have Budget tell Ximenes that funds are just not available and that he should attempt to work out with the members of his Committee putting his staff on their respective payrolls (in effect having the agencies loan staff to the Committee)."[28] Once again, Ximenes was running his operation on a shoestring with no hard money, no budget line, and no secure resources. Ximenes took immediate action as advised, trying to cobble together $40,000 from each of his committee members in other offices to keep his own office solvent through the end of the fiscal year.[29]

This patchwork system of funding would continue through the following year until Ximenes resigned as chair of the Inter-Agency Committee on Mexican American Affairs in April 1969. The brief burst of momentum he had enjoyed in January 1968 was utterly depleted over the tumultuous final year of the Johnson presidency. The ambitious visions of the Great Society, including the Inter-Agency Committee on Mexican American Affairs, faded quickly. By June 10, 1968, Ximenes received news that the House Appropriations Committee had severed funding for all interdepartmental boards, commissions, and councils, including his own.[30] The tenuous funding for Ximenes's office had been shut off just one year after its formation.

In January 1969, following the dramatic outcomes of the presidential election, Ximenes found himself once again appealing to the administration for official word on the status of his office. In a January 3, 1969, memo to Larry Levinson, special assistant to the president, Ximenes wrote: "Please let me know the legal status of the Cabinet Committee on Mexican American Affairs. As you know, the Committee was created by Memorandum by President Johnson. In the absence of a new Memorandum by President Elect Nixon, can we continue to exist and expend funds?"[31] Ximenes's office was stripped bare. According to Middleton, speechwriter for Johnson and later director of the LBJ Presidential Library, at the close of his administration, Johnson cleared out the totality of his administration's papers. With Johnson went the archive of his presidency, including the foundational documents of the Inter-Agency Committee on Mexican American Affairs. Until the Watergate indictment during the Nixon administration, presidential administrative papers from George Washington to Lyndon Johnson were the legal property of the president himself. "On the last day of the Johnson Administration, trucks pulled up to the White House and denuded the White House Central Files, carried all the material down to Austin, and stored it exactly the same way," recalled Middleton.[32]

With Johnson's departure from the White House, Ximenes's office had been promptly denuded and his funding cut. His cabinet committee members were replaced with Nixon's appointees. Califano then obstructed Ximenes's efforts to draft legislation to give a statutory basis for the Inter-Agency Committee on Mexican American Affairs and to enlarge its functions.[33] By April, as his underfunded and underrecognized office foundered with neglect from the Nixon administration, Ximenes was making national headlines in protest. An April 2, 1969, *Los Angeles Times* article reported, "In almost two years since former president Lyndon B. Johnson created the committee and named Ximenes chairman, the 49 year old New Mexican has not been able to convince the establishment that Mexican-Americans are really there."[34]

According to the report, "Ximenes related that during the last two years he had seen top officials in Washington who, not realizing he was talking about a group of American citizens, expected him to describe problems in Mexico."[35] The blatant disregard for his office and entrenched discrimination that persisted in the federal government, industry, and private foundations infuriated Ximenes. "That kind of reply is enough for me to want to go out and hit someone," *Los Angeles Times* journalists quoted Ximenes as saying.[36] The frailty and impotency of the Inter-Agency Committee on Mexican American Affairs under President Nixon's administration had become abundantly clear, so Ximenes resigned. Nevertheless, he hung onto the role of EEOC commissioner during the Nixon administration for another three years as an acolyte of LBJ's Great Society. Ximenes had held his position as chair of the Inter-Agency Committee on Mexican American Affairs for less than two years. In that position he nevertheless left a historical trace.

Memory Building and the Inter-Agency Committee on Mexican American Affairs

As Johnson's Great Society began to collapse, Ximenes took on the task of recording the El Paso Hearings. He approached the act of memory building as a scholar and a researcher by foregrounding two priorities: the need to make knowledge for present purposes and the need to compose an archive to shape public memory. The final document, *Testimony Presented at the Cabinet Committee Hearings on Mexican American Affairs*, represents the most comprehensive portrait of Mexican American citizens bearing witness to their civic experiences across all facets of U.S. society ever recorded in the annals of post–World War II Mexican American civil rights history. The proceedings represent everyday Mexican American citizens giving voice to their own journeys and engaging in the process of deliberative democracy. The fifty testimonies featured in this publication demonstrate the rhetorical work of bearing witness, crafting persuasive arguments, and making appeals to the highest offices of national decision makers. As instrumental rhetoric, the proceedings also offer pragmatic action plans for implementing legislation, making policy, and funding programs.

Testimony Presented at the Cabinet Committee Hearings on Mexican American Affairs was published in the months immediately following the October 1967

El Paso Hearings. The document was edited and approved by Ximenes in his capacity as chair of the Inter-Agency Committee on Mexican American Affairs. It was widely circulated to the participants and witnesses who gave testimony at the hearings and to leaders of the major Mexican American organizations, including emergent Chicano groups such as MAPA and MAYO. The intended audience for this document also included public officials responsible for administering government programs and implementing the recommendations of the El Paso Hearings.

The proceedings of the El Paso Hearings represent the most significant archival record available that was published by the short-lived office of the Inter-Agency Committee on Mexican American Affairs. The proceedings contain the distillation of transcriptions from two thousand pages of testimonies by more than fifty witnesses as well as an introductory statement written by one of those witnesses, Doris J. Armijo. Ximenes had constructed the rhetorical work of the El Paso Hearings to reflect the voice and dignity of Mexican American citizens.

The scope of the *Testimony* reached further than any other prior official document into the needs and problems facing Mexican American populations. Its release was accompanied by a presidential statement from Johnson and press conferences by Ximenes. As an exemplar of the literacy of community activism, the *Testimony* reflects the productive tensions of the El Paso Hearings, an exercise in agonistic pluralism and community building. The document is especially remarkable in the ways it evidences four types of social power: ascribed, acquired, transgressive, and transformative. As Doris Armijo summarizes in the introduction, "the resulting composite picture formed by this testimony contains several basic themes: Concrete proposals were made in the areas of agriculture; labor; health; education and welfare; the war on poverty and the general improvement in the economic and social condition of the Mexican American."[37]

Armijo's introduction adroitly reflects the cultural rhetorical ecology of the moment, accommodating the discourse of Mexican American reform for an institutional-level Anglo-dominant audience. The document efficaciously bridges the disparate subject positions of cabinet-level officials with those of everyday citizens. The redistribution of social power through education, labor, commerce, housing, and criminal justice reform was the overarching rhetorical aim of this document. Echoing Constitution-era discourse, Armijo declares, "Before Cabinet officers of our Nation, these representatives of Mexican American citizens gave testimony reflecting positive attitudes and action for consideration and incorporation into our governmental policy and social structure."[38]

The manifestos of resistance that preceded this event and the constellation of testimonies bearing witness to historical inequities giving rise to it are carefully embedded within the text. The memo of resolutions sent by Corky Gonzáles to President Johnson after the 1966 Albuquerque EEOC walkout is not directly referenced but clearly implied (chapter 5). Political critique of Anglo-dominant hegemony is also evidenced throughout the proceedings. Armijo's introductory remarks assert, "Foremost in importance is [*sic*] the long acknowledged but long ignored cultural differences. Since our programs have been geared, in great measure, toward the Anglo American population, the Mexican American has been left behind surrounded by all the implications that non-growth can have in a progressive industrial society such as ours. The witnesses pointed out that these differences must be understood and considered in every aspect of our efforts."[39] As evidenced in the proceedings, advancing bilingual education in the U.S. public school system was a key issue foregrounded at the El Paso Hearings. In sum, the *Testimony* provided a template for translating the experience, vision, and leadership of Mexican American citizen scholars into action plans for influencing public policy and changing social structures.

The proceedings of the El Paso Hearings predated the foundational Chicano manifestos of the late 1960s including the *Plan del Barrio* (1968), *Plan de Santa Barbara* (1969), and *Plan Espiritual de Aztlán* (1969).[40] The El Paso Hearings constructed a public space for cultivating Mexican American solidarity and exercising compassionate listening on the borders of a hundred-year-old binational struggle. At the same time as the Chicano movement and Reies López Tijerina's New Mexico land grant movement were advancing the jeremiad rhetorics of revolt, the 1,200 or more participants at the El Paso Hearings told their stories and generated practical action plans. The militancy of revolutionary rhetoric was transformed for a brief moment into dialogue and productive disputation. While Ximenes and the Inter-Agency Committee on Mexican American Affairs worked to coalesce the discursive strands of testimony, the fabric of the Mexican American community was fraying. The counterdiscourse of Mexican American civil rights rhetoric was rapidly reinventing itself across generational, class, and ideological lines. As Ximenes exercised rhetorical authority in the White House, maintaining a tenuous hold on the office of the Inter-Agency Committee until April 1969, an emergent counternarrative captured the Chicano collective imagination and public memory.

Using the public rhetoric of testimony helped to shift transgressive power toward transformative power. The healing process necessary for this kind of shift relied on the rhetorical concept of *phronesis* and civic wisdom, reflective of Ximenes's handling of the Daughters of the American Revolution flag exchange ceremony in 1957 (chapter 3). Moreover, the act of giving witness as demonstrated through the hearings invoked the rhetorical resources of *enargia*, making palpable and present the lived experience of the speakers. There was no other public occasion, before or after the 1967 El Paso Hearings, that coalesced as many community stakeholders, public and private foundation decision makers, high-level government officials, and grassroots leaders on behalf of Mexican American issues.

Recovering the Agonistic Pluralism of Cold War Reformers

Lessons learned from the 1967 White House Cabinet Committee Hearings on Mexican American Affairs in El Paso have historical and global implications. Getting into the sinew of government leadership and policy making was as much a vital step in institutionalizing social reform for the Mexican American constituency in the United States in the 1960s as it was for black citizens in postapartheid South Africa in the 1990s. The legacy of the post–World War II Mexican American civil rights movement that waged sustained resistance to the internal colonization of native peoples by white hegemonic political and economic systems suggests powerful alignments with the struggle in South Africa led by figures such as Desmond Tutu and Nelson Mandela. These parallel stories of shaping democracy and public memory merit deeper consideration for promoting global humanitarian models of self-governance.

The enduring question facing leaders seeking to transform oppression into social justice is how to resolve both the violence of the oppressor and the rage of the oppressed toward productive and sustainable reforms. The *Testimony* seeks to do that kind of rhetorical work. It reflects the concept of *querencia* that Ximenes struggled to advance through his community organizing projects in New Mexico through the 1950s. It also reflects the notion of *ubuntu* in the Nguni group of African languages that Tutu describes as the collective ethical assertion of a people that "my humanity is caught up, is inextricably bound up, in yours."[41] But these kind of cross-cultural alignments cannot be fully explored without the recovery of the larger narrative of Mexican American civil rights reform, a narrative that includes the collective voices of the 1967 El Paso Hearings.

For a brief moment it seemed like the tide of public opinion and the president's public display of support for Spanish-speaking citizens was finally moving in a productive direction. Moreover, it appeared that Ximenes finally had the rhetorical platform and the rhetorical power he wanted to enact substantive change. For the five years following the El Paso Hearings, Ximenes used his federal platform as an EEOC commissioner to make numerous nominations and recommendations for the appointment of Mexican Americans to government positions and to institute and chair EEOC hearings on everything from the labor rights of airline stewardesses, to negative stereotypes of Spanish-speaking groups in the film industry and media, the absence of people of color in the federal administration, and the implementation of affirmative action policies in industry and government. Ximenes exposed the full spectrum of ideological oppression, structural violence, and racial discrimination in U.S. society through the apex of the civil rights era.

Representing the Spanish-speaking population in the national census was an issue Ximenes thought critical to the development of social programs for all Spanish-speaking groups. In 1969 Ximenes lobbied the Census Bureau to include ethnolinguistic identity as a category for the 1970 census. The Census Bureau approved the inclusion of a question on the 1970 census form to indicate languages other than English used at home. Ximenes also recommended including a question regarding ethnic self-identification for the 1970 census. Ximenes's recommendations shaped census-taking practices over the next decade.[42] In a March 1, 1971, follow-up memo to the EEOC about the findings of the 1970 census, Ximenes later reported:

> About 55 percent of Spanish surnamed in the United States are bilingual and 20 percent speak only Spanish and another 20 percent speak only English. . . .
>
> Persons of Spanish origin were classified into five categories: Mexican, Puerto Rican, Cuban, Central and South American, and "other Spanish." The Spanish origin population was estimated to be about 9.2 million of whom about 5 million (55 percent) were of Mexican origin; 1.5 million (15.8 percent) were Puerto Rican, a half-million, Cuban, another half million other Latin American; and 1.6 million (17.1 percent), "other Spanish."
>
> Persons of Spanish origin numbered about 5 percent of the Nation's total. Four out of five on them were born in the United States, the Commonwealth of Puerto Rico, or in the outlying areas of the U.S. Overall, Spanish was reported as the mother tongue of 6.7 million persons and the current language of 4.7 million persons, making it second only to English as the language most commonly spoken in the United States.[43]

Ximenes not only pressed the federal government to account for the national origin of Spanish-speaking citizens but to catalog the ethnolinguistic identities of those groups.

The evolution of a panethnic term for Spanish-speaking Americans eventually took hold in the 1970s as a bureaucratic move toward identifying the Latin American diaspora in the United States for both census-taking purposes and commercial marketing interests. Factors influencing the adoption of a construct to categorize U.S. Spanish-speaking groups as a cohort (the broad usage of the cover term *Hispanic* for diverse Latino/a subgroups) were the result of these converging social, political, and media influences. The first incidence of the U.S. Census Bureau's inclusion of the category of "non-white Hispanic," however, did not occur until the 1980 census.[44] Affirmative action policies on behalf of nonwhite Hispanic populations evolved over time along with the federal ethnolinguistic labeling process.

This bureaucratically constructed racial category became a standard term for Spanish-origin groups in the United States beginning in the 1980s, eventually adopted by public institutions, including educational institutions, to designate minority status and provide Title VI civil rights protections for Spanish-speaking communities as historically underserved populations. Ximenes's insistence on the inclusion of Puerto Rican populations in the U.S. census-taking process helped to illustrate the ethnolinguistic diversity and magnitude of the presence of Spanish-speaking populations in the United States by 1970, and it prefigured the federal government's recognition of Spanish-speaking groups as populations under Title VI protections. Well aware that Spanish-speaking populations were neither confined to the Southwest nor defined by the same grievances, Ximenes convened the Midwestern Conference on Mexican American and Puerto Rican Affairs in Detroit in October 1968, one year after the El Paso Hearings. Spanish-speaking constituencies from Michigan, Illinois, Indiana, Ohio, Iowa, and Wisconsin were invited to address the problems and needs of Latino groups throughout the Midwest.[45]

Keeping the Conversation Going

Ximenes took on Frito-Lay beginning in 1968, battling corporate leaders for the next three years and resisting the perpetuation of dehumanizing images of Mexican Americans.[46] The showdown culminated in 1971 with EEOC hearings that exposed the racist icon of the "Frito Bandito" in a public forum. The media had a heyday punning about the showdown between Ximenes, poised as the erudite, articulate, and sophisticated EEOC commissioner, and his adversary, the gun-toting outlaw cartoon character.[47] Ximenes also monitored the EEOC hearings that addressed the complaints of stewardesses against the airline industry, which required that female employees remain young and unmarried; they became ineligible for employment if they gained weight or were over the age of thirty-two.[48] The EEOC finally ruled in favor of the stewardesses in June 1968 in one of the earliest women's rights victories in the emerging feminist movement.

Ximenes counseled corporate executives and federal administrators on the implementation of the new civil rights legislation. He attacked the hiring practices in U.S. banking industries, rebuking Security Pacific Corporation for failing to recruit people of color. "What advice would you give the black and brown people in this audience," Ximenes reportedly said during a March 14, 1969, EEOC hearing in Los Angeles, "to tell their children who might want to go into banking as a career?"[49] Ximenes took on the inequities of the national higher education system, testifying before the Subcommittee on Executive Reorganization with a bold assertion: "The educational system has succeeded in eliminating the Mexican American from the graduating classes of the Universities. The school system now produces a preponderant number of angry high school Mexican American drop-outs and a pitiful number of college graduates."[50] Ximenes contributed to the development of affirmative action policies and bilingual education programs, and he advocated for the representation of Mexican Americans in all branches of federal government. He helped to write the $7 million bilingual education bill that Congress approved in early 1969, noting that $40 million was needed to serve the bilingual children in the U.S. educational system. On March 14, 1969, Ximenes told *Los Angeles Times* reporters, "We have a hell of a long way to go in bilingual education. We are just beginning to produce the materials necessary to make 'Juanito' proud of his heritage in a system which pays attention only to the 'Johnnys' in our society."[51] In a speech to the Mexican American Law Student Association on March 19, 1970, at the Ghost Ranch in Abiquiú, New Mexico, Ximenes revealed his perceptions of the intractability of poverty, racism, and linguistic discrimination in U.S. society. Evoking the images and stories he portrayed in his earliest community-organizing public addresses, Ximenes describes:

> The domestic problems confronting the politician and public administrator in the 1970s are the same ones we failed to solve in the 1960s. Hunger, employment discrimination, civil rights, sex discrimination, quality education, inner city decay, pollution, and population control. These problems are inter-related, but some appear to have a possibility of solution whereas such issues as discrimination and civil rights appear to lack a handle . . .
>
> In 1968, during a study on migrancy, hunger, and rural poverty, a Mexican American farm worker was asked what the saddest thing in his life

would be. His answer was, "I haven't stopped to think about it because the more you think about it the sadder it will become. If I stopped to think about it—maybe my inability to work. But I haven't stopped to think about it because it's like death. . . ."

In Texas, a Mexican American seventh grader wrote an essay on her experience in school. "In the first through the fourth grade," she wrote, "if the teachers caught us talking Spanish we would have to stand in the 'black square' for an hour or so. During the fifth and sixth grade they charged us a penny for each Spanish word we said, and that really kept me from talking the language."[52]

Ximenes uses the art of storytelling and the narrative technique of testimony to depict the soul of the story and the people he serves. Like the testimonies delivered at the 1967 El Paso Hearings, Ximenes privileges the voices of everyday people to represent their own experience and to frame the larger political arguments. Ximenes engages all three dimensions of the rhetorical art of storytelling—the narrative self, the reflective self, and the rhetorical self—to do the work of public persuasion.

If there was a moment in Ximenes's public career that defined him, satisfied him, and represented him as he wished to be known, it was this five-year period beginning with his White House appointment in June 1967 through the December 1972 Civil Rights Symposium. Ximenes had struggled for three key things throughout his seasoned rhetorical career: the acquisition of rhetorical power, the exercise of civic self-representation, and the authority of social position to act as a public advocacy agent. It was what his father José Jesús Ximenes modeled to him. It was what his World War II generation expected of him. It was what his community demanded of him. In a July 2, 1970, letter to Héctor García on EEOC letterhead, Ximenes confides:

> I do not know what the future will bring to persons like you and those of us who believe in civil rights. I do know that the very fabric of a democratic society hangs in the balance. I do know that a non-democratic society spells death for the minorities. I do know that to maintain a free society the burden and sacrifice is placed on a very few. . . .
>
> Please be assured that I will put forth every ounce of effort, intelligence, and courage to gain equal employment for the Mexican Americans, Blacks, Indians, Puerto Ricans, and women of this land.[53]

The access and the authority to wield rhetorical power, Ximenes discovered time and again, is a shifting target.

The Closing of the Great Society

The rhetorical alacrity Ximenes demonstrated through the closing stages of the Great Society is exemplified in the numerous speeches and addresses he delivered between 1968 and 1972 at EEOC hearings throughout the country. In one example, Ximenes performs the role of storyteller in his opening remarks during the September 22, 1972, U.S. Postal Service's National Employment Opportunity Conference, recounting through exemplification and narration a specific event of institutionalized discrimination. He foregrounds this story to an audience of government bureaucrats in order to cultivate collective understanding and empathy toward a common commitment to action. He also demonstrates alacrity for transcultural repositioning with adept use of humility, humor, understatement, narrative, dialogue, and solidarity markers. Ximenes details his experience working as a mediator for Mexican American workers:

> Equal employment opportunity is undoubtedly an important area of human effort in our nation. I began this kind of effort only about 20 years ago as a student at a university. I discovered that the announcements of opportunity did not include Mexican Americans. I discovered that the persons that wrote and spoke about employment and accepted employment applications didn't have the Mexican American in mind at all.
>
> I remember quite vividly my first feeble attempts at helping another person to get a job that he claimed was not given to him because he was a Mexican American. I called the manager of the plant and said, "I understand you won't give Mr. Martinez a job because he is a Mexican American." He said, "No. That is not what I said; I said I wouldn't give him a job because he is Mexican and furthermore don't bother me."[54]

In this narrative excerpt, Ximenes demonstrates his skill for disarming resistance by exposing the absurdity of racism. He invites his audience of Anglo male bureaucrats to laugh with him as well as to laugh at their administrative counterpart in this story. Rather than elevating himself above his audience on the higher moral ground, Ximenes provides a self-effacing example of his own naïveté in this story as well as the ignorance of the racist manager. Ximenes levels the rhetorical playing field, using a particular case to illustrate larger principles and common values. Moreover, Ximenes violates the expectation bias of his audience.

He knows his audience expects to hear the kind of blaming and shaming rhetorical moves typical of affirmative action advocates speaking on behalf of historically underrepresented groups. Ximenes, in contrast, avoids deploying hyperbolic representations and overstated generalizations that overwhelm audiences with information about systems beyond their control. In contrast, he invites them to laugh at him and the manager as the key actors in this anecdote (and, indirectly, allows them to laugh at themselves). Ximenes exposes the stigma of the Other and the frequently unarticulated historical ambivalence toward *latinidad* that permeated the attitudinal climate of the dominant public sphere of the Cold War United States. In sum, not only does Ximenes construct himself as rhetor, enhancing his ethos and disrupting expectations, but he constructs his audience with the confidence that they are capable of exercising good thinking and right action. He operates under the assumption that his Anglo-American audience is both educable and flexible; to know the right thing is to do the right thing. This assumption, however, went against the ideological grain of the historical moment.

Ximenes keenly understood the rhetorical synthesis necessary for incorporating marginalized voices into the national discourse. He shifted fairly seamlessly between the nation-changing discourses of the social activist and the nation-maintaining discourses of the public administrator. The protean rhetorical work of his leadership drew on a repertoire of disparate and often conflicting ideological constructs and cultural material. His peculiar way of synthesizing the available means of persuasion across very diverse if not precarious rhetorical situations (from the 1957 flag exchange ceremony to the 1967 El Paso Hearings), all of which resolved in largely efficacious outcomes, distinguished Ximenes as one of the great rhetors in the pantheon of postwar civil rights activists. Ximenes stands among those recognized and not-yet-recognized figures whose acquisition and circulation of discursive power not only changed the social conditions of local communities but of the nation as a whole. Ximenes remembers: "Just before his assassination, Martin Luther King, Jr., led the African American garbage workers' strike to respond to the complaints of the garbage workers to the City of Memphis in 1968 over issues very similar to what I did in the beginning of my confrontation with the City of Albuquerque in 1954."[55] The reverberations of social reform that rippled across the nation through the civil rights era were not confined to one group. Each strand of reform rhetoric contributed to the civic DNA of social transformation that was ultimately reflected in the 1972 Civil Rights Symposium.

The Final Act of LBJ

Ximenes's remarks at the December 11, 1972, LBJ Presidential Library Symposium on Civil Rights raised questions about overlooked contributors to civil rights as he sought to call attention to the binaries of race and the construction of history. Additionally, Ximenes's remarks illustrated his persistent struggle to make present those groups and individuals who were either absent or had been erased from the rhetorical moment. Ximenes remembers:

> My last meeting with the President was at the December, 1972, Civil Rights Symposium. Johnson brought together the champions of civil rights for one last time at the LBJ Library. Chief Justice Earl Warren, Vice President Humphrey, Roy Wilkins, Julian Bond, Representative Henry Gonzales, Clarence Mitchell, and I and others participated in panel discussions on civil rights. President Johnson attended the symposium against the orders of his physician. The President popped some glycerin pills in his mouth and barely made it to the podium to give the closing remarks. Before the President died in January, 1973, he sent a letter of thanks for my participation in the symposium. He mentioned Floresville in his letter and knew it would bring back memories of his early campaigns in Wilson County. Now we were friends forever.[56]

In his final days, Johnson struggled to secure his historical legacy and his rhetorical relevancy. The 1972 Civil Rights Symposium represented a key moment in constructing the public memory of the civil rights era. On December 11, 1972, Johnson reflected on his role in U.S. civil rights reform during his closing remarks for the event. Johnson reasserted his commitment to equal rights for all social groups, harkening back to his 1963 Gettysburg speech:

> A decade ago, in the year 1963, we observed the 100th anniversary of the signing of the [Emancipation] Proclamation. On Memorial Day of that fateful year, I was called upon as Vice President to speak at Gettysburg Cemetery where, a century before, words had been spoken which all of us have long remembered. On that occasion, I said this: "Until justice is blind to color, until education is unaware of race, until opportunity is unconcerned with the color of men's skins, emancipation will be a proclamation but not a fact. . . . When I spoke those words as Vice President, I could not know that the future would present me shortly with the opportunity and the responsibility to contribute toward fulfilling the fact of emancipation."[57]

With the tragedies of 1968 and the nadir of the final days of his presidency—the assassinations of Martin Luther King Jr. and Bobby Kennedy, the Vietnam War, and the reelection of Richard Nixon—still searing the nation's memory, Johnson reiterated his words spoken at Gettysburg in 1963 to celebrate the achievements of 1960s civil rights reform. He sought to imprint the legacy of his presidency in public memory as well as to pass down his charge to future generations to continue the work of the World War II generation of reformers.

What followed Johnson's delivery of his 1963 Gettysburg address (but is not mentioned here in his 1972 Civil Rights Symposium remarks) was a tidal wave of social turbulence and change. In brief, the Great Society policies of the Johnson administration launched more public programs, instituted more equal rights protections, and advanced more educational access initiatives from Head Start to college for more citizens than ever before in U.S. history. But Johnson lists none of these achievements. Instead the rhetoric of place plays a critical role in marking the significance of Johnson's actions, the present and past. Johnson's final public remarks on his contributions to civil rights history do not include direct claims about his legacy or his unprecedented record of reform. He deferred to the moment and the place to speak for him.

Johnson keenly understood the symbolic value of moment, memory, and place. Johnson had learned that rhetorical lesson early in his political career after he intervened in the controversial case of a Mexican American soldier denied burial in his hometown of Three Rivers, Texas. As a junior senator, Johnson had personally arranged for Private Félix Longoria to be honored with an Arlington National Cemetery funeral in January 1949 (chapter 1). It was a watershed moment for Johnson as well as Mexican Americans during the postwar era. "Metaphorically, synecdochically, and metonymically, the burial of Private Félix Longoria evoked an unprecedented response in the American public," placing the young Texas senator in the national limelight and bringing the plight of Mexican American citizens into sharper national focus.[58]

These moments, like the March on Washington and the arrest of Rosa Parks, form the sedimentary layer of U.S. civil rights history. For Johnson, civil rights reforms throughout U.S. history, especially those enacted during his presidency, were teleologically linked by events, peoples, places, and moments. While some rhetorical scholars argue that Johnson's 1963 Memorial Day Gettysburg address signaled his public commitment to civil rights reform, it was the 1949 Félix Longoria case that initiated Johnson into the national debate on civil rights and represented his first bold public act on behalf of race and equal access.

We will never know which factors were most potent. Certainly, the shift in Johnson's public stance on civil rights was influenced by multiple factors. Nevertheless, the cultural rhetorical ecologies of Johnson's narrative and of Ximenes's remain marked by their connection to place and sense of belonging in the geographies of their own memories. For Johnson and Ximenes, the narrative of U.S. civil rights history was firmly embedded in the shared geographies of memory that extended back to South Texas (Cotulla and Floresville) and included the U.S.-Mexico border sites of El Paso and the Chamizal. In his December 14, 1972, letter to Ximenes, Johnson writes:

> Dear Vicente: I have never been prouder of anyone from Floresville in all my life—your remarks at the Civil Rights Symposium were both meaningful and eloquent, and so justly deserved the applause they received.
>
> Your contribution of time, ability, and esteem is deeply appreciated by me, and I know everyone that attended the Symposium feels the same.
>
> With fondest regards and all good wishes to you and yours for a Happy Holiday Season. Sincerely, LBJ.[59]

Through the tendrils of their common alliances, stretched, stressed, and strained for over forty years but never severed, Johnson struggled to construct meaning for his own story. The letter was among the few exchanges of personal correspondence between Johnson and Ximenes, the only other display of affection from Johnson having been delivered to Ximenes via telegram on April 17, 1965, at the Palacios Funeral Home in Floresville, Texas, upon the death of Vicente's father, José Ximenes. On that rare occasion Johnson wrote, "Lady Bird and I know the sadness of losing a loved one. Please know that you and those near and dear to you are in our prayerful thoughts. Lyndon B. Johnson."[60] Tejano connections ran deep for both men. Like Ximenes's, Johnson's ego and self-esteem were directly tied to his legacy as a public figure.

Johnson had almost completely removed himself from the public eye and retired to his ranch in the Hill Country outside Johnson City, Texas. He routinely evaded the ominous task of writing his memoirs and instead turned his attention to the operations of the ranch, the management of his birth home as a national historical site, and the establishment of the Lyndon B. Johnson Presidential Library in Austin. Somehow the task of writing his own story, lifting the veil between the shadow and ego, was beyond him. "History became comically reduced to a constant and watchful eye on the birth house," biographer Doris Kearns Goodwin observes. "[Johnson] wanted more people to see his birth house than any other presidential home. In afternoon walks to the birth house, Johnson liked to check the different license plates to see how many states were represented; he seemed to get a great deal of pleasure from the knowledge that people were coming from all over to see this memorial to his childhood."[61]

Casting about for four years after vacating the White House in dejection and shame, Johnson worried incessantly about how history would portray him. Goodwin notes:

When the Lyndon Baines Johnson Library opened, Johnson repeatedly said that he wanted more people to come to it than had come to any other presidential library in the country. He pleaded with his staff to open the doors early in the morning and keep them open late at night. Asked to supply daily attendance figures, knowing that Johnson would be angry at them if the figures were low, the staff—in a painful similarity to another staff in another place—tended, gradually at first and then more and more regularly, to escalate the body count.

Through the license plates and attendance reports, Johnson seemed to be searching for hints of his fate; the number of visitors serving as a finger in the wind, suggesting which way the historical breeze was going to blow.[62]

The *telos* of Johnson's political career that began in the rocky hardscrabble hills of the Pedernal directly shaped his narrative construction of his role in the civil rights period.

Certainly, Johnson enacted the narrative arc of Hill Country populism. His hero's journey had led him from the poverty and shame of his father's Hill Country dirt farm to the White House. In his mind, he had done right by his people, the Texas constituency that voted him into office and then elected him to the presidency. All told, he delivered on the promises of his 1964 Great Society speech and his 1965 Voting Rights Act speech. And along the way, he also got rich. All the wealth and power that Johnson had accrued over the course of his lifetime, however, failed to give him what he wanted most at the end of his life. What he wanted and struggled to achieve was a meaningful place in history. Johnson wanted to matter.[63]

Johnson's identity remained thoroughly enmeshed with the construct of the Great Society. In remarks to his biographer, Johnson often personified the vision of Great Society as a beautiful woman. He frequently mourned the demise of the Great Society as he mourned his own mortality. As Goodwin observes, Johnson's fate seemed inextricably tied to the Great Society. "And when she dies," he concluded, "I, too, will die."[64] Goodwin poignantly depicts Johnson's final hours in this portrait:

> On January 20, 1973, Nixon was inaugurated for a second term. The next day a cease-fire was announced in Vietnam—the long war was finally coming to an end. Later that day a new Nixon plan was announced for the dismantling of the Great Society. The following day, on January 22, 1973, Johnson had what was diagnosed as a fatal heart attack. . . . At 3:50 P.M., he had called the ranch switchboard and asked the Secret Service men to come at once. Before they reached his room, he had died.[65]

Throughout Johnson's bold and brash life story, distinction was always far more important than intimacy. And so it seems to follow, considering Johnson's need for distance, that in the final act of his personal narrative Johnson would die alone, surrounded by the tarnished symbols and fading accoutrements of power. Sealed off from the world, his death played out like a script. He exercised control over his own story to the very end. It is no less significant that Johnson's remarks at the 1972 Civil Rights Symposium would represent his last public appearance.

The loss of power and position affected Johnson and Ximenes deeply and differently. Ximenes had held the brass ring of power for only a brief time. He knew all along that it was tied to Johnson's shirttail and went wherever Johnson went. Ximenes wore the ring of power, moving about the hallowed halls of the White House and opening the doors and windows like some kind of harrowing of hell, letting all his *'manos* enter the intimate circle of political insiders. Johnson's renunciation speech meant the end of the party, literally and metaphorically. For Ximenes, the White House years were the apex of his public career. Ximenes knew that if his father had survived to see him at his June 9, 1967, swearing-in ceremony that José's blessings would have been with him. The moment was too short, but somehow it was enough, and it would be the centerpiece of his narrative script for the rest of his life.

But it was not enough for Johnson. Johnson and Ximenes did not share the same sense of class position, racial identity, ethnolinguistic heritage, religious background, or community connection. Johnson always regarded himself as separate, if not above, his communities of belonging. He was better than his people. As such, Johnson cultivated the stance of the noble benefactor throughout his life. His acquisition of political power, rhetorical authority, and social position was largely pursued to benefit himself and his own ego needs, primarily, and the needs of others, secondarily. His desire for power was insatiable. And his loss of power was intolerable. Johnson benefited and suffered from an excess of hubris and unbridled ambition driving him from the earliest years as a frustrated college student and transforming him over time into the benevolent tyrant.

Ximenes shared Johnson's tenacity and determination, reveling in the role of the diva and the dignitary whenever the occasion offered him that opportunity. In contrast to Johnson, however, Ximenes largely regarded himself as part of his community of belonging, an integral piece of the greater whole. As a result, Ximenes cultivated a deep capacity for reverence—respect and a sense of something greater than himself. He never severed himself from his family, his community, his roots, his faith, or his own story as "Joe's boy." His hubris was always tempered by a greater share of humility. His devilish

Hermes shadow was always counterbalanced by his generous humanity. His vulnerability lived in divine tension with his strength. He died surrounded by his children, a quiet death. Curled like an infant, a knitted cap on his head, Ximenes left the world much like he entered it—small and frail.

Neither Johnson nor Ximenes shared the same narrative arc of their self-ascribed hero's journey. Ximenes's hero's journey returned him, not to the isolation of an expansive self-fashioned kingdom, but to what Martin Luther King Jr. termed the "beloved community." He returned from his epic journey to a quiet and relatively humble existence of unassuming public service. Ximenes lived in the modest adobe home in Albuquerque, serving as chair of the Albuquerque Human Rights Board from 1977 to 1988. His legacy of public service to the Mexican American community was recognized in 1972 with the Aztec Award by the Mexican American Opportunity Foundation. He was presented the State of New Mexico Distinguished Service Award in Albuquerque in 1981 and the Common Cause Public Service Achievement Award in Washington, D.C., in 1982.

Ximenes became a founding board member for the New Mexico Youth Conservation Corps Commission at the age of seventy-two. He was first appointed by New Mexico governor Bruce King in 1991 and reappointed to the Youth Conservation Corps Commission by Governor Bill Richardson in 2003. Reflective of his earliest years in public service, Ximenes also participated in the national alumni groups of FDR's Civilian Conservation Corps until the age of ninety. He had come full circle, returning to the values of public service that he had cultivated in his youth at the Richard Kleberg Civilian Conservation Corps Camp in Seguin, Texas. He and María remained active members of their neighborhood Catholic church until their last days.

In contrast to Johnson's retirement years, Ximenes never engaged in any personal pursuits that might be considered frivolous or self-indulgent. He had no passions or hobbies aside from politics. There were no whirlwind trips overseas, no camping, no fishing, no hunting excursions. There were no fancy cars, no audacious ranch, no whimsical road trips, no golf, no gambling or even bingo at the local Albuquerque casinos. There were no pets or pastimes to whittle away his time, energy, or money. The death in 1978 of their eldest child, Steven, at the age of thirty-two, had taken the wind out of Vicente and María's sails. Helping to raise their only grandchild, Teresa Ximenes, became their primary concern following Steven's death. The loss of Steven prompted Vicente's permanent retirement and retreat to a private life in Albuquerque.

After returning to New Mexico after his final Washington, D.C., stint as the commissioner of the White House Fellows program under President

Jimmy Carter (1977–81), Ximenes confined himself to the business of his own family and his local community. Vicente and María eventually helped to raise Teresa's baby, great-granddaughter Chloe Ximenes-Merrill, who joined the Ximenes household on Monroe Street in 1994. The rough and tumble of local Albuquerque politics, lobbying on behalf of the New Mexico Youth Conservation Corps and the Albuquerque Human Rights Commission, was as much work as Ximenes wanted. In their final days, Ximenes's life trajectory shared very little with Johnson's, even though the former's career arc had been so deeply affected by the latter's. Everything that truly connected the two men happened in the beginning, during their early years in Floresville, and extended for those fleeting moments in Washington, D.C., in the eighteen months between June 1967 and January 1969 when everything seemed possible.

All in all, Johnson and Ximenes shared a common network of South Texas relationships, social democratic political convictions, New Deal liberal sensibilities, and a strong connection to home and place. Out of a deep sense of fidelity to Johnson; their *buen amigo* Héctor García; his own father, José Ximenes; and their mutual mentor Sam Fore, Vicente Ximenes was both willing and able to offer Johnson a revered place in the story of Mexican American civil rights reform. Ximenes gave Johnson what few contemporaries were willing or able to give him. Beneath the overarching trope of the Cotulla school days, Ximenes, in some small but significant way, helped make the final days of Johnson's journey more meaningful. Johnson's December 14, 1972, letter to Ximenes was penned only a month before his sudden death. At the end of his life and the closing of the Great Society, Ximenes answered Johnson's deepest nagging existential question: With whom will I stand? Ximenes continued standing with Johnson when few others did.

Ximenes represented an affirmation of the glory days of the Great Society as Johnson's bodacious political project was gradually starved into oblivion. It was not García whom Johnson summoned to the table at the 1972 Civil Rights Symposium; it was Ximenes. Johnson's omission of García from the list of speakers had deeply offended the good doctor.[66] Politically, Ximenes had increasingly distanced himself from the AGIF through the 1970s and 1980s. The AGIF became more politically conservative over time—a target of critique for Chicano activists. Unlike Ximenes, García failed to acknowledge the Chicano youth movement and failed to see that the polarization between the Mexican American generation and the Chicano generation represented a harbinger of deep divisions within *la raza*. Moreover, Ximenes had watched García's personal and professional life deteriorate under the AGIF's demands on García's time, finances, and health. Ironically, the nadir of the Johnson administration paralleled the nadir of the AGIF. García simply did not have the rhetorical cachet in 1972 that he had enjoyed in the previous decade. He became increasingly embittered and embattled as political power shifted away from him and the AGIF.

Ximenes, however, had stayed the course of the Great Society vision. He had become the public symbol of Mexican American achievement during the "high tide of liberalism."[67] The achievements and resounding approval of the 1967 White House Cabinet Committee Hearings on Mexican American Affairs became all the more important over the following years as significant measures of success for both Ximenes and Johnson. As the Nixon administration ushered in a second term of dismantling the Great Society programs and policies, Johnson found satisfaction in the fact that Ximenes had carried on as commissioner for the EEOC through 1971 and then as vice president for field operations of the National Urban Coalition through 1973. Although Ximenes had resigned in 1969 as chair of the Inter-Agency Committee on Mexican American Affairs, he still prevailed.[68] Ximenes fought the good fight.

Significantly, Ximenes took a key role in the rhetorical moment of the 1972 Civil Rights Symposium, representing the narrative of the Mexican American civil rights movement in the larger national story. At the symposium Ximenes called for a more capacious narrative that included not only Mexican Americans but women's rights activists as well. He acknowledged his friend and *compadre* Héctor García, as well as his other post–World War II contemporaries in the Mexican American civil rights movement. Ximenes took on the mantle of the esteemed elder statesman. At last, Johnson was not only willing to give Ximenes that platform; he wanted and needed Ximenes on that platform. In turn, Ximenes's presence and the narrative he constructed somehow restored and redeemed Johnson.

In each sphere of his rhetorical career, Ximenes cultivated an "open space for democracy."[69] From his formative experiences in Floresville, Texas, to his Washington, D.C., appointments, Ximenes promoted a dynamic discursive system of circulation. We see Ximenes's civic rhetorical impulse evidenced in events across his life: his public protest at his Floresville High School graduation in 1939 (chapter 1), the 1954 AGIF labor rights campaign on behalf of Albuquerque garbage workers (chapter 3), the 1957 Daughters of the American Revolution flag exchange (chapter 3), the 1964 Viva Johnson campaign and Alliance for Progress program in Quito, Ecuador (chapter 4), the 1965 Great Society Conference and the 1967 White House Cabinet Committee Hearings on Mexican American Affairs (chapter 5). A decorated war veteran, Ximenes approached the fight for civil rights with the tenacity of a warrior. Ximenes's multiple spheres of belonging, those personal and public spaces of rhetorical engagement, helped him to cultivate a complex cultural ecological perspective toward political life and an intuitive understanding, if not reverence, for ecotones of difference.[70]

The notion of ecotone is an apt metaphor for describing the cultural rhetorical ecologies of Ximenes's experiences of civic life. Ximenes occupied the edges of culture for his entire life: academic, civic, and professional. He immersed himself in every sphere of belonging, even as he retained his connections and investments in other spheres. He also experienced and provoked tremendous social change in each space of his public life. He learned how to circulate and thrive within the many disturbance ecologies he entered, discovering how ultimately to "set into play a succession of generating events."[71] Ximenes became an expert at organizing and supporting human communities through the economies of public rhetoric—the circulation of discursive energy systems. Unlike Johnson, Ximenes did not set himself apart from the communities he served. He was, indeed, part of the very disturbance ecologies he cultivated, as well as those he resisted.

The efficacious nature of Ximenes's approach to political practice was both his strength and his undoing. This was as true at the University of New Mexico in 1961 when President Popejoy asked for his resignation as it was for the Inter-Agency Committee on Mexican American Affairs in 1969 when President Nixon starved Ximenes's office into oblivion. The generativity of Ximenes's ecological approach to leadership represented a serious threat to monolithic political structures and hegemonic energy systems. In every case Ximenes had to learn to navigate the consequent conflicts of bringing competing systems into contact. He could not control the outcomes of his actions or the dynamic process of the larger systems, but he did take responsibility for his role and his actions within his spheres of influence. He did not shirk from conflict or hide from the consequences. As exemplified at the 1972 Civil Rights Symposium that wrapped up that year, Ximenes always showed up.

Conclusion: Vicente Ximenes—Engaging Public Rhetoric, Cultural Ecologies, and Civic Literacies in the Twenty-First Century

Ximenes delivered the keynote address for the seventy-fifth anniversary celebration of the Civilian Conservation Corps (CCC) for the CCC Alumni Chapter 141 in Albuquerque on April 2, 2008. He was eighty-eight years old. I listened as Ximenes and this enthusiastic gathering of New Mexico octogenarians remembered March 31, 1933, the day that President Franklin Roosevelt signed the Emergency Conservation Act, the legislation leading to the formation of the CCC. All CCC camps closed without fanfare on December 8, 1941, the day after the bombing of Pearl Harbor. The sudden closing left a huge vacuum. Ximenes remembers:

> The day after Pearl Harbor the CCC camps were closed and we all marched off to war. It was as if the Civilian Conservation Corps died and no one came to the funeral to deliver the eulogy. We left the communities where we worked without saying goodbye or for them to say thanks and to wish us well. The commander did not call everyone out one last time to the parade grounds to lower the flag for the last time and bid farewell. The shutdown of the camps was so quick and the vacuum quickly filled with the need to mobilize for war that few felt the transition. Years later the CCC Alumni felt a need to recall a part of our lives that had been important to us.
>
> We remember a time in the history of our country when we took a quantum leap to develop and protect our natural and human resources. People from the world can see, feel, and touch what the spirit of cooperation can accomplish when the creativity of young people is allowed to flourish. I believe it was democracy in action when our nation undertook the greatest peacetime public works program in the world. A peacetime public works program that involved more than three million men plus an estimated four other persons per enrollee that received a benefit from the money sent home. . . . We were the original practicing conservationists of our land, water, and natural resources.[1]

Ximenes's description of the last hours of the CCC could very well have been a metaphorical depiction of the closing of the Great Society. The final days of the CCC were as ominous and haunting as the last gasps of the Johnson administration. Ximenes was among the last believers in the Great Society to leave the White House after Johnson cleared out the White House Central Files and shipped them to Austin, Texas, in January 1969. It was as if the Great Society had died, and "no one came to deliver the eulogy."

Recovering the memories and the contributions of the CCC became a primary preoccupation for Ximenes in the final decades of his life. The loss of the CCC was a gaping hole that needed to be filled—not only for him personally but for perpetuity.[2] To Ximenes the CCC represented the alignment of important core values for him, for his generation, and for the nation. The workers of the CCC were more than stewards of the land, building roads and fences, planting trees, fighting erosion, and protecting forests, lakes, and streams. They were citizen scholars writing, remembering, recording, and inscribing their experiences of America. They were communities doing the everyday work of democracy.

Ximenes found solace and meaning among these few survivors of the World War II generation, the last remaining direct beneficiaries of FDR's CCC public works programs. It was not with the local chapter of the American Legion, Veterans of Foreign Wars, or the American GI Forum (AGIF) that Ximenes wished to spend his last days but with the Albuquerque Roadrunner CCC Alumni Chapter 141. The generative work of the CCC had set the foundation for his seventy-year career of public service beginning in 1939, and it was what continued to nourish him through the latter years of life.

Altogether, Ximenes spent more than two decades recovering the legacy of the CCC and reinvigorating its principles and practices through the New Mexico Youth Conservation Corps (YCC). In 1992 Ximenes and CCC alumni lobbied the New Mexico state legislature for $150,000 to establish the YCC. The bill was passed, and the New Mexico YCC Commission was established by Governor Bruce King to provide oversight for public works projects throughout New Mexico. By 1998 the YCC had grown into a $2 million per year program supporting urban and rural projects. Olivia Ximenes served with her father on the YCC Commission through its formative years.

Some of the sites for the earliest New Mexico YCC projects included locations in Zuni Pueblo, Albuquerque, the Sandia Mountains, Sumner Lake State Park, Silver City, Taos, Portales, and Santa Rosa.[3] The New Mexico YCC cut hiking trails, created open spaces for wildlife, designed nature areas at schools, restored fire-scorched forests, and cleared brush. Ximenes's efforts on behalf of the CCC didn't end with the developments of the New Mexico YCC.

In November 1998 Ximenes and CCC alumnus Carl Walker worked with a cohort of CCC supporters to complete construction on the largest adobe building in the nation. The Old Santa Fe Trail Building had been partly built sixty years earlier in 1938 by the CCC, but construction ceased for lack of funding. Reminiscent of his early community organizing days building the AGIF headquarters in Albuquerque, Ximenes was once again busy carrying adobe bricks to build the headquarters for yet another organization. At the age of seventy-nine, Ximenes alongside other former CCC workers set out to finish the old Works Progress Administration project and finally dedicate the building that would become the New Mexico headquarters of the National Park Service.[4]

In 2002 Ximenes and CCC Alumni Chapter 141 member Roy Lemons launched the lengthy process of drafting and ushering Senate Resolution 207 through the legislative process with the support of Senator Jeff Bingaman to designate March 31st as National Civilian Conservation Corps Day.[5] The resolution took six years to pass. The U.S. Senate finally passed the National Civilian Conservation Corps Day resolution in March 2008, just in time to mark the organization's seventy-five-year anniversary. It would not be an act of overreaching to call March 31, 1933, the first national Earth Day. Ximenes and the CCC alumni considered this to be the case. Ximenes had cultivated his public service identity with the CCC. His reverence for open spaces, his abiding sense of *querencia* for his birth state of Texas and his adopted home state of New Mexico, never left him. In Ximenes's mind, environmental justice was a civil rights issue. Ximenes shared these enduring sentiments with other prominent environmentalists of his era.

Edward Abbey, environmental activist, author, and inspiration for Earth First!, was Ximenes's contemporary and former classmate at the University of New Mexico (UNM) from 1948 through 1951. Abbey earned a BA in English and philosophy and then pursued an MA in 1954.[6] They probably never met each other. Nonetheless their individual contributions to twentieth-century American public culture were profoundly shaped by their common New Mexico roots. Ximenes and Abbey were on parallel courses that diverged dramatically by the 1960s. The comparisons are remarkable. Both men loved New Mexico and shared a passion for the high desert landscape that had become their adopted homes. Both cultivated a deep concern for nature. Both men were writers, activists, and leaders. Both pressed the limits of the Cold War rhetorical imagination. Both Ximenes and Abbey traveled widely before returning to the Southwest to the place they called home. But the similarities end there. Ximenes rooted himself in the place very differently than Abbey did. Abbey died at the age of sixty-two on March 14, 1989, his life cut short by hard living and poor health. He was buried in a secret grave in the high desert marked with a hard-carved tombstone that bears his name: "Edward Abbey (1927–1989) 'No Comment.'"[7]

Ximenes would have never tolerated such rhetorical brevity or irreverent anonymity. Ximenes's life was far from over at the age of sixty. In striking contrast to his fellow UNM alumnus and environmentalist, Ximenes had come full circle in New Mexico, back to the place and the communities that had so profoundly shaped his vision and experience. By the late 1980s, Ximenes had fully reclaimed the adobe home on Monroe Street he had left behind after President John F. Kennedy dispatched him to Quito, Ecuador, in 1961. Like the mythic Odysseus, Ximenes had finally come home. But his work was far from done. He was a young man in his late twenties when he first arrived in New Mexico with María and their first child, Steven, in 1947. After building their lives in Albuquerque for more than a decade, they were tossed about by the political currents of the Kennedy and Johnson years. Ximenes didn't return home to his adopted state until he was an elder statesman in his sixties. He would spend another thirty years fully engaged with this place.

The cultural rhetorical ecology and landscape of the region satisfied something very deep inside him. The huge vacuum left by the sudden closure of the CCC in 1941 was not unlike the huge vacuum left by the sudden collapse of the Great Society in 1969. Ximenes filled the void left by the sudden disappearance of the CCC by cultivating a network of intergenerational YCC programs across the state of New Mexico. He regenerated the experiences and connections he most valued, living close to the landscape and the communities he loved.

There is a published photograph of Ximenes, circa 1939, seated behind a heavy carved wooden desk on which rests a large office-sized Underwood typewriter.[8] An old telephone with its tulip-shaped mouthpiece and receiver hanging in its cradle sits on the desk to Ximenes's left. A full-length wood-paned window separates the thin slice of the outside world from the inside. On the wall of the wood-paneled office directly behind a twenty-year-old Ximenes in starched uniform are framed watercolor prints of forest scenes, a mounted clock, and a framed photograph of President Franklin D. Roosevelt peering down on the young CCC recruit. The surrounding furniture and file cabinets recede into the shadows; only the sober countenance of the white-haired FDR and the almost quizzical visage of young Ximenes are illuminated, peering out from the dark chamber of the military-like office space. The caption reads, "Vicente Ximenes sits under a portrait of President

Franklin Roosevelt in this undated photo. Roosevelt was founder of the Civilian Conservation Corps, which Ximenes says profoundly influenced his life."[9] The image is iconic.

As *topos* this 1939 photograph captures what would become the key themes of Ximenes's life, memes inscribed within the assemblage of objects situated inside this time frame of his youthful life. Literacy, ecology, and civic engagement represent the recurring primary colors, the tropological threads weaving throughout Ximenes's life and work. The typewriter, the crisply pressed uniform, FDR's paternal gaze, the paintings of mountain landscapes shrouded in wispy clouds and pine boughs beside a wood-paned window peering out onto a stark horizon were the defining tropes he would fill with meaning again and again.

Literacy

The growing dilemma facing Ximenes throughout his rhetorical career both at home and abroad was how to resist and to reconcile his complicity with the social systems and government administrations that supported and promoted policies of structural violence within and beyond U.S. borders. Acting as an agent of the expansionist agenda of Kennedy's Alliance for Progress from 1961 to 1964 and then as a representative of Johnson's emerging administration culminating in his leadership role with the Equal Employment Opportunity Commission (EEOC) from 1967 on into the Nixon administration through 1971, Ximenes had to negotiate the conflicting ideological territory of these respective political regimes on behalf of Spanish-speaking communities.

Ximenes quickly realized, as physician Paul Farmer argues in *Pathologies of Power: Health, Human Rights, and the New War on the Poor*, that "civil rights cannot really be defended if social and economic rights are not."[10] Moreover, Ximenes discovered that to be a citizen of a nation (and a community) is to be always-and-already implicated and impacted by the histories and pathologies of the past. This dilemma represents what one might call the original sin of citizenship: we are held accountable for the actions of our predecessors and our compatriots. Through the cultivation of a counterpublic, Ximenes provided a way and a means for coming to terms with his own Faustian pact with the dominant social group.

The demand for social reform is a continuous cycle, requiring persistent observation, analysis, critique, and responsive action informed by the lived experience of the poor. Because the oppression of one group by another remains endemic to systems of power, the burden of promoting public engagement and exercising civic judgment represents a continuous social struggle toward justice. Justice is a process, not an end result or product. Herein lies the herculean task of the activist and the rhetor: conditioning the rhetorical situation to enact public attitudes to move social action.

In *The Rhetorical Career of César Chávez* Hammerback and Jensen advance the notion of "reconstitutive discourse" to characterize the rhetorical efficacy of farmworker and labor rights activist César Chávez. The authors contend, "Discourse that reconstitutes the character of the audience contains rhetorical qualities and invites rhetorical processes particularly appropriate and in some cases indispensable for the task of changing character."[11] Chávez, according to Hammerback and Jensen, exploited the contemplative nature of reconstitutive rhetoric to promote solidarity around common values with strong appeals to pathos. Chávez's message was largely moralistic and his methods were highly dramatistic, seeking to promote identification and stir conversion in the hearts and minds of his audience.

The notion of reconstitutive discourse is far less productive to the analysis of the rhetorical career of Ximenes, however. Ximenes was never concerned with changing the character of his audience. Like most of his cadre of post–World War II reformers, Ximenes employed a pragmatic discourse focused on stirring action, not evangelizing or inciting moral conversion. Although Ximenes engaged in sustained moral protest against the inequities facing his people, he was more interested in working with his adversaries than converting them. He triangulated the available means of persuasion in circulation, cultivating a different hermeneutic of the public sphere. Ximenes's rhetoric was pluralistic, generative, and practical, aligning the discourses of American pragmatism, deliberative democracy, and New Deal liberalism. Ximenes eschewed the dramatism and pathos that propelled rhetorical figures like Héctor García (and the historic Félix Longoria incident) and César Chávez (and the poignant farm labor hunger strikes) into the national consciousness.

To be an effective leader, therefore, Ximenes had to exercise agency through his various appointments in order to influence public attitudes and civic judgment. Ximenes learned to use a broad array of public discourses and literacies to move public opinion toward social outcomes that would benefit marginalized groups. In effect, Ximenes's rhetorical representation of Mexican Americans in a national leadership position and his acquisition of unprecedented levels of prominence in the White House recalibrated the expectations and attitude toward Spanish-speaking citizens. Ximenes's administrative roles and his exercise of authority in the public sphere changed the discursive dynamics of national politics and disrupted the dominant cultural stereotypes that previously erased and denigrated Mexican-origin peoples in the national consciousness. What Ximenes achieved as an exceptional orator and writer was the capacity to negotiate multiple public spheres by invoking varying discursive registers, literacy practices, linguistic codes, and rhetorical genres for different audiences.

Ecology

The first overarching question of Ximenes's public life was, how do we live in right relationship with our different spheres of belonging—economically, environmentally, politically, and culturally? He found the answer to that question through his own culture and the ethic of *querencia* (love for his land, his home, his family, his community). However, living in the racist social conditions of South Texas complicated the answer to that question with the violence of racism. The second overarching question for Ximenes then became, how do we as citizens transform systems that erase and exploit us? He spent a lifetime answering that question. Ximenes's story offers a few important take-away insights on both of these questions.

Navigating power (ascribed, acquired, transgressive, and transformative) demands embodied presence. Identity formation is not a virtual, out-of-body process. Leaders must be consubstantiated with their own cultural rhetorical ecologies. Belonging is the consummate rhetorical act. How do we transform systems that erase and exploit us? Ximenes's story suggests that social transformation evolves out of engaged resistance, embodied engagement, symbolic action (metonymic alignment), a sustained narrative, and an enduring bond to a beloved community. We can see this evidenced most profoundly in the 1967 White House Cabinet Committee Hearings on Mexican American Affairs in El Paso. Ximenes cultivated a public space in the cultural rhetorical ecology of the U.S.-Mexico border to foreground the voices of the *mexicano* diaspora. He created a platform to enact what it means to be a Mexican American citizen in the United States. He allowed the members of the community to bear witness to their own lives and experiences of reconciling the losses of the dispossessed.

Ximenes, a self-authorizing, self-fashioned change agent, remained connected to something greater than himself. He acted on the world as the world acted on him. And so it seems that leaders must be transformed as they make the journey of changing their spheres of belonging. Dramatic sacrifice is also demanded. Critics of Obama's two-term presidency have suggested that his legacy lacked the luster of greatness for his having come to the presidency without making "a notable sacrifice for his views."[12] Ximenes intuitively understood the demands of sacrifice that would be required of the young aspiring and charismatic senator from Illinois who first dazzled the nation at the 2004 Democratic National Convention. "He's very promising but he still needs to be tested," Vicente thoughtfully observed as we celebrated Obama's first inauguration on January 20, 2009.[13] Vicente's opinion of this nation's first black president was informed by his own well-seasoned vantage point as a public servant.

Ximenes's tenure as a federal administrator evolved amid two of the most turbulent moments in postwar U.S. history. He was part of the expansive mesh, the "ecological thought" of the Great Society through its early period of articulation and final days of implementation.[14] In the dark ecology of LBJ's bipolar administration (the simultaneous escalation of devastating destruction in the Vietnam War and the robust generation of U.S. social programs and civil rights reform), Ximenes found a way to enact a model of restorative justice on the borders of the Americas and advance the social democratic vision of the Great Society long after its political death. Ximenes's capacity for paradox, and his own experience living in tension between deep conviction and deep doubt, set the parameters for his rhetorical career. In sum, Ximenes again and again constructed a deliberative space for giving witness to the experience of living on both sides of the U.S.-Mexico border and for hearing the voices of individuals seeking full civic inclusion in America's political life.

The exodus of tens of thousands of refugees fleeing the increasingly violent and unsustainable political economy of Central America since 2014 is an environmental as well as a human rights issue. A 150-year legacy of U.S. imperialism throughout Latin America continues to manifest itself through entrenched political corruption and the economic stronghold of intractable drug cartels that exploit the natural and social resources of Latin American nations. The villages and pueblos throughout Mexico and Central and South America are becoming so toxic and uninhabitable that men, women, and children are willing to risk the threat of incarceration and death by crossing the sun-scorched desert to reach the U.S. border.

In an article published in the *Albuquerque Journal* titled "Living in Limbo," the personal narratives of South Texas residents document the precarious border politics, which will become even more difficult and deadly in this post-Obama moment. The complexities of a shifting border are poignantly reflected in the human ecology of stories like these. *Albuquerque Journal* reporter Richard Marosi writes:

> The Homeland Security Department last year put up a tall steel barrier across the fields from [the house of Pamela Taylor and her husband]. The government calls it the border fence, but it was erected about a quarter

mile north of the Rio Grande, leaving Taylor's home between the fence and the river. Her two acres now lie on a strip of land that isn't Mexico but doesn't really seem like the United States either. . . . "My son-in-law tells people we live in a gated community," joked [Pamela] Taylor.[15]

Community resistance among Brownsville, Texas, residents delayed construction after the Secure Fence Act of 2006 was passed by Congress. Rising tensions within this largely Mexican American working-class border city of 172,000 complicated the land acquisition process and slowed the construction of the quasi-secure/quasi-permeable fence. In the end the government had to initiate condemnation proceedings against more than one hundred residents, many of whom were aged, poor farmers whose families had resided in the region since the original Spanish land grants. The impact on the region's geobiological and human ecologies has been substantial.

In the process of erecting the tall metal fence, construction workers leveled thriving orchards; plowed over family gardens of okra, squash, and tomatoes; drained freshwater lakes; and razed driveway access to personal residences. The Nature Conservancy charges that the fencing on the Southmost Preserve ruptures the migratory corridor of many forms of wildlife. At the local farm of Debbie and Leonard Loop, situated on the boundaries of Brownsville, Texas, and Mexico, this farming couple tend their nine-hundred-acre citrus orchard on the U.S. side of the fence while their son Ray Loop raises soybeans, sunflowers, and watermelons on the "Mexican" side of the fence. Separated by automatic gates that lock during high security alerts, Debbie Loop reflects, "It's an eerie feeling crossing that [boundary]."[16]

Civic Engagement

Ximenes lived by the mantra of the pragmatist. In his own everyday experience, Ximenes believed that action was not only the opportunity but the duty of the engaged citizen. The guiding principle of Ximenes's entire public life could be summed up succinctly in these words: "In the face of uncertainty and incomplete information, don't just stand there, move things around."[17] And moving things around is what he did best: he moved ideas, people, policies, resources, power, money, and opportunity. Rhetoric was his lever and his fulcrum.

Ximenes's cultivation and mobilization of New Mexico counterpublics, alliances formed across cultural and class lines, were efficacious and durable enough to persist after his international appointments in Ecuador and Panama. Ximenes extended the rhetorical imagination of the AGIF nationally and internationally, spreading the influence of the AGIF into Latin America with charity drives and fund-raising efforts on behalf of Quito's schools. In turn, Ximenes found himself at problematic cross-purposes with America's Alliance for Progress program, navigating the conflicting agendas of Kennedy's humanitarian program for Latin America's poor combined with an anti-Communist political-military campaign and free market capitalism.

Ximenes's transnational journey promoting human and civil rights across the Americas illustrates how social movements like the Cold War Mexican American civil rights movement are not only interrelated but interdependent with conditions elsewhere. Social activism demands catalysts as well as constellations of discourses (sermonic, instrumental, and deliberative) to sustain it. Narrow representations that focus only on the sermonic or literary rhetoric of influential leaders fail to represent the full cultural rhetorical ecology of the situation and the continuous discursive loops that move toward social reform. An invigorated public life demands inclusion of the full range of rhetorical practices of citizenship.

Ximenes's story demonstrates that the struggle for civic inclusion is also the struggle for power and the recognition of the consequences of power. The enduring issues of the twenty-first century—environmental justice, global health issues, immigration (transnational citizenship), deep capitalism, structural violence, and institutionalized racism—are the same issues Ximenes engaged with in the twentieth century. Ximenes grappled adeptly with the acquired power of earned privilege, the ascribed power of hereditary privilege, the transgressive power of resistance, and the transformative power of reconciliation. None of these, alone or together, eradicated the human suffering that moved Ximenes to action. In the end he changed the cultural rhetorical ecology of his spheres of belonging because he was willing to take the risk of changing himself through the exercise of power.

The history of Mexican American civil rights reform remains integral to the U.S. democratic process of constituting what Dryzek calls a "flourishing oppositional civil society"[18] Moreover, Ximenes's adroit implementation of the 1967 El Paso Hearings was the first and only moment in post–World War II history to successfully bring all stakeholders (grassroots activists and cabinet-level administrators) across interest groups together in dialogue about Mexican American social and political concerns. Ximenes's story illustrates that democracy is always a work-in-progress and no one gets to claim sole authorship.

At the first glimpse of success, at that shining moment of possibility in the months immediately following his landmark joint appointment as commissioner of the EEOC and chair of the Inter-Agency Committee on Mexican

American Affairs, Ximenes offered a pragmatic, long-view perspective on the civil rights struggle to the AGIF convention in Denver, Colorado, on August 2, 1967. His words, tinged with his characteristic playful wit and practical wisdom, invoked the kind of optimism and vision the Mexican American community would need to endure the backlash and reversals that Ximenes knew would inevitably follow this moment of jubilation. His words still ring true fifty years later. Ximenes reflects:

> As you already know, our people have, for many years, been victims of discrimination, poverty and disease. A great philosopher once said, "If we gathered all the afflictions of the world and put them in a bundle, and each individual came and took his share, everyone would go away satisfied with his just portion." What this philosopher was saying, in other words, is that in real life some people have more problems than others. This is exactly the point I want to make today. Our people for too long and unjustly so, have carried more than their portion of the troubles of our society. However, we now find ourselves on the threshold of a new era. Many opportunities have been presented to us; many more will come.
>
> But one must understand that these opportunities are not the product of one day's work. Benefits have been long in arriving. If we do not live to reap the rewards of our work, at least our children will.[19]

Ximenes's words suggest a vision of civic engagement that reminds citizens that the sustainability of human and natural resources for future generations is the first principle of survival. Civic education for future leaders, or what my friend and colleague Juan Guerra calls "citizens-in-the-making," demands an understanding of rhetoric as the work of cultivating deep and durable relationships within our cultural rhetorical ecologies of belonging.[20] The global issues facing twenty-first-century generations—biodiversity depletion, climate refugees, natural resource scarcity, and disparate economic development conditioned by competing geopolitical forces—will continue to stress and profoundly complicate the cultural rhetorical ecologies of future citizens tasked with leadership roles in business, government, law, education, science, engineering, and health and medicine.

The legacy of Vicente Ximenes illustrates again and again the value of an engaged presence that comes from belonging to viable communities and practicing the rhetorics of the everyday. Ximenes and his contemporaries were not flawless citizens. They were engaged citizens. They helped to change the national conversation. Ximenes demonstrated that rhetoric is as much about right relationship as it is right action and right words. The essence of discursive democracy is not only exercising the vote and participating in public deliberation, but it is taking a leadership role in shaping the collective narrative, national policy, and public memory. Ximenes, García, and the AGIF rallied together for Mexican American access to the ballot as well as the political platform. They positioned key leaders in precarious but influential roles within the dominant social structures to change the story, enact policy, and build an archive to document the journey. Together they enacted discursive democratic practices, acting on the conviction that deliberative processes allow citizens to discover their political interests, to make sense of the issues that influence their lives, to cultivate public opinions, and to take positions on problems.

Vicente Ximenes and the history of mid-twentieth-century civil rights reform reveal that social movements must become part of the sinew of governing organizations in order to effect enduring institutional change. They must shape and exercise the muscle and connective tissue of policy and practice from the inside out. It is not enough to stir a movement for social change. Activists must implement and administer institutional transformation. Recognizing the role of postwar reformers, Henry Cisneros delivered a September 28, 2007, keynote address in honor of Ximenes titled "A Giant in Mexican American History." Cisneros asserts:

> The Latino progression is one of the most important dynamic forces in the United States. There are major trends which we can see will shape our country—globalization, the continuing evolution of technology, the aging of the population, the migration of populations across America. . . .
>
> A drive by a schoolyard today in almost any major American city reveals a population of children playing in the schoolyard that reflects the shape of the American future captured in the many faces of minority children. Many of those children are Latino, not just in New Mexico, Texas or California; not just in Arizona, Colorado or Florida, but in Arkansas, Georgia, North Carolina, Nebraska, Illinois, New York, and Washington State. All across America as this process unfolds Latinos will take our place among the shapers of America's destiny. Because we love this country, we want to work for it and make it greater. As we do, let us remember the pioneers, the visionaries, the courageous few, those who were unwilling to settle for lives of discrimination and segregation, and who used their skills for the benefit of a people and a nation. Vicente Ximenes is foremost among those who have worked to create the better life that we enjoy today.[21]

The need for Latino and Latina leadership at every level of U.S. society is no less critical today than it was for Ximenes's generation.

End of an Era

Ximenes's story is not a perfect morality tale. It is a story of mixed successes, incomplete efforts, failed promises, and incremental change. Ximenes's journey tells emerging democracies in South Africa and elsewhere that the United States incorporated and enfranchised a nation of immigrants through the *paideia* of everyday democratic participation, literacy education, economic opportunity, civic engagement, and the acquisition of political power extending beyond the local to the national. However, Ximenes's story also serves as a cautionary tale reminding emerging democracies and aspiring citizens that the United States did not incorporate and enfranchise a nation of immigrants uniformly or equitably. The burden of acquiring rhetorical efficacy rests on each new generation of citizens-in-the-making.[22]

Ximenes's legacy, furthermore, illustrates that democracy is not only a way of governing but a way of knowing. Ximenes's role as a citizen scholar points to the need for cultivating citizens capable of engaging agonistic pluralism in both government and education because no one (not one political perspective or disciplinary lens) has the total picture. Democracy in governance and knowledge making demands agonistic pluralism—citizens adept at opening up discursive tensions through diverse critical thinking processes and competing intellectual resources in the sciences, humanities, social sciences, arts, medicine, business, engineering, and law. To practice rhetorical arts toward conditioning our environments for health and wholeness (in the *oikos* and the *polis*) demands thinking, learning, writing, and speaking across communities. Learning to live in right relationship with each other and our environments is the great ecological narrative, the great human drama.

When Vicente was nominated for a UNM honorary doctorate in 2008, the other nominee for UNM's honorary degrees was none other than Ximenes's nemesis, Reies López Tijerina of the infamous Rio Arriba courthouse raid. Vicente was devilishly delighted to hear that his nomination received the unanimous support of the UNM Board of Regents. He had beat out the fiery land grant agitator and former charismatic preacher, a public figure once described as having the "tongue of a Latin Moses" for UNM's Honorary Doctorate in Humane Letters.[23] I remember escorting Vicente to the platform at the "Pit" for the May 2008 commencement ceremonies. He would have liked to deliver the commencement address to the restless crowd of thousands but was instead reverently hooded by then president David Schmidly. The irony of the moment wasn't lost on either Vicente or me given how the stalwart former UNM president Popejoy had once demanded Vicente's resignation

from the UNM Bureau of Business Research over fifty years earlier. Over
the next six years, I wrote Ximenes's story while he continued living it. Every
person with whom I spoke, grassroots community members as well as high-
level government officials, echoed the same sentiment: Vicente Ximenes is
a historical figure *sin iguales*.

History is the rupture of the linear narrative, the counternormative, the
traumatic event. For both the postwar Mexican American civil rights activists
and the post-civil-rights-era Chicano intellectuals, the traumatic event of
exclusion never ended. It is continuously reproduced in language politics,
educational gatekeeping policies, the immigration struggle, border violence,
media representations, and the public imagination. The political dramas of
the new millennium continued to stir Ximenes. But he kept his focus on his
home and his home state, and the New Mexico YCC, even though his inner
diva missed the thrill of the political stage and the allure of the limelight.

Even in his nineties, Ximenes continued to hear the call of *el duende*, the
animating magic of consubstantiating desire, and the creative pulse of what
Martin Luther King Jr. once called the beloved community.[24] I remember
Vicente walking out to greet me on one occasion in the La Vida Llena reception area with a slight limp, still favoring one foot after his recent surgery
debacle. Vicente wryly informed me about the cataract surgery he would
have soon. "Let's hope they operate on the correct eye," I remember telling
him as I hugged him good-bye. He laughed with an impish appreciation
for the ironies and absurdities of life. "Yes, let's hope," he quipped, pointing
down at his foot. I can still picture him shaking his head and recalling a
previous surgery mishap when he woke up from anesthesia to discover that
the surgeons had operated on the wrong foot.

There should be a second book, a companion piece, to this one capturing
his dialogue and laughter. His flickering light was still evident to the residents of La Vida Llena Retirement Center as he sang "Bésame" to María
accompanied by a ragtag band of mariachis in the cafeteria cluttered with
wheelchairs and walkers on Cinco de Mayo in 2009. It was the last Cinco
de Mayo he would ever share with María.[25] In the words of Federico García
Lorca, "In that gathering of muses and angels—beautiful forms and beautiful smiles—who could have won but [his] moribund *duende*, sweeping the
ground with its wings of rusty knives."[26]

Our last lunch together was on President Obama's second inauguration
day, January 21, 2013. Vicente greeted me at the reception area of La Vida
Llena as he had for the past nine years, his eyes bright and smiling, his silver
hair pulled back in a ponytail, wearing blue jeans and his 2008 Obamanos
t-shirt. He steadied himself with a walker. The jaunty carved-wood cane

was no longer sufficient for keeping his balance. I knew he was failing. We chatted our way through the cafeteria-style dining room with our trays. He served himself soup, salad, and a scoop of stewed prunes with an impish smile. "Things aren't working as well as they used to," he laughed. He was ninety-three years old and had survived a minor stroke and a few trips to the intensive care unit over the past year. The e-mail conversations between us had stopped. No longer quick to reply to my e-mail or phone calls, Vicente was letting go. The loss of María on September 26, 2009, had been taking its toll on his health and his soul for the past three years.

I kept in touch through his children, Rick, Ana, and Olivia, getting regular updates on his health through the final years of his life. I visited Vicente once in the La Vida Llena rehabilitation and recovery unit, where the ladies swooned over him and vied for a place at his dining room table. He charmed them all, every smitten white-haired woman in the room. He hadn't lost his infectious smile or sense of humor—even after weeks of hospitalization and physical therapy to regain his strength and mobility.

As we reflected on Obama's second presidential victory during our final lunch together, Vicente was eager to hear how the book was progressing. I hadn't seen Vicente since my trip to the National Archives and the Library of Congress in Washington, D.C., in May 2012. We talked about my last swoop through the archives and revisions made to earlier drafts of the manuscript. At our last lunch in January 2013, we discussed the 2012 presidential election, the Democratic National Convention keynote address by Julian Castro, and the promising future of the young and exciting Castro brothers. Vicente hugged me good-bye, and somehow we both knew we would never see each other again. I received a few more e-mails over the next few months before all communication ended. Vicente had another, more debilitating stroke.

On December 5, 2013, Vicente celebrated his ninety-fourth birthday with his family and most-intimate friends, the same day that South Africa civil rights activist and twentieth-century contemporary Nelson Mandela died at the age of ninety-five. I remembered listening to the National Public Radio program the evening of Mandela's eighty-eighth birthday driving back from Floresville, Texas, and the Ximenes family home on that first research trip in July 2006. In my mind, driving through the mesquite pastures of South Texas, I pictured Vicente Ximenes and Nelson Mandela on parallel journeys. The idea that these two leaders, born within eighteen months of each other in different corners of the world, had shared a parallel journey was not too far fetched. Born under some unnamed common star, these two men died within months of each other.

Late on a snowy night, February 24, 2014, Rick called me to come to the hospice unit at Presbyterian Hospital in downtown Albuquerque. My husband, Ross, drove me down the mountain pass from our home in the Sandias on that snowy night to say good-bye to my good friend. I sat with Vicente, unconscious and struggling to breathe, waiting with his family over the next three days. Vicente died on February 27, 2014.[27]

The year 2014 was a watershed moment for commemorating a number of key moments in our national collective memory. The year 2014 marked the fiftieth anniversary of Lyndon B. Johnson's Great Society speech, the 1964 Civil Rights Act, and the 1964 Wilderness Act. Since my first phone call to Vicente during my campus visit to UNM in February 2004, I had never imagined life here in this beautiful place without him. Vicente was New Mexico to me: the turbulence, the mystery, the whimsy, the beauty. I remembered again how we chatted together as I stood gazing out the windows of the top floor of the historic La Posada Hotel (now the Hotel Andalúz) in downtown Albuquerque as an amethyst sun set over the pink granite mountains. And in that moment when all things seemed possible, I became mesmerized by the magnificence of the place and magic of Vicente's story.

For those of us coming of age during the civil rights era who witnessed the cataclysmic events of 1968, in spite of all the bold visionary claims of the 1960s generation, neither the metaphorical Age of Aquarius nor the utopian Aztlán unfolded over the decades that followed. The rhetoric of presence—presence with self, others, and the ecology of relationships within which we circulate; how we live and engage these concentric and interconnected spheres of belonging—is ultimately transformative. The capacity for self-reflection is essential. Ximenes knew this. He understood how rhetoric intrinsically conditions cultural rhetorical ecologies of belonging. What most intrigued me about Ximenes, throughout our friendship that spanned more than a decade, over the course of countless conversations and through the final hours of his life, was the total lack of cynicism and nihilism in Ximenes's concept of the past, present, and future.

The story of Vicente Ximenes illustrates that justice and generativity evolve out of two very different energy systems: the *telos* of justice is restitution and reparation; the *telos* of generativity is reconciliation and transformation. Social reform movements of the twentieth century, like the Mexican American civil rights movement, demonstrate the need for invoking both systems. Desmond Tutu and Nelson Mandela recognized the difference between these two energy systems when seeking to move the nation toward healing in postapartheid South Africa. Justice alone is insufficient. Reparation is not enough to heal the fissures of oppression, dehumanization, and the structural violence of racism.

The power of Ximenes's story rests in the humanity, luminosity, and generosity of his life journey. The rhetorical situations of his life shifted as dramatically as a New Mexico summer sky—balmy and endless; violent and stormy; roiling, shifting shadows punctuated by silver-bellied clouds. The continuity of his identity and the circularity of his narrative remain as paradoxical as his capacity for change and adaptation to whatever life circumstances came his way. Ever the opportunist and the diva, there was no occasion Ximenes didn't find ripe for the picking. He could always find a connection. Ximenes was willing to be the unabashed Hermes figure, sharing his shape-shifting journey with so many people—his vulnerability, his strength, his humor, his humility were his gifts. His fatal flaws serve as a mirror, a reflection transforming us and exposing us to ourselves. Ximenes remained forever fascinated by charismatic leaders, intrigued by the shadows of powerful men. He excused the devil in them all because he kept close counsel with the *daimon* in himself. He enjoyed flirting with power. Politics sated his desire for action. Rhetoric was his *pharmakon* that he measured liberally but carefully, understanding rhetoric as both a balm and a poison.

Ximenes could somehow pull off the persona of the audacious diva and the impish altar boy, ever the middle son—the charmer, the mediator who just wanted everyone to get along. He generally endeared himself to everyone, but knew full well that there were many along the way whom he would inevitably and invariably annoy or altogether alienate. He was not only resolved to this fact of political life; he almost reveled in it as the evidence of having truly engaged the good fight—the rough and tumble of democracy. When I told him about the handwritten marginalia on the memos entombed in the presidential archives labeling him "LBJ's wetback" and "Califano's wetback," he smiled. He took a bit of satisfaction in the information, not so much because of some enduring animosity but as confirmation that he had indeed been a worthy adversary in the nation's hallowed halls. Fate spared him an epic fall from grace, but it didn't reward him with iconic hero status either. He was the good man speaking well, the network operator, the community organizer, the merchant's son behind the counter trading in the social and material goods of everyday life. "Joe's boy."

Notes

Selected Bibliography

Index

Notes

Foreword

1. Michelle Hall Kells, *Héctor P. García: Everyday Rhetoric and Mexican American Civil Rights* (Carbondale: Southern Illinois University Press, 2006).

2. Juan C. Guerra, "Out of the Valley: Transcultural Repositioning as a Rhetorical Practice in Ethnographic Research and Other Aspects of Everyday Life," in *Reframing Sociocultural Research on Literacy: Identity, Agency, and Power*, ed. Cynthia Lewis, Patricia Enciso, and Elizabeth Birr Moje (Mahwah, NJ: Erlbaum, 2007), 140.

3. Cynthia L. Selfe, "The Movement of Air, the Breath of Meaning: Aurality and Multimodal Composing," *College Composition and Communication* 60, no. 2 (2009): 645.

4. Chantal Mouffe, *The Democratic Paradox* (New York: Verso, 2009).

Acknowledgments

1. Michelle Ballif, "Writing the Event: The Impossible Possibility for Historiography," *Rhetoric Society Quarterly* 44, no. 3 (Summer 2014): 244.

2. Kells, *Héctor P. García*.

3. Jeff Felts, prod., *Justice for My People: The Héctor P. García Story* (Corpus Christi, TX: KEDT-TV, 2002).

4. Vicente Ximenes, interview with author, October 30, 2011.

5. Ralph Cintron, "Thinking Freedom Right/Left" (keynote address, Watson Conference, Louisville, KY, October 20, 2012).

6. Terry Tempest Williams, *The Open Space of Democracy* (Eugene, OR: Wipf & Stock, 2004).

7. Héctor Galán, Henry Cisneros, and Sylvia Morales, prods., *¡Chicano! History of the Mexican American Civil Rights Movement* (Los Angeles: National Latino Communication, 1996); Paige Martinez, dir., *El Senador: The Life and Career of Dennis Chávez* (Albuquerque: Center for Regional Studies at the University of New Mexico, 2003).

8. José Vasconcelos, *La Raza Cósmica* (Mexico D.F.: Espasa Calpe, 1948).

9. Segments of the introduction have been published in Michelle Hall Kells, "Vicente Ximenes and LBJ's Great Society: The Rhetorical Imagination of the American GI Forum," in *Leaders of the Mexican American Generation: Biographical Essays*, ed. Anthony Quiroz (Boulder: University Press of Colorado, 2015),

253–75. Segments of chapter 3 have been published in Michelle Hall Kells, "What's Writing Got to Do with It? Citizen Wisdom, Civil Rights Activism, and 21st Century Community Literacy," *Community Literacy Journal* 7, no. 1 (Fall 2012): 89–110. Segments of chapter 6 have been published in Michelle Hall Kells, "Landscapes of Civic Literacy: The Rhetoric of Remembering," *JAC* 29, nos. 1–2 (Spring 2010): 451–64.

Introduction: The Cultural Rhetorical Ecology of the Mexican American Civil Rights Movement

1. To honor the authenticity of Ximenes's texts, I have not edited nonstandard orthographic features and have made sparing use of bracketed annotation. Variations in the orthographic representation of Spanish words and the use of accent marks are reproduced from the originals. In deference to Ximenes's rhetorical authority over his texts, I have translated the Spanish (and Tex-Mex) lexicon only when the primary source omits explication in English. In some cases, like the 1968 "Key Note Address to the Twentieth Annual Convention of the American GI Forum," Ximenes rhetorically engages in code-switching (as well as code-mixing or code-meshing), using English excerpts as acts of elucidation rather than as direct translations of the Spanish.

2. Vicente Ximenes, "Key Note Address to the Twentieth Annual Convention of the American GI Forum" (Corpus Christi, TX, August 8, 1968), Vicente T. Ximenes Personal Papers.

3. J. Mills Thornton III, "Commentary," in *The Civil Rights Movement in America*, ed. Charles W. Eagles (Jackson: University Press of Mississippi, 1986), 150.

4. William E. Leuchtenburg, *The White House Looks South: Franklin D. Roosevelt, Harry S. Truman, Lyndon B. Johnson* (Baton Rouge: Louisiana State University Press, 2005), 395.

5. Leuchtenburg, *White House Looks South*, 395.

6. Juan Gómez-Quiñones and Irene Vásquez, *Making Aztlán: Ideology and Culture of the Chicana and Chicano Movement, 1966–1977* (Albuquerque: University of New Mexico Press, 2014), xxii.

7. Jacquelyn Dowd Hall, "The Long Civil Rights Movement and the Political Uses of the Past," *Journal of American History* 91, no. 4 (March 2005): 1233–63.

8. Renee C. Romano and Leigh Raiford, eds., *The Civil Rights Movement in American Memory* (Athens: University of Georgia Press, 2006).

9. Cornel West, *The American Evasion of Philosophy: A Genealogy of Pragmatism* (Madison: University of Wisconsin Press, 1989), 3.

10. Minrose Gwin, *Remembering Medgar Evers: Writing the Long Civil Rights Movement* (Athens: University of Georgia Press, 2013).

11. John M. Ackerman and David J. Coogan, eds., *The Public Work of Rhetoric: Citizen-Scholars and Civic Engagement* (Columbia: University of South Carolina Press, 2010). Ackerman and Coogan argue that the recent turn in rhetorical studies toward an inquiry of civic engagement presses academics as citizen scholars to go beyond the "comfortable imaginations and accoutrements of academic life" (9).

12. Ackerman and Coogan, *Public Work of Rhetoric*, 9.

13. West, *American Evasion of Philosophy*, 4.

14. West, *American Evasion of Philosophy*, 7.

15. Raúl Yzaguirre, "Liberty and Justice for All: Civil Rights in the Years Ahead," in *Latinos and the Nation's Future*, ed. Henry Cisneros (Houston: Arte Público Press, 2009), 27.

16. Barack Obama, "Remarks by the President at the LBJ Presidential Library Civil Rights Summit" (address, Lyndon B. Johnson Presidential Library, Austin, TX, April 10, 2014), accessed August 9, 2017, http://www.whitehouse .gov/the-press-office/2014/04/10/remarks-president-lbj-presidential-library-civil -rights-summit.

17. Ballif, "Writing the Event."

18. Ballif, "Writing the Event," 246.

19. Florence R. Krall, *Ecotone: Wayfaring on the Margins* (Albany: State University of New York Press, 1994). Examining the construct of *ecotone*, Krall maintains, "Much like the ecotones in biotic communities, [cultural ecotones] may be rich and dynamic transitional zones and may provide great learning as well as suffering" (4).

20. Michel de Certeau, *The Writing of History*, trans. Tom Conley (New York: Columbia University Press, 1988), 58; Paul Ricoeur, *Memory, History, Forgetting*, trans. Kathleen Blamey and David Pellauer (Chicago: University of Chicago Press, 2004), 137.

21. de Certeau, *Writing of History*, 69.

22. Hayden White, *Metahistory: The Historical Imagination of Nineteenth-Century Europe* (Baltimore: Johns Hopkins University Press, 1973).

23. I invoke the Greek term *liturgia* here to describe Ximenes's life and work, drawing on classical Athenian constructs for the cultural spaces of the public stage, rhetorical dramatism, and the notion of liturgy as the work of the people.

24. Jacqueline Jones Royster, *Traces of a Stream: Literacy and Social Change among African American Women* (Pittsburgh: University of Pittsburgh Press, 2000), 13.

25. For further analysis of the World War II Mexican American generation, see Mario T. García, *The Mexican American Generation: Leadership, Ideology, and Identity, 1930–1960* (New Haven, CT: Yale University Press, 1989).

26. For an extensive overview of Mexican American leaders, events, and accomplishments, see Matt S. Meier and Margo Gutiérrez, eds., *Encyclopedia of the Mexican American Civil Rights Movement* (Westport, CT: Greenwood Press, 2000).

27. Vicente Ximenes, guest lecture (University of New Mexico, Albuquerque, NM, October 9, 2006). Vicente T. Ximenes Personal Papers.

28. For further examination of the War on Poverty, see David Zarefsky, *President Johnson's War on Poverty: Rhetoric and History* (Tuscaloosa: University of Alabama Press, 1986).

29. Recipients of the Vicente Ximenes Scholarship in Public Rhetoric and Community Literacy include Bernadine Hernandez, Genevieve Garcia de Mueller, Christine Garcia, Melisa Garcia (no relation), Dan Cryer, and Anjanette Griego.

30. Debra Dominguez, "Speaking Up: Human-Rights Advocate Honored for Lifetime of Activism," *Albuquerque Journal*, May 27, 2005, C1–C2.

31. See Aimee Ortiz, "CNN Van Jones Calls This Election a 'White-lash,'" *Boston Globe*, November 9, 2016, accessed August 9, 2017, https://www.boston globe.com/news/politics/2016/11/09/cnn-van-jones-calls-this-election-white -lash/JOl8B19wnlnOLjuddRCSvK/story.html. The term *white-lash* was deployed by news commentator Van Jones following the 2016 presidential election to describe the landmark alt-right Republican victory and ascendancy of Donald Trump to the White House.

32. Owen J. Dwyer and Derek H. Alderman, *Civil Rights Memorials and the Geography of Memory* (Chicago: Center for American Places at Columbia College, 2008).

33. Ximenes, guest lecture, October 9, 2006.

34. Rick Nathanson, "Front-Line Warrior," *Albuquerque Journal*, February 2011, Mature Life section, 4, 12.

35. Hugh Davis Graham, *The Civil Rights Era: Origins and Development of National Policy 1960–1972* (New York: Oxford University Press, 1990), 7.

36. Graham, *Civil Rights Era*, 227.

37. Graham, *Civil Rights Era*, 226–27.

38. For an excellent history of interracial relationships in Texas, see Neil Foley, *Quest for Equality: The Failed Promise of Black-Brown Solidarity* (Cambridge, MA: Harvard University Press, 2010).

39. Joseph Califano, memo, June 9, 1967, Office Files of Joseph A. Califano, box 16, Lyndon B. Johnson Presidential Library (hereinafter cited as LBJ Library).

40. Joseph A. Califano Jr., *The Triumph and Tragedy of Lyndon Johnson: The White House Years* (New York: Simon & Schuster, 1991), 136–37.

41. Califano, memo, June 9, 1967.

42. Charles Maguire to Will Sparks, memo, February 19, 1968, WHCF Subject File EX HU2, box 7, LBJ Library.

43. Mouffe, *Democratic Paradox*, 19.

44. David Hiley, *Doubt and the Demands of Democratic Citizenship* (New York: Cambridge University Press, 2006).

45. John Dewey, "The Ethics of Democracy," reprinted in *Pragmatism: A Reader*, ed. Louis Menand (New York: Vintage Books, 1997), 192.

46. Henry Cisneros, "A Giant in Mexican American History" (keynote address, University of New Mexico Civil Rights Symposium, Albuquerque, NM, September 28, 2007).

47. Henry Cisneros, "An Overview: Latinos and the Nation's Future," in *Latinos and the Nation's Future*, ed. Henry Cisneros (Houston: Arte Público Press, 2009), 4.

48. Ximenes, guest lecture, October 9, 2006.

49. Albert O. Hirschman, *The Rhetoric of Reaction: Perversity, Futility, Jeopardy* (Cambridge, MA: Harvard University Press, 1991), 115.

50. Ximenes, guest lecture, October 9, 2006.

51. "Willard Wirtz: Mediator Was Secretary of Labor for Kennedy, Johnson," *Albuquerque Journal*, April 26, 2010, A6; Julie Pace, "Obama Praises Civil Rights Champion Height," *Albuquerque Journal*, April 30, 2010, A6.

52. Martin Luther King Jr., *Where Do We Go from Here: Chaos or Community?* (Boston: Beacon Press, 2010), 4.

53. For a complete list of featured speakers and events, see Lyndon B. Johnson Presidential Library, "We Shall Overcome": Civil Rights Summit, April 8–10, 2014, accessed August 9, 2017, http://www.civilrightssummit.org/.

54. Rick Nathanson, "Artesia Divided on Detainees," *Albuquerque Journal*, July 4, 2014, A1, A4.

55. Devon Peña, ed., *Chicano Culture, Ecology, Politics: Subversive Kin* (Tucson: University of Arizona Press, 1998).

56. Mouffe, *Democratic Paradox*, 102.

57. Graham, *Civil Rights Era*, 7. Graham offers the phrase "the new American administrative state" to represent the constellation of executive agencies established during the civil rights era to implement new antidiscrimination policies.

58. King, *Where Do We Go from Here*, 93.

59. For further examination of Héctor P. García's criticism of Lyndon B. Johnson's presidential administration, see Kells, *Héctor P. García*, 196.

60. Graham, *Civil Rights Era*, 7.

61. For a more detailed examination of the "won cause" notion of civil rights history, see Dwyer and Alderman, *Civil Rights Memorials*.

1. "Chente": Interrogating Histories, Negotiating Rhetorics

1. Ximenes, guest lecture, October 9, 2006.

2. Ricoeur, *Memory, History, Forgetting*, 137.

3. The term *terroir* refers to the complex interrelationship of soil and climate in a micro-bioregion that influences the cultivation of agricultural products such as grapes, chilies, tomatoes, and beans. The term is most frequently used to characterize the cultivation of grapevines for wine production. For a metaphorical application of terroir to the notion of rhetorical situation, see Thomas Rickert, *Ambient Rhetoric: The Attunements of Rhetorical Being* (Pittsburgh: University of Pittsburgh Press, 2013).

4. Peña, *Chicano Culture, Ecology, Politics*.

5. For an extensive examination of the character of Lyndon B. Johnson and his formative influences, see Robert A. Caro's multivolume biography: Robert A. Caro, *Lyndon B. Johnson: Path to Power* (New York: Vintage Books, 1990); Robert A. Caro, *Lyndon B. Johnson: Master of the Senate* (New York: Alfred A. Knopf, 2002).

6. For further examination of the Hermes archetype, see Lewis Hyde, *The Gift: Imagination and the Erotic Life of Property* (New York: Vintage Books, 1983), 246–49. Hermes was the mythological Greek god of trade and commerce. He is also the conceptual namesake of hermeneutics. The proverbial network operator and deity of social exchange, Hermes represents a trickster and transgressive figure who promotes the circulation of economic power. He is the spirit of the open road and the traveler. He is the patron of both merchants and thieves.

7. Manuel Castells, *The Power of Identity*, 2nd ed. (Malden, MA: Wiley-Blackwell, 2010), 7.

8. For richly nuanced critical explorations of culture and identity in Greater Mexico, see José Limón, *American Encounters: Greater Mexico, the United States, and the Erotics of Culture* (Boston: Beacon Press, 1999).

9. See Rodolfo Acuña, *Occupied America: A History of Chicanos*, 3rd ed. (New York: Harper & Row, 1988), 21. Acuña's portrayal of cultural identifications and national allegiances further delineates the complicating factors that influenced the U.S.-Mexican War (features instantiated within the collective memory of the Ximenes family as survivors, victims, and victors).

10. "History of Wilson County," *Wilson County Centennial 1860–1960: Official Centennial Program*, n.d., n.p., Wilson County Public Library.

11. "History of Wilson County."

12. See David Montejano, *Anglos and Mexicans in the Making of Texas, 1836–1986* (Austin: University of Texas Press, 1987), 5.

13. Neil Foley, *The White Scourge: Mexicans, Blacks, and Poor Whites in Texas Cotton Culture* (Berkeley: University of California Press, 1997), 4–5.

14. Ximenes, guest lecture, October 9, 2006.

15. Frederick B. Pike, *The United States and Latin America: Myths and Stereotypes of Civilization and Nature* (Austin: University of Texas Press, 1992), 180.

16. Pike, *United States and Latin America*, 181.

17. Paul Farmer, *Pathologies of Power: Health, Human Rights, and the New War on the Poor* (Berkeley: University of California Press, 2003).

18. Michelle Roberts, "Early Ranch Structure Buried Again," *Albuquerque Journal*, December 26, 2009, C1.

19. "Biography of José Jesus Ximenes," Wilson County Historical Society, n.d., n.p., Vicente T. Ximenes Personal Papers.

20. "Biography of José Jesus Ximenes."

21. Julie Leininger Pycior, *LBJ and Mexican Americans: Paradox of Power* (Austin: University of Texas Press, 1997), 25.

22. Vicente Ximenes, keynote address (University of New Mexico Civil Rights Symposium, Albuquerque, NM, September 28, 2007), Vicente T. Ximenes Personal Papers.

23. Jessica Enoch, *Refiguring Rhetorical Education: Women Teaching African American, Native American, and Chicano/a Students, 1864–1911* (Carbondale: Southern Illinois University Press, 2008), 132.

24. Enoch, *Refiguring Rhetorical Education*, 133.

25. Ximenes, keynote address, September 28, 2007.

26. Ximenes, keynote address, September 28, 2007.

27. Vicente Ximenes, interview with author, January 31, 2005.

28. Vicente Ximenes, interview with author, February 4, 2006.

29. Ximenes, keynote address, September 28, 2007.

30. Caro, *Path to Power*, 230.

31. Sam Fore Keach, "Death Comes Peacefully to 'Mr. Sam' at Home," *Floresville Chronicle-Journal* (Floresville, TX), December 29, 1966, 1.

32. Diana Bancroft Borse, "Sam Fore: An Enduring Model" (senior thesis, Texas A&M University–Kingsville, December 1997), South Texas Archives.

33. Elma Fore, interview by David G. McComb, July 12, 1971, AC 76–50, OH Mrs. Sam Fore Jr., University of Texas Oral History Project, National Archives and Records Service, LBJ Library.

34. Ximenes, interview with author, January 31, 2005.

35. John Connally to Lyndon Johnson, letter, May 24, 1939, LBJA Selected Names File; Sam Fore to John Connally, letter, September 16, 1940, LBJA

Selected Names File; Sam Fore to Frank Knox, Secretary of the Navy, letter, September 16, 1940, LBJA Selected Names File, box 15, LBJ Library.

36. See Teachers Temporary Certificate for Lyndon Johnson, June 1, 1928, LBJA Subject File, box 73, LBJ Library. Johnson received a Teachers Temporary Certificate, which allowed him to teach in "third class and unclassified high schools of the public schools of Texas."

37. Ximenes, guest lecture, October 9, 2006.

38. Robert Kleberg Jr., interview by David McComb, July 9, 1969, AC 79–86, OH Robert Kleberg, University of Texas Oral History Project, National Archives and Records Service, LBJ Library.

39. Doris Kearns Goodwin, *Lyndon Johnson and the American Dream* (New York: St. Martin's Griffin, 1991), 67.

40. Goodwin, *Lyndon Johnson*, 67.

41. Caro, *Path to Power*, 160.

42. Goodwin, *Lyndon Johnson*, 53.

43. Lyndon B. Johnson, clerk hire forms, November 24, 1931, to July 25, 1935; Robert H. Harper to Lyndon B. Johnson, letter, Office of the Clerk, House of Representatives, Disbursing Office, March 27, 1962, LBJA Subject File, box 73, LBJ Library.

44. Fore, interview with David G. McComb, July 12, 1971.

45. Ximenes, interview with author, February 4, 2006.

46. "Real Cowboy Graces the Halls of Congress," *American Business Survey*, January 1932, 3, LBJA Subject File, box 73, LBJ Library.

47. Caro, *Path to Power*, 220.

48. Ximenes, interview with author, January 31, 2005.

49. Vicente Ximenes, interview featured in *American Experience: The Civilian Conservation Corps*, produced and directed by Robert Stone (2009; Boston: WBGH Boston, 2010), DVD.

50. Ximenes, interview featured in *American Experience*.

51. Ximenes, keynote address, September 28, 2007.

52. Ximenes, guest lecture, October 9, 2006.

53. Vicente Ximenes, interview with author, July 26, 2011.

54. Caro, *Path to Power*, 345.

55. Press release, The Works Program: National Youth Administration, July 27, 1935, LBJA Subject File, box 28, LBJ Library.

56. Lyndon Johnson to John J. Corson, letter, September 22, 1935, LBJA Subject File, box 73, LBJ Library.

57. Vicente Ximenes, interview with author, July 4, 2010.

58. Vicente Ximenes, interview with author, February 8, 2007.

59. Zaragosa Vargas, *Labor Rights Are Civil Rights: Mexican American Workers in Twentieth-Century America* (Princeton, NJ: Princeton University Press, 2005), 135.

60. Ximenes, keynote address, September 28, 2007.

61. Caro, *Path to Power*, 718.

62. Zaragosa Vargas, "Emma Tenayuca: Labor and Civil Rights Organizer of 1930s San Antonio," in *The Human Tradition between the Wars, 1920–1945*, ed. Donald Whisenhunt (Wilmington, DE: Scholarly Resources, 2002), 171.

63. Vargas, "Emma Tenayuca," 178.

64. E. P. Curtis, Colonel, USAAF, Chief of Staff, General Orders No. 120, Awards of Distinguished Flying Cross, Headquarters Northwest African Air Forces APO # 650, June 20, 1943, Ximenes Papers, box 4, LBJ Library.

65. Lloyd Jojola, "Maria Ximenes: Wife Helped American GI Forum," *Albuquerque Journal*, September 17, 2009, B3.

66. Ximenes, interview with author, July 26, 2011.

2. New Mexico and the Political Imagination of the American GI Forum

1. Vicente Ximenes to Héctor P. García, letter, September 8, 1951, Semi-Processed Papers, Dr. Héctor P. García Papers (hereinafter cited as HPG Papers).

2. See Ellen Schrecker, *The Age of McCarthyism: A Brief History with Documents* (New York: Bedford/St. Martin's, 2002), 17.

3. Vicente Ximenes University of New Mexico Bachelor of Arts in Education Certificate, June 5, 1950, Ximenes Papers, box 4, Folder Certificates and Photographs, LBJ Library.

4. Limón, *American Encounters*, 53.

5. Julian Samora, ed., *La Raza: Forgotten Americans*, 3rd ed. (Notre Dame, IN: University of Notre Dame Press, 1969); George I. Sánchez, *Forgotten People: A Study of New Mexicans* (Albuquerque: University of New Mexico Press, 1996).

6. Vicente Ximenes, interview with author, February 6, 2006.

7. Héctor P. García to Dennis Chávez, letter, July 13, 1941, Semi-Processed Papers, HPG Papers.

8. "Speech Delivered by Senator Dennis Chavez before the American GI Forum of Texas at Austin, Texas," box 138, folder 28, HPG Papers.

9. Arthur Schlesinger Jr., "The Evolution of the National Government as an Instrument of Attaining Social Rights," in *Toward New Human Rights: The Social Policies of the Kennedy and Johnson Administrations*, ed. David C. Warner (Austin: Lyndon B. Johnson School of Public Affairs, University of Texas at Austin, 1977), 13.

10. Vasconcelos, *La Raza Cósmica*, 10.

11. Richard D. Belian, letter to the editor, *New Mexico Magazine*, November 2012, 76.

12. Kells, *Héctor P. García*, 83.

13. Kells, *Héctor P. García*, 28.

14. Kells, *Héctor P. García*, 83.

15. For further examination of the political and historical evolution of the AGIF, see Carl Allsup, *The American G.I. Forum: Origins and Evolution* (Austin: Center for Mexican American Studies, University of Texas at Austin, 1982); Patrick J. Carroll, *Felix Longoria's Wake: Bereavement, Racism, and the Rise of Mexican American Activism* (Austin: University of Texas Press, 2003); Ignacio M. García, *Héctor P. García: In Relentless Pursuit of Justice* (Houston: Arte Público, 2002); Pycior, *LBJ and Mexican Americans*; Henry A. J. Ramos, *The American GI Forum: In Pursuit of the Dream, 1948–1983* (Houston: Arte Público, 1998).

16. Chaim Perelman and Lucie Olbrechts-Tyteca, *The New Rhetoric: A Treatise on Argumentation* (Notre Dame, IN: University of Notre Dame Press, 1969), 14.

17. Vicente Ximenes, interview with author, February 23, 2010.

18. See Mouffe, *Democratic Paradox*. Chantal Mouffe's notion of agonistic pluralism reconfigures the role of difference and dissent in a deliberative democracy. According to Mouffe, "envisaged from the point of view of 'agonistic pluralism,' the aim of democratic politics is to construct the 'them' in such a way that is no longer perceived as an enemy to be destroyed, but as an 'adversary,' that is, somebody whose ideas we combat but whose right to defend those ideas we do not put into question. This is the real meaning of liberal-democratic tolerance" (101).

19. Mouffe, *Democratic Paradox*, 101.

20. See Peña, *Chicano Culture, Ecology, Politics*. According to Chicano scholar Devon Peña, "in disturbance ecology, life is by nature chaotic and fragmentary rather than orderly and successional. From the vantage point of this new ecology, there is no universal truth about the social construction of nature that we call 'ecosystem' other than perhaps the unpredictability of human interference in the natural cycles of disturbance and regeneration" (4).

21. Naomi Quiñonez, "Rosita the Riveter: Welding Traditions with Wartime Transformations," in *Mexican Americans and World War II*, ed. Maggie Rivas-Rodriquez (Austin: University of Texas Press, 2005), 245.

22. Ximenes, interview with author, February 4, 2006.

23. For further examination of racial dynamics through the history of New Mexico, see Thomas E. Chávez, *New Mexico: Past and Future* (Albuquerque: University of New Mexico Press, 2006); Laura E. Gómez, *Manifest Destinies: The Making of the Mexican American Race* (New York: New York University Press,

2007); Phillip B. Gonzales, *Forced Sacrifice as Ethnic Protest: The Hispano Cause in New Mexico and the Racial Attitude Confrontation of 1933* (New York: Peter Lang, 2001).

24. Gómez, *Manifest Destinies*, 158.

25. For a historical examination of the panethnic labels of *Hispanic* and *Latino*, see G. Cristina Mora, *Making Hispanics: How Activists, Bureaucrats, and Media Constructed a New American* (Chicago: University of Chicago Press, 2014).

26. Ximenes, interview with author, February 4, 2006.

27. Ximenes to Héctor P. García, September 8, 1951.

28. Suzanne Forrest, *The Preservation of the Village: New Mexico's Hispanics and the New Deal* (Albuquerque: University of New Mexico Press, 1998), 10.

29. Acuña, *Occupied America*, 279.

30. Forrest, *Preservation of the Village*, 10.

31. Forrest, *Preservation of the Village*, 7.

32. Forrest, *Preservation of the Village*, 22.

33. Forrest, *Preservation of the Village*, 22.

34. For further discussion, see Joe S. Sando and Herman Agoyo, eds., *Po'Pay: Leader of the First American Revolution* (Santa Fe, NM: Clearlight Publishing, 2005).

35. Luci Tapahonso, "They Moved Over the Mountain," in *Here First: Autobiographical Essays by Native American Writers*, ed. Arnold Krupat and Brian Swann (New York: Random House, 2000), 344.

36. For additional information about the political career of Senator Dennis Chávez, see Martinez, dir., *El Senador*; Kevin Allen Leonard, "Dennis Chávez: The Last of the *Patrones*," in *The Human Tradition in America between the Wars, 1920–1945*, ed. Donald W. Whisenhunt (Wilmington, DE: Scholarly Resources, 2002), 105–20.

37. Vicente Ximenes quoted in Martinez, dir., *El Senador*.

38. Isabelle Tellez quoted in Martinez, dir., *El Senador*.

39. Laura Pulido, "Ecological Legitimacy and Cultural Essentialism: Hispano Grazing in Northern New Mexico," in Peña, *Chicano Culture, Ecology, Politics*, 122.

40. Pulido, "Ecological Legitimacy and Cultural Essentialism," 125.

41. Forrest, *Preservation of the Village*, 174.

42. Lynne Marie Getz, "Lost Momentum: World War II and the Education of Hispanos," in Rivas-Rodriguez, *Mexican Americans and World War II*, 101.

43. Forrest, *Preservation of the Village*, 75.

44. Ximenes, guest lecture, October 9, 2006.

45. Vicente Ximenes, letter to editor, December 20, 1951, box 141, folder 2, HPG Papers.

46. Ximenes, letter to editor, December 20, 1951.

47. Vicente Ximenes to Héctor García, letter, February 12, 1952, Semi-Processed Papers, HPG Papers.

48. Vicente Ximenes to Héctor García, letter, August 8, 1952, Semi-Processed Papers, folder 1, HPG Papers.

49. Vicente Ximenes to Héctor García, letter, August 17, 1952, Semi-Processed Papers, folder 1, HPG Papers.

50. Vicente Ximenes, interview with author, March 14, 2010.

51. See Schrecker, *Age of McCarthyism*, 98.

52. Ximenes, keynote address, September 28, 2007.

53. Vicente Ximenes, interview with author, February 8, 2006.

54. Ximenes, interview with author, February 4, 2006.

55. Ximenes, keynote address, September 28, 2007.

56. Vicente Ximenes, interview with author, January 26, 2010.

57. Lloyd Jojola, "Maria Ximenes: Wife Helped American GI Forum," *Albuquerque Journal*, October 17, 2009, B3.

58. See Parker J. Palmer, *The Company of Strangers: Christians and the Renewal of America's Public Life* (New York: Crossroads Publishing, 1981). Sociologist Palmer examines the centrality of voluntary associations in the health of public life. He argues, "A healthy public life not only protects people from power, but empowers them to guide government and hold it accountable" (94).

59. Acuña, *Occupied America*, 278.

60. *Salt of the Earth*, produced by Paul Jerrico and Sylvia Jerrico, directed by Herbert J. Biberman, (1954; Independent Productions/International Union of Mine, Mill, & Smelter Workers; Alpha Video Distributors, 2004).

61. Ximenes, interview with author, March 14, 2010.

3. The Public Rhetoric of Vicente Ximenes: Citizen Scholars and Mexican American Civil Rights Activism

1. For a catalogue of the classical five canons of rhetoric (invention, arrangement, style, delivery, and memory), see Aristotle, *On Rhetoric: A Theory of Civic Discourse*, trans. George A. Kennedy (New York: Oxford University Press, 1991).

2. Vicente Treviño Ximenes, University of New Mexico Certificate of Master of Arts, June 4, 1953, Ximenes Papers, box 4, Folder Certificates and Photographs, LBJ Library.

3. Marilyn M. Cooper, "The Ecology of Writing," in *Writing as Social Action*, ed. Marilyn M. Cooper and Michael Holzman (Portsmouth, NH: Boynton/Cook, 1989), 7.

4. Vicente Ximenes, "The New Mexico Welfare Situation," *American GI Forum News Bulletin* (Austin), January 1956, 1, Vicente T. Ximenes Personal Papers.

5. For further analysis of the metaphorical construction of genre as semiotic ecology, see Anis Bawarshi, *Genre and the Invention of the Writer: Reconsidering the Place of Invention in Composition* (Logan: Utah State University Press, 2003); Amy J. Devitt, *Writing Genres* (Carbondale: Southern Illinois University Press, 2004).

6. Mora, *Making Hispanics*, 3.

7. For further examination of the cultural practices of *curandismo*, see Eliseo Torres, *Curandero: A Life in Mexican Folk Healing* (Albuquerque: University of New Mexico Press, 2003).

8. Mora, *Making Hispanics*, 2.

9. Mora, *Making Hispanics*, 2.

10. Mora, *Making Hispanics*, 2.

11. Martin J. Medhurst, "Eisenhower's 'Atoms for Peace' Speech: A Case Study in the Strategic Use of Language," in *Cold War Rhetoric: Strategy, Metaphor, and Ideology*, eds. Martin J. Medhurst, Robert L. Ivie, Philip Wander, and Robert L. Scott (East Lansing: Michigan State University Press, 1990), 29.

12. "Archbishop Bryne Commends New Mexico Forum's Work," *American GI Forum News Bulletin* (Austin), June 1953, 1, HPG Papers.

13. "U.S. Senator Dennis Chavez Commends New Mexico Forum," *American GI Forum News Bulletin* (Austin), August 1954, 2, HPG Papers.

14. "U.S. Senator Dennis Chavez Commends New Mexico Forum," *American GI Forum News Bulletin*.

15. Ximenes, interview with author, March 14, 2010.

16. Ximenes, "The New Mexico Welfare Situation," 7.

17. Kells, *Héctor P. García*, 57.

18. Vicente T. Ximenes, *Housing in New Mexico* (Albuquerque: University of New Mexico Division of Research, 1954); *Natural Gas in New Mexico: New Mexico Studies in Business and Economics* (Albuquerque: University of New Mexico Bureau of Business Research, 1954); *Wages in the Construction Industry of New Mexico* (Santa Fe: State Labor Industrial Commission, 1954); *Income by Counties in New Mexico: New Mexico Studies in Business and Economics* (Albuquerque: University of New Mexico Bureau of Business Research, 1956); *Demand for Dentists in New Mexico* (Santa Fe: New Mexico Department of Public Health, 1957); *1957 Income by Counties in New Mexico* (Albuquerque: University of New Mexico Bureau of Business Research, 1958); *1958 Directory of New Mexico Manufacturing and Mining* (Albuquerque: University of New Mexico Bureau of Business Research, 1958).

19. David R. Hiley, *Doubt and the Demand of Democratic Citizenship* (New York: Cambridge University Press, 2006).

20. Hannah Arendt, "Lying in Politics: Reflections on the Pentagon Papers," in *Crisis of the Republic* (New York: Harcourt Brace, 1972), 6.

21. George I. Sánchez to Héctor P. García, letter, October 27, 1951, box 141, folder 12, HPG Papers.

22. George I. Sánchez advanced this rhetorical trope in a chapter titled "Step Children of a Nation" in his monograph *Forgotten People*.

23. Carlos Kevin Blanton, *George I. Sánchez: The Long Fight for Mexican American Integration* (New Haven, CT: Yale University Press, 2014), 15.

24. For further discussion of the rhetorical and intellectual legacy of George I. Sánchez and his contemporaries, see Meier and Gutiérrez, *Encyclopedia of the Mexican American Civil Rights Movement*.

25. See Philippa Strum, *Mendez v. Westminster: School Desegregation and Mexican-American Civil Rights* (Lawrence: University Press of Kansas, 2010).

26. Vicente Ximenes, interview with author, May 25, 2010.

27. Sánchez, *Forgotten People*.

28. Sánchez, *Forgotten People*, 13.

29. For further information on the history of LULAC, see Craig Kaplowitz, *LULAC: Mexican Americans and National Policy* (College Station: Texas A&M University Press, 2005).

30. Cynthia E. Orozco, "LULAC Has Long History in New Mexico," *Albuquerque Journal*, July 16, 2010, A9.

31. Kaplowitz, *LULAC*, 26.

32. Carlos Vásquez, *Barelas: A Través de los Años: A Pictorial History* (Albuquerque: National Hispanic Cultural Center, 2010), 53.

33. See Neil Foley, *Quest for Equality: The Failed Promise of Black-Brown Solidarity* (Cambridge, MA: Harvard University Press, 2010).

34. A copy of the LULAC constitution is available in Richard A. García, *Rise of the Mexican American Middle Class, San Antonio, 1929–1941* (College Station: Texas A&M University Press, 1991), 268–69.

35. Kaplowitz, *LULAC*, 34.

36. Ximenes, guest lecture, October 9, 2006.

37. Elaine Tassy, "NAACP Albuquerque Branch Celebrates 100 Years," *Albuquerque Journal*, January 11, 2015, B1.

38. Clete Daniel, *Chicano Workers and the Politics of Fairness: The FEPC in the Southwest, 1941–1945* (Austin: University of Texas Press, 1991).

39. Vargas, *Labor Rights Are Civil Rights*, 159.

40. For a copy of the FEPC Executive Order 8802: Establishing the Fair Employment Practices Committee of June 25, 1941, see appendix C in Richard

Griswold del Castillo, ed., *World War II and Mexican American Civil Rights* (Austin: University of Texas Press, 2008).

41. "New Mexico Forum Seeks Bill to Outlaw Public Discrimination," *American GI Forum New Bulletin*, March 1953, 4, HPG Papers.

42. Vicente Ximenes, interview with author, October 29, 2004.

43. For an examination of the history of Jewish peoples in New Mexico, see Stanley M. Hordes, *To the Ends of the Earth: A History of the Crypto-Jews of New Mexico* (New York: Columbia University Press, 2005).

44. Vicente Ximenes, interview with author, July 7, 2010.

45. Ximenes, interview with author, May 25, 2010.

46. "U.S. Senator Dennis Chavez Commends New Mexico Forum," *American GI Forum News Bulletin*, August 1954, 4, HPG Papers.

47. "Anti-Discrimination Bill Passes New Mexico Legislature," *American GI Forum News Bulletin* (Austin), March 1955, 1, HPG Papers.

48. Ximenes, guest lecture, October 9, 2006.

49. Vicente Ximenes, interview with author, February 16, 2010.

50. Ximenes, interview with author, March 14, 2010.

51. "Albuquerque Forum Asks Civil Service for City Workers on Garbage Department," *American GI Forum News Bulletin*, September 1953, 2; "Albuquerque Forums Get Joe Valencia Back on City Job," *American GI Forum News Bulletin*, October 1953, 2; "Albuquerque GI Forums Gain Great Victory as Merit System Extended to Garbage Men," *American GI Forum News Bulletin*, November 1953, 2; "Albuquerque Departmental Investigation Sought by Ximenez," *American GI Forum News Bulletin*, December 1953, 2; "Albuquerque Forum Wins Another Tussle over City Employee," *American GI Forum News Bulletin*, February 1954, 2, HPG Papers.

52. "New Mexico Board Plans Headquarters," *American GI Forum News Bulletin*, September 1953, 2, HPG Papers.

53. "New Mexico Building Fund Drive," *American GI Forum News Bulletin*, November 1953, 2, HPG Papers.

54. Vicente Ximenes, interview with author, June 30, 2007.

55. "Louis Tellez and Isabelle Orgaz Announce Plans for Albuquerque Wedding," *American GI Forum New Bulletin*, March 1955, 2, HPG Papers.

56. Ramos, *American GI Forum*, 29.

57. Vicente Ximenes letter to Héctor P. García, December 15, 1957, Semi-Processed Papers, HPG Papers.

58. Ximenes, interview with author, March 14, 2010.

59. Allsup, *American G.I. Forum*, 98.

60. Vicente Ximenes, interview with author, March 4, 2008.

61. Ximenes, interview with author, March 4, 2008.

62. Allsup, *American G.I. Forum*, 99.

63. Héctor P. García, "A Brief History of the American GI Forum in the US," Album 1.1, HPG Papers.

64. "Racial Issue Halts Lincoln Day Affair," *Amarillo Globe-Times*, n.d., n.p., box 146, folder 20, HPG Papers.

65. Mary Whitlock Blundell, "Ethos and Dianoia Reconsidered," in *Essays on Aristotle's* Poetics, ed. Amélie Oksenberg Rorty (Princeton, NJ: Princeton University Press, 1992), 168.

66. Paul Woodruff, *Reverence: Renewing a Forgotten Virtue* (New York: Oxford University Press, 2001), 165.

67. Vicente Ximenes, interview with author, March 9, 2008.

68. Héctor P. García letter to Vicente Ximenes, February 23, 1957, box 146, folder 20, HPG Papers.

69. Ignacio M. García, *Viva Kennedy: Mexican Americans in Search of Camelot* (College Station: Texas A&M University Press, 2000), 18.

4. Latinidad: *The Question of Democracy and the Americas*

1. Vicente Ximenes, "Message to American GI Forum of Chicago," 1958 American GI Forum National Convention Program Brochure, box 138, bolder 26, HPG Papers.

2. Ximenes, "Message to American GI Forum of Chicago."

3. Ximenes, "Message to American GI Forum of Chicago."

4. Ximenes, "Message to American GI Forum of Chicago."

5. Raymond Williams offers the construct of the "structure of feeling" in *The Long Revolution* (New York: Harper & Row, 1961).

6. C. G. Jung, *The Undiscovered Self,* trans. R. F. C. Hull (New York: Little, Brown, 1958), 120–21.

7. Irwin Unger and Debi Unger, *LBJ: A Life* (New York: John Wiley & Sons, 1999), 218.

8. Paul Schutzer, "A Veep's Anger: 'Don't You Want the Truth?'," *Life*, May 18, 1958, 20–25.

9. Thomas Skidmore, Peter H. Smith, and James N. Green, *Modern Latin America*, 8th ed. (New York: Oxford University Press, 2014), 224.

10. Skidmore, Smith, and Green, *Modern Latin America*, 452.

11. Skidmore, Smith, and Green, *Modern Latin America*, 123.

12. Dennis Chávez, "Address of Senator Dennis Chavez before the GI Forum, Chicago, Illinois," May 17, 1958, box 138, folder 26, HPG Papers.

13. Chávez, "Address of Senator Dennis Chavez before the GI Forum."

14. Chávez, "Address of Senator Dennis Chavez before the GI Forum."

15. Chávez, "Address of Senator Dennis Chavez before the GI Forum."

16. John F. Kennedy, "The New Frontier," Remarks of Senator John F. Kennedy Accepting the Democratic National Presidential Nomination, July 15, 1960, Pre-Presidential Papers, 1960 Campaign Press and Publicity, box 1032, Speeches and Statements Folder, 1958–60, John F. Kennedy Presidential Library.

17. Unger and Unger, *LBJ*, 249.

18. "Remarks of John F. Kennedy," September 12, 1960, Pre-Presidential Papers, Senate Files, box 1, Speeches and the Press, 1953–60 Folder, John F. Kennedy Presidential Library.

19. García, *Viva Kennedy*, 95.

20. García, *Viva Kennedy*, 96.

21. Héctor P. García, "Confidential Report for Senator Lyndon Johnson," June 10, 1960, Unprocessed, "LBJ 1969," box 1, folder 6, HPG Papers.

22. Hector P. García, interview by David G. McComb, July 9, 1969, AC74–277, University of Texas Oral History Project, National Archives and Records Service, LBJ Library.

23. Ramos, *American GI Forum*, 31.

24. Allsup, *American G.I. Forum*, 68.

25. John F. Kennedy quoted in "Senator Chavez Charges of Spanish-American Snub Brings Some Appointments," *AGIF News Bulletin*, March 1961, 1–2, Semi-Processed Papers, HPG Papers.

26. Ximenes, interview with author, July 4, 2010.

27. "Hector P. Garcia Cross Reference Sheet," White House Files, White House Name File, box 946, "Garcia" Folder, John F. Kennedy Presidential Library.

28. Zeke Duran to John F. Kennedy, letter, January 18, 1961, Semi-Processed Papers, HPG Papers.

29. García, *Viva Kennedy*, 122.

30. García, *Viva Kennedy*, 109.

31. "Ximenes Named to Quito Post," press release, n.d., Semi-Processed Papers, HPG Papers.

32. Ximenes, interview with author, July 4, 2010.

33. Ximenes, interview with author, July 4, 2010.

34. "Address by Honorable Robert F. Kennedy Attorney General to the United States to the North Carolina Cold War Seminar," May 17, 1963, Asheville, NC, Robert F. Kennedy Papers, Speeches 1961–64, box 2, John F. Kennedy Presidential Library.

35. Vicente Ximenes to Héctor P. García, letter, June 21, 1963, Semi-Processed Papers, HPG Papers.

36. "Your Contribution to Operation Amigo Is a Strike against Communism," promotional flyer, box 102, folder 21, HPG Papers.

37. Héctor P. García to Vicente Ximenes, letter, April 6, 1962, box 101, folder 21, HPG Papers.

38. "Veteranos de guerra de E.U. envían ayuda económica a escolares de esta ciudad," *El Comercio* (Quito, Ecuador), April 26, 1962, n.p., Semi-Processed Papers, HPG Papers.

39. For further examination of human rights activism in Latin America and Liberation Theology, see Farmer, *Pathologies of Power*; Christian Smith, *The Emergence of Liberation Theology* (Chicago: University of Chicago Press, 1991).

40. The name of this fictional television character, ironically and coincidentally, was the same as Vicente's father, José Ximenes, only spelled differently.

41. An examination of this cartoon is available in Foley, *Quest for Equality*.

42. Statements of the John F. Kennedy Presidential Library, "U.S. Latin American Friendship," *U.S. Latin American Exhibit: 40th Anniversary Exhibit*, John F. Kennedy Presidential Library. The library and museum mounted a special exhibit commemorating the fortieth anniversary of the Alliance for Progress from May 26 to September 1, 2001. The author viewed the exhibit on July 12, 2001.

43. Héctor P. García to Vicente Ximenes, letter, November 29, 1963, Semi-Processed Papers, HPG Papers.

44. Unger and Unger, *LBJ*, 251.

45. Unger and Unger, *LBJ*, 276.

46. Unger and Unger, *LBJ*, 278.

47. Unger and Unger, *LBJ*, 278.

48. Unger and Unger, *LBJ*, 290.

49. Goodwin, *Lyndon B. Johnson*, 170.

50. "On Presidential Campaign Organization—Democratic," *Congressional Quarterly Fact Sheet*, October 9, 1964, DNC Collection, box 19, DNC Organization Folder, LBJ Library.

51. Vicente Ximenes to Craig Raupe, memo, "Viva Johnson Clubs," n.d., box 168, folder 17, HPG Papers.

52. For additional information, especially for interdisciplinary curricular material about the civil rights era and Freedom Summer with an emphasis on Fannie Lou Hamer and the Mississippi Freedom Democratic Party, see Bruce J. Diernefield, *The Civil Rights Movement* (Essex, England: Pearson, 2004): 95–107.

53. For further discussion of the Viva Kennedy campaign, see García, *Viva Kennedy*.

54. Ximenes, interview with author, February 6, 2006.

55. Department of State, Agency for International Development, clearance form, May 3, 1966. The form reports that Ximenes was employed by USAID from October 1961 to September 1964 in Ecuador. He resigned from the agency

to become the national coordinator for the Democratic National Committee of the Southwest. Following the 1964 campaign, he was employed as an inspector for the Office of Economic Opportunity from February to August 1965 before returning to USAID in Panama as deputy mission director at FSR-2 pay grade of $19,612 per annum. John Macy Files, box 659, LBJ Library.

56. Lyndon Johnson, 1964 DNC acceptance speech, August 27, 1964, Office Files of Bill Moyers, box 124, LBJ Library.

57. Ximenes, interview with author, May 25, 2010.

58. James M. Smallwood, "Viva Johnson: LBJ and the Transformation of the Hispanic Community of Texas," *Journal of South Texas* 15, no. 2 (Fall 2002).

59. "On Presidential Campaign Organization—Democratic," *Congressional Quarterly Fact Sheet*, October 9, 1964.

60. Ximenes, interview with author, May 25, 2010.

61. Pycior, *LBJ and Mexican Americans*, 148.

62. Vicente Ximenes to Craig Raupe, memo, n.d., box 168, folder 17, HPG Papers.

63. "Ximenes, Ramos Lead Viva Johnson Clubs," *AGIF News Bulletin*, November 1964, 1, Semi-Processed Papers, HPG Papers.

64. *Johnson y Humphrey*, 1964 campaign brochure, "Continuemos. Adelante. Viva," Ximenes Papers, box 4, LBJ Library.

65. Ximenes to Craig Raupe, memo, n.d., "Viva Johnson Clubs."

66. Ximenes, interview with author, May 25, 2010.

67. Juan C. Guerra, "Writing for Transcultural Citizenship: A Cultural Ecology Model," *Language Arts* 85, no. 4 (2008): 296–304.

68. Juan C. Guerra, "Emerging Representations, Situated Literacies, and the Practice of Transcultural Repositioning" in *Latino/a Discourses: On Language, Identity, and Literacy Education*, ed. Michelle Hall Kells, Valerie Balester, and Victor Villanueva (Portsmouth, NH: Heinemann-Boynton/Cook, 2004), 8.

69. Smallwood, "Viva Johnson," 74.

70. Ximenes to Craig Raupe, memo, n.d., "Viva Johnson Clubs."

71. See Jeffrey M. Pilcher, *Cantinflas and the Chaos of Mexican Modernity* (New York: Rowman & Littlefield Publishers, 2000).

72. Ximenes, interview with author, May 25, 2010.

73. Vicente Ximenes, interview with author, January 30, 2011.

74. Ximenes to Craig Raupe, memo, n.d., "Viva Johnson Clubs."

75. Ximenes, interview with author, January 30, 2011.

76. Pycior, *LBJ and Mexican Americans*, 151.

77. Vicente Ximenes, interview with author, July 26, 2010.

78. Robert Canino, Viva Johnson Campaign memo, November 10, 1964, PL2/PR 1 Collection, box 108, folder PL2/PR1 11/21–11/30/64, LBJ Library.

79. Ximenes to Craig Raupe, memo, n.d., "Viva Johnson Clubs."

80. Ximenes to Craig Raupe, memo, n.d., "Viva Johnson Clubs."

81. Ximenes, interview with author, May 25, 2010.

82. Ximenes, interview with author, May 25, 2010.

83. Ximenes, interview with author, May 25, 2010.

84. Ximenes, interview with author, May 25, 2010.

85. Vicente Ximenes to John F. Kennedy, letter, November 11, 1960, John Macy Files, box 659, LBJ Library.

86. Vicente Ximenes to Louis Martin, memo, February 15, 1965, Vicente T. Ximenes Personal Papers.

87. Ximenes, interview with author, July 4, 2010.

88. Guest list, Great Society participants, June 1, 1965, Vicente Ximenes Papers, box 4, LBJ Library.

89. "'Mexican-Americans' Attend 'Great Society' Conference," *Democrat* (Washington, D.C.), June 14, 1968, 4.

90. Carlos Rivera to Marvin Watson, memo, August 30, 1965, WHCF Name File, box 176, LBJ Library.

91. "Forum Members Prominent at Great Society Conference," *Forumeer*, July 1965, Semi-Processed Papers, HPG Papers.

92. Robert Dallek, *Flawed Giant: Lyndon Johnson and His Times, 1961–1973* (New York: Oxford University Press, 1999), 293.

93. Vicente Ximenes, interview with author, July 25, 2010.

94. Ximenes, interview with author, July 4, 2010.

95. "LBJ's Message to National Convention," *Forumeer*, September 1965, 2, HPG Papers.

5. Constructing the "Great Society": The Topoi *of the 1967 El Paso Hearings*

1. Vicente Ximenes, "The Alliance for Progress in Ecuador," n.d., Semi-Processed Papers, HPG Papers.

2. Ximenes, "Alliance for Progress in Ecuador."

3. Skidmore, Smith, and Green, *Modern Latin America*, 179.

4. Adam Smith's comments on the notion of the "great society" from *The Wealth of Nations* (book 4, chapter 2) are quoted in Marvin E. Gettleman and David Mermelstein, eds., *The Great Society Reader: The Failure of American Liberalism* (New York: Random House, 1967), 14.

5. Remarks of President Johnson, University of Michigan Commencement, May 22, 1964, Statements of Lyndon Baines Johnson, May 20–23, 1964, box 106, LBJ Library.

6. For discussion of the influences on Johnson's Great Society speech, see Gettleman and Mermelstein, *Great Society Reader*, 13–15.

7. Caro, *Path to Power*, 49.

8. The most poignant and human portrait of Lyndon Johnson's relationship with his father, Sam Johnson, is found in Goodwin's authorized biography, *Lyndon Johnson*, 35–45.

9. For an analysis of Graham Wallas, see Terence H. Qualter, *Graham Wallas and the Great Society* (New York: St. Martin's Press, 1979).

10. Qualter, *Graham Wallas*, 11.

11. Remarks of President Johnson, University of Michigan Commencement.

12. See Sidney M. Milkis and Jerome M. Mileur, eds., preface to *The Great Society and the High Tide of Liberalism* (Boston: University of Massachusetts Press, 2005), xiii.

13. Pericles's funeral oration is available in Thucydides, *The History of the Peloponnesian War*, trans. Richard Crawley (1910; repr., New York: E. F. Dutton, 1950).

14. Milkis and Mileur, *Great Society*, xii.

15. Remarks of President Johnson, University of Michigan Commencement.

16. Milkis and Mileur, *Great Society*, xiii.

17. See Wilson Carey MacWilliams, "Great Societies and Great Empires: Lyndon Johnson and Vietnam," in Milkis and Mileur, *Great Society*, 216.

18. MacWilliams, "Great Societies and Great Empires," 215.

19. MacWilliams, "Great Societies and Great Empires," 215–16.

20. Remarks of President Johnson, University of Michigan Commencement.

21. See Goodwin, *Lyndon Johnson*, 211.

22. Remarks of President Johnson, University of Michigan Commencement.

23. Remarks of President Johnson, University of Michigan Commencement.

24. Lyndon Johnson quoted in Goodwin, *Lyndon Johnson*, 216.

25. Goodwin, *Lyndon Johnson*. Goodwin catalogs a long list of those who were promised to benefit from the Great Society:

> So the agenda was established: the Great Society would offer something to almost everyone: Medicare for the old, educational assistance for the young, tax rebates for business, a higher minimum wage for labor, subsidies for farmers, vocational training for the unskilled, food for the hungry, housing for the homeless, poverty grants for the poor, clean highways for commuters, legal protection for the blacks, improved schooling for the Indians, rehabilitation for the lame, higher benefits for the unemployed, reduced quotas for the immigrants, auto safety for drivers, pensions for the retired, fair labeling for consumers, conservation for the hikers and campers, and more and more and more. (216)

26. White House Press Release on Conference on Equal Employment Opportunity, August 5, 1965, Office Files of John Macy, Ex-General—EEOC, box 782, LBJ Library. This press release includes the program for the White House Conference on Equal Employment that convened August 19–20, 1965.

27. "Dr. Hector Garcia Presents Statement to the President," *Forumeer*, October 1965, 1, HPG Papers.

28. "Remarks by the President at the President's Conference on Equal Employment Opportunity," August 20, 1965, Statements of Lyndon B. Johnson—August 18–26, 1965, box 158, LBJ Library.

29. H.R. 7152 Title VII Civil Rights Act of 1964, Office Files of Mike Manatos, box 6, LBJ Library.

30. S. 1750. A Bill, 88th Congress, First Session, Office Files of Mike Manatos, box 6, LBJ Library.

31. White House Press Release on Equal Employment Opportunity Commission, July 26, 1965, Office Files of John Macy, Ex-General—EEOC, box 782, LBJ Library.

32. "Report of the White House Conference on Equal Employment Opportunity," August 19, 1965, WHCF Subject File EX-HU 2-1 MC, box 46, LBJ Library.

33. Graham, *Civil Rights Era*, 215.

34. Kaplowitz, *LULAC*, 100.

35. Kaplowitz, *LULAC*, 101.

36. For further examination of the Chicano rhetoric of Corky Gonzáles, see "'No Revolution without Poets': The Rhetoric of Rodolfo 'Corky' Gonzales," ed. John C. Hammerback, Richard J. Jensen, and José Angel Gútierrez, *A War of Words: Chicano Protest in the 1960s and 1970s* (Westport, CT: Greenwood Press, 1985), 53–80.

37. Rudolph Corky Gonzales to Lyndon B. Johnson, telegram, April 5, 1966, HU2 Files, box 14, LBJ Library.

38. Harry McPherson Jr. to Rudolph C. Gonzales, letter, May 25, 1966, HU2 Files, box 14, LBJ Library.

39. Carlos Rivera to Marvin Watson, memo, March 30, 1966, WHCF Subject File EX HU 2-1 Employment, box 43, LBJ Library.

40. Franklin Roosevelt Jr. to Lyndon Johnson, letter, April 7, 1966, WHCF Subject File EX-HU 2-1 MC, box 46, LBJ Library.

41. David North to Joseph Califano, "Report of the Task Force on Problems of Spanish Surname Americans," November 15, 1966, Office Files of James Gaither, box 327, LBJ Library.

42. For further examination of U.S. policies on race and citizenship, see Ian F. Haney López, *White by Law: The Legal Construction of Race* (New York: New York University Press, 1996).

43. Rudolph Corky Gonzales to Lyndon B. Johnson, telegram, April 5, 1966.

44. Gómez-Quiñones and Vásquez, *Making Aztlán*, 117–18.

45. "'Huelga' Battle Cry of Delano Strikers," *Forumeer*, April 1966, 1, 4, HPG Papers.

46. John C. Hammerback and Richard J. Jensen, *The Rhetorical Career of César Chávez* (College Station: Texas A&M University Press, 1998), 83.

47. "8,000 March on Sacramento," *Forumeer*, May 1966, 1, 4, HPG Papers.

48. Kells, *Héctor P. García*, 139–49.

49. "M-A Leaders Seek Meeting with LBJ," *Forumeer*, May 1966, 1, HPG Papers.

50. Edward C. Sylvester Jr. to Clifford Alexander Jr., Special Counsel to the President, memo, May 3, 1966, "Mexican American Unity Conference, Los Angeles, California," April 28–29, 1966, WHCF Subject File EX-HU2/MC, box 22, LBJ Papers.

51. Regarding the appointment of Ximenes to the EEOC, Joseph Califano recommended to President Johnson that he "actively take charge of the Mexican American problem and keep it away from the White House." Quotations are available in Graham, *Civil Rights Era*, 227.

52. Joseph Califano Jr., memo, May 24, 1966, WHCF Subject File EX-HU2/MC, box 22, LBJ Library.

53. Joseph A. Califano Jr., *The Triumph and Tragedy of Lyndon Johnson: The White House Years* (New York: Simon & Schuster, 1991), 136–37.

54. Pycior, *LBJ and Mexican Americans*, 168–69.

55. Kaplowitz, *LULAC*, 104–5.

56. "News Conference at the White House with Robert Fleming," May 26, 1966, Diary Backup Special Files, box 35, LBJ Library.

57. "An Embattled Conference," *New York Times*, June 2, 1966, n.p., Statements of Lyndon B. Johnson—June 4–8, 1965, box 149, LBJ Library.

58. "To Fulfill These Rights," Council's Report and Recommendations to the Conference, June 1–2, 1966, HU2/MC, box 22, LBJ Library.

59. Jack Jones, "Answer Is Silence: How about That White House Conference? Latins Wonder," *Los Angeles Times*, n.d., n.p., WHC Subject File EX HU2/MC, box 23, LBJ Library.

60. David North to Joseph Califano, memo, February 15, 1967, WHCF Subject File EX HU2/MC, box 23, LBJ Library.

61. Marvin Watson to Lyndon Johnson, letter, February 3, 1967, WHCF Subject File Ex HU2/MC, box 23, LBJ Library.

62. Vicente Ximenes, interview with author, May 31, 2003.

63. Héctor García to Lyndon Johnson, letter, September 22, 1966, LBJ box, HPG Papers.

64. García to Lyndon Johnson, letter, September 22, 1966.

65. García to Lyndon Johnson, letter, September 22, 1966.

66. Joe Dominquez to Lyndon Johnson, letter, March 3, 1967, LBJ box, HPG Papers.

67. Marvin Watson to Lyndon Johnson, telegram, December 12, 1966, John Macy Files, box 659, LBJ Library.

68. Graham, *Civil Rights Era*, 226.

69. "Biographies of the Members of the Equal Opportunity Commission," May 10, 1965, Office Files of John Macy, Ex-General—EEOC, box 782, LBJ Library.

70. Kaplowitz, *LULAC*, 226.

71. Graham, *Civil Rights Era*, 226.

72. The name "Eileen Hernandez" was the full name published in the May 10, 1965, White House press release announcing the EEOC nominations. However, her name is listed as "Aileen Hernandez" in Kaplowitz, *LULAC*, and in Graham, *Civil Rights Era*. Consistent with the current scholarship, the name "Aileen Hernandez" has been used here.

73. "Extension of Remarks of Honorable Edward R. Roybal of California in the House of Representatives," *Congressional Record*, April 27, 1967: A2081, John Macy Files, box 659, LBJ Library.

74. Bert Corona to Lyndon Johnson, telegram, June 9, 1967, John Macy Files, box 659, LBJ Library.

75. James Falcon to John Macy, memo, November 3, 1966, John Macy Files, box 659, LBJ Library.

76. James Falcon to John Macy, memo, January 4, 1967, John Macy Files, box 659, LBJ Library.

77. Oral History of Clinton Anderson, OH AC74-68, November 11, 1969, LBJ Library. Paralleling Lyndon Johnson's political career, Senator Anderson from New Mexico held office from 1949 to 1973.

78. Vicente Ximenes, interview with author, February 19, 2006.

79. Ximenes, interview with author, May 31, 2003.

80. Ximenes, interview with author, January 31, 2005.

81. Lyndon B. Johnson, memo, June 9, 1967, reproduced in "Inter-Agency Committee on Mexican American Affairs, 1967–1968," Brochure, Inter-Agency Committee on Mexican American Affairs, Washington, D.C., Vicente T. Ximenes Papers, box 4, LBJ Library.

82. Ximenes, interview with author, February 19, 2006.

83. "Remarks of the President at the Swearing-In Ceremony for Vicente T. Ximenes," June 9, 1967, box 95, folder 79, HPG Papers.

84. Vicente Ximenes, letter to author, May 31, 2003.

85. Bruce Spinks, "Discrimination in Pay Decried," *Corpus Christi Caller*, July 3, 1967, 1, 14.

86. Graham, *Civil Rights Era*, 227.

87. Graham, *Civil Rights Era*, 7.

88. García, *Viva Kennedy*, 111.

89. Vicente Ximenes quoted in Pycior, *LBJ and Mexican Americans*, 202.

90. Vicente Ximenes, "Road to Sotomayor Started in 1961," *Albuquerque Journal*, June 3, 2009, A9.

91. Lawrence Levinson to Tom Johnson, memo, June 19, 1967, WHCF Subject File EX HU2/MC, box 23, LBJ Library.

92. Ximenes, interview with author, May 31, 2003.

93. Ximenes, interview with author, February 19, 2006.

94. Ximenes, interview with author, February 19, 2006.

95. Ximenes, interview with author, January 31, 2005.

96. Ximenes, interview with author, February 19, 2006.

97. Felix Salinas, interview with author, July 4, 2008.

98. Vicente Ximenes to Lawrence Levinson, memo, June 19, 1967, WHCF Subject File EX HU2/MC, box 23, LBJ Library.

99. Phillip S. "Sam" Hughes, Deputy Director Bureau of the Budget, to Willard Wirtz, memo, June 30, 1967, WHCF Subject File EX HU2/MC, box 23, LBJ Library.

100. Felix Salinas, Special Assistant to the Chair of Inter-Agency Committee on Mexican American Affairs, to White House Cabinet Committee Members, letter, July 21, 1967, Ximenes Papers, EEOC 1967 Files, box 4, LBJ Library.

101. "Bien Hecho" Inter-Agency Committee on Mexican American Affairs Brochure, Ximenes Papers, EEOC 1967 Files, box 4, LBJ Library.

102. Proceedings of the American GI Forum of the U.S. National Convention Brochure, August 2–6, 1967, Semi-Processed Papers, HPG Papers.

103. White House Press Conference of Vicente Ximenes, September 12, 1967. Semi-Processed Papers, HPG Papers.

104. Ximenes, interview with author, May 31, 2003.

105. Vicente Ximenes, interview with author, February 18, 2006.

106. For further analysis of the rhetorical space of the Chamizal memorial, see Brian J. McNely, "*La Frontera y el Chamizal*: Liminality, Territoriality, and Visual Discourse" in *The Responsibilities of Rhetoric*, ed. Michelle Smith and Barbara Warnick (Long Grove, IL: Waveland Press, 2010), 96–114.

107. Milkis and Mileur, *Great Society*, xv.

108. Ximenes, interview with author, May 31, 2003.

109. Vicente Ximenes quoted in Pycior, *LBJ and Mexican Americans*, 213. Pycior reports that dozens of Chicano activists gathered in El Paso during the

hearings for the concurrent meetings to protest both the Vietnam War and the Johnson administration.

110. Carlos Truan, interview with author, October 13, 2006.

111. Ralph Guzmán, "Ethics in Federally Subsidized Research—the Case of the Mexican American," *Testimony Presented at the Cabinet Committee Hearings on Mexican American Affairs, El Paso, Texas, October 26–28, 1967* (Washington, D.C.: Inter-Agency Committee on Mexican American Affairs, 1967), 245–46, Ximenes Papers, EEOC 1967 Files, box 4, LBJ Library.

112. *Testimony Presented at the Cabinet Committee Hearings on Mexican American Affairs*, 161.

113. García, *Héctor P. García*, 274.

114. César Chávez quoted in Pycior, *LBJ and Mexican Americans*, 204.

115. George Sánchez quoted in Pycior, *LBJ and Mexican Americans*, 203.

116. For further examination of Reies López Tijerina's resistance rhetoric and the land grant movement, see "'The Tongue of a Latin Moses': The Rhetoric of Reies Lopez Tijerina," in Hammerback, Jensen, and Gútierrez, *War of Words*, 11–31.

117. Ximenes, interview with author, May 31, 2003.

118. Martin Salazar, "Bullets Flew at Courthouse in Land Grant Fight," *Albuquerque Journal*, June 3, 2007, reprinted January 20, 2015, A3.

119. Colleen Heild and Thom Cole, "Reies Lopez Tijerina: A Hero to the Chicano Movement," *Albuquerque Journal*, January 20, 2015, A1.

120. Ximenes, interview with author, May 31, 2003.

121. Lauro García Jr., "Presentation," *Testimony Presented at the Cabinet Committee Hearings on Mexican American Affairs*, 161.

122. Vicente Ximenes to Lyndon B. Johnson, memo, January 25, 1968, Ximenes Papers, EEOC 1967 Files, box 4, LBJ Library.

123. Ximenes, interview with author, May 31, 2003.

124. Vicente Ximenes, interview with author, February 20, 2006.

125. Meier and Gutiérrez, *Encyclopedia of the Mexican American Civil Rights Movement*, 254.

6. Public Memory and the Reconstruction of History: The 1972 Civil Rights Symposium

1. Vicente Ximenes quoted in Robert C. Rooney, ed., *Equal Opportunity in the United States: A Symposium on Civil Rights* (Austin: University of Texas Press, 1973), 139–43.

2. National Committee to Honor Commissioner Vicente T. Ximenes, program brochure, Equal Employment Opportunity Commission, July 1, 1971, Semi-Processed Papers, HPG Papers.

3. Oral History Interview of Harry Middleton, August 1994, OH Harry Middleton, AC 06-27, LBJ Library; Rooney, *Equal Opportunity*, 2.

4. Ximenes quoted in Rooney, *Equal Opportunity*, 139–43.

5. National Committee to Honor Commissioner Vicente T. Ximenes, program brochure.

6. Vicente Ximenes, "Seeking a Path Out of Poverty for Chicanos," *Agenda* (Winter 1974): 26–29, Semi-Processed Papers, HPG Papers.

7. Paulo Freire, *Pedagogy of the Oppressed*, trans. Myra Bergman (New York: Seabury Press, 1970), 95.

8. For a more comprehensive retrospective on the Chicano movements, see Gómez-Quiñones and Vásquez, *Making Aztlán*.

9. See Kells, *Héctor P. García*, 28. The label "militant Moses" was coined by a journalist in reference to Héctor García to describe his ardent jeremiad rhetorical style.

10. See Mark Kurlansky, *1968: The Year That Rocked the World* (New York: Random House, 2004).

11. Kurlansky, *1968*, xviii. In his retrospective, Kurlansky observes that four historic factors merged to create 1968: the civil rights movement, the youth generation, the war, and live television.

12. Gettleman and Mermelstein, *Great Society Reader*.

13. Vicente Ximenes to Lyndon Johnson, memo, November 7, 1967, EX FG 686/A, box 386, LBJ Library.

14. *El Continental* (El Paso), October 30, 1967, 1, EX FG 686/A, box 386, LBJ Library.

15. "Job Well Done," *El Paso Times*, October 30, 1967, A4, EX FG 686/A, box 386, LBJ Library.

16. Charles Maguire to Will Sparks, memo, February 19, 1968, WHCF Subject File EX HU2, box 7, LBJ Library.

17. Charles Maguire to Will Sparks, memo, February 19, 1968.

18. Larry Levinson to Jim Jones, memo, February 21, 1968, Statements of LBJ, box 266, LBJ Library.

19. Vicente Ximenes, press release, February 23, 1968, Diary Backup 1/24/68–1/31/68, box 91, LBJ Library.

20. Lyndon B. Johnson, presidential statement, February 23, 1968, Diary Backup 1/24/68–1/31/68, box 91, LBJ Library.

21. Kells, *Héctor P. García*, 208.

22. Gettleman and Mermelstein, *Great Society Reader*.

23. Walter Cronkite quoted in Kurlansky, *1968*, 61.

24. Vicente Ximenes quoted in Kells, *Héctor P. García*, 219.

25. Lyndon B. Johnson, Statements of the President, box 274, LBJ Library.

26. Larry Temple, memo, Comments of Cabinet Members, March 31, 1968, Office Files of James Gaither, box 22, LBJ Library.

27. Joseph Califano to Jim Gaither, memo, April 3, 1968, Office Files of James Gaither, box 22, LBJ Library.

28. Califano to Jim Gaither, memo, April 3, 1968.

29. Vicente Ximenes to Bertrand Harding, memo, Office of Economic Opportunity, April 4, 1968, Office Files of James Gaither, box 22, LBJ Library.

30. Joseph Califano to Lyndon Johnson, memo, June 10, 1968, WHCF Subject File Gen FG 687, box 45, LBJ Library.

31. Vicente Ximenes to Larry Levinson, memo, January 3, 1969, WHCF Subject File Gen FG 687, box 45, LBJ Library.

32. Oral History Interview of Harry Middleton, August 1994.

33. Joseph Califano to Jim Gaither, memo, January 11, 1969, WHCF Legislation/FG 687, box 45, LBJ Library.

34. Stuart H. Loory, "36 Foundations Refuse Bids to Meeting on Mexican Americans," *Los Angeles Times*, April 2, 1969, 3, 31, box 131, folder 50, HPG Papers.

35. Loory, "36 Foundations Refuse Bids."

36. Loory, "36 Foundations Refuse Bids."

37. Doris J. Armijo, introduction to *Testimony Presented at the Cabinet Committee Hearings on Mexican American Affairs*, xi.

38. Armijo, introduction to *Testimony Presented at the Cabinet Committee Hearings*, xi.

39. Armijo, introduction to *Testimony Presented at the Cabinet Committee Hearings*, xi.

40. For further information on these foundational Chicano movement manifestos, see Meier and Gutiérrez, *Encyclopedia of Mexican American Civil Rights Movement*, 182–83.

41. For additional information on the Truth and Reconciliation Commission in postapartheid South Africa, see Nelson Mandela, *Long Walk to Freedom: The Autobiography of Nelson Mandela* (New York: Little, Brown, 1995); Philippe-Joseph Salazar, *An African Athens: Rhetoric and the Shaping of Democracy in South Africa* (Mahwah, NJ: Lawrence Erlbaum, 2002); Desmond Tutu, *No Future without Forgiveness* (New York: Doubleday, 2000), 31.

42. Vicente Ximenes to Héctor García, letter, May 9, 1969, box 103, folder 17, HPG Papers.

43. Vicente Ximenes, memo, "Census Survey Information," Equal Employment Opportunity Commission, March 1, 1971, Semi-Processed Papers, HPG Papers.

44. Mora, *Making Hispanics*.

45. Press release, "Midwestern Conference on Mexican American and Puerto Rican Affairs to Be Held in Detroit, Michigan, October 19, 1968," Office of Inter-Agency Committee on Mexican American Affairs, October 7, 1968, Semi-Processed Papers, HPG Papers.

46. "Mexican American Affairs Agency Chairman Deplores Ethnic Slurs in Advertisement," Press release of the Inter-Agency Committee on Mexican American Affairs, September 16, 1968, Semi-Processed Papers, box 149, folder 6, HPG Papers.

47. "Angry Mexican-Americans Take Aim at the Frito Bandito in Suit," *Pensacola Journal*, January 1, 1971, D4, HPG Papers.

48. For further discussion about the issues of sex and age discrimination addressed by the EEOC in 1968, see Cynthia Harrison, *On Account of Sex: The Politics of Women's Issues* (Berkeley: University of California Press, 1989), 204; Graham, *Civil Rights Era*, 158–59; Kurlansky, *1968*, 310–11.

49. Jack Jones, "U.S. Hearing Assails Networks on Minority Hiring Practices," *Los Angeles Times*, March 15, 1969, 1.

50. "Statement of Vicente Ximenes before the Subcommittee on Executive Reorganization," press release, June 12, 1969, *EEOC News Bulletin*, Semi-Processed Papers, HPG Papers.

51. Ruben Salazar, "Latin-American Gains under Johnson Hailed," *Los Angeles Times*, March 15, 1969, Part 2, Semi-Processed Papers, HPG Papers.

52. Vicente Ximenes, "Speech to Mexican American Law Students Association," (National Issues Conference, Abiquiú, NM, March 19, 1970), Semi-Processed Papers, HPG Papers.

53. Vicente Ximenes to Héctor García, letter, July 2, 1970, Semi-Processed Papers, HPG Papers.

54. Vicente Ximenes, "Address to Post Office Department's National Equal Employment Opportunity Conference," September 22, 1967, box 130, folder 27, HPG Papers.

55. Ximenes, interview with author, February 19, 2006.

56. Ximenes, guest lecture, October 9, 2006.

57. Lyndon B. Johnson quoted in Rooney, *Equal Opportunity*, 163.

58. Kells, *Héctor P. García*, 97.

59. Lyndon B. Johnson to Vicente Ximenes, letter, December 14, 1972, Semi-Processed Papers, HPG Papers.

60. Lyndon B. Johnson to Vicente Ximenes, telegram, April 17, 1965, WHCF Name File, box X-1, LBJ Library.

61. Goodwin, *Lyndon Johnson*, 363.

62. Goodwin, *Lyndon Johnson*, 363–64.

63. See Goodwin, *Lyndon Johnson*. As Goodwin observes, "yet no amount of determined thought nor even the ranch—where his power was more absolute than ever before—could protect Johnson from the harsh judgments he received in the final years from the world. He agonized over reports in the papers about the course of the war in Vietnam and the fate of the Great Society" (365).

64. Goodwin, *Lyndon Johnson*, 365–66.

65. Goodwin, *Lyndon Johnson*, 365–66.

66. Kells, *Héctor P. García*, 222.

67. See Milkis and Mileur, *Great Society*.

68. Vicente Ximenes, to D. G. Coronado, telegram, May 29, 1969, Semi-Processed Papers, HPG Papers.

69. Williams, *Open Space for Democracy*.

70. Krall, *Ecotone*. As Krall observes, in natural landscapes, the "edges where differences come together are the richest of habitats" (4).

71. Krall, *Ecotone*, 4.

Conclusion: Vicente Ximenes—Engaging Public Rhetoric, Cultural Ecologies, and Civic Literacies in the Twenty-First Century

1. Vicente Ximenes, "Continuing the CCC Legacy" (keynote address, Seventy-Fifth Anniversary of the Civilian Conservation Corps Celebration, CCC Alumni Chapter 141, Albuquerque, NM, April 2, 2008), Vicente T. Ximenes Personal Papers.

2. Timothy Egan, *The Worst Hard Time* (New York: Houghton Mifflin Company, 2006).

3. Gilbert Gallegos, "YCC Founder Builds Experience for Workers," *Albuquerque Tribune*, May 8, 1996, 1.

4. Sarah Van Cott, "A Legacy of Building," *Albuquerque Tribune*, November 4, 1998, C1.

5. Jan Jonas, "Commendation for Conservation," *Albuquerque Tribune*, March 12, 2002, A1–A2.

6. Sean Prentiss, *Finding Abbey: The Search for Edward Abbey and His Hidden Desert Grave* (Albuquerque: University of New Mexico Press, 2015), 29.

7. Prentiss, *Finding Abbey*, 22–23.

8. Jonas, "Commendation for Conservation," A2.

9. Jonas, "Commendation for Conservation," A2.

10. Farmer, *Pathologies of Power*, 9.

11. Hammerback and Jensen, *Rhetorical Career of César Chávez*, 45.

12. David Bromwich, "What Went Wrong: Assessing Obama's Legacy," *Harper's*, June 2015, 32.

13. Ximenes, interview with author, January 20, 2009.

14. Timothy Morton, *The Ecological Thought* (Cambridge, MA: Harvard University Press, 2010).

15. Richard Marosi, "Living in Limbo," *Albuquerque Journal*, March 13, 2011, B5–B6.

16. Marosi, "Living in Limbo."

17. Ximenes, interview with author, January 20, 2009.

18. John S. Dryzek, *Deliberative Democracy and Beyond: Liberals, Critics, Contestations* (New York: Oxford University Press, 2002), 113–14.

19. "Address by Vicente Ximenes at the American GI Forum National Convention," August 2, 1967, Semi-Processed Papers, HPG Papers.

20. Juan C. Guerra, "Enacting Institutional Change: The Work of Literacy Insurgents in the Academy and Beyond," *JAC* 34, nos. 1–2 (2014): 71–95.

21. Henry Cisneros, "A Giant in Mexican American History" (keynote address, University of New Mexico Civil Rights Symposium, Albuquerque, NM, September 28, 2007).

22. Juan Guerra expands on this term "citizens-in-the-making" in Juan C. Guerra, *Language, Culture, Identity, and Citizenship in College Classrooms and Communities* (Urbana, IL: NCTE-Routledge, 2015).

23. Hammerback and Jensen, *War of Words*.

24. Martin Luther King Jr., *The Autobiography of Martin Luther King, Jr.*, ed. Clayborn Carson (New York: Hachette Books, 1998), 123.

25. Lloyd Jojola, "Maria Ximenes: Wife Helped American GI Forum," *Albuquerque Journal*, September 17, 2009, B3.

26. Federico García Lorca quoted in Frederick Smock, "On *Duende*: Reading Federico García Lorca," *Writer's Chronicle* 45, no. 1 (September 2012): 70.

27. Nicole Perez, "Vicente Ximenes, Rights Activist Dies at 94," *Albuquerque Journal*, March 2, 2014, B2.

Selected Bibliography

This listing includes sections for archival collections; books; and articles, dissertations, and theses.

Archival Collections

Nettie Lee Benson Latin American Collection, General Libraries, University of Texas, Austin.

Dr. Héctor P. García Papers, Special Collections and Archives, Mary and Jeff Bell Library, Texas A&M University–Corpus Christi.

Lyndon B. Johnson Papers, Lyndon B. Johnson Presidential Library, University of Texas, Austin.

J. Cloyd Miller Library Special Collections, Western New Mexico University, Silver City, New Mexico.

John F. Kennedy Papers, John F. Kennedy Presidential Library, University of Massachusetts, Boston.

Library of Congress, Washington, D.C.

National Archives, Washington, D.C.

Robert F. Kennedy Papers, John F. Kennedy Library, University of Massachusetts, Boston.

Silver City Public Library, Silver City, New Mexico.

South Texas Archives, Texas A&M University–Kingsville, Texas.

Vicente T. Ximenes Personal Papers, Albuquerque, New Mexico.

Wilson County Public Library, Floresville, Texas.

Books

Acuña, Rodolfo F. *Occupied America: A History of Chicanos.* 3rd ed. New York: Harper & Row, 1988.

Allsup, Carl. *The American G.I. Forum: Origins and Evolution.* Austin: Center for Mexican American Studies, University of Texas at Austin, 1982.

Behnken, Brian D. *Fighting Their Own Battles: Mexican Americans, African Americans, and the Struggle for Civil Rights in Texas.* Chapel Hill: University of North Carolina Press, 2011.

Blanton, Carlos Kevin. *George I. Sánchez: The Long Fight for Mexican American Integration.* New Haven, CT: Yale University Press, 2014.

Caro, Robert A. *Lyndon B. Johnson: Master of the Senate.* New York: Alfred A. Knopf, 2002.

———. *Lyndon B. Johnson: Path to Power.* New York: Vintage Books, 1990.

Castells, Manuel. *The Power of Identity.* 2nd ed. Malden, MA: Wiley-Blackwell, 2010.

Dallek, Robert. *Flawed Giant: Lyndon Johnson and His Times, 1961–1973.* New York: Oxford University Press, 1999.

Foley, Neil. *Quest for Equality: The Failed Promise of Black-Brown Solidarity.* Cambridge, MA: Harvard University Press, 2010.

García, Ignacio M. *Viva Kennedy: Mexican Americans in Search of Camelot.* College Station: Texas A&M University Press, 2000.

———. *White but Not Equal: Mexican Americans, Jury Discrimination, and the Supreme Court.* Tucson: University of Arizona Press, 2009.

García, Mario T. *The Mexican American Generation: Leadership, Ideology, and Identity, 1930–1960.* New Haven, CT: Yale University Press, 1989.

Gettleman, Marvin E., and David Mermelstein, eds. *The Great Society Reader: The Failure of American Liberalism.* New York: Random House, 1967.

Gómez, Laura. *Manifest Destinies: The Making of the Mexican American Race.* New York: New York University Press, 2007.

Gómez-Quiñones, Juan, and Irene Vásquez. *Making Aztlán: Ideology and Culture of the Chicana and Chicano Movement, 1966–1977.* Albuquerque: University of New Mexico Press, 2014.

Goodwin, Doris Kearns. *Lyndon Johnson and the American Dream.* New York: St. Martin's Griffin, 1991.

Graham, Hugh Davis. *The Civil Rights Era: Origins and Development of National Policy, 1960–1972.* New York: Oxford University Press, 1990.

Griswold del Castillo, Richard. *World War II and Mexican American Civil Rights.* Austin: University of Texas Press, 2008.

Hiley, David. *Doubt and the Demands of Democratic Citizenship.* New York: Cambridge University Press, 2006.

Hirschman, Albert O. *The Rhetoric of Reaction: Perversity, Futility, Jeopardy.* Cambridge, MA: Belknap Press of Harvard University Press, 1991.

Kaplowitz, Craig. *LULAC: Mexican Americans and National Policy.* College Station: Texas A&M University Press, 2005.

Kells, Michelle Hall. *Héctor P. García: Everyday Rhetoric and Mexican American Civil Rights.* Carbondale: Southern Illinois University Press, 2006.

Meier, Matt S., and Margo Gutiérrez. *Encyclopedia of the Mexican American Civil Rights Movement.* Westport, CT: Greenwood Press, 2000.

Milkis, Sidney M., and Jerome M. Mileur, eds. *The Great Society and the High Tide of Liberalism.* Boston: University of Massachusetts Press, 2005.

Montejano, David. *Anglos and Mexicans in the Making of Texas, 1836–1986.* Austin: University of Texas Press, 1987.

Mouffe, Chantal. *The Democratic Paradox.* New York: Verso, 2009.

Orosco, Cynthia. *No Mexicans, Women, or Dogs Allowed: The Rise of the Mexican American Civil Rights Movement.* Austin: University of Texas Press, 2010.

Peña, Devon, ed. *Chicano Culture, Ecology, Politics: Subversive Kin.* Tucson: University of Arizona Press, 1998.

Pilcher, Jeffrey M. *Cantinflas and the Chaos of Mexican Modernity.* New York: Rowman & Littlefield Publishers, 2000.

Pycior, Julie Leininger. *LBJ and Mexican Americans: The Paradox of Power.* Austin: University of Texas Press, 1997.

Quiroz, Anthony, ed. *Leaders of the Mexican American Generation: Biographical Essays.* Boulder: University Press of Colorado, 2015.

Ricoeur, Paul. *Memory, History, Forgetting.* Translated by Kathleen Blamey and David Pellauer. Chicago: University of Chicago Press, 2004.

Romano, Renee C., and Leigh Raiford, eds. *The Civil Rights Movement in American Memory.* Athens: University of Georgia, 2006.

Strum, Philippa. *Mendez v. Westminster: School Desegregation and Mexican-American Rights.* Lawrence: University Press of Kansas, 2010.

Unger, Irwin, and Debi Unger. *LBJ: A Life.* New York: John Wiley & Sons, 1999.

Vargas, Zaragosa. *Labor Rights Are Civil Rights: Mexican American Workers in Twentieth-Century America.* Princeton, NJ: Princeton University Press, 2005.

West, Cornel. *The American Evasion of Philosophy: A Genealogy of Pragmatism.* Madison: University of Wisconsin Press, 1989.

White, Hayden. *Metahistory: The Historical Imagination in Nineteenth-Century Europe.* Baltimore: Johns Hopkins University Press, 1973.

Articles, Dissertations, and Theses

"Albuquerque Departmental Investigation Sought by Ximenez." *American GI Forum News Bulletin*, December 1953, 2.

"Albuquerque Forum Asks Civil Service for City Workers on Garbage Department." *American GI Forum News Bulletin*, September 1953, 2.

"Albuquerque GI Forums Gain Great Victory as Merit System Extended to Garbage Men." *American GI Forum News Bulletin*, November 1953, 2.

"Angry Mexican-Americans Take Aim at the Frito Bandito in Suit." *Pensacola (FL) Journal*, January 1, 1971, D4.

Ballif, Michelle. "Writing the Event: The Impossible Possibility for Historiography," *Rhetoric Society Quarterly* 44, no. 3 (Summer 2014): 243–55.

Borse, Diana Bancroft. "Sam Fore: An Enduring Model." Senior thesis, Texas

A&M University–Kingsville, December 1997. South Texas Archives and Special Collections.

Dyer, Stanford P., and Merrell A. Knighten. "Discrimination after Death: Lyndon Johnson and Felix Longoria." *Southern Studies: An Interdisciplinary Journal of the South* 18 (Winter 1974): 411–26.

Gallegos, Gilbert. "YCC Founder Builds Experience for Workers." *Albuquerque Tribune*, May 8, 1996, 1.

Green, George Norris. "The Felix Longoria Affair." *Journal of Ethnic Studies* 19, no. 3 (1991): 22–34.

Hall, Jacquelyn Dowd. "The Long Civil Rights Movement and the Political Uses of the Past." *Journal of American History* 91, no. 4 (March 2005): 1233–63.

Heild, Colleen, and Thom Cole. "Reies Lopez Tijerina: A Hero to the Chicano Movement." *Albuquerque Journal*, January 20, 2015, A1.

Houston, Romona Allaniz. "African Americans, Mexican Americans, and Anglo Americans and the Desegregation of Texas, 1946–1957." PhD dissertation, University of Texas, Austin, 2000.

Jojola, Lloyd. "Maria Ximenes: Wife Helped American GI Forum." *Albuquerque Journal*, September 17, 2009, B3.

Keach, Sam Fore. "Death Comes Peacefully to 'Mr. Sam' at Home." *Floresville (TX) Chronicle-Journal*, December 29, 1966, 1.

"LBJ's Message to National Convention." *Forumeer*, September 1965, 2.

Meighan, Tyrone. "Dr. Hector P. Garcia." *Corpus Christi (TX) Caller Times*, July 3, 1993.

"Mexican-Americans Attend 'Great Society' Conference." *Democrat* (Washington, D.C.), June 14, 1968, 4.

Miller, Carolyn R. "Genre as Social Action." *Quarterly Journal of Speech* 70 (1984): 151–67.

Morgan, Ernest. "A Profile of Dr. Hector Garcia: A Man of Controversy." *Corpus Christi (TX) Caller Times*, December 12, 1966.

"Nation Honors Latin-American: Three Rivers Soldier Buried in Arlington." *Austin American-Statesman*, February 17, 1949.

"New Mexico Board Plans Headquarters." *American GI Forum News Bulletin*, September 1953, 2.

"New Mexico Building Fund Drive." *American GI Forum News Bulletin*, November 1953, 2.

"New Mexico Forum Seeks Bill to Outlaw Public Discrimination." *American GI Forum New Bulletin*, March 1953, 4.

Orozco, Cynthia E. "The Origins of the League of United Latin American Citizens (LULAC) and the Mexican American Civil Rights Movement in Texas with an Analysis of Women's Political Participation in a Gendered Context, 1910–1929." PhD dissertation, University of California, Los Angeles, 1992.

Perez, Nicole. "Vicente Ximenes, Rights Activist Dies at 94." *Albuquerque Journal*, March 2, 2014, B2.

President Lyndon B. Johnson Has a Lifetime Record of Personal Concern and Public Assistance to Americans of Mexican or Spanish Origin. Viva Johnson Organization of the Democratic National Committee, 1964. Pamphlet.

Pycior, Julie Leininger. "*La Raza* Organizes: Mexican American life in San Antonio as Reflected in *Mutualista Activities*." PhD dissertation, University of Notre Dame, 1979.

Roberts, Michelle. "Early Ranch Structure Buried Again." *Albuquerque Journal*, December 26, 2009, C1.

Rooney, Robert C., ed. *Equal Opportunity in the United States: A Symposium on Civil Rights*. Austin: University of Texas Press, 1973.

Salazar, Martin. "Bullets Flew at Courthouse in Land Grant Fight." *Albuquerque Journal*, June 3, 2007. Reprinted January 20, 2015, A3.

Smallwood, James M. "Viva Johnson: LBJ and the Transformation of the Hispanic Community of Texas." *Journal of South Texas* 15, no. 2 (Fall 2002).

Testimony Presented at the Cabinet Committee Hearings on Mexican American Affairs, El Paso, Texas, October 26–28, 1967. Washington, D.C.: Inter-Agency Committee on Mexican American Affairs, 1967.

"U.S. Senator Dennis Chavez Commends New Mexico Forum." *American GI Forum News Bulletin* (Austin), August 1954.

"Ximenes, Ramos Lead VIVA JOHNSON Clubs." *American GI Forum News Bulletin*, November 1964, 1.

Ximenes, Vicente. "The New Mexico Welfare Situation." *American GI Forum News Bulletin*, (Austin), January 1956, 7.

Index

Italicized page numbers indicate figures.

Abbey, Edward, 253–54
Ackerman, John, 3, 273n11
acquired power, defined, 28. *See also*
   social power, overview
Acuña, Rodolfo, 69
ADL (Anti-Defamation League), 119,
   122–24
advertising images, 237
AGIF (American GI Forum): Albuquerque EEOC conference walkout, 189; Chávez affiliation, 60–61;
   and Civil Rights Symposium, 218;
   Easter Sunday March, 192–93; El
   Paso Hearings, 207, 211; establishment context, 61–63, 64; Johnson
   administration expectations, 187–88;
   Longoria case, 63–64; McCarthyism
   problem, 55, 56; meeting sites, 128;
   national chairman election, 129, 131;
   national conventions, 128, 138–41,
   143–45, 261; state convention, 1–2,
   55, 60–61; suitability for Ximenes,
   57–60, 61, 64–66; Unity Banquet,
   193; waning influence, 220–21,
   248–49
AGIF (American GI Forum), New
   Mexico: coalition building, 84–85,
   108–9, 119–20, 121–24; as community building, 85–86, 130–31; DAR
   flag controversy, *94*, 132–36; headquarters construction, *93*, 128–31;
   issue selection process, 109–10; labor
   activism, 82–83, 86–88, 120–21,
   123–28; Latin America support
   activity, 155–56; LULAC approach

contrasted, 118–19; membership
   growth, 81, 83–84; national level
   participation, 129, 131–32, 136–37;
   organizational meeting, 78–79;
   power broker conflicts, 81; resistance
   factors summarized, 66–69, 77–78;
   state conventions, 109; statement
   about motivations, 79–80; surveillance concerns, 79, 84; Ximenes
   family concerns, 81–82
agonistic pluralism, 20, 66, 85, 128,
   182, 263, 280n18. *See also* El Paso
   Hearings
agropastoral system, changes, 75–76
airline industry, EEOC hearings,
   237–38
Albuquerque Human Rights Board,
   247
Albuquerque Journal, 10, 79–80, 151,
   205, 258–59
Albuquerque United Nations Human
   Rights Award, 109
Albuquerque walkout, EEOC conference, 189–91, 195, 234
Alianza Federal de Mercedes, 211–12
Alliance for Progress program,
   94–96, 153–57, 158–59, 162, 164, 168,
   180–82, 288n42
Alumni Chapter 141, CCC, 247,
   251–53
Amador, Albert, 119, 123
American Business Survey, 42–43
American Encounters (Limón), 58
American Evasion of Philosophy
   (West), 3

ichelle Hall Kells, an associate professor of rhetoric and writing in the Department of English at the University of New Mexico, is the author of *Héctor P. García: Everyday Rhetoric and Mexican American Civil Rights* and the lead editor of both *Attending to the Margins: Writing, Researching, and Teaching on the Front Lines* and *Latino/a Discourses: On Language, Identity, and Literacy Education*. Her research interests include public rhetoric (civil rights and environmental discourses), sociolinguistics (language diversity), and community literacies.